Puritans and Adventurers

Puritans
and
Adventurers

Change and Persistence
in Early America

T. H. Breen

New York   Oxford
OXFORD UNIVERSITY PRESS

Copyright © 1980 by Oxford University Press, Inc.

Library of Congress Cataloging in Publication Data

Breen, T. H.
  Puritans and adventurers.

  1. Massachusetts—History—Colonial period, ca.
1600–1775—Addresses, essays, lectures.   2. Virginia—
History—Colonial period, ca. 1600–1775—Addresses,
essays, lectures.   3. Puritans—Massachusetts—
Addresses, essays, lectures.   I. Title.
F67.B83   974.4′02   80-12364
ISBN 0-19-502728-0
ISBN 0-19-503207-1 (pbk.)

Printed in the United States of America
printing, last digit: 10 9

For Three Teachers:
Edmund S. Morgan,
J. H. Hexter, and John Morton Blum

Acknowledgments

Of the nine essays in this volume, seven have been previously published in scholarly journals. Chapter I first appeared in the *William and Mary Quarterly*, 3rd ser., XXXII (1975). It received the annual award sponsored by the National Society Daughters of Colonial Wars for the best article published by the *William and Mary Quarterly* in 1975. Chapter II first appeared in *Past and Present: A Journal of Historical Studies*, no. 57 (Nov. 1972), World Copyright: The Past and Present Society, Corpus Christi College, Oxford (England). I am indebted to T. H. Aston, Editor of *Past and Present*, for permission to reprint this essay. "Moving to the New World" was published in the *William and Mary Quarterly*, 3rd ser., XXX (1973). It too won the prize for the outstanding article (1973) to appear in that journal. I thank my co-author, Stephen Foster, for allowing me to include this piece in the present collection. Chapter IV appeared in *The New England Historical and Genealogical Register*, CXXXII (1978), copyright © 1978 by The New England Historic Genealogical Society. I thank Ralph J. Crandall, Editor of *The New England Historical and Genealogical Register* for allowing re-publication of this article. Chapter VI was originally published in *The South Atlantic Quarterly*, LXXVIII (1979), in slightly different form. It was entitled, "Looking Out for Number One: Conflicting Cultural Values in Early Seventeenth Century Virginia," copyright © 1979 by Duke University Press. Chapter VII originally appeared as "A Changing Labor Force and Race Relations in Virginia, 1660–1710," *Journal of Social History*, VII (1973–1974), and is reprinted by permission. And "Horses and Gentlemen" was published in the *William and Mary Quarterly*, 3rd ser., XXXIV (1977). Chapter IX was prepared specifically for a conference held at the Newberry Library, May 1978, and sponsored by the Illinois Chapter of the Society of Colonial Wars. I thank George Milnor, Chapin Litten, and Dutton Morehouse for permission to include this essay in the present collection, and for their support of research in colonial American history.

I have made minor revisions in Chapters II, VI, and VIII. These changes mainly involved the addition of specific examples in support of my arguments.

In researching and writing these essays, I received generous backing from the American Philosophical Society, the American Council of Learned Societies, the Guggenheim Foundation, the Institute for Advanced Study, the Otis Fund of Wheaton College, Norton, Massachusetts, and the History Department at Northwestern University.

Many people have provided suggestions and criticism along the way, and as they all know, I appreciate their contribution. Stephen Foster sharpened my understanding of Puritanism, and on many occasions, patiently reworked my clumsy prose. Josef Barton taught me a new way of looking at culture that was at once rigorous and humane. Susan C. Breen reminded me of the importance of writing for men and women who have not spent their lives studying seventeenth-century America. The others who assisted in this project were Leonard Barkan, Richard R. Beeman, George E. Breen, Paul J. Bohannan, Louis G. Carr, George M. Fredrickson, Robert Gilmour, Thomas William Heyck, Stephen Innes, Peter Laslett, Kenneth A. Lockridge, Michael McGiffert, Russell R. Menard, Sheldon Meyer, John Murrin, Chester Pach, James Sheehan, John Shy, Lacey Baldwin Smith, Thad Tate, E. P. Thompson, Lawrence William Towner, James Walsh, Robert Wiebe, R. Hal Williams, Peter H. Wood, Hal Worthley, and Clarence Ver Steeg. To the three men to whom this volume is dedicated, I owe a debt that I am only beginning to repay.

T. H. B.

Evanston, Illinois
March 1980

Contents

Introduction

These essays—two of which are published here for the first time—explore the origins and subsequent development of quite different early American cultures, Massachusetts and Virginia. The idea for this collection occurred to me over a decade ago. At that time, I had just begun rummaging through the colonists' "cultural baggage," bundles of custom and tradition, habits of mind that the settlers carried across the Atlantic Ocean. Along with other historians working in this period, I assumed that the migrants' English background played an important role in shaping social institutions in America. My research abundantly confirmed that belief. What I had not anticipated was the complexity of the story. I discovered not one, but many English backgrounds, and where I expected to find changing values in the New World, I encountered persistence.

The comparative cultural history of these particular colonies presented problems that I would probably not have faced had I attempted to contrast the development of vastly dissimilar societies, say Virginia and Cuba or Massachusetts Bay and New France. Since England's mainland colonies cooperated in fighting a revolution and establishing a new nation, one is tempted to homogenize early American culture, to stress common elements that prepared the way for later events. From this perspective, of course, colonial Massachusetts and Virginia shared a single tradition, a deep commitment to Protestantism, the English language, economic and political dependence upon the same mother country, just to name a few. But this approach exaggerates the significance of shared values of people living in different parts of colonial America as well as the eventual cultural solidarity of the Founding Fathers. In my investigations I attempted to explain why men and women who settled in these two regions created and then maintained strikingly different patterns of institutional behavior. Local cultural variation—indeed the existence of enduring sub-cultures—turned out to be more important in understanding everyday life in Massachusetts and Virginia than did broad cultural similarities.

Interpreting these differences presented quite another problem. Not a few colonial historians have noted—indeed, celebrated—the existence of distinct values in these two seventeenth-century societies. The Virginians usually come off poorly in comparison to the founders of the Bay Colony. Governor John Winthrop and his followers, we learn, traveled to America on a noble mission. They subscribed to an intricate theology, Puritanism, that gave meaning to a broad range of daily activities. They built towns, championed education, developed a body of thought now called "the New England mind." No wonder Richard Beale Davis in a recent prize-winning study, *Intellectual Life in the Colonial South 1585–1763*, complained that modern scholars have slighted the South in general and Virginia in particular by portraying "the Puritan religious mind as the source of the American intellectual tradition and thus of the American spirit" (xxiii). Davis may exaggerate, but it is certainly true that many scholars depict the culture of early Virginia as little more than a negation of New England culture. Unlike the Bay Puritans, the lazy planters failed to establish towns, a printing press, a strong religious system. The list could be extended, but there is no need to do so. To insist that Chesapeake settlers should have acted like New Englanders, people who traveled to America under vastly different circumstances, blinds the historian to the more subtle aspects of cultural transfer and persistence. In any event, the alleged absence of values cannot explain patterns of public behavior in early Virginia.

This book, therefore, has two distinct goals. First, the essays compare—albeit implicitly—the experiences of early Virginians and Bay Colonists. In several chapters, I explore values that shaped the Virginians' social institutions and argue that a coherent body of attitudes and beliefs, ideas and norms had as profound an effect upon the development of Virginia as Puritanism had upon that of Massachusetts Bay. And second, perhaps because of my growing interest in cultural anthropology, I have tried to sketch out a general framework in which one might analyze cultural transfer for the whole of colonial America, in other words, a consideration of the precise character of the migrants' Old World background, the extent to which it influenced institutional decisions made in entirely new surroundings, the role of environmental factors and just plain luck in forming social institutions, and finally, the relation between changing institutional forms and persistent cultural values. Since my comments about the process of cultural transfer are scattered throughout the present volume, it may be helpful to indicate the general lines of my argument, however briefly, in this introduction.

The character of the colonists' Old World background—most people who appear in this book were English—depended in large part upon the region from which they originated and the timing of their decision to emigrate. It was once taken for granted that the settlers' English heritage was static and that regardless of when they arrived in America, they brought the same general "cultural baggage," a collection of commonplace beliefs about common law and social structure. But a spate of local studies recently published by English historians has revealed the weakness of such an interpretation. In fact, as we now know, early seventeenth-century England contained many distinct social environments. Some English people cultivated fields in isolated farming villages, others raised livestock. Some lived in cities, working as tradesmen or artisans, and still others drifted from place to place, the rogues and vagabonds that Jacobean gentlemen feared so much. As Stephen Foster and I explain in "Moving to the New World," it makes a great difference in understanding the transfer of culture to state exactly which local culture one is studying, the culture of London or the culture of East Anglian farming communities, the culture of Kent or that of Yorkshire.

Moreover, as I argue in "Persistent Localism" and "The Covenanted Militia," Stuart England was changing so rapidly, especially in politics and religion, that it is essential to ascertain the precise timing of the migrant's departure for America. A man or woman who lived in Norfolk, Suffolk or Essex after 1626, for example, had recent vivid experiences that someone who had departed earlier would not have had and probably would not have even understood. The Puritanism of a person who left East Anglia in 1637 was different from the Puritanism of one who sailed in 1630 or 1642.

The point is clearly that we should define as closely as possible the *specific context* of migration. Only then can we make sense out of a group's behavior in the New World, unraveling what was an adjustment to an unfamiliar physical environment from what was a conscious effort to reform or replicate local English practices. The same general rule undoubtedly holds for the African backgrounds of early American blacks. As anthropologist Sidney Mintz explains in his *Caribbean Transformations*, the invention of a general "African tradition" may simply reveal that researchers have failed "to pin down specific origins for words, traits, beliefs, values, and material objects" (27).

Apart from differences in their English cultural heritage, the people who settled in Massachusetts and Virginia also found themselves living in very different physical environments that imposed their own limits upon Old World aspirations. Colonial historians usually take for granted climate, soil types, natural resources, flora and fauna. Such indifference, however, is unwarranted. Some environments obviously were more conducive than were others to the smooth transfer of local English cultures. As I explain in "Chance and Design," the founders of New England were fortunate to land in an area much like the one that they had just departed. The Bay colonists raised the same crops and breeds of livestock as they had in England; their environment did not call forth extraordinary adjustments in lifestyle.

If Winthrop's fleet had sailed by chance up the James River in Virginia or the Ashley in South Carolina, the Puritans would still have attempted to create a "city on a hill," but the results of their efforts would have been far different from—and one suspects much less successful than—what they actually were in Massachusetts Bay. By the same token, the accidental discovery that tobacco could be produced profitably on scattered riverfront plantations preserved the central features of seventeenth-century Virginia culture—its competitiveness, individualism, and materialism—for without the planters' realistic expectation of striking it rich in America, the first colonies would have been abandoned in short order. The various New World environments did not determine the shape of colonial cultures. Rather, they set general parameters on the institutional expression of English values in the New World.

Once they arrived in Massachusetts or Virginia, the colonists neither replicated immemorial English custom nor gave themselves over to frontier democracy. The process was far more involved than either of these familiar explanations of cultural transfer would suggest. The settlers created institutional structures that responded to specific local conditions they had experienced in England on the eve of departure, conditions which in some cases the migrants thought were in desperate need of reform. Decisions about institutional forms, of course, took environmental realities into account, and in each colony the relation between Old World background and New World environment was slightly different. I discovered, however, that regardless of local peculiarities, each group of colonists attempted to bring coherence to the various institutions they established in America. A common set of values—attitudes about popular participation in the formulation of public policy or assumptions about human nature just to cite two examples—affected the shape of church, state, and militia. It is in "Persistent Localism," "The Covenanted Militia," and "Looking Out for Number One" that I develop the concept of *institutional parallelism* most fully. The notion that the colonists created each of their institutions strictly according to its own logic and that colonial historians can study these institutions separately, as if they were so many tunnels unrelated to the rest of society, closes off opportunities to see connections between general value systems and actual institutional policy.

As anyone who reads these essays will discover, military affairs figure prominently in my discussion of institutional parallelism. This focus reflects a conscious research design. In both colonies, military matters occupied a large percentage of the settlers' time, and when they debated whether common soldiers should elect officers or discussed a citizen's obligation to preserve his neighbor's life and property from enemy attack, they kept remarkably full records. These documents enabled me to compare institutional development in Massachusetts and Virginia. Equivalent comparisons from other less complete sources are inevitably more conjectural.

When I began this project, I assumed that in the design of military organizations and the formulation of military policy, the colonists had less chance to experiment than they did in other aspects of their lives. After all their very survival depended upon a strong defense, and it seemed as if one colony's militia would look pretty much like that of any other. But common sense proved an inadequate guide. Military practices in Virginia differed significantly from those of Massachusetts

Bay, and I encountered innovations in institutional structure that seemed totally incomprehensible until I realized that they were expressions of a system that included the church as well as the state. Indeed, the organization of the early Massachusetts trainbands had more in common with the polity of the Congregational churches in the same colony than it did with the structure of the loose, unreliable military forces of Virginia.

In other essays, I have analyzed the relation between change and persistence in colonial American society. In both colonies major changes occurred over the course of the seventeenth century. The labor force in Virginia became more African and less free; an American-born planter elite achieved political dominance over other Virginians. In Massachusetts people clashed over the limits of popular participation in public affairs, and some institutions were clearly less open on the eve of the Glorious Revolution than they had been in John Winthrop's time. No one disputes that these shifts took place. The question is how to interpret them. Do they reveal a profound transformation of values or are they merely surface adjustments, changes that tend to obscure persistent ideas, attitudes, and beliefs?

For me this question is largely artificial. While writing this book, I became convinced that colonial historians have overestimated the importance of change in pre-Revolutionary America. They are often too eager to hustle the colonists down the road toward modernization. As cultural anthropologists have shown, institutional forms can change in traditional societies, often quite dramatically, without altering the value system upon which these institutions are based. There are scores of examples of this phenomenon. Political changes, even the violent overthrow of a chief, or a shift from one form of agriculture to another can actually reinforce a people's commitment to a particular world view.

Such examples were very much on my mind when I wrote "Horses and Gentlemen" and "Of Time and Nature." Change suddenly did not seem to me antithetical to persistence. They existed together; one was a function of the other. Take the case of Virginia. Colonial historians have understandably stressed the centrality of change in the development of this colony, pointing out well-documented shifts in its economic relationship to the mother country, its political structure, and its demographic composition. But from my perspective, it appeared as if these changes were intricately bound up with the persistence of certain deep values, indeed, to an enduring structure of assumptions and attitudes that had elicited some of these changes in the first place. People found different ways to communicate old values and thus, when the great planters staked enormous bets on the quarter horses in the late seventeenth century, they simply evolved a new, socially acceptable means to express their aggressive individualism. A similar argument can be made for the Bay Colony. As I suggest in "War, Taxes and Political Brokers," the changes in institutional forms that occurred in Old Charter Massachusetts do not in themselves indicate that Puritanism had lost its hold upon the members of this society.

Reflections upon change and persistence aroused my curiosity about another aspect of seventeenth-century society, one that I explore in several chapters in this book. Put simply, I wondered how pieces of these particular societies fit together. How did various levels of authority—local, county, colonial—relate to one another? How were local units integrated into larger social structures? How did persons whose material interests were clearly in conflict—the great planters and dependent laborers of Virginia for example—achieve coherence?

As I attempted to answer these questions, I was forcefully reminded that these were extremely fragile societies. Villagers in England and America discovered periodically that they no longer understood or shared the goals of the central government. Severe strains often connected with war broke the links that normally tied one level of authority to another. Such crises involved personal tragedies, for the men who had traditionally mediated differences between local and central government suddenly found themselves rejected by their constituents. They lost the confidence of the townspeople; national or colonial leaders withdrew their support. During the late 1620s the deputy lieutenants of Essex fell into this unhappy position and cried out that they had been deserted by "our Neighbours . . . whom wee were able to pursuade much by love, and our tenents whom wee used to Command." The difficulties confronting brokers in periods of rapid institutional change is a theme explored in "Persistent Localism," "The Covenanted Militia," and most thoroughly in "War, Taxes, and Political Brokers." And certainly, a sensitivity to the specific needs and aspirations of different groups in society led me to a new understanding of the dynamics of Bacon's Rebellion. These insights are discussed in "Changing Labor Force and Race Relations."

This book represents one person's attempt to understand early American culture. I anticipate that some men and women working in this period will find interpretations with which they disagree. That is all to the good. My intention in publishing the collection was to share a particular way of looking at values and institutions, at persistence and change, and if these essays provoke others to think about culture and society from a fresh perspective, the effort will have been a success.

Puritans and Adventurers

I

Persistent Localism:
English Social Change
and the Shaping
of New England Institutions

SEVERAL ESSAYS IN this collection had already been published when I began to write this piece. It appears first because it discusses the specific background of New England settlement comprehensively and at the same time raises themes central to the entire volume.

If Charles I is remembered at all today, it is as an ineffectual monarch who lost his head on the chopping block. During the first years of his reign, however, he brought considerable energy to his position. He instituted or tried to institute far-reaching changes in civil, ecclesiastical and military affairs. These unprecedented, often arbitrary policies disrupted the fabric of local society, and they were a major preoccupation of the men and women who moved to Massachusetts Bay. One cannot fully understand the institutional decisions that the colonists made in America unless one realizes how gravely Stuart centralization threatened established patterns of daily life in England's local communities.

This essay was well received, but some readers missed an important point that I had tried to make. The English background of many migrants, humble men and women about whom we know very little, was not the English background of John Winthrop or other members of the colonial gentry. The two groups did not disagree on fundamentals, especially not on the role of religion in their society. Rather, their perception of localism was different. Winthrop's experiences in England had been largely on the county level, and when he attempted to strengthen the hand of the Bay magistrates, to keep the colony's villages from spinning off in a dozen different directions, he found himself unwittingly portrayed as an enemy of the local communities.

I

The purpose of this investigation is to reconsider the relationship between ideas and institutions in seventeenth-century New England. Intellectual historians such as Perry Miller simply took it for granted that Puritanism was responsible for the shape of social institutions in Massachusetts Bay and left it up to other historians to work out the exact interplay between the two.[1] The task, however, has proved more difficult than it may once have appeared.[2] Recent research has expanded our knowledge of the colony's institutions—its towns, churches, and families. At the same time, intellectual historians have analyzed in ever greater detail the subtleties of Puritan thought.[3] But while this growing body of scholarship is in many ways impressive, it has failed to explain how Puritan ideas affected Massachusetts social institutions.

Without denying the centrality of Puritanism in the history of New England, this study suggests that the religious beliefs that the colonists carried with them to the New World cannot in themselves account for either the original form or the subsequent development of specific institutions in Massachusetts Bay. Since there seems no reason to doubt the important role of ideas in the founding of that society, our goal will be to determine whether another set of ideas might not explain more adequately the peculiarities of the colony's social development.

It is the thesis of this essay that vague generalizations about the world the colonists left behind have obscured our understanding of the formation of New England institutions precisely because such generalizations neglect the colonists' institutional experiences in the mother country immediately prior to emigration. The towns and churches of Massachusetts were shaped by Charles I's ill-advised attempt to increase his authority by attacking local English institutions. The people who accompanied Governor John Winthrop came from diverse regions within England, some from populous commercial centers such as London and Norwich, others from isolated rural communities, but regardless of where they originated, most had been affected in some personal way by the king's aggressive effort to extend his civil and ecclesiastical authority. Between 1625 and 1640 his government made what appeared to many

Englishmen—not just Puritans—to be a series of arbitrary attempts to dominate county and local affairs, to assert the king's influence in matters that his predecessors had wisely left alone. Throughout the kingdom his subjects suddenly found themselves forced to defend what they had come to regard as traditional institutional forms.

The experience of having to resist Stuart centralization, a resistance that pitted small congregations against meddling bishops, incorporated boroughs and guilds against grasping courtiers, local trainbands against demanding deputy lieutenants, and almost everyone in the realm against the collectors of unconstitutional revenues, shaped the New Englanders' ideas about civil, ecclesiastical, and military polity. The settlers departed England determined to maintain their local attachments against outside interference, and to a large extent the Congregational churches and self-contained towns of Massachusetts Bay stood as visible evidence of the founders' decision to preserve in America what had been threatened in the mother country. And if the argument of this chapter is correct, it may offer a clue to disputes that divided the colonists as soon as they were safely out of Charles's reach. In fact, as we shall see, the settlers' English experience helps explain the bitter controversies between Winthrop and the local freemen who regularly elected him to office.

II

Historians of Massachusetts Bay have usually included in their analyses of the colony's social institutions something called the "English background." But one finds little recognition in their writings, especially in survey accounts of early American settlement, that the migrants' ideas about social institutions might have been influenced by the timing of their departure or by the particular locality form which they had originated.[4]

Seventeenth-century English society was neither stagnant nor uniform. The men and women who moved to New England during the 1630s had different institutional experiences in the mother country— different attitudes, different memories—from those of people who had already migrated to Virginia or who would eventually transfer to Pennsylvania. Throughout the century unstable political leadership, internal wars, and economic crises either altered or threatened to alter England's social institutions—its government, its churches, its army—and if one is to understand why a particular group of colonists behaved in a certain manner, one must recapture its specific English background. The critical period may have been no more than a few years preceding emigration in which rapid social and political change produced new ideas, raised fresh expectations, or generated bitter memories.

When the colonial historian contemplates seventeenth-century English society, his attention is naturally drawn to the confrontations between king and Parliament, to the affairs of court, to civil war and rebellion, and it is easy to suppose that all Englishmen must have followed these dramatic occurrences with eager interest. From this perspective the colonists' English background becomes a narrative of how people reacted to the major events of their times. But the focus here is skewed. For many men and women who moved to America the constitutional and religious battles at the national level only indirectly influenced their thinking about social institutions.

By and large the English people lived in small agricultural communities.[5] This fact does not necessarily transform our analysis into a fragmented discussion of the peculiarities of each community. It is still possible to generalize about the ways in which inhabitants of boroughs and villages across the English countryside responded to what they perceived as outside threats, the most serious usually coming from the king himself. For this purpose it is not sufficient to catalog the arbitrary decisions that Charles I made during the late 1620s. Nor is it enough to chronicle plagues and depressions. Instead, an attempt must be made to discover what kinds of common institutional experiences people living in isolated communities throughout England were having at this time, to comprehend how they reacted to what appeared to be an unprecedented level of external interference in local affairs. It is in these scattered but shared confrontations that one will find the specific English background relevant to the founding of Massachusetts Bay.

New England's social institutions appear in large part to have been shaped by Charles's efforts to expand his civil and ecclesiastical authority by curtailing the autonomy of local English institutions, efforts that forced people to think about protecting what they regarded as traditional rights from a meddling king. Charles became monarch in 1625, and Englishmen throughout the realm soon felt the impact of his policies upon their daily lives. What kind of society did the new king disturb? What were the institutions of the mother country like before he attempted to centralize his power? The answer, of course, would have been different depending on where one lived and what one's experiences had been. People felt local attachments to various levels of English society, to country villages, incorporated boroughs, religious groups, and county communities. To understand how these local bonds affected the settlement of Massachusetts Bay it is necessary to consider each level separately.

We know a good deal about the character of the English countryside, the hamlets, and scattered manor houses. A thoughtful description has been offered by the English historian Alan Everitt, who contends that the three distinguishing attributes of much of seventeenth-century English country society were its diversity, its insularity, and its continuity.[6] Everitt argues that the people living in what he calls "local communities" throughout England had little interest in events that occurred outside their own immediate environment. National politics had no place in these agricultural villages, and the lives of most persons were bound up in the simple "affairs of buying, selling, making love, marrying, bringing up a family, and with all those thousand little concerns that tied together the bonds of family life."[7] Each region developed its own special skills and crafts, its own unique farming practices.

Given the primitive state of communications in the early seventeenth century, one might attribute such strong local attachments solely to physical isolation. While isolation was certainly a major influence, there is evidence that the reign of James I was accompanied by a heightened sense of "local loyalty" or particularism. The Tudors had clipped the wings of over-mighty nobles but had neglected to establish a reliable centralized royal bureaucracy in the villages and country shires. In the absence of a strong national bureaucracy local leaders filled the vacuum, stressing as they did so the importance of local autonomy.[8] And in those communities which possessed no "gentlemanly household," the yeomen or husbandmen were apt to run everything themselves.[9] Almost everyone in the English countryside before 1625 had a stake in maintaining the customary routine of agricultural life.

Some seventeenth-century Englishmen lived in incorporated boroughs, small to middling size cities like Boston, Ipswich, Norwich, and Great Yarmouth, whose ancient royal charters gave them special rights of self-government. At the time Charles became king an incorporated borough might elect a mayor and burgesses, enforce local ordinances, hold fairs, and determine the qualifications for freemanship.

Although these boroughs, usually regional trade centers, were less insular than the country villages, they were no less diverse in character. Some were narrow oligarchies; others allowed fairly broad participation in civil affairs. Many corporations also exercised ecclesiastical patronage and, as in the instance of Great Yarmouth, jealously guarded "the right of choosing their own minister." [10] Because the boroughs, especially those engaged in foreign commerce, were often havens for nonconformists, the selection of ministers frequently fell to men of Puritan leanings—a fact that neither escaped nor pleased Charles and Archbishop William Laud. What is important to note here, however, is not the widespread nonconformity but the corporations' sense of their own continuity and independence. As the mayor and burgesses of Boston explained, their city was an "ancient borough" and "from time immemorial . . . a body corporate." [11] Like their rural neighbors, the freemen of the boroughs had an obvious interest in preserving their autonomy from outside interference.

Charles also inherited a peculiar religious situation. Some of the ablest historians of this century have examined the origins of New England Congregationalism, and there is no need to review their work. One recent essay, however, merits special attention. Patrick Collinson has investigated what he calls the "popular protestantism" of pre-Civil War England, and some of his findings, tentative though they are, should cause historians to reconsider the adequacy of any interpretation that regards congregational polity as the invention of a few Cambridge-educated divines. Collinson argues that after the Hampton Court Conference of 1604 Protestant dissent split into a "fragmented sectarianism," characterized by scores of little religious groups that "agreed as to the *delenda* but not as to the *agenda* of the further reformation." [12] Many of these bodies appear to have been voluntary organizations in which the members, not the ministers, decided matters of discipline and theology. Collinson recognizes that the Reformation contained other tendencies besides congregationalism. Nevertheless, as he observes, "it is hard to see how the movements generated within popular protestantism, left to themselves, can have had any other end." [13]

The important words here are "left to themselves." In the fifteen or so years before Laud decided to bring the nonconformists into line, dissenters had become better entrenched and more diverse, especially in the incorporated boroughs. During this period James I had done little to make good his threat of 1604 to harry the Puritans out of the land, and the sects may have grown accustomed to a certain measure of independence, of self-determination, and, perhaps it is fair to say, of congregationalism.[14] Although the men and women involved probably composed only a small fraction of the English population, they would be disproportionately represented in the settlement of Massachusetts Bay.[15] Charles's religious troubles resulted not only from his blundering efforts to punish dissenters, but also from his decision to institute such a policy after "popular protestantism" had had so many years to establish itself. The members of these little Protestant sects must have been as concerned as other Englishmen in the period before 1625 about the need to preserve local autonomy.

Another level of English society is also relevant to the specific background of Massachusetts Bay—the county communities. If town and country dwellers of the early 1620s felt a sense of political loyalty to anything beyond a few local institutions, it was likely to have been more to a county community than to the English nation as a whole. Within the shires a network of interrelated gentry families usually stood between the king and his subjects. Because the Tudors failed to replace the unpaid local gentry with salaried crown officials, "local particularism grew step by step with the growth of the central government." The gentry dominated county affairs, drilled the trainbands, sat on the quarter courts, served in Parliament, and by the time Charles became king it is difficult to imagine how any monarch could have successfully challenged their authority. They acted as mediators, rationalizing royal policies to farmers and borough freemen while simultaneously lobbying for county interests at court. If the monarch alienated these powerful gentry families, he lost effective contact with thousands of ordinary Englishmen living in places like Norfolk and Kent. Indeed, in the early decades of the seventeenth century the English body politic was composed of sets of loosely connected county elites, each of which placed its own rights and prerogatives before those of the crown. In some cases, provincial leaders self-consciously developed an idealized county history, a mythical heritage that provided all believers with a sense of regional identity.[16]

It is difficult to establish how many men and women felt a part of these county communities; if a village had no resident gentry family or were extremely isolated, the county identification may have been small. Perhaps it was only the gentry themselves who perceived politics in this manner. The point is that the existence of county communities heightened the particularism that seems to have been present at other levels of English society. The natural instinct of the local ruling gentry was to preserve an independent heritage, a set of old customs and privileges, against all outside threats. It is important to remember that while few of the men who colonized Massachusetts Bay had been county leaders of the first rank, several dozen at least had been associated with the ruling gentry and carried to the New World political impressions formed within England's county communities.

Charles disrupted these local institutions. He came to power in 1625 determined to strengthen the court, curtail religious dissent, and build an efficient army—in short, to centralize his authority at the expense of the local and county communities. As Lawrence Stone has observed, the king's plans were in keeping with the growth of royal absolutism throughout Europe. In fact, if his actions are viewed from the perspective of the Continent, it appears that "the objectives and methods of Charles, Laud, and Strafford were precisely those in which the future lay."[17] Although historians can now explain why Charles's dreams of absolutism were doomed from the start—why in the face of deeply rooted traditions of common law and representative government he could never have become an English Louis XIV—his subjects feared he might succeed.

Charles went about his business with a humorless rigor disturbing to persons grown accustomed to James's easygoing ways. Even though the new king declared that he was defending his rightful prerogatives against parliamentary encroachment, his approach and methods looked, at least to some people, like radical innovations, and on all the levels of English society that we have examined his efforts to increase royal control upset customary patterns of life.[18] His policies threatened the autonomy of the county communities, the dissenting congregations, the incorporated boroughs, and the thousands of local communities that had formerly ignored national politics. Previous monarchs had sometimes been forced to remind excessively independent Englishmen of their responsibility to the throne. But Charles attacked across the board, and his ill-conceived reforms created more enemies than one king could handle.

Insufficient funds continually plagued Charles's government; all his plans seemed to require more money than Parliament was willing to grant. His disastrous military expeditions on the coast of France, his ever-growing number of court favorites, and his personal extravagance put tremendous strains on the exchequer. He asked his subjects for free gifts and, when that failed, for forced loans. By the 1630s the king was demanding ship money from areas traditionally exempt from such levies. Much has been written about the collection of these unconstitutional revenues, and there is no need to recount the bitter struggle between Charles and Parliament over this issue. What is important is that the king's unprecedented efforts to obtain money alienated Englishmen of all types. He unwittingly helped to break down the diversity and isolation of English society by creating a grievance that affected everyone.[19]

The king's innovations were by no means restricted to unparliamentary taxation. He had the misfortune to rule during a period of general economic instability. Unemployment was high, especially in the textile regions. In the late 1620s serious food shortages developed, and groups of "lewde and dissolute persons" were reported wandering about the countryside. Charles and his advisers became convinced that unless something were done to relieve the suffering, rioting would spread throughout the depressed areas.[20] Such fears were not without foundation. In 1629, for example, an Essex court hanged a woman and three male companions for breaking into a house in broad daylight and stealing some corn, "the woman saying 'come, my brave lads of Maldon, I will be your leader, for we will not starve.' "[21] In an effort to preserve order, the Privy Council took control of local poor relief. It forbade the export of certain grains and directed justices of the peace to levy rates that might be used to provide employment for indigent workers. While these orders were well intended, the Council's actions were without precedent. According to one historian of English poor relief, "the Central Authority set in motion the whole local machinery for the execution of the poor law." County officials resented the increased work load, and some of them even questioned whether they possessed constitutional authority to collect poor relief. The king's plans to pacify the poor, like his schemes to find additional revenue, were regarded by many Englishmen as another indication of growing absolutism, another assault on local independence.[22]

The early years of Charles's reign brought disturbing efforts at religious innovation, both theological and institutional. Not only was the Arminianism of Laud offensive to England's Calvinists, but his ecclesiastical reforms aroused the antagonism of villagers and gentry alike in many parts of the realm.[23] Laud was determined to force religious dissenters to conform to the Anglican service, and he urged his bishops to report any deviation from accepted ecclesiastical practice. Some bishops dragged their feet, but others were eager to please their superior. These men visited local congregations, broke up conventicles, and challenged respected ministers. Indeed, they attacked "popular protestantism" wherever they found it. In Hampshire angry villagers protested Laud's actions as "an unwonted, dangerous, and unwelcome innovation." [24] People in other local communities agreed.

Laud's ecclesiastical officers also attempted to destroy "that ratsbane of lecturing" frequently found in the incorporated boroughs. Again, what men perceived as established local traditions were disturbed. According to one historian, when the king and his archbishop attacked the lectureships, "they were tampering not with a recent innovation but rather with an institution that in many places had been rooted in the life of the community for several generations." [25] Laud's interference agitated people who wanted to preserve accustomed forms of worship and drove them into alliance with persons who resented the king's economic and political meddling. [26]

Nothing created greater dislocation in the English countryside than Charles's military policies. Early in his reign the king decided to commit troops to the Continental wars. James had regarded overseas expeditions as an extravagance, but the wisdom of his position escaped Charles. He recklessly plunged ahead. Throughout the kingdom soldiers were pressed into service, marched to coastal cities, and dispatched to French battlefields from which few returned alive. The military companies consisted of the dregs of English society—misfits, troublemakers, men too poor to buy their way out of the army. The recruits often did not receive the "coat and conduct money" that might have sustained them on their journey to the port towns. The shortsightedness of this policy soon became apparent. Desperate bands of soldiers wandered from village to village disturbing the peace, assaulting people, and raping women. [27]

Although many examples could be cited to show how Charles's unprecedented military innovations upset local institutions, the case of Great Yarmouth is sufficient to the purpose. When the deputy lieutenants of Norfolk called for twenty soldiers from Great Yarmouth, the bailiffs of that city responded with surprise that "it had not been used or known, time out of mind, that any land soldiers had been pressed in Yarmouth, it being a frontier town [that is, exposed to attack from the sea] and of special importance to the kingdom, and consisted principally of seafaring men." Soon after, one hundred Irish troops were sent into the town and, in the language of the day, "billeted there during His Majesty's pleasure." Unfortunately for this nonconformist center, the Irish turned out "to be all Papists," and the city watch had to be strengthened. Every householder turned out with musket and pike, not to ward off foreign invaders, but to protect their lives and property from Charles's own troops. And Great Yarmouth got off easily in comparison with other places where there were serious riots. It would have been far better for the king not to have angered England's boroughs and local communities in this way. His policies only served to widen the growing gap between royal government and local authority.[28] In the end he discovered that while he could frighten his subjects, he could not control them.

Resentment against the king's interference in local affairs was by no means restricted to the poor and the humble. His policies steadily undermined the loyalty of the great gentry families that dominated England's county communities. He expected them as deputy lieutenants to develop what he termed a "perfect militia." He ordered them as justices of the peace to supervise poor relief.[29] It was they who often ended up paying his illegal revenues, and when their spokesmen in Commons complained too strongly, Charles decided he could rule without Parliament's help.

The increased work load, the financial strain, even the constitutional crisis might have been borne had not Charles's policies threatened to alter traditional social relationships within the county communities themselves. The gentry discovered that by putting the king's directives into effect they alienated local support. Suddenly in the late 1620s some of them found themselves in a defensive position before the very people from whom they had always received deference.[30] Local loyalties were important, far too important to lose over a foolish "perfect militia" or some other royal scheme. Charles warned the county leaders that "ther remissnes in executing thes our commands geves encouragement to the inferior sort of people," but despite such admonishments, men of better quality—"the High sheriff, deputy Lieutenants and Justices of peace, and under them the constables and other inferior officers"—concluded that it was better to have friends at home than to try to please the king.[31]

The changes that took place in the incorporated boroughs are not entirely clear; historians have not given the problem adequate attention. It is known, however, that after 1621 the House of Commons tried to revive parliamentary elections in a number of boroughs that had long since stopped sending representatives, usually because of local poverty. The franchise in these towns was broadly defined, sometimes all householders being included, so that there was little likelihood that the crown could determine which men were sent to Parliament from these constituencies.[32] But Charles was apparently unwilling to accept this state of affairs without a fight. After 1626 royal courts instituted *quo warranto* proceedings against the charters of several boroughs. Great Yarmouth reported that courtiers were plotting to "have the antient and laudable custom of choosing two bailiffs altered." In 1629 its townsmen took up a subscription to defend their charter before King's Bench. A writ of *quo warranto*, issued against the corporation of Boston in 1627, charged local officials "with Having usurped" privileges and liberties "to the injury of the King's prerogatives." In 1631 the borough of Ipswich suddenly was forced "to make defense, and to procure confirmation of the Charter." In most of these cases the towns preserved their corporate rights after long and expensive court battles.[33] The judicial outcome is less important than the fact that the king's attacks on the "ancient boroughs" seemed part of a general assault on England's local institutions. And it is probably not insignificant that a good many New Englanders originated in Boston, Ipswich, Great Yarmouth, and Norwich—all boroughs that had been forced to combat royal intervention.[34]

In reaction to the king's continued interference in local affairs—his attacks on "popular protestantism," his disruption of the county communities, his assault on the corporate boroughs—a few thousand English men and women chose to leave the country. To these people Charles must have seemed perfectly capable of establishing himself as an absolute ruler: the future of local society appeared dark to those who followed John Winthrop in 1630, and to the emigrants of the mid-1630s the situation must have looked nearly hopeless.[35] Their response was essentially defensive, conservative, even reactionary.

There is a substantial body of information about how other people—not necessarily Puritans—reacted to the disruption of local communities and traditional ways of life by some outside authority. Invariably, the beleaguered groups assumed a defensive stance, resisting, sometimes with force, any alteration of accepted routine. Historian J. H. Elliott discovered that the population of sixteenth- and seventeenth-century

Europe deeply resented innovation. Indeed, the participants in violent risings seemed "obsessed by *renovation*—by the desire to return to old customs and privileges, and to an old order of society."[36] England was no exception to the rule. In her comments on the Civil War, Joan Thirsk observes that "the great majority of the gentry and peasantry, in their almost morbid anxiety to preserve the traditional fabric of local society, generally stood side by side."[37] It appears that the same local communities that resisted Charles ultimately defeated Oliver Cromwell for he too tried to force them to change their ways—to make them integral parts of a centralized nation-state.[38] These examples suggest that the English countryside was filled with traditionally oriented men and women, who, like turtles, pulled back into the safe and familiar shell of local custom at the first sign of danger.

The results of this conservative response would appear in the social institutions of New England. The colonists' experiences under Charles had heightened their sense of tradition, and whether they came from small country villages or sizable corporate boroughs, whether they were humble yeomen or influential county leaders, they shared a desire to preserve a customary way of life. That they were willing to travel three thousand miles to achieve that goal reveals how strongly some of them felt about the disruptions of local institutions. Like the Catholic proprietors who in the late 1630s tried to create a vast feudal manor in Maryland, the Bay colonists looked to America as a place to escape the dislocating effects of social change.

These observations are not intended to imply that all colonists were of one mind about social institutions in the New World. They were not. The settlers' English background produced both unity and diversity. On the one hand, the people who transferred to New England during the 1630s were obviously influenced by the same general threats to local autonomy. This common experience helped to create broad areas of agreement about the character of New England society. On the other hand, the migration itself created diversity. New Englanders had crossed the Atlantic not as individual adventurers but as self-selected groups. Respected civil and religious leaders often recruited their neighbors, and it was not unusual for persons from the same small village to stay together once they reached Massachusetts. This type of migration, called "chain migration," meant that each group possessed separate and distinct memories of life in the mother country.[39] Stuart policies had affected them in different ways. Habits and traditions, attitudes toward land division, town government, church membership—all these things were in part the product of a specific environment. While Massachusetts society was still in its formative stages, therefore, each community was forced to work out the relationship between its own particular English heritage and a more general English background that it shared with other Bay communities. Seen in this light, New England was not a single, monolithic "fragment" separating off from the mother country. It was a body of loosely joined fragments, and some of the disputes that developed in the New World grew out of differences that had existed in the Old.[40]

III

The early migrants to Massachusetts Bay were anxious to recapture a traditional way of life. Left behind were interfering Stuart officials and troublesome Anglican bishops. The very openness of New England made it possible for the colonists to transform social ideas into actual institutions. Each group of immigrants had an opportunity to create an independent community, a village in which local institutions might be safe from outside interference. The settlers' commitment to the preservation of local autonomy led almost inevitably to social diversity, and within a decade after Winthrop's arrival, a score of towns had taken root in Massachusetts, each developing institutions slightly different from those of its neighbors.

But the preservation of local institutions involved New Englanders in difficulties that no one anticipated. The immigrants were so obsessed with local autonomy that almost without being conscious of it, they created institutions that looked very little like those they had left behind in the mother country. The settlers realized that within a locality broad participation in civil, military, and ecclesiastical affairs would help to secure local independence from central authority, and voluntarism quickly became the hallmark of Massachusetts society.[41] The colonists had no use for democracy, but they believed that anyone who possessed a voice in local concerns thereby acquired a responsibility to the community as a whole. Indeed, the person who enjoyed such a privilege would find it in his best interests to defend those elements that had been threatened in England—continuity, independence, and insularity.

The irony was that the New Englanders' social goals forced them unwittingly to accept significant social change. In elections of all sorts they opened the franchise to men who would have been excluded in almost every English borough and town. In the early years of settlement the need for such alterations seemed perfectly obvious. Winthrop and the first assistants of the Massachusetts Bay Company could legally have become a narrow oligarchy selecting themselves anew year after year. But Winthrop encouraged a considerable expansion in the number of voters, a group that could and later did drop him from the governorship.[42] The people who enlarged the franchise do not seem to have been as much concerned with creating an ideal Puritan commonwealth as with averting absolutism. To appreciate how the settlers' English backgrounds influenced social institutions, one has only to examine the towns, churches, and trainbands established in Massachusetts Bay during the 1630s. In each case, parallel forms developed which strongly suggest that socio-cultural experiences in the mother country after 1625 were a major determinant in the way of the colonists organized New England society.

Colonial historians have only recently come to appreciate the diversity of New England towns.[43] Some evidence suggests that Winthrop wanted the settlers of 1630 to form one large fortified community, but whatever his ideas may have been, the colonists quickly went their separate ways.[44] Historians who have traced the development of the early towns have been struck by local differences. Intensive studies of Andover, Dedham, Hingham, and Sudbury reveal how misleading it is to speak of *the* New England town. Some of the communities experienced bitter feuds; others were quite stable. Some were more commercially oriented than others. There was no uniform method of dividing lands, running town meetings, or laying out house lots. Edward Johnson surveyed the villages of Massachusetts Bay and discovered that while people in some places clustered around the meetinghouse, those in other communities were relatively dispersed. In Concord, for example, he found that the "buildings are conveniently placed chiefly in one straite streame [streete]. . . ." But in Newbury the "houses are built very scattering, which hath caused some contending about removall of their place for Sabbath-Assemblies." And when Johnson visited Salisbury he observed that "the people of this Towne have of late placed their dwellings so much distanced the one from the other, that they are like to

divide into two Churches."[45] In other words, even in the earliest years
of settlement some towns allowed "outlivers" to erect homes away from
the center of the village.[46]

What the towns of Massachusetts Bay had in common was a desire to
preserve their individual autonomy. New England villagers often
bound themselves together by written covenants, promising to uphold
certain clearly stated principles. Historians have analyzed these covenants, but few have seen them as an indication of the colony's reactionary origins. These voluntary agreements provided villagers with a sense
of local identity, a rationale for excluding outsiders, and a means of
achieving continuity between present and future generations. Moreover,
the covenants served a more immediate function. By promoting harmony and homogeneity, they helped to ward off the kind of external interference that had been so troublesome in the mother country. Many
town covenants contained a section specifically committing townsmen
to settle their disputes through love and friendly arbitration. While this
provision seems an expression of Christian charity, it also reduced the
likelihood that colonial magistrates would intervene in local affairs.[47]
And by screening potential inhabitants—indeed, by accepting in some
cases only those people who had emigrated from a particular English
district—many towns avoided the contention that conflicting backgrounds and traditions might have bred.[48] Each individual was under
strong peer-group pressure to give his first loyalty to the town, and, as
one might expect, New England's local communities resisted anything
that threatened established routine.

The Congregational churches were another institution that revealed
the effect of the English background on the character of Massachusetts
society. Historians have exaggerated the intolerance of the colony's ministers and magistrates. Although, to be sure, such outspoken critics of
the New England Way as Roger Williams and Anne Hutchinson were
exiled, Congregational orthodoxy, compared to other seventeenth-century religious systems, allowed a relatively wide range of opinion on
questions of polity and theology.[49]

Because the settlers insisted on local control over religious affairs, it is
not surprising that significant differences developed among the
churches. In fact, the Congregational system itself fostered diversity.[50]
New Englanders who had resented Laud's interference refused in
America to recognize any ecclesiastical authority beyond the local community. Colony-wide synods could recommend—even cajole—but they

could not order individual congregations to alter religious procedures. In the words of the Cambridge Platform of 1648, the churches were "distinct, and therefore may not be confounded one with another: and equall, and therfore have not dominion one over another."[51] Only in the most extreme cases did the political leaders of Massachusetts involve themselves in local church matters, and then only reluctantly. Normally, the church-members of a village selected their minister, set his salary, and determined ecclesiastical policy. One colonist, Thomas Lechford, described in 1642 some of the ways in which the churches varied. The Boston congregation, for example, was ruled "by unanimous consent," while in Salem decisions required only "the major part of the church." Moreover, Lechford found that "some Churches have no ruling Elders, some but one, some but one teaching Elder, some have two ruling, and two teaching Elders; some one, some two or three Deacons. . . ."[52] It was not only in details of polity that congregations exercised their discretion. Even in the earliest years of colonization, some towns such as Newbury favored presbyterian forms of worship.[53]

Some contemporaries in the mother country regarded the Bay colonists as religious innovators, experimenting with extreme types of separatism. These English critics were correct on one count. In the early 1630s there were few precedents for the ecclesiastical system that developed in Massachusetts. In 1644 one colonial minister, William Hooke, admitted, "It is a truth, we saw but little in comparison of what we now do, when we left our Native homes."[54] But what the people back in England failed to understand was that the colonists regarded Congregationalism as a means to restore the Protestant faith and preserve true religion from outside interference. Because they were safely beyond Laud's reach, they enjoyed an opportunity to do in the 1630s what was denied Englishmen until the 1640s. The New Englanders gave the church back to the local communities. And in so doing they were responding not only to the freedom of their new environment but also to specific conditions that they had experienced in England. New England's Congregational churches, like its towns, were the result of the general antipathy that the colonists felt toward Stuart centralism.[55]

The colonists also created a system of defense. Military organizations by their very nature would seem to demand a highly centralized chain of command. If the New Englanders had been willing to compromise their desire for local autonomy, one might expect them to have done so in the formation of their militia. But the shape of this social institution was not so very different from that of the Congregational churches and the town governments. All of them stressed local control, even if that meant an unprecedented degree of popular participation in the selection of leaders.[56]

In England it had been Charles's appointed officers, usually his deputy lieutenants, who had most frequently disrupted country life. They had been responsible for the king's "perfect militia," for the collection of unparliamentary levies, and for the billeting of unwelcome troops. With such experiences in mind the settlers of Massachusetts Bay insisted upon placing as many local controls on the military as security would allow. The colonial government could dispatch an army against the Indians, but the militia itself was a village institution. Not only did the townsmen drill together, they also chose their own officers. As early as 1632 Winthrop reported that "a proposition was made by the people, that every company of trained men might choose their own captain and officers."[57] By the mid-1630s local trainband elections had become common practice throughout the colony. Although the Massachusetts General Court claimed ultimate authority in the selection of officers, the legislators seldom rejected a name, and local nomination amounted to final selection.

Some military men thought that the New Englanders had lost their good sense. One veteran of European campaigns complained that the Massachusetts system would destroy discipline. Voluntarism had no place in matters of defense, and the colony's organization appeared to this person, at least, a wrong-headed innovation.[58] But the colonists were not concerned with winning Continental wars; they were far more conscious of the meddling deputy lieutenants who had made life so unpleasant in England. It was the king's appointed officers, not the elected New Englanders, who were viewed as the true innovators. The immigrants merely restored the trainbands to community control. Once the militia had been transformed into a local structure, it became highly unlikely that it could be used to oppress the settlers. And it is not surprising that a survey of Massachusetts records reveals no instance in which the colony's rulers attempted to employ the militia as a police force, as a tax collector, or as an instrument of social control.

The colonists' English background affected life in Massachusetts in another way that no one expected. Instead of promoting unity, it became a source of dissension, especially in political and ecclesiastical matters, and within a few years the settlers were forced to confront the unpleasant realization that they were not all interested in preserving the same things in the New World. Like their contemporaries in the mother country, a majority of the New Englanders seem to have been concerned primarily with what occurred in their own villages. They built homes, sowed crops, made love, and for the most part gave scant attention to the actions of the colony's central government. As one colonist explained, "Plantations in their beginning have worke enough, and find difficulties sufficient to settle a comfortable way of subsistence, there beinge buildings, fencings, cleeringe and breakinge up of ground, lands to be attended, orchards to be planted, highways and bridges and fortifications to be made."[59] But other men such as Winthrop appear to have regarded Massachusetts Bay as a sort of American "county community." These people naturally defined "local" in larger terms than did the other colonists, and when they were forced to curb the independence of certain local institutions, they found themselves suddenly cast in the role of Charles I. Ironically, tensions between central authority and local custom had followed the settlers to the New World.

The division was most apparent in political affairs. Indeed, at the same time that the colony's local institutions were taking shape, the central government was a continuous source of conflict. A year seldom passed without Bay rulers accusing each other of some abuse of power, and on one occasion at least jealousy and anger sparked an attempt to impeach Winthrop. These political battles have been closely examined, and much is known about their intellectual content.[60] So far, however, no historian has adequately explained the social origins of these disputes. Since all the colonists involved presumably had similar religious views, one is forced to look elsewhere for the roots of dissension. Why, indeed, did an elected governor and court of assistants find it so difficult to work in harmony with an elected house of deputies representing the towns of Massachusetts Bay? Had the local communities carried their contempt for external authority to such an extreme that they were unwilling to tolerate the slightest outside interference in their affairs?

In most of these controversies Winthrop and a small group of like-minded magistrates were pitted against an outspoken but loosely connected body of village representatives. The reasons for these fights were complex, but one of them no doubt was the way in which the governor and his allies defined "local" interests. Although Winthrop had not been a leader of the first rank in his native English county, Suffolk, he counted among his friends some of the most powerful gentry families in the shire. His business dealings carried him regularly from his home at Groton Manor to London, and he knew firsthand how a county community operated. The most influential members of the gentry (in Suffolk they would have been the Barnardistons and Barringtons) acted as mediators between England's central government and the specific interests of their county.[61] When they spoke of preserving independence or complained of royal interference, they usually had the shire in mind.

The actions of Winthrop and a few other men of similar experience suggest that they arrived in America intent on reproducing a county community. In this smaller New World pond they may well have regarded themselves as bigger fish and assumed the role and responsibilities of the leading gentry of Massachusetts Bay. Although they were elected to office annually by the colony's freemen, they saw themselves as natural rulers—as persons prepared by God, training, and status to act in the colonists' best interests. The New England county elite received advice from the people with ill grace, viewing any attempt to limit their discretionary powers as a personal insult.[62] The Winthrops of Massachusetts believed that the voters should trust the gentry's judgment in much the same manner as in the mother country. These notions about the government and society grew out of a special English background, and to Winthrop's chagrin they were challenged by groups within the colony who conceived of "local" autonomy in rather different terms.

Most settlers were willing to trust this self-styled county elite, but only up to a point. They had gone through too much in England, traveled too far, raised their expectations about local autonomy too high to do simply as Winthrop and his friends desired. In any case, the colonists found it difficult to regard these leaders as mere county gentry. The nature of this authority seemed quite different from that of the Barringtons and Barnardistons. They issued important executive orders, served in the highest courts, and claimed broad powers and privileges on the basis of a royal charter granted to the Massachusetts Bay Company. No one, of course, confused John Winthrop with Charles Stuart, but it seemed clear that the governor spoke for the central government as opposed to the local communities. Almost as soon as the migrants arrived in the New World they sought ways to control the magistrates' discretionary powers and to ensure that civil rulers in Massachusetts understood that the ultimate source of political authority was a collection of independent corporate towns speaking through their elected delegates.

One of the better illustrations of the division between New England's county elite and the local communities occurred in 1632, when the Massachusetts Court of Assistants, a small group of magistrates selected at large by the colony's freemen, levied a tax to finance a fortification at Newtown (later renamed Cambridge). This act met with immediate resistance in neighboring Watertown, where the town's minister and its leading elder summoned the villagers together and admonished them that "it was not safe to pay moneys after that sort, for fear of bringing themselves and posterity into bondage." [63] The people of Watertown concluded that they had been taxed without adequate representation.

Winthrop rejected this argument out of hand. The assistants, he explained, were like members of Parliament in that they represented the interests of the voters who had chosen them. But Winthrop missed the point of the Watertown protest. When it came to matters of taxation, these villagers wanted someone in the legislature who represented the interests not of the entire colony but of their own locality. People living in other communities apparently shared this view, for despite assurances from Winthrop that a colony-wide elite would govern fairly, the Massachusetts freemen insisted in 1634 on having local representatives participate in the legislative process. [64] In a historic decision the General Court ordered that each town select two or three men who "shalbe hereafter soe deputed by the freemen of [the] severall plantacions, to deale in their behalfe, in the publique affayres of the commonwealth." [65] A good many New Englanders in the 1630s obviously would have asked with William Pynchon of Springfield, "If magistrates in N. E. should ex officio practise such a power over mens proprieties, how long would Tyrany be kept out of our habitations?" [66]

The clash between local and county views of government authority reached a dramatic climax in 1645. In the spring of that year the militiamen of Hingham selected a West Country migrant, Anthony Eames, as their captain. For reasons that remain unclear, however, Eames fell out of favor with his neighbors, and the trainband held a second election, this time choosing Bozone Allen. At this point Winthrop, then the colony's deputy governor, stepped in and accused Allen's supporters of fomenting insubordination to lawful authority. Allen's followers countered in no uncertain terms that by intervening in a local affair Winthrop had exceeded his legitimate powers, and the disgruntled Hinghamites organized an unsuccessful attempt within the Massachusetts General Court to impeach him. Throughout the controversy the inhabitants of Hingham insisted that they were defending local autonomy against unwarranted outside interference.[67] Hingham reacted to what it perceived as a threat to its independence much as the English local communities reacted first to Charles and then to Cromwell. And like the members of Parliament, the village representatives serving in the Massachusetts legislature tried to assert their rights through impeachment. Winthrop came out of this trial with his reputation intact, but Hingham had served notice that civil power flowed up from the local communities, not down from a county elite.

By the 1650s the Bay colonists had sorted out their various English backgrounds. Unexpected problems had been confronted, and compromises made. But for most of them the trip to the New World had been an overwhelming success. The Massachusetts countryside at mid-century appeared remarkably like the traditional English society which they had sought to preserve from Stuart intervention. One historian has termed New England's little settlements "peasant utopias"—a description that captures their backward-looking character.[68] Most of them went years without significant change in institutional forms or procedures. The townsmen regarded the village as the center of their lives; indeed, most were married and buried in the places of their birth. The vast undeveloped lands to the west had little appeal. Seldom has a conservative movement so fully achieved its aims.

II

The Covenanted Militia
of Massachusetts Bay:
English Background and
New World Development

THIS ESSAY EXPLORES the distinctive origins of the Massachusetts militia and in so doing further develops several themes presented in "Persistent Localism," particularly the concept of institutional parallelism. The great nineteenth-century English historian, S. R. Gardiner, was one of the first scholars to appreciate how seriously Charles's military policies in the late 1620s upset the entire nation. Since the publication of Gardiner's monumental *History of England,* others—most notably Lindsay Boynton—have extended our knowledge of the disruption of the English countryside between 1625 and 1628. The king's misguided efforts to create a "perfect militia" and his stubborn determination to wage war on the continent sparked a storm of constitutional and religious protest. Colonial American historians have concentrated their research largely upon other aspects of English society, especially upon the rise of Puritanism, and have overlooked the profoundly negative impact that the Stuart military system had upon those men and women who emigrated to Massachusetts Bay. After they had successfully replaced Charles's "perfect militia" with their own "covenanted militia," the colonists confronted a quite different institutional problem, the need to define the limits of popular participation in the election of officers. This debate continued for the rest of the seventeenth century.

I

A major problem for anyone examining seventeenth-century colonial society, and probably other, more modern societies as well, is to establish a connection between the settlers' experiences in the Old World and the shape of their social institutions in America. The difficulty arises when one attempts to define an English background with precision, for there is a danger that the colonial historian will seize upon influences so general—an Elizabethan world view or immemorial English custom just to cite two examples—that he will be unable to elucidate obvious differences in the character of various early American settlements. How, in fact, does one explain why early seventeenth-century English migrants formed such strikingly dissimilar societies in the Chesapeake and New England? To answer this question, it is necessary to consider conditions in specific shires and boroughs on the eve of colonization, to develop a greater appreciation of how local practices within the mother country varied with time and place.[1] Such close study demonstrates that broad generalities about English tradition and Elizabethan social ideas obscure the anomalous circumstances surrounding the founding of each colony.

A second problem is to assess what the development of a specific social institution, be it church, state, or militia, indicates about a colonial society as a whole. The pitfall to be avoided here is what Professor J. H. Hexter calls "tunnel history," a narrow focus upon one aspect of human activity without reference to man's other pursuits.[2] To avoid this pitfall, one must take a broader view. One must analyze the intricate relationships between different institutions and compare their function, growth, and structure. The colonial historian might consider, for example, whether New World institutions were founded upon a single organizing principle or whether each developed independently. This approach could produce a more accurate picture than is presently available of the character of early American society and might even shed light on such disputed matters as the growth of democracy and the decline of Puritanism. This essay examines one particular institution, the militia of Massachusetts Bay. It is not intended as an exercise in military history, but as a suggestion of how one might deal with the problems of defining English background and interpreting New World development.

In the perennial debate about the character of early New England society, historians have seldom considered the militia. The reason for their omission is clear. The trainbands of the Bay Colony appeared to them to have been less innovative than were the Puritan church and state. It was in the meeting houses, not on the training fields, that the founders seemed to depart most dramatically from English institutional models and to experiment with popular participation in the selection of civil and ecclesiastical leaders. By comparison, the militia was regarded as a vestige of the Old World, a medieval organization that changed little either during the transfer to America or over the course of the seventeenth century.[3]

This view of the militia requires substantial modification. The migrants who traveled to Massachusetts Bay designed their military system in response to the specific experiences that they had had in England. The Bay Colony militia was not a product of the free air of America or an attempt to reproduce an ancient military organization in a new environment. Rather, it represented a self-conscious rejection of the policies of Charles I.

A reexamination of the Massachusetts system of defense also reveals that it was as much an expression of Puritan social ideas as were the New England town meetings and the Congregational churches. The history of the village trainbands paralleled the development of other, more obviously Puritan institutions. Throughout the Old Charter period, 1629–1684, the leaders of the Bay Colony attempted to define the limits of popular participation in civil and ecclesiastical affairs. The results of these efforts rarely pleased everyone. Some demanded a greater voice in the selection of officials and in the determination of public policy, while others, such as the Reverend Samuel Stone, urged parishioners to stand silent before their "speaking aristocracy."[4] The militia in Massachusetts was at once a reflection and a product of this larger debate, and a fuller study of trainband politics enriches our understanding of the nature of the Puritan experiment in the New World.[5]

II

The story of the Massachusetts militia begins not with the Anglo-Saxon "fyrd," nor with the medieval assize-at-arms, but with certain military reforms effected under Queen Elizabeth. By making the office of the Lord Lieutenant more important than had any of her predecessors, she transformed overmighty nobles into officers of the Crown and reduced the possibility that their retainers would be employed against the state. Since the queen never possessed a standing army, she insisted on bringing the militia, the nation's only domestic armed force, tightly under her control. She commissioned Lords Lieutenant to direct the trainbands and to defend England's shires against potential foreign invaders.[6] These individuals, or in some cases deputies, appointed all lesser officers.[7] The trainbands themselves were made up of able-bodied men drawn from the middle class. One Essex Deputy advised his captain to accept into the militia only "good freeholders, fermers & housholders or the sones of such meete for the service." While poorer persons and those of "base Condision" did not receive regular training, they were the first to be levied for overseas expeditions, a service from which few returned alive.[8]

Under Elizabeth and her successor, James I, the Lieutenancy acquired some additional administrative responsibilities such as selling Virginia lottery tickets, but the position retained its original military character.[9] In Stuart times, however, the Lords Lieutenant grew too fond of life at court, many of them doubling as Privy Councillors, and their duties fell increasingly to deputies who were prominent members of the local gentry.[10] They served as important mediators between the central and county governments, and though the men who became deputies received no fees or salary for their work, they do not seem to have regarded the office as a great burden so long as James ruled the nation.[11]

The reason, of course, was that James possessed little interest in military matters, and throughout his reign, he studiously avoided expensive foreign wars that would have forced him to summon Parliament. Even after a Catholic army drove his Protestant son-in-law, Frederick the Elector, out of the Palatinate, James hesitated to raise English troops. In the counties his indifference to military affairs meant that the deputies often cancelled training and overlooked faulty arms. The quality of the trainbands decayed so much during these years that one Lord Lieutenant aptly described James's musters as a "May game."[12] The king not only saved revenues, he also left undisturbed countless local communities throughout the realm. The men and women who inhabited these villages escaped the terrifying sight of sick and hungry soldiers marching off to almost certain death. And no householder was confronted with the dismal prospect of quartering desperate, armed strangers in his own home.

Charles I broke with the past. He came to the throne in 1625 determined to reform his father's military system. Not only did Charles commit English troops to the Continental wars, he also called for the formation of what he termed "a perfect Militia."[13] The king sent Low Country veterans into the counties to assist in the training of the militia, and he ordered a modernization of all weapons.[14] While Charles addressed his orders to the Lords Lieutenant, it was the deputies who put the new plans into effect, and in the years after 1625 they became the most active, the most visible, and the most despised royal officers in the land.[15]

Between the middle of 1624 and the end of 1627 the Lords Lieutenant or persons acting in their name levied approximately fifty thousand men into military service. About ten thousand troops were pressed each year, just about double the annual levy under Elizabeth.[16] According to contemporary observers, the soldiers came from the dregs of English society. Reports from the south coast noted that recruiters pressed the "poorest and unablest men."[17] An Irish officer serving in the Spanish army reviewed a group of English deserters in 1625 and concluded—as many Englishmen would have done—that these soldiers had "been gathered compulsorily of the most basest sort of rascalitye."[18] English officers echoed these sentiments. A captain scolded the deputies in one county for pressing "about 130 of the basest beggars and the poorest boyes and lowsey Rascalls that I did ever see sent for Souldiers." The writer confessed, "I cannot blame you although you desired to rid your Countrie of them for 16d a man [press money] for I protest before god if halfe of them were my souldiers, I would give 16d a man to have them taken from mee."[19]

As soon as the deputies levied their quota, men called conductors marched the recruits to coastal cities such as Harwich, Southampton, and Plymouth. These journeys were disorderly, terrifying experiences for everyone involved, and as rumors of each new military disaster raced through the countryside, control of the recruits became increasingly difficult. Some draftees killed or mutilated themselves rather than follow the Duke of Buckingham to the Isle of Ré. Scores of men deserted or rioted. Indeed, by 1627 conductors sometimes arrived at their destination without a single soldier. Their entire column, often more than a hundred conscripts, had disappeared along the country roads.[20]

After the defeat of an English expedition at Ré in 1627, Charles announced that the army would *not* be disbanded as most people expected. The idea was to keep the forces intact so that they could launch a second attack the next year. The king's decision turned out to be a monumental blunder. No previous monarch had ever attempted to maintain large numbers of idle troops on English territory. There was no money in the Exchequer to support them, no buildings in which to house them. To make matters worse, the soldiers were in a nasty mood.[21] In November the Privy Council warned the deputies of Northamptonshire that the returning men might run from the colors. The deputies were instructed to monitor road traffic, to challenge suspicious looking groups of men, arresting their leaders if necessary, and to draw up local trained bands in emergencies.[22] Another directive from the Council asked commanders ". . . to cause the soldiers to march together, and not to spoil or do any misdemeanors or use any violence."[23] Such orders had little effect. Charles managed to set the remnants of an English army against the English people. The sight of this ragged force served as a constant reminder of Buckingham's ineptitude, of the bankruptcy of the king's foreign policy, and the presence of these troops in the boroughs and villages in itself became a fresh grievance against the Crown.

The deputies' plight in this period can better be appreciated when one remembers that Parliament refused to back Charles's ill-planned, expensive military adventures. After Commons failed to vote him his normal subsidies, the king turned to his subjects asking first for free gifts, and when that scheme collapsed, for forced loans.[24] The collection of these unparliamentary taxes often became the deputies' responsibility. In addition to benevolences and loans, Charles ordered his deputies to raise special funds called "coat and conduct money." In previous reigns the Crown had supplied these sums, which were used to clothe and transport soldiers to the seacoast.[25] Charles's Privy Council regularly promised prompt repayment of such monies, but with the Exchequer empty, few Englishmen expected to be reimbursed.[26] Unwittingly perhaps, the king and his favorites had transformed the character of the Elizabethan Lieutenancy. What had been conceived as an institution of defence under the queen had now become an instrument of government buttressing Charles's prerogative power.[27]

Charles also expected the deputies to billet his troops. The task was impossible. Sick, unpaid soldiers returned from France and Spain anticipating decent treatment from their government. Instead the deputies sent them to live in the homes of those who could least afford the burden. Some deputies saw the inequity of this quartering system, but they protested that there was little they could do: "Persons of better ability absolutely refuse to receive them [the soldiers]."[28] The short-sightedness of this policy immediately became apparent. Angry bands of soldiers wandered through the countryside disturbing the peace, assaulted people, and, on one occasion at least, attacked a town which failed to house them in the manner they desired.[29] English men and women regarded these strangers as aliens, unwanted visitors sent by Charles, and to people already unhappy with the king's civil and religious policies, quartering seemed a cruel and unnecessary innovation. "This Kingdome," Sir Walter Earle explained, "never knew this wrong [forced billeting]: In Qu: E: [Queen Elizabeth's] tyme, there were soldiers but none were forced on us."[30]

Surveying the damage done by the king's army to the English population, Sir John Eliot exclaimed "little difference doe I find betweene theise and the old Romaine soldiers, can this people give supply that are not masters of themselves."[31] The beleaguered deputies attempted to restore order through martial law, but civilians found to their great surprise that they were hauled before the military courts along with the soldiers. Had there been a clear national emergency or had the civil courts been closed, the use of martial law within England might have made sense, but since neither was the case, it appeared that the deputies were bent upon undermining traditional English liberties.[32] These officers had already assisted in the collection of unparliamentary taxes; now they threatened the common law.

In some counties Deputy Lieutenants increased their unpopularity by making the military a religious as well as a constitutional grievance.[33] The heavily Puritan counties of Essex, Suffolk, and Norfolk were important staging areas for English and Irish troops bound for the Continent, and the Stuart military system may have seemed a greater hardship in these shires than it did in other parts of England. On February 10, 1628, the anxious deputies of Essex advised the Privy Council: "Our Countrie doth much grieve, that since itt cannot be avoyded but that they must have souldiers, that theire fortune is soe badd, that of all the Regiments that is placed with them, which is soe many wayes offensive above others, as beinge Irish, not English of a contrary Religion. . . ." The deputies were certain that the number of Catholic troops stationed in their county was "more than dubble . . . [that] which is placed in any [other] shire, and every day encreasinge."[34]

In 1626 the deputies of Norfolk in an ill-conceived attempt to make their trainbands more perfect, ordered militiamen to practice "archery, running, wrestling, leaping, football playing, casting the sledge hammer, and playing at cudgels." Moreover, they explained that church wardens would see that these exercises were carried out immediately following Sunday services. The Norfolk deputies simply adopted James's Declaration of Sports, an anti-Puritan document encouraging Sabbath recreation, for their own purposes, and while there is no record of protest, the local Puritans probably did not appreciate the benefits of Sunday exercise.[35] The billeting of Irish Catholic regiments in East Anglia exacerbated religious tensions. In one Essex village a number of persons died in a battle that occurred after Protestant children tied red crosses on the tails of their dogs and ran the animals in front of resident Irish troops.[36] These incidents possess special importance for the colonial historian because it was from East Anglia and the surrounding region that many future New England settlers came, and they seem to have been among the people most adversely affected by Stuart military policy.

Some of the more perceptive Deputy Lieutenants understood that the king's demands not only had a pernicious effect on the character of their office, but also undermined their position of leadership within the counties. The deputies of Essex wrote in February 1628 that they had been deserted by many "of our Neighboures with whom wee were able to pursuade much by love, and our tenents whom wee used to Command." These deputies were convinced that if the Crown continued to extract forced loans, billet Irish soldiers on the people, and rely on martial law, it would reap a bitter harvest, and the deputies would find themselves "opposed not by a few private men, but by a generall Consent."[37]

The Parliament of 1628 proved the Essex deputies to have been correct. All at once the growing rage at Charles's military policies exploded.[38] One speaker after another rose to complain of the evils done by the Deputy Lieutenants. Sir Robert Phelips, a leading spokesman for reform, expressed a common sentiment: "I stand upp to performe that dutie I owe to the Countrie that sent mee hither. I was entreated by our Countrymen, that what ever wee did wee would bring securitie against the oppression of the deputie lieutenants."[39] Parliament made some headway with the Petition of Right, curbing abuses in martial law and billeting. The crucial question of whether the king or the Parliament would control the militia remained, however, and the attempt to answer it eventually precipitated civil war.[40]

III

The Puritans who sailed with John Winthrop in 1630 believed there were many things wrong in England and the "perfect militia" was not least among them. The leaders of the Massachusetts Bay Company knew, long before any settlers left for the New World, that they would have to provide for the colonists' defense. The grisly memory of the Virginia Indian massacre of 1622 haunted company planners, and they hired military experts, veterans from the wars in the Low Country, to fortify the commonwealth and to train the settlers in the arts of war.[41]

It soon became apparent, however, that these professionals represented only a temporary solution to the colony's military needs. The experts were expensive and showed only moderate interest in building a city on a hill. One employee, a German surveyor of ordinance named Jost Weillust, succumbed to homesickness and returned to Europe as quickly as possible.[42] Daniel Patrick and John Underhill, both fresh from campaigns in the Netherlands, lasted longer in the Bay Colony than did any of the other Company appointees, but neither man was a Puritan. Captain Patrick chased after women other than his wife, and according to Governor Winthrop, "perceiving that he was discovered, and such evil courses would not be endured here, and being withal of a vain and unsettled disposition, he went from us."[43] Captain Underhill showed early promise and was even elected to the Massachusetts General Court. But Underhill's reputation suffered after his neighbors noticed that he frequented the house of a beautiful young woman. His actions were all the more suspicious since he insisted upon locking the door from the inside whenever he paid a visit. The Captain admitted the evil appearance of his behavior, but protested that he and the woman had been "in private prayer together." The colony's rulers relieved Underhill of his military command after he became an Antinomian. Later he confessed to having committed adultery, and one suspects the Bay magistrates were not at all surprised.[44]

The behavior of soldiers like Patrick and Underhill may well have persuaded Massachusetts leaders of the need for a system of defense drawing upon the colony's own, non-professional personnel. In any case, the Company abandoned the costly practice of hiring military experts. During the 1630s the larger towns of Massachusetts formed trainbands that included most males over sixteen, be they freemen or non-freemen. At first the General Court assumed complete authority not only to select local militia officers, but also to define their "dutyes and powers." The colonists apparently made no attempt to exclude persons from the militia because they were poor or because they were servants, and the Bay trainbands may have represented a broader cross section of society than did their English counterparts.[45] The New Englanders drilled together several times a year, but they seldom went into battle as a unit. During emergencies, such as Indian attacks, the Massachusetts General Court raised special fighting companies from the ranks of the various village trainbands.[46]

During these early years of settlement, the colonists' attitude towards their militia was a product of their experiences in Stuart England as well as their belief in the covenant as the organizing principle of society. The colonists arrived in the New World aware of the need for military reform but without exact plans about what to do. It was not long, however, before the spirit of participation which was evident in the election of ministers and magistrates infected the militia as well. The reason is not difficult to understand. The New Englanders built churches, towns, indeed, the entire commonwealth upon the contractual model. In these compacts the individual voluntarily promised to obey scriptural or civil law in exchange for benefits accruing from being a part of the larger group. The essential ingredient in this contract was free choice, for the Puritans believed that meaningful obedience could only grow out of voluntary consent, never out of coercion. With this principle in mind, the Reverend Thomas Hooker insisted that the man who desired to enter a social covenant had "willingly [to] binde and ingage himselfe to each member of that society . . . or else a member actually he is not."[47] Like the Congregational churches and the New England town meetings, the trainbands were covenanted organizations based on voluntarism. And because of the large number of persons, freemen as well as non-freemen, who participated in military elections, New Englanders had no cause to fear that their militia would abuse its power by oppressing the towns or by collecting arbitrary taxes as the appointed Deputy Lieutenants had done. The freemen of Charlestown merely repeated what became a conventional piece of seventeenth-century wisdom when they declared that the free choice of leaders in civil, ecclesiastical, and military affairs "hath rendered us the most happy people that wee know of in the world."[48]

The colonists' desire for a covenanted militia became apparent within a few years after the original settlement. They aspired neither to create a professional officer corps nor to copy the system that they had known in England. Instead, they advocated a new kind of militia, one that allowed popular participation in the selection of leadership. As early as 1632, Governor Winthrop reported, "A proposition was made by the people, that every company of trained men might choose their own captain and officers."[49] It is not certain who made this request, but the proposal came at a time when many New Englanders were demanding a greater voice in civil affairs. The minister of the Watertown church, for example, gathered his parishioners and warned them that if they paid a certain tax levied by the Governor and Assistants, they might bring "themselves and posterity into bondage." He argued that only the people's elected representatives could make such assessments. Winthrop persuaded the Watertown group that the Governor and Assistants were a sort of little parliament and that no colonist need fear for his liberties. The Governor also convinced the persons who had called for trainband elections to drop their petition.[50]

Winthrop slowed, but did not halt, the expansion of participation in civil and military affairs. After 1634 representatives elected by the freemen of each town became a part of the General Court, and in 1636, on the eve of the Pequot war, the colonial legislature passed a law permitting each regiment and company to nominate officers and to present these men to the Council for confirmation. The circumstances surrounding the passage of the militia act are obscure. There is no evidence, however, that the decision was forced upon the Bay rulers. Puritan leaders probably concluded that the men who elected representatives and ministers should also choose military personnel. All freemen and those non-freemen who had taken the residents' oath were allowed to participate in trainband nominations, and since Bay rulers seldom rejected a name, nomination amounted to election. The General Court did stress, however, that the nominees had to be freemen, in other words, members of a Congregational church.[51] As one Puritan writer explained, "There are none chosen to office in any of these Bands, but such as are freemen supposed to be men indued with faith in Christ Jesus."[52]

Reaction to the new law varied. Captain Underhill, the military professional, was annoyed when the Salem militia put the ordinance into effect, appointing in Underhill's words "a Captaine, Lieutenant, and Ensigne . . . after such a manner as never was heard of in any Schoole of warre; nor in no Kingedome under heaven." In a petition to the Governor and Assistants, the Captain warned, "For my parte, if there should not be a reformation in this disordered practise, I would not acknowledge such Officers." Indeed, he predicted that martial discipline as he had experienced it would dissolve.[53] No doubt, many career officers on the Continent would have shared Underhill's indignation at such disordered practices, but in New England he found no support. The Puritans were already familiar with civil and ecclesiastical elections, and they apparently took this military innovation in their stride. Trainbands throughout the colony soon began to present names to the Council for confirmation. When the militia company of Ipswich needed a lieutenant and an ensign in 1639, it nominated four men, two of whom had previously served as sergeants. The Ipswich soldiers observed diplomatically that it was the Council's right to select whomever it pleased, but they wanted the Council to know "that *the major part of them* did rather desire the 2 Sergeants." The Council really had no choice. The two other nominees were not freemen and therefore ineligible for commission.[54]

During the 1640s and early 1650s the General Court extended the military franchise. In 1643 the members of the legislature announced that the office of major general, the colony's highest military position, would be filled by the vote of the freemen. On the county level, the freemen were given the right to select a sergeant major, an officer in charge of regimental affairs. Two years later the General Court decided that additional persons should be allowed to participate in the choice of sergeant majors, and it ordered that "*not onely* freemen but *all* that have taken the oath of fidelity, or shall take it before the election, (except servants or unsettled persons), may have liberty of their votes." The law contained what seems an extremely liberal procedure permitting any soldier who had not taken the fidelity oath to do so immediately preceding the selection of officers. In 1647, apparently in response to specific queries about the size of the franchise, the legislators explained that even those freemen ordinarily exempt from training could take part in military elections.[55]

It was clear that most New Englanders regarded the inclusiveness of the military franchise as an important element in the Massachusetts polity. Indeed, when the London pamphleteer John Child took the magistrates of Massachusetts to task for barring non-freemen from civil and military matters, Edward Winslow responded that Child was badly misinformed. The English author had "falsely charge[d] the government with denying libertie of votes where they allow them, as in choyce of military officers, which is common to the non-freemen as with such as are free."[56] In 1652 the Massachusetts legislature made yet another change in the militia law, this time declaring that "all Scotsmen, Negers, & Indians inhabiting with or servants to the English, shalbe listed, & are hereby enjoyned to attend traynings." The Scots, blacks, and Indians may conceivably have voted for local trainband officers. What little evidence is available suggests that they did participate, but until much more is known about local practices in this period, it would be unwise to regard the covenanted militia as a melting pot for different races and nationalities.[57]

Confusion over the extent of the trainband's authority to determine its own officers contributed to one of the colony's more serious constitutional crises. During the years when the military franchise was expanding, some militiamen either forgot, or, what is more likely, ignored the fact that they had power only to nominate the lesser trainband officers, captains, lieutenants, and ensigns. However, the law on this point was clear. The General Court or one of the County Courts could disallow the choice of any company. Since the colonial magistrates tended to confirm most names presented to them, it was probably natural for soldiers to assume that the will of the majority expressed in elections would not be overruled. In the spring of 1645 the Hingham militia chose Anthony Eames as its captain. Soon after the election Eames offended a good many of his neighbors, exactly how is not certain, and the trainband held a second election. This time the Hingham captaincy went to Bozone Allen. Since Eames did not resign, the town found itself with two captains, and when both appeared for training, the militia split into factions. The dissension soon spread to the Hingham church. At this point Governor Winthrop stepped in, accusing Allen's supporters of insubordination, a serious charge in seventeenth-century Massachusetts. Allen's party countered that, by intervening, the Governor had exceeded his proper authority, and they organized an unsuccessful attempt within the General Court to impeach him. Throughout the controversy, the inhabitants of Hingham advocated local autonomy. They were especially annoyed by outside interference in their militia affairs. One disgruntled Hingham soldier declared that he would "die at the sword's point, if he might not have the choice of his own officers." While this threat revealed a misunderstanding of colony law, it also demonstrated that in one town at least participation in the selection of leadership had become an essential part of the militia system.[58]

There were other elements that distinguished the Massachusetts militia from its English counterpart. The early Puritans carefully regulated those powers which the state transferred to the military. From the time of the founding, Bay leaders rigorously separated military and political affairs, and the Massachusetts records reveal no instance in which rulers employed the militia as a police force. Elected civil officers, both on the colonial and the local level, kept watch on the trainbands, vigilant lest the soldiers assume unwarranted powers.[59] In 1638 a group of prominent Boston gentlemen proposed to the government the formation of a private artillery company, more of a club than a military unit, but the magistrates balked because they realized, to use their words, "how dangerous it might be to erect a standing authority of military men, which might easily, in time, overthrow the civil power." Puritan rulers acceded to this request only after the petitioners had promised complete obedience to the colony's civil leaders.[60]

In the General Court of May 1645 several parties consisting of some of the colony's highest military officers requested permission to establish three private companies similar to the one formed earlier in Boston. The petitioners came from towns throughout the counties of Essex, Middlesex, and Old Norfolk. They asked for liberty to determine their membership, to elect their officers, to govern their own affairs, and to drill "as often as they please." The stated goal of these organizations was the advancement of military arts, but one suspects that the private companies had a social function as well. Winthrop, always suspicious of special military privilege, disapproved of the plan, and in his journal he noted that

> the military officers prevailed with much importunity to have the whole power of those affairs committed to them; which was thought by diverse of the court to be very unfit, and not so safe in times of peace; but a *great part* of the court being military officers, and others not willing to contend any further about it, the order passed, and the inconvenience whereof appeared soon after, and will more in future times.

To the historian's immense frustration, Winthrop never returned to this topic or bothered to explain what problems the private companies created. Moreover, in the absence of additional evidence, it is difficult to ascertain what the Governor meant when he observed that a "great part" of the 1645 General Court were military officers.[61] An analysis of the membership of the legislature from 1634 to 1684 reveals that approximately one-third of the General Court in any given year used military titles. During the 1640s there appear to have been somewhat fewer officers in the General Court, about one-quarter in each legislature. During the 1660s and 1670s the percentage rose, sometimes going as high as 60 percent.[62] But whatever the exact proportion of military men may have been in 1645, Winthrop clearly had no use for independent military power, and judging by the subsequent failure of these private companies to become more than paper organizations, it would seem that many colonists agreed with him.

IV

From its inception the covenanted militia contained seeds of its own dissolution. Even as the military franchise was expanding during the 1640s, some Puritans began to have doubts about the wisdom of broad participation in trainband politics. To be sure, they believed that the people were entitled to select the persons who would run the militia, but in no covenanted institution, be it church or state, did they condone faction. The very notion of competition for office angered Governor Winthrop, who explained in 1642, "If this past for good doctrine, then let us no longer professe the Gospell of Jesus Christ, but take up the rules of Matchiavell, and the Jesuits, for Christ sayeth Love is the bond of perfection and a kingdome or house devided cannot stand."[63] Yet in practice well-meaning men in Massachusetts did disagree at election time, and in various trainbands throughout the commonwealth the choice of a captain or ensign frequently bred dissension. In 1647 the selection of a new captain for Roxbury opened a deep split between the older and younger men of the village. The younger militiamen decided to cast their votes for a soldier who had recently fought in the English Civil War and who probably entertained them with stories about battles against the king's army. The newcomer failed to impress the older men of Roxbury, however, and they supported for the captaincy "a godly man and one of the chief in the town." The issue generated much "discontent and murmuring," and although the older men eventually won the contest by more than twenty votes, the other side pursued its case before the General Court. The controversy cooled somewhat when it was belatedly discovered that the candidate of the younger men had not yet become a freeman and was therefore ineligible for office.[64] In Newbury an argument within the local church carried over into military matters, and between 1647 and 1669 the town's squabbling inhabitants found it almost impossible to settle upon an officer.[65]

One of the more serious disputes within the colonial militia occurred in Ipswich. Sometime in late February 1664, Major General Daniel Denison ordered a company of local soldiers to clear a field of logs and stumps in preparation for a general training day. When several men grumbled about their unpleasant task, Samuel Hunt, a person dressed in "a leather paire of britchs and a flaske hanged on a chaine," spoke up. He observed that Denison had overreached his legal authority and that no one in Ipswich need carry out the Major General's order. Hunt added confidently that "if any punishment should be upon those that refused to obey that command, he did know that it would breed a great disturbance, in the country, for he did know that there were hundreds in the country of his mynd." Apparently, the willingness of some soldiers to hear him out encouraged Hunt, for he was soon describing other militia problems. He and his neighbors desired greater "liberty" in choosing officers, and if the government did not meet their demands, they threatened to lay down their arms, form a company of their own, and elect new officers. Unfortunately for the institutional historian, Hunt did not give many details about the local militia practices. His arrest may have dampened his enthusiasm for the cause. Depositions gathered for his trial indicate that he wanted more frequent elections, no doubt, to remove men like Denison more easily. For his "mutinous and seditious words," the Essex County Court disfranchised and fined Hunt, a sentence that the colony's General Court later upheld on appeal. The leader of this abortive Ipswich mutiny seems to have been impetuous, but he was not a crank. There may well have been "hundreds in the country" who shared his opinions about militia elections, but who refused to confront the Major General. Fifteen of Hunt's friends later petitioned the County Court in his behalf, noting that, although he had broken the law, he was still a "neighbourly" individual, "human frailities excepted."[66] Other Massachusetts towns suffered similar disputes, and as the contention spread, civil magistrates were often forced to intervene. As the Essex County Court observed, "there was wanting that full concurrence and mutual satisfaction that were to be desired in the establishment of such public officers."[67]

As the dissension within the trainbands grew, it apparently struck some persons that the very openness of military elections created controversy, indeed, that the militia might be suffering from an excess of democracy. Not only were the laws governing participation in the selection of officers too liberal, they were also ignored. In 1652 the General Court had to disallow trainband elections in Suffolk County because certain unqualified persons had cast votes.[68] The Bay rulers discovered the Suffolk fraud, but what about the other counties? In how many cases had persons who had little interest in the colony's covenant with God outvoted the freemen? At what point should Puritans curb voluntarism?

During the 1650s men who thought the time for restricting trainband elections had already arrived began pestering the General Court for reform. The Bay legislature briefly considered disfranchising all non-freemen except those whom the freemen had specifically selected to participate in militia politics. Nothing came of this proposal.[69] Another plan presented would have increased the freemen's power in military affairs at the expense of that of the non-freemen. Five prominent citizens advised the General Court that in elections wherein "scotch, servants, Irish, negers, and persons under one and Twenty years have liberty to voat," the freemen should have a double vote. After all, the petitioners argued, it was the freemen "who undergoe all the burdens of this Commonwelth."[70] This particular scheme did not become law, but the movement to limit the military franchise seems to have gained adherents as the years passed. In 1656 the Massachusetts legislature responded to what it called the need for the "better ordering and settling" of the colony's military companies and ruled that henceforth only freemen, householders, and persons who had already taken the oath of fidelity could take part in the election of officers. Moreover, the new law dropped Indians and blacks from the militia altogether. This ordinance did not bring harmony to the village trainbands, witness the Hunt mutiny, but it did represent a significant retreat from the inclusiveness of earlier decades.[71]

The movement away from broad participation in military affairs received an unexpected boost from England. Soon after the Restoration, officials in the mother country began to review practices in the Puritan

colonies more closely than they had ever done before, and the covenanted militia was one of the things that caught their attention. The
king's Council for Foreign Plantations learned from a sea captain in
1660 that "2 thirds of the soldiers [in Massachusetts] are non-freemen,
who tho' at present they obey the command of their officers, would
. . . be glad to have officers by the King's commission." [72] The Bay
magistrates who were none too happy about the Stuart return would
have preferred the captain to have kept his opinions to himself. Unfortunately, from their point of view, English administrators became increasingly interested in Massachusetts, and in 1664 a group of royal
commissioners were sent to investigate conditions in New England.
Henry Bennett, secretary of state, wrote in their private instructions that
the Bay militia "should bee putt under an officer nominated or recom-
mended by us; and it may be, if they [the colony's rulers] consider their
Charter, they will not find that they have in truth, the disposall of their
owne Militia as they imagine." Bennett believed that if the commissioners employed "skill & dexterity," one of their number, George
Cartwright, might become the colony's major general. [73] Once in
America the commissioners revealed a singular lack both of skill and
dexterity, but even if they had possessed these attributes, there was no
chance that the people of Massachusetts would select Cartwright to high
military office. [74] Most Puritans were determined to resist outside interference. There could be no denying, however, that England posed a
serious threat to the colony's former independence, and common sense
seemed to dictate that Bay leaders should remove, or at least mask, as
many charter violations as possible.

In 1668 the General Court, responding to internal and external pressures, abolished local trainband elections altogether, claiming full authority to "nominate, choose, [and] appoint" commission officers. [75]
The freemen still selected a major general, the colony's highest ranking
officer, but the non-freemen no longer possessed a voice in determining
military leadership. No one recorded the arguments presented in favor
of this act, but several elements seem to have contributed to its passage,
the pressure from England, the fear of social disorder, and the belief
that non-freemen should be excluded from elections. An early version
of the law drafted by the upper house described military elections as occasions of "much division amongst particular companies." In its final
form, however, the legislators mentioned only the colonists' desire to
abide by the terms of the king's charter, a document which the
members of the General Court now chose to read with tortuous

literalism. [76] Nowhere did the civil leaders of Massachusetts state that they wanted to curtail the participation of non-freemen in trainband affairs, but some contemporaries were certain that this had been the legislature's intent. [77]

Whatever the Court's motives may have been, citizens complained that the change deprived them of their liberties, and the freemen of Charlestown in particular begged their rulers to preserve the privilege of election which they had come to regard as an "undoubted right." A committee of the General Court informed the Charlestown petitioners that the trainbands had never enjoyed the right to *choose* officers, only to *nominate* them. [78] This explanation, while technically correct, must have come as a surprise to men who regarded participation in the choice of officers as accepted New England practice.

In the remaining years before the Glorious Revolution, the rulers of the Bay Colony enacted no additional legislation affecting participation in the selection of military leadership. The Massachusetts legislature continued to appoint all officers with the exception of the major general. In 1675 in the midst of King Philip's War the colonial government admitted that it was having difficulty collecting adequate information about potential officers, and it asked the town militia committees to recommend "useful & fitt persons for that service." This change in procedure in no way undermined the law of 1668, however, for militia committees were composed of previously appointed officers and local members of the General Court. [79] Unless these men solicited the opinions of rank and file soldiers, and there is little evidence that they did, there was no way villagers could influence the choice of trainband officers.

V

The question that remains to be resolved is what, if anything, the history of the covenanted militia indicates about the development of Massachusetts society in general. Was the retreat from an earlier commitment to participatory procedures solely a military phenomenon and therefore of little value in enriching our understanding of other institutions? Or did the evolution of the trainbands and attitudes toward them reflect larger social trends?

Unless the colony's militia laws are interpreted as part of a larger effort to define the limits of voluntarism, they will seem no more than a series of false starts and contradictions. From the time the Puritans arrived in the New World there was a tension within their social thought. They believed that the people, at least the most godly among them, should select the heads of church, state, and militia. But the founders also insisted on maintaining harmony in the commonwealth, for as Winthrop explained, "We must be knitt together in this worke as one man."[80] During the first two decades the Puritans had relatively little difficulty reconciling their desire for social unity with their acceptance of popular participation in the choice of leaders. It was during this period that the colonists showed a great burst of social inventiveness, a willingness to experiment with institutional forms unknown in the mother country. They gave church members liberty not only to elect ministers but also to determine local ecclesiastical policy. After 1631 every adult male church member could take part in civil elections and, because most adults in Massachusetts belonged to a church, the potential vote was proportionally larger than that of contemporary England. Historians are not certain how many persons had a voice in village politics, but the number surely was not small. Social harmony could always be preserved by banishing persons unwilling to accept the Congregational Way. In fact, when dissenters such as Roger Williams and Anne Hutchinson departed for Rhode Island, they left behind a homogeneous society in which highly participatory institutions flourished. As long as Puritan leaders could exile opposition, they had no reason to fear elections, even within the militia. The colony's voters shared a common ideology, and although they might disagree on the merits of a particular candidate, they usually chose men dedicated to transforming Massachusetts into a city on a hill.[81]

During the 1650s the character of Massachusetts society began to change. Social unity and order, once taken for granted, somehow seemed to be slipping away, and Puritans lamented, in the words of one Congregational minister, that "after many years of his fatherly tenderness toward us," the Lord has turned "our healthiness into sicklynesse, our sweete union to much disunion."[82] Throughout the Bay community at this time the historian senses a loss of confidence, a retreat from an earlier commitment to voluntarism, and a suspicion of colonists who failed to become church members and therefore failed to become freemen. By any modern standard Restoration Massachusetts was a tranquil, cohesive society, but contemporaries seem to have been conscious only of dissension. They contrasted their performance with the apparent harmony of Winthrop's generation and were depressed by the results. There was an uneasiness about the growing number of persons who were lukewarm, even hostile, to the colony's special errand in the New World. Religious dissenters could no longer be exiled as they were in former times. An attempt to banish the Quakers only served to anger English administrators and to endanger the Massachusetts charter. Faced with these conditions many Puritans seem to have turned inward, concerning themselves with the salvation of their own immediate family and showing only moderate interest in the conversion of the unregenerate. Indeed, as one historian has explained, "theology became the handmaid of genealogy."[83]

The institutions of Puritan society reflected these tensions. In the churches, for example, some ministers criticized broad participation in ecclesiastical business, and a few tried unsuccessfully to reduce their parishioners' power. A man in Newbury described the issues that were at stake in his congregation, and perhaps other congregations as well: "As for our controversy it is whether God hath placed the power in the elder [the minister], or in the whole church, to judge between truth and error, right and wrong, brother and brother, and all things of church concernment."[84] In civil government there were similar signs of a pulling back from an earlier inclusiveness in political affairs. During this period the members of the General Court decided that it was unwise to allow so many non-freemen to vote in village elections. They ruled that only those non-freemen specifically selected by the town's freemen could take part in choosing local officials. The reasons for this action are unclear. The legislators may have regarded the non-freemen as a threat or as a cause of social division. Whatever their thinking, Massachusetts authorities made it increasingly difficult for non-freemen to vote in town meetings, and in 1670 the General Court quadrupled the amount of property required for local franchise.[85]

What is important to stress here is the parallel development of different colonial institutions. The examples from church and state suggest that the various attempts to limit the militia franchise, culmination in the law of 1668, were an expression of a general movement to limit popular participation in public affairs, a movement that, in military affairs at least, brought the colonists almost full circle. By the 1680s the trainbands of Massachusetts Bay looked more like those of Caroline England than they had at any other time since Winthrop sailed for the New World.[86]

III

Moving to the New World:
The Character of
Early Massachusetts Immigration

WHILE I WAS working on this volume, Professor Stephen Foster and I discovered that our scholarly interests temporarily overlapped. We both wanted to know what sort of men and women elected to move to New England. What had been the character of their lives before they decided to emigrate? How did the transfer affect their callings? Their social mobility? Their longevity?

The answers to these questions frequently surprised us, for the people who left East Anglia and Kent for Massachusetts Bay in 1637 turned out to have been somewhat older and more urban than we had expected. This investigation reinforced my conviction—discussed more fully in the general introduction to this collection—that Early American historians must explore the settlers' specific backgrounds, paying close attention to the precise timing of departure and the exact place of origin, if they are to understand fully the dynamics of cultural transfer.

I

The early migrants to New England remain a puzzling group. Who were these men and women who crossed the Atlantic to settle Massachusetts Bay? Why did they come? And what effect did the New World have upon the character of their lives?

Often asked, these questions are still difficult to answer with precision, as anyone with experience of seventeenth-century record keeping can testify. Lack of hard statistical data has forced most accounts of the Great Migration to rely heavily on statements drawn from the Puritan leadership. Ordinary folk appear in the story only haphazardly: the contents of some probate inventory or snatches from the odd surviving letters to relatives back in England will be used to give substantiation to the official claims of a Winthrop or a Cotton.[1]

What is needed now is a new and systematic analysis of the mass of the ordinary settlers who moved to New England during the 1630s.[2] Such a study should properly begin with the English origins of the migrants and then follow them through their experiences in the New World. Yet with the exception of Sumner C. Powell's work on Sudbury, Massachusetts, the existing literature is surprisingly silent about the migrants' previous life in the mother country. Recent intensive demographic explorations of individual New England towns, valuable as they are in other respects, inevitably slight the migration itself. The new town-studies usually begin not with the migrant in England but with the townsman in New England, and since they focus on a particular village, they cease to follow individual settlers once they leave this town for another locality.[3] These local studies would gain a new dimension from complementary investigations into the experiences of entire groups of migrants irrespective of the place or places in which they happened to settle.[4]

Fortunately, surviving lists of migrants do make possible the systematic study of early Massachusetts immigration. Englishmen departing the realm prior to the Civil War were required to present the royal customs officers with evidence that they had taken the oath of allegiance to the king and conformed to the established church. Some emigrants may well have ignored the regulations, and the records of many more have certainly been lost, but registers giving the names of well over two thousand of the first settlers of New England still exist, and many contain important supplementary information about age, vocation, and place of origin.[5]

Most of these lists were collected and printed by John Camden Hotten in 1874. Fifty years later Colonel Charles Edward Banks attempted to rearrange the names on the Hotten lists by family and shipload, publishing the reordered registers with a short analytical introduction as *The Planters of the Commonwealth*. Hotten's version of the lists is the more reliable, but whichever source is used, any attempt to generalize from these lists to the whole of the New England migration can be extremely misleading.[6] Banks correctly noted that he and Hotten had collected *only* the names of those emigrants appearing on extant registers with whatever biases the accidental survival of one list rather than another may have introduced.[7] The existing lists are not in any sense a random sample, and attempts to treat them as such have led to some dubious conclusions. For example, one attempt to measure changes in the place of origin of New England immigrants during the 1630s discovered an apparent shift away from Essex and Suffolk after 1636 and an increasing predominance of Norfolk migrants in 1637 and 1638.[8] The change in question, however, may actually only be the result of full reporting from the port of London in 1635 but not after and equally full reporting from the Norfolk port of Great Yarmouth in 1637 but not before. Ships, of course, had sailed from Yarmouth before 1637 and continued to sail from London after 1635, but their passenger lists disappeared before either Hotten or Banks could collect them. Similarly, the repeated efforts to assign the bulk of the Great Migration to East Anglia as a whole run afoul of the same difficulty: relatively complete recording for London and the East Anglian ports without equally detailed West and North Country port records, which, if they had survived, might have swelled the roll of emigrants from those parts of England.[9]

Inconsistent recording makes generalizations about vocation equally difficult. On some lists every adult male gave a specific occupation, but on most only ministers, conscious of their status, bothered to record a calling, so that a straightforward count of all the trades listed in Hotten would end with the conclusion that more than one out of every seven adult male emigrants leaving East Anglia for New England were clergymen. Even those who claim that Massachusetts was a theocracy would find this statistic hard to accept.[10]

Yet the lists have much to tell about the Great Migration if they are not abused by uncritical extrapolation from the whole of the record without regard for the varying utility of the different parts. Careful analysis of limited sections of the material can yield conclusions more limited in their turn but more reliable for the specific groups under consideration. In particular, the year 1637 stands out for its relatively complete data. One hundred ninety-three emigrants who departed that year from Great Yarmouth in Norfolk and another eighty who sailed from Sandwich in Kent listed their age, profession, place of origin, and probable distination for the benefit of the royal customs officers. Some passengers leaving in other years gave their occupation or place of origin, but it was only in 1637 that *every* adult who gave his name also gave such full additional information about himself and his family. There had not been such careful recording before and there would not be again.[11]

A total of 273 migrants constitutes too small a number for us to claim with confidence that they reflect the overall character of the Great Migration. But limited as it is, this group provides some useful suggestions about the types of persons who emigrated before the Civil War as well as about their motives for doing so. Comparison of the experience of these settlers in the New World with their counterparts in the Old can also put to the test various theories about the effect of migration on family structure, vocational patterns, and social relationships. Our conclusions about the economic and spatial mobility of the 1637 group do challenge some historiographical commonplaces, but further, more extensive studies of seventeenth-century migration will have to determine the representative quality of these particular settlers.[12]

II

Turning to the lists themselves, even a casual examination calls into question the classic picture of migration to the New World: a predominantly male movement of young, single unattached persons, that is, individuals free both of strong ties to their homes and of constitutional infirmities that would preclude a difficult journey. On the contrary, most of the 1637 emigrants were grouped into relatively small nuclear families consisting of two parents, a few children, and sometimes one or more servants. Men and women were about equal in number, and only a handful of the families included grandparents or in-laws. The Sandwich list consists of twelve male heads of families and their wives, thirty-one children, twenty-two servants, and only three single men (traveling without a family). The comparable figures for Yarmouth are twenty-nine male heads of households and their wives, eighty-six children, thirty-four servants, five single men, and eight single women or female heads of families. Whatever disruptions migration may have inflicted on the nuclear family structure in other times and places, they were not much in evidence in the migration to New England in 1637.[13] Moreover, if this pattern holds true for the rest of the migration, the absence of large numbers of single unattached men in early New England could have contributed to social stability and helped Massachusetts to avoid the type of recurring internal conflict that plagued colonies like Virginia, where, according to one recent historian, women "were scarcer than corn or liquor."[14]

Migration is often assumed to be an affair of the young, but the Yarmouth examiners left enough material about age to establish that this was not a particularly youthful group of colonists. Although among the servants, as might be expected, almost all of the men were between the ages of eighteen and twenty-two, with heads of households the case was quite different. Almost half of the twenty-five men whose ages were recorded were in their thirties, another eight were forty or older, while only five were in their twenties.[15] Nor were the women appreciably younger: a large minority of the wives, in fact, were older than their husbands. Seventeenth-century life spans being what they were, the nine men and women who were fifty or over in 1637 had little reason to suppose that they had many years to live when they removed to America. Nicholas Busby, aged fifty, managed to live until 1657, but Richard Carucar at sixty and Thomas Paine at fifty survived their arrival in Massachusetts by less than three years, and Benjamin Cooper, aged fifty, did not live to see the end of the voyage.[16]

Most migrants fared better. Despite some early deaths among the older settlers, New England (unlike contemporary Virginia) turned out to be an unusually healthy place in which to live. Of the fifty-six men whose death dates are known, thirty-two were alive in 1670 and five were still alive in 1695, fifty-eight years after their voyage to the New World.[17]

Revealing as the lists are about individual settlers, they throw no light on how they came to embark together on the same ships. Groups of prospective colonists may have chartered a ship, or a captain may have announced his intention to sail to New England and then waited for a full contingent of passengers. The manner of putting together boatloads of migrants is still an unsolved problem, but whatever the actual practice, the 1637 emigrants did not have to travel far in order to find a Massachusetts-bound vessel.[18] Virtually all those who left a record of their English home came from towns or parishes close to the port of embarkation. All the passengers on the Sandwich list originated in the northeastern section of Kent: the westernmost came from Faversham, the southernmost from the North Downs. A majority lived in a still smaller area, the triangle bounded by Canterbury, Dover, and the port of Sandwich itself which is traditionally called East Kent. The Yarmouth emigrants originated mainly in the city of Norwich, the lowland regions around Yarmouth, or the port of Yarmouth itself. Those of the emigrants who came from Suffolk were exclusively residents of the coastal and lowland towns in the north of the shire, which were oriented toward Norwich and Yarmouth across the county line, and only two of the emigrants on the Yarmouth list originated outside East Anglia.

The northeastern part of East Anglia (the lightloam region) and East Kent had a good deal in common.[19] Both regions were located in shires containing disproportionately high percentages of England's town dwellers and industrial workers. In both areas the chief industry was cloth working, particularly the production of the lighter worsteds and "new draperies" introduced into England in the previous century by Protestant refugees from the Low Countries.[20] Yet despite the importance of the cloth trade, Norfolk, High Suffolk, and Kent remained predominantly rural and agricultural, and agriculture meant primarily raising grain rather than dairying in both the East Anglian lightloam and East Kent. Agriculture in both areas was relatively advanced, however, and High Suffolk in particular may have been the most progressive farming region in seventeenth-century England.[21]

With such an agrarian background the Yarmouth and Sandwich colonists might be expected to conform fairly closely to the pattern of occupational distribution noted by a recent study of West Country migration in the latter half of the seventeenth century: few poor laborers, a large majority of husbandmen and yeomen, and a small but significant number of craftsmen.[22] In point of fact, while there were no laborers whatever among those who listed their occupation, the order of occupational frequency differs dramatically from the West Country men. Most of the East Anglians and Kentish men were urban and most were artisans. Excluding servants, forty-two of forty-nine men gave their occupation, and only eleven were farmers as against eight weavers, four cordwainers, four carpenters, two each of joiners, tailors, coopers, and mariners, as well as a brewer, a shoemaker, a grocer, a locksmith, a minister, a butcher, and a calender. The cities of Norwich and Great Yarmouth between them accounted for well over half the East Anglian emigrants, and Canterbury, Sandwich, and Dover for the majority of the men from Kent. At least thirteen adult males on the 1637 lists and very probably more were freemen of incorporated boroughs.[23]

Freemanship did not necessarily indicate that an individual was more wealthy or prominent than the average yeoman.[24] But many of the urban migrants were clearly reasonably well off, a few more than that. Edward Johnson, a Canterbury joiner, also owned enough land in the county of Kent (let to others) to make him the equal of a very substantial Kentish yeoman.[25] Nicholas Busby, Francis Lawes, and Michael Metcalfe, all freemen weavers of Norwich, merited the distinction of being among the ten individuals cited by name in the Long Parliament's indictment of the former bishop of Norwich for driving into exile the most important tradespeople of his diocese, some of whom had provided work for "an hundred poor people." Wren denied the prominence of most of the ten, Busby and Lawes included, but even he admitted that Metcalfe was "of some estate."[26]

Rich or poor, none of the migrants was hopelessly ruined at the time of his decision to leave England for America. Here again, their ages are worth remembering. Most of the male heads of households were five or more years past their apprenticeship, all were old enough to be launched on a career, most were too young to have been driven to desperation by the incapacities of age or misfortune.[27] Instead of consisting of adventurers or of the dispossessed, the 1637 group was made up mainly of families headed by urban tradesmen somewhere in mid-career who apparently chose to exchange their settled English vocations for life in a pioneer agricultural community of uncertain prospects.[28] So unlikely a choice calls for an explanation, however difficult it may be to discuss the subject of personal motivation with any kind of exactness.

Acting on the assumption that happy people do not emigrate, historians have usually begun their histories of the Great Migration by turning to whatever might have made men unhappy in East Anglia and Kent in 1637. The economy of both regions, it has been noted, depended heavily on the clothtrade, which for some time had suffered severely from the disruption of traditional continental markets and the blunders of government policy. There had been sharp contractions in the volume of the trade in 1618, 1621, and from 1629 to 1631, while a serious outbreak of the plague in London, Norwich, Sandwich, and many other cities in 1636 and 1637 had suspended commerce for

months at a time, a major setback to a recovery already painfully slow
and uneven.[29]

On top of depressions and epidemics came harassment by overzealous
church officials. Bishop Matthew Wren held the diocese of Norwich
(which comprised the shires of Norfolk and Suffolk) from the fall of
1635 to the spring of 1638. During this brief period he enforced cere-
monialism and deprived nonconformist clergy with so much enthusiasm that at the calling of the Long Parliament he was impeached and
spent eighteen years as a prisoner in the Tower. Wren's enemies in Parliament claimed among other things that his "rigorous prosecutions and
dealings" had driven three thousand families from the diocese of Norwich.[30] Certainly, his policy took a heavy toll among the clergy of his
diocese: Wrentham, Norwich, Yarmouth, and Hingham, towns which
supplied the bulk of the East Anglian emigrants of 1637, also sent seven
ministers into exile in New England and another two to Holland.[31] Nor
were the Puritan laity any happier under the bishop's administration: his
policy provoked civic discord in both Yarmouth and Norwich as well as
an increase in conventicle keeping, and when his officers arrived in
Ipswich in 1637 full-scale rioting broke out.[32] Kent had a less spectacu-
lar ecclesiastical history in the same period, but the shire did contain
well-entrenched nonconformist and Separatist movements dating back
to Elizabethan days and still vital at the time of the Civil War; as the
diocese of Archbishop Laud himself, Canterbury was hardly a haven for
Puritans.[33]

After cataloguing the woes of English society in the 1630s (which
were obviously considerable), traditional historiography has turned to a
ferocious debate over the primacy of economic as against religious discontent in producing the migration.[34] But put in less abstract terms, in
terms of the individual experiences of the migrants rather than of imper-
sonal religious and economic "factors," the whole attempt to separate
one cause from another appears not merely hopeless but unhistorical—a
question badly posed. Given the unusually strong appeal of nonconformity to town dwellers and artisans, there was likely to be a marked
congruence between disgruntled tradesmen and disgruntled Puritans:
people falling into one category would frequently fall into the other,
and there is no way to distinguish between them.[35] The traditional
either/or dichotomy—*either* religion *or* economics—makes no sense.

Take the case of William Ludkin, a locksmith from the city of Norwich. While we can establish that the Norfolk clothtrade experienced violent fluctuations, we cannot meaningfully argue that Ludkin moved to Massachusetts in 1637 because the impoverished weavers of Norwich could not afford locks. On the other hand, neither can we say persuasively that he left Norwich because he had come to dislike altar railings and ceremonies in his own parish of St. Clements and because a respected preacher named Thomas Allen in a nearby parish had been forced to flee to the Bay Colony for resisting Wren's innovations.[36] Ludkin was one of the better recorded migrants, and yet he has left us only his name, age, occupation, and an inventory taken at the time of his death in 1652. None of this data reveals whether Ludkin the locksmith was also Ludkin the Puritan, and if he was, which role was the more important in his decision to leave England.[37]

Whatever motive was suggested for Ludkin's removal, the assertion would fail for lack of conclusive evidence. But incomplete documentation is only part of the problem. Motivation appears straightforward enough in a man like the Norwich master weaver Michael Metcalfe. Unlike his shipmates, Metcalfe left a detailed memorial of his particular troubles. He was a parishioner of the suspended Thomas Allen and was himself in trouble with the ecclesiastical courts in 1633 and again in 1636 for failing to bow at the name of Jesus. Evidently a strong-willed man, Metcalfe defended himself with such asperity that a church official threatened him, "Blockhead, old heretic, the Devil made you, I will send you to the Devil." Following this exchange Metcalfe found it prudent to depart the realm and set down his reasons, all religious, in a circular letter addressed "to all the true professors of Christ's gospel within the city of Norwich." "Therefore, seeing what the Lord hath done unto thee," he intoned, "O! Norwich: prepare to meet thy God."[38]

Metcalfe, then, becomes a religious refugee while the absence of a similar statement from Ludkin could permit him to be pictured as an aspiring craftsman moving west in order to move up the social scale. But if it should have turned out that Metcalfe had also left a record of business failure, we might have been tempted to say with a Suffolk episcopal official that "as soon as any one doe purpose to breake or is become much indebted he may flye into new England and be accompted a religious man for leaving of the kingdome because he cannot indure the ceremonies of the church."[39] And by the same token if evidence existed to link Ludkin with Metcalfe's "professors," we could plausibly rank him among the persecuted Puritans whatever his financial situation. Our difficulty is not just that we do not know enough about the Metcalfes and Ludkins, for if the problem of motivation is posed as a choice between two mutually exclusive impulses, religious or economic, then complete records for every individual migrant would not explain the Great Migration. In addition to insufficient evidence, the problem is also one of interpretation.

Rather than seeking to separate the historically inseparable, a more fruitful account of the migration should begin with the actual relationship between religious and economic conditions in the regions which supplied the migrants, and it must consider other possible motives for emigration as well as other possible destinations the emigrants might have chosen. Instead of ending the discussion with general statements about hard times in the clothworking areas, it may legitimately be asked how hard they were and for whom, and what the available alternatives were for those affected by them.[40]

In the case of the 1637 migration the colonists originated in towns which differed from other clothworking centers in that they contained large foreign congregations and were also well on the way to recovery from the earlier depressions. One hundred sixty-four of the 273 migrants came from Norwich, Yarmouth, Canterbury, or Sandwich, all cities which had been the chief refuges (outside of London) for the Fleming, Walloon, and Dutch Protestants who fled the Spanish armies in the Low Countries in the latter half of the sixteenth century. The Protestants from the Continent imported both their religion and their skills into England, accentuating the native nonconformity of their new homes at the same time that they turned them into centers for the manufacture of "new draperies." Coarser but cheaper than the traditional broadcloth, these mixed and worsted fabrics would be the economic salvation of England in the course of the seventeenth century as the market for the "old draperies" declined and new markets opened for light and inexpensive fabrics. Much of the instability in the cloth trade in the 1630s reflected the transition from old to new clothmaking, a transition in which the worsted weaving areas, especially Norfolk, would lead at the expense of large parts of the West Country, Yorkshire, and central East Anglia. To argue, then, that depression was the primary inspiration for the Kentish and East Anglian migration of 1637, and that religion amounted to little more than the social cement that bound the migrants together inverts the actual order of importance of the facts: the 273 colonists in question came from the most Protestant and comparatively the least blighted sections of the clothworking areas.[41] Contemporaries were well aware that tradesmen in the coastal towns made good Puritans and that Puritan tradesmen were especially likely to become New England colonists. And so the hostile, albeit careful, subdean of Westminster Abbey, Peter Heylin, noted acidly that the people "in many great trading towns which were near the sea" were "long discharged from the bond of ceremonies" and already organized into congregations, so that "it was no hard matter for those [suspended] Ministers and Lecturers to persuade them to remove their dwellings and transport their trades. . . . New England was chiefly in their eye, a Puritan plantation from the beginning, and therefore fitter for the growth of the Zwinglian or Calvinian gospel than any country whatsoever."[42]

Heylin saw only a portion of the truth, and that hazily. The majority of urban artisans of Puritan sympathies never seriously considered leaving England despite *both* the state of the clothtrade *and* Archbishop Laud. To present economic and religious discontent as mutually exclusive not only obscures their real relationship, but it errs by ignoring additional causes for emigration. Neighborhood squabbles, family quarrels, a desire for adventure and similar personality traits, all of these motives and more figured in the exodus of Englishmen from their native land. Among the 1637 emigrants perhaps Thomas Oliver chose to follow his fellow parishioner Michael Metcalfe out of respect for the latter's courage and integrity, and the three Batchellor brothers of Kent may have left together to keep up their family ties.[43] Such reasons are less accessible today than the more obvious economic and religious discontents, but the men who actually took part in the Great Migration felt their weight when they made up their minds to leave their country.

Having chosen migration, our 273 then made a second and in many ways more remarkable decision, to go to New England, an underdeveloped agricultural colony where few of them would ever again practice the crafts which had given them income and status in the Old World. Their destination was not forced upon them: they could just as easily have moved to the Netherlands, the most economically advanced area in the whole of Europe, where every kind of craft and especially that of worsted weaving was in high demand. Wages in the Netherlands were so much in advance of the prevailing English level that the cynical Bishop Wren thought the Dutch had deliberately bid them up to drain England of its skilled labor, and the government of Charles I, alarmed at the growing size of the English community in Holland, came up with the fantastic plan of resettling the expatriates in New England or Virginia.[44] But in 1637 the real choice was between New England and Holland, and it was no foregone conclusion. In the same six months of that year that 193 people left Yarmouth for Massachusetts, another 414, the bulk of them artisans, sailed from the same port, bound for Holland.[45]

The Netherlands offered employment for skilled craftsmen and an even more palatable form of religion for disgruntled nonconformists, but it was New England which possessed special attraction for men unhappy with the new Laudian regime in the Church of England. By 1637 the eccentricities of Massachusetts church government were well known to interested parties back in England, indeed too well known for some. Moderate nonconformists in the mother country complained that reports of New England Congregationalism had encouraged enthusiastic imitators in England and thereby opened the entire nonconformist movement to the charge of Separatism.[46] One correspondent of Governor John Winthrop warned him in May 1637 that "the whole kingdome begins, or rather proceeds, to be full of prejudice against you, and you are spoken of disgracefully and with bitterness in the greatest meetings in the kingdome, the Pulpitts sound of you both at Visitacions and Assises, and the Judges begin to mention you in theyre charges."[47]

A church way which seemed excessive to the moderates and pure anathema to the Laudians could also have been a powerful magnet to enthusiasts already made restless by episcopal rigor and the slump in trade. There is no sure evidence that the Yarmouth and Sandwich emigrants inclined to congregationalism before their departure, but they certainly found the New England Way appealing once they had arrived. Despite admissions procedures that had grown increasingly more restrictive since 1630, about half and possibly more of the adult males in the migration became church members in Massachusetts, usually within a few years of their arrival.[48] Some carried their religious zeal too far even for the established authorities of the Bay Colony, who were no fonder of schism and heterodoxy than was Peter Heylin. For example, Mary Oliver, formerly of Norwich, had been cited with her husband before Bishop Richard Corbett in 1633; once settled in Salem, she took Roger Williams's part against the Bay Colony elders with such vehemence that she quickly ran afoul of the Massachusetts General Court. Later, in 1644, her ardent advocacy of eccentric religious views brought her a public whipping. Less spectacularly but similarly, Adam Goodens, who as a boy living near Great Yarmouth was a frequenter of conventicles as early as 1628, as a young man of twenty in New England found the Providence of Roger Williams more suitable to his constitution than the Massachusetts of John Winthrop and moved there in 1638.[49]

There were undoubtedly some worldlings in the New England migration, even in that select portion of it examined in this essay. But one should not mistake initial indifference for sustained hostility. Reviewing the settlement of the colonies in 1648, John Cotton observed that the churches of New England were the means of conversion "of sundry elder and younger persons, who came over hither not out of respect to conscience, or spiritual ends, but out of respect to friends, or outward inlargements: but have here found that grace, which they sought not for."[50] Cotton in his way was shrewder than some later commentators: he neither denied the mixed motives that brought some people to New England nor much worried about them provided church and state were arranged so that his inadvertent Puritans were likely to find "that grace, which they sought not for."

Perhaps with such cautions about motivation in mind it will become easier to discuss without preconception the experiences of the immigrants once arrived in New England. The impact of the New World on seventeenth-century Englishmen is most easily approached by sticking to specifics, that is, by examining the nature and degree of changes in mobility, social status, and vocation brought on by the Atlantic passage. Seventeenth-century Boston was not half the size of Norwich, nor was it prior to 1700 even as large as Canterbury, and the other New England towns were substantially smaller than Boston, so that dramatic alterations in the life style of the migrants might be expected as a consequence of their new, less populous, more rural environment.[51] In fact, the changes for the first generation do not seem to have been very great.

In their initial choice of New England homes the Kentish and Norfolk groups fell into divergent patterns. The East Anglians tended to bunch together, settling mostly in Essex County at first and then spreading northwards into Old Norfolk County (most of which is now in New Hampshire) or, less frequently, drifting south into Plymouth Colony. The emigrants from Kent were more dispersed from the start and generally began their New England careers in Suffolk or Middlesex counties. Hingham, Dedham, Watertown, Charlestown, and Dorchester all received a portion of the 1637 influx, but no one moved to Cambridge or Roxbury and only a few initially settled in Boston.[52] Differences in the areas of settlement should not obscure a fundamental similarity between the East Anglian and Kentish colonists: the individuals in both groups moved about a good deal in their first twenty-five years in the New World. Considering the high rate of geographic mobility in Elizabethan and Stuart England, a comparable pattern in Massachusetts is, perhaps, not so surprising.[53] Seventeen of the eighty-one adult males cannot be traced at all, and another five have left such scanty records that they too must be excluded from the count. Of the fifty-nine men remaining, twenty-four moved at least once *after* their original settlement, four twice, three three times, and one particularly peripatetic individual completed four moves. These figures do not include purely nominal removals, such as the legal separation of Malden from Charlestown, Wenham from Salem, or Topsfield from Ipswich, and, if anything, understate the extent of spatial mobility in early New England. The twenty-seven men with only one recorded location include several who did not live long enough to get in a second move and several more whose disappearance from their town's records probably indicates another move rather than an unrecorded death.

Some of the colonists, as might be expected, made their first move soon after arrival, probably leaving hastily chosen first homes for more attractive locations they had learned of only after settling in or near their port of disembarkation: Robert Page moved to Hampton in Old Norfolk after only a short time in Salem, Jarvis Boykett left Charlestown for New Haven within a few years of his first settlement. But others continued shifting about well into the 1640s. John Yonges, the only minister in the 1637 group, left to found Southold, Long Island (named for his birthplace in Suffolk) in 1646, taking with him another of the Yarmouth emigrants, Philomen Dickinson, an established tanner in Salem.[54] So dramatic a venture as the founding of a new town on Long Island was, however, unusual: on the whole the 1637 migrants confined their moves to previously settled villages or to the lands nearby, and the vast empty acreage of western Massachusetts never seems to have tempted any of them.[55]

Internal migration on this scale did not pass unnoticed even at the time, and not all observers were sympathetic. Giles Firmin wrote bitterly in 1639 of men who "range from place to place on purpose to live

upon the Country."[56] Firmin was too jaundiced to see the social significance of the process he was criticizing, but the career of Thomas
Dagget, although an extreme instance, throws some light on why so
many people took to moving about. Dagget was a servant who made
good by dint of the main chance and two rich widows. He was about
thirty when he arrived in Salem in 1637 with his master, the Norwich
calender Thomas Oliver, and stayed in his first home for a few years at
most; by 1642 at the latest he was living in Concord in Middlesex
County, for in that year his wife's death is recorded on the town
records. The following year, 1643, he moved to Weymouth (then in
Suffolk County) where he promptly married the widow of William
Frey. Through his new wife's inheritance from her late husband,
Dagget found himself a proprietor of Weymouth, and by 1648 he was
respectable enough to be elected selectman, a clear sign of status in any
New England community. But four years later Dagget's second wife
passed away, and he continued his southward migration, this time settling in Marshfield in Plymouth Colony, where he married another
widow in 1654 and finally settled down to spend the rest of his days
there as a selectman, tax collector, and leading citizen.[57] Dagget apparently had become an ever bigger fish by seeking ever smaller ponds,
a technique which may well account for the attraction comparatively
underpopulated areas such as Plymouth and New Hampshire held for
the migrants of 1637 who had first settled in the more populous coastal
towns.

Men could occasionally remain in one spot, even a well-developed
one, and still prosper. Without ever leaving Salem, John Gedney, a
Norwich weaver, acquired considerable land, held important town offices, and founded a dynasty considerably more prominent in early New
England history than that of Dagget.[58] Fortune, however, usually favored the mobile, who if they failed in three towns might yet make good
in a fourth. While Gedney flourished at Salem, his fellow weaver and
fellow parishioner at Norwich, William Nickerson, brought his own
stormy career to a more or less triumphant conclusion by methods strikingly similar to those of the ex-servant Dagget, down to a good marriage, except that Nickerson surpassed even Dagget in frequency of removal. Settling first in Ipswich, he moved on to Yarmouth on Cape
Cod in 1640, briefly transferred to Boston in 1657 to wind up the estate
of his well-to-do father-in-law Nicholas Busby, returned to Yarmouth
again two years later and stayed there until 1672 when he trekked even

farther out on the Cape to found Chatham. Along the way Nickerson speculated in Indian lands with such relentless energy that he was almost constantly in trouble with the Plymouth Colony authorities. Although his business dealings once landed him in the stocks, he still managed to amass over four thousand acres on the Cape, ending his days as Chatham's leading citizen and, for want of a settled minister, as its religious teacher as well.[59]

Geographic mobility sometimes had less happy consequences. John Roper, a Norfolk carpenter, settled in Dedham and failed, moved to Charlestown and failed, and then decided to try his luck in the frontier town of Lancaster where he seemed to be succeeding at last when in 1676 the Indians wiped out the entire town.[60] Others on the 1637 lists found that ambition involved conflict with the law. Samuel Greenfield, still another of the Norwich weavers, lived briefly in Salem and Ipswich but then moved to more congenial surroundings in Old Norfolk County, settling in Hampton in 1639 and moving to Exeter a few years later. Greenfield too had a taste for land speculation and quickly became a leading citizen of Exeter and one of its selectmen in 1644. He was also in trouble with the Essex County Court in 1639 for illegally appropriating his stepchildren's legacy, and in 1649 he was up before the same court "for singing a lascivious song and using unseemly gestures." Later the same year he made another attempt on his stepchildren's money by forging a bill of sale; this time his misdemeanors landed him in the Boston jail, at which point he disappears from New England history.[61]

Despite their varied fates, Dagget, Nickerson, Roper, and Greenfield had all responded to the same lure, leaving the older, more settled towns for small, outlying villages where they would enjoy the advantages of firstcomers. But others of their shipmates turned to the city of Boston for personal advancement, finding in its steady expansion the same opportunities and more. Jonathan Gill began life in New England as the servant of the Kentish yeoman Nicholas Butler, but while Butler went on to achieve prominence on Martha's Vineyard, Gill took the opposite tack and moved first to Dorchester and then to Boston itself, dying in 1678 as "Mr." Johnathan Gill, millowner, substantial landholder, and prosperous merchant with an estate in excess of £1,600.[62] Boston could be the scene of this provincial variant on the Dick Whittington story because alone among the New England towns it could recreate the urban way of life most of the 1637 migrants gave up in coming to the New World; it was the one community where men trained in a craft might still practice it or at least avoid obligatory farming. William Ludkin, the Norwich locksmith, spent a few years in Hingham and then bought a smith's shop in Boston. At his death in 1652 he left an estate of only £158, but he had distinguished himself by being one of the few 1637 immigrants to maintain his original trade.[63] Another Norwich freeman, the weaver Nicholas Busby, after a brief stay in Newbury, tried his hand at farming in Watertown, but then, still game at the age of fifty-nine, he too moved to Boston, bringing his looms with him, to set up as a merchant trading primarily in cloth. His new life was not quite that of Norwich master weaver, but it was probably close enough: Busby served a turn as Boston constable in 1649 and died in 1657, leaving a substantial £973, although his two looms so carefully transported across the Atlantic were now valued at only £4.[64]

Boston, however, could only accommodate a limited number of colonists. For most of the Norfolk and Kentish emigrants the move to the New World carried with it a change in vocation, usually a transition from a skilled craftsman in England to a farmer in America. The psychological effects of such a shift are not easily determined. Perhaps the freemen artisans in the 1637 group were already prepared to give up their old callings; perhaps the limited vocational opportunities of Massachusetts came as a shock. Whatever the case may have been, most of them found new callings successfully, but the process of adjustment sometimes required time.

The clothworkers as members of the most industrialized sector of the English economy encountered the greatest difficulty in keeping up their trades in Massachusetts, and yet it was these men who made the most stubborn efforts to retain their original vocation. To the end of their lives they proudly called themselves "weaver" on every offical document, even if like William Nickerson living far out on Cape Cod they probably had not put their looms to commercial use in years. Busby received a government bounty for making some cloth in 1643 and continued to weave small quantities until his death: his probate record shows £6 of cloth still on his looms. Another former weaver, John Pearce of Watertown, apparently ever hopeful, took on a young apprentice in 1656, promising that "with the trade of weaving, he is . . . to instruct him." Pearce retained a small "shop" with looms in Watertown, but he was primarily a farmer, just as Busby was primarily a merchant.[65]

The failure of clothworking is a mystery. Massachusetts possessed a considerable resource in the persons of so many trained weavers. Its population obviously required cloth. Yet despite repeated encouragement from the General Court, every attempt to establish a textile industry in the Bay Colony ended shortly after it began. The inhabitants of Rowley, many of whom were experienced English weavers, took the lead in the first great drive to create an indigenous textile industry in 1643. Three years later, however, they were still paying premium prices to Boston merchants for imported fabrics. "The greatest want (for the present) if not our only," complained Rowley's minister Ezekiel Rogers, "is Clothing."[66]

One wonders why so much determination produced so little. Part of the trouble may have been a labor shortage. Like all seventeenth-century trades, clothworking was extremely specialized and fragmented, while the "new draperies" in particular were also an unusually "labor intensive" industry. Although Massachusetts had a large body of immigrant weavers, it quite possibly lacked the necessary number of combers, throwers, carders, calenders, and the like to complement their skills.[67] Equally, there probably was never enough wool for them to weave. Ezekiel Rogers boasted in 1646 that "we are about getting sheepe, which doe thrive here exceedingly well."[68] It was an empty boast. Sheep appear periodically on Massachusetts inventories (among others, Abraham Toppan, a former Yarmouth cooper, kept twenty-four head at Newbury), but they are far inferior to other types of livestock both in number and assessed value.[69] This lack of interest in sheep, in turn, may be the product of the English origins of the migrants. The 1637 group came from areas where livestock was raised primarily for meat rather than for dairying, and the settlers may have followed their former preferences in the New World. If so, then sheep would probably take up too much land and demand too much care for too little return in meat to make them a viable substitute for cattle or swine as an important source of food.[70]

Whatever the reasons, English clothworkers became New England farmers or occasionally, like Busby, found alternative trades. Coopers, cordwainers, and (surprisingly) shoemakers and tailors had little better luck in keeping their English vocations. The mariners and carpenters possessed skills still very much in demand, but even they used their crafts only to supplement a basically agricultural way of life. In its early years the New England economy was too primitive to support substantial vocational specialization, so that, willing or not, for the artisan emigrant the trip to Massachusetts Bay turned into a movement back to the land.[71]

The eight husbandmen and three yeomen who left England in 1637 were spared this vocational transition, and it is worth noting that they became far and away the single most successful occupational group in New England. Four of the eleven died within a few years of their arrival; all were probably advanced in years and, judging from probate records and the number of their servants, at least three of them were already men of considerable property before their emigration.[72] The surviving seven farmers prospered in New England. Nicholas Butler of Eastwell in Kent became a founder of a settlemant on the Vineyard, Henry Smith of Norfolk served Medfield as selectman for thirteen terms, and no less than three of the seven were founders of Hampton, each serving the town in turn as selectman and deputy to the Massachusetts General Court.[73] The most needed skills in New England brought a high reward to those fortunate enough to possess them.[74]

Despite the effects of vocational changes and the potential for social disruption inherent in so much geographic mobility, the status relationships established in the mother country remained basically intact. For the most part the masters on the 1637 lists flourished in the New World while their former servants remained humble. For every Dagget, Gill, or other servant made good, there were several men like Samuel Arres, who came to Ipswich with his master John Baker and lived there for the next forty years without accomplishing anything of note. By contrast, Baker put his old Norwich trade of grocer to use by keeping an ordinary (an eating-house or tavern), acquired a large amount of property in Ipswich and Topsfield, took to calling himself "Mr.," and finally in 1682 attained the office of selectman.[75] The disparity in officeholding is in itself one indication of the difficulty the servants encountered in raising their status. Twenty-seven nonservants were chosen to some post in New England, while only seven former servants could boast the same honor. Six of these nonservants were elected deputies to the Massachusetts General Court, a position of importance in the Bay Colony, but none of the servants ever held an office beyond the village level. Yet in the original migration of 1637 adult male nonservants had outnumbered male servants by a ratio of less than four to three.

The servants provide the darkest element in the entire story of the colonists of 1637. Thirty-six male servants are known by name, but seventeen have left little or no other record of their existence after their initial entry on the ship lists (as against only five nonservants in the same category). Brief entries in probate records reveal that the disappearance of two servants can definitely be ascribed to early deaths, but there is no way of knowing how many others suffered the same fate without leaving an estate to be recorded.[76] The journal of an earlier migrant to New England, however, may be suggestive. Governor William Bradford of New Plymouth kept a record of the mortality among the Pilgrims in the first awful winter of 1620–1621: in spite of the advantages of youth the death toll was much higher among servants than masters.[77]

Less unhappy explanations for sparse recording of the missing seventeen might include early return to England, removal to another colony, or merely an obscure life in New England. None of these theories, however, indicates much of a success story for almost half the thirty-six men who sailed from Yarmouth or Sandwich as servants. Several of the nineteen remaining who left some record of their life in New England have done so mainly on account of their collisions with the authorities. John Pope was censured for foolery with women in 1640 and presented for excessive wages in 1643.[78] Isaac Hart was bound over for good behavior in 1640 and convicted of stealing a cow in 1656 and again in 1658, while on still another occasion he was admonished "for divers naughty speeches against the Court."[79] The principal achievement of another servant, John Granger, seems to have been the fathering of Thomas Granger, who was executed by the Plymouth Colony government after one of the most bizarre trials on record in the history of early New England.[80]

Even some of the servants who prospered did so mainly with the help of influential relatives already established in Massachusetts before their arrival. Samuel Lincoln of Hingham and William Moulton of Hampton were able to reap the benefits of the dominant positions of their families in their respective towns, but their careers no more bear testimony to New England as a land of opportunity than do the more sordid records of Hart and Pope.[81]

For most of the 1637 migrants prominence in the New World had followed substance in the Old. Edward Johnson, founder of Woburn, power in the lower house of the Massachusetts General Court, and author of the chronicle entitled *Wonder-Working Providence*, had been a substantial landholder in Kent, the son of the clerk of St. Gregory's

Parish, Canterbury, and a freeman of that city. John Gedney of Salem was originally a Norwich freeman capable of bringing over four servants, while Nicholas Butler of Martha's Wineyard had been a Kentish yeoman with five.[82]

There were exceptions. Samuel Greenfield proved quite clearly that not every Norwich weaver lived a long happy life in New England. Again, one might have expected more from the pugnacious Michael Metcalfe, who had been bold and learned enough to dispute theology with an episcopal court. Even Bishop Wren thought him an important if seditious inhabitant of his diocese. Yet Metcalfe's career in Dedham was anticlimactic: one term as selectman, a brief turn as town schoolmaster toward the end of his life, and an estate of £364.[83] Perhaps the cantankerousness that stood him in such good stead in his personal war against prelacy in Norfolk was less useful in the more peaceful environment of Dedham. Matcalfe, in any case, is not typical of the 1637 group. Records of estates, lists of town officers, even the use of honorific titles all point in the same direction: social status could be transferred across the Atlantic without major disruptions.

In summary, several characteristics about the 1637 migration stand out in spite of sometimes inadequate information. The men on the passenger lists were for the most part urban artisans who gave up their English callings to become farmers in New England. Their motives for moving to the New World were mixed, but for most, religion was probably not incidental. Moreover, their patterns of physical and social mobility in America apparently paralleled those of the England of their birth.

Conceivably this group of migrants may have been atypical, but at this stage of research it is not really possible to define what was typical and what eccentric. This much can be said, however: there is no obvious indication that the 1637 group is unique. The passenger lists are not top-heavy with the names of ministers and magistrates; indeed, the most remarkable attribute of most of the men prior to their decision to emigrate was their apparent ordinariness.[84] Nor is there anything singular in their trades or origins. Contemporary commentators on English economic policy knew well enough that the country was losing valuable skilled labor to the Continent and the colonies. Reflecting on the previous two decades, a pamphleteer in 1641 lamented that the tradesmen and artificers of the nation had suffered under a "multiplicity of vexations" which "did impoverish many thousands and so afflict and trouble others that great numbers, to avoid their miseries, departed out of the kingdom, some into New England, and other parts of America, others into Holland, where they have transported their manufacture of Cloth."[85] The author of this complaint knew whereof he spoke: a standard genealogical work lists ninety-one men who identified themsclvcs as clothworkers on Bay Colony records prior to 1650 as well as equally impressive contingents from other crafts.[86] The average migrant may not have been a craftsman, but a significant proportion of the Great Migration must have consisted of men drawn from urban and artisan backgrounds.

A large number of such people among the early colonists might help to answer some of the continuing problems of New England history. New Englanders may have adopted an unusual system of land division, for example, in part because many of them were amateurs at agriculture.[87] The urban origins of so many migrants also suggest one way in which the migration was recruited: from among neighbors already grouped into loosely organized congregations. One Canterbury parish, St. George's, provided a strikingly large number of the Kentish emigrants, and it was the home of Edward Johnson, who had already been to New England once before his return there in 1637. Perhaps he spent his sojourn back in England informing his fellow parishioners about the nature of the American settlement. The proposition is supported by Johnson's own account of the promotion of the New England migration. Often regarded as fanciful rhetoric, he may have intended it as self-description: "This Proclamation [from Christ] being audibly published through the Ile of Great Brittaine by sundry Herraulds, which Christ had prepared for that end: the rumour ran through Cities, Townes and Villages."[88]

We offer these possibilities as suggestions only. The New England migration lasted for twelve years and involved over fifteen thousand people. Conclusions based on the lives of only 273, all of whom arrived in a single year, obviously cannot be too generously applied to the Great Migration as a whole. However, examining this one unusually well-documented group establishes in outline the character of one form of migrant, the urban artisan of Puritan leaning. The frequency of this type of settler and the relevance of his experience to early New England history are questions awaiting further detailed research. At least the men and women who left England in 1637 have had their story told, and this may help us to understand the entire movement of which they formed one part.

IV

Transfer of Culture: Chance and Design in Shaping Massachusetts Bay, 1630–1660

THIS ESSAY DEVELOPED logically out of "Persistent Localism" and "The Covenanted Militia." The persistence of local English values in Massachusetts was so remarkable that it made me curious about the role the New World environment played in facilitating the transfer of culture. To be sure, it is necessary to know that certain East Anglian settlers arrived in Massachusetts Bay eager to right Charles's many institutional wrongs. But what would have occurred if they had landed by chance in a more tropical part of America? To what extent did elements in the New World over which they had little or no control influence their designs? These questions forced me to examine a range of factors—length of the growing season, density of the Native American population, availability of precious natural resources—that I had previously taken for granted.

I

In 1676 William Berkeley, royal governor of Virginia, learned that Indians had overrun the Puritan settlements of New England. While the governor apparently had the good grace not to applaud the Indians in

This essay first appeared in The New England Historical and Genealogical Register, CXXXII (1978), copyright © 1978 by the New England Historic Genealogical Society, and is reprinted by permission.

public, he wrote privately to friends announcing the happy intelligence. Throughout the English Civil Wars, Berkeley and members of the Virginia gentry remained loyal to the Stuarts, and they never forgave the Puritans for raising the standard against the beloved Charles I. To the leading Virginia planters, Puritanism became synonymous with rebellion and regicide, and the men and women who followed those whom Berkeley regarded as fanatical preachers to Massachusetts Bay received no pity in their hour of defeat.[1]

But if men in the southern colonies agreed that New England was a hot-bed of sedition, they conceded that the Puritans had accomplished something in their pattern of settlement which the planters had not. The southerners envied the Bay colonists' establishment of scores of towns which, the Virginians and others of their region believed, formed the basis of Massachusetts's striking prosperity. These local communities appeared to be vital centers of commerce. However much Berkeley and people like him despised Puritanism, they spent considerable time and energy during the seventeenth century in an unsuccessful attempt to break out of the plantation economy and create towns throughout the South.[2]

The purpose of this chapter is not to demonstrate the superiority of the early New England social structure or to compare systematically the towns of Massachusetts and the plantations of Virginia and Carolina. The goal is rather to understand more fully the foundations of localism in seventeenth-century New England society. By examining the ways in which the New Englanders transferred the traditional agricultural communities they had known in England to the New World, one learns more not only about the development of the Bay Colony, but also about localism as a general historical phenomenon. The transfer of localism to Massachusetts was complex, a mixture of chance and design, an amalgam of well-laid plans and dumb luck. Both elements were essential to the successful reestablishment of Old World local communities in America.

During the 1630s thousands of men and women moved to New England. This so-called Great Migration drew people from all parts of England, but these settlers still had much in common. They shared the dominant cultural values of the time, and this general background—what historians sometimes term the migrants' cultural baggage—has understandably received close scholarly attention. There is no question that this common body of ideas and beliefs, assumptions and customs helped shape the character of the society that the immigrants founded in the New World. Like the people who remained in the mother country, the settlers were children of the Reformation, aggressive Protestants contemptuous of anything that smacked of Catholicism. They revered England's ancient constitution, hated its enemies—especially Spain—and cherished the memory of Good Queen Bess. Indeed, for the most part the colonists' notions about economics, politics, and society were indistinguishable from those of their countrymen who never contemplated moving to the New World.

This dominant culture, however, does not reveal the source of the settlers' tenacious commitment to localism once they reached America. As we have seen in Chapter I, to understand this aspect of their lives, we need to focus our attention not only upon English culture as a whole, but also upon hundreds of sub-cultures that flourished in the provinces, in areas such as Yorkshire, Kent, East Anglia, and the West Country. In these districts before the mid-1620s decisions made by the royal government in London seldom had great impact, since men and women in the scattered, self-contained agricultural villages that characterized these regions gave their first loyalty to their own communities. It was here that most of them were born, and it was here, too, that they acquired meaningful social identity: they and their neighbors farmed as their ancestors farmed, they shared in village folk customs, and they viewed outsiders with suspicion if not outright hostility. In fact, most sixteenth- and early seventeenth-century English communities insisted upon the preservation of traditional ways of life and upon the maintenance of customary institutional forms. In this respect, the rural population of Elizabethan England was no different from peasant communities that can still be found in certain parts of the world today.

Wise monarchs disturbed the fabric of local society only at their peril. Charles I, who became king in 1625, tried to do so and failed; his policies broke with those of his predecessors and, therefore, seemed arbitrary to his subjects. His ill-conceived plans to centralize authority and to standardize local civil, military, and ecclesiastical practice interfered with village autonomy. Charles was following the example of contemporary Continental monarchs who were also attempting to curb the independence of provincial magnates and peasant villagers, but unlike the kings of France and Spain the English king lacked the means and temperament to effect such vast reforms. He sent military officers to drill the local trainbands, but these expensive strangers only irritated village inhabitants who were not interested in Charles's reckless overseas adventures.[3] Bishops of the Church of England, acting with the king's blessing, tried to force local congregations throughout the nation to conform to general Anglican ceremonies and prayer books, and when village preachers protested against what one historian has termed "an Arminian revolution"—as they did most vociferously in Puritan strongholds—the bishops moved aggressively to silence criticism.[4] In civil matters Charles demanded extravagant new taxes and unconstitutional loans. When the elected members of Parliament questioned the need for these levies, the monarch decided he could rule just as well without their assistance.[5]

These policies threatened the continuity of local society. Englishmen in the 1630s and 1640s, of course, would discover that Charles had overreached himself. Without a standing army of his own, he could not coerce his subjects; without their love, he could not count on their obedience. But in the late 1620s the outcome of the king's ambitious drive to centralize authority was by no means clear, and it is not surprising that those people who migrated to New England tried as best they could to preserve traditional community life. In this sense, the Great Migration was a conservative movement.[6]

By 1660 three distinct attributes characterized the local communities of Massachusetts Bay: stability, diversity, and independence. With the exception of Boston, which was already developing into an important commercial center, these villages were inward-looking.[7] Migrants had established local customs and procedures with surprising speed, and as one reads through the records of these communities, one easily forgets that at most the towns were only twenty years old. They seem to have already laid down the type of deeply rooted traditions that are usually associated with peasant villages whose past is measured in centuries rather than in decades. Rates of spatial mobility were low. New Englanders stayed put, and their sons and daughters married into the community becoming part of an elaborate kin network that provided them with social identity. They were socialized into village folkways and ritual patterns of behavior, and it is neither surprising nor unwarranted that several colonial historians have recently described these people as "peasants."[8]

The second characteristic, diversity, sprang not only from the differences between the particular English subcultures that established particular towns, but also from the peculiarities of environment. Some towns were classical nuclear communities from the time of their founding; others allowed families to live at some distance from each other.

Some villages practiced open-field farming well into the late seventeenth century; others quickly converted to compact individual holdings. In church affairs, some local congregations tolerated greater ministerial domination than did others. In some communities the selectmen possessed broad discretion in making decisions about the common good; in others the town meeting narrowly circumscribed the selectmen's power. There is no need to extend the list, though it would be easy enough to do so. The New England town was as varied in form as were the rice and tobacco plantations of the southern mainland colonies. The towns' relative independence from the central authority, of course, reinforced their stability and preserved their diversity.

II

Thus far in the analysis of localism the transfer of culture has focused largely upon the settlers' conscious design. We have seen that groups of villagers throughout England moved to Massachusetts Bay in part to preserve a traditional way of life threatened by an interfering monarch. Surely, the colonists' intentions are crucial to an understanding of the shape of early New England society. The explanation for the patterns of settlement in that society, however, is not quite so simple. Other people over the centuries have been uprooted from rural communities, but few have been able to replicate so fully the traditional life they left behind in the Old World. Conditions beyond their control have usually forced them to modify their plans, and before long they found themselves parts of a totally unfamiliar social order.[9] Because early New Englanders accomplished something so unusual, we should examine the elements beside the strength of their determination that contributed to the smooth transfer of localism to the Bay Colony. We can discern at least six separate factors at work here.

The first factor operating in the migrants' favor was the environment. To be sure, it was somewhat colder than it had been in the mother country, but the length of the growing season, the range of the soil types, and the amount of annual rainfall were roughly similar to conditions the settlers had known in the English countryside. Francis Higginson, a minister who arrived in Salem in 1629, explained "The Temper of the Aire of *New-England* is one speciall thing that commends this place. Experience doth manifest that there is hardly a more healthfull place to be found in the World that agreeth better with our English bodyes." Higginson assured English readers that Indian corn or maize grew with a minimum of physical labor, and he speculated "There is not such greate and plentifull eares of Corne I suppose any where else to bee found but in this Country."[10] More important to the average English farmer, however, were reports of the successful cultivation of English corn, in other words, wheat, oats, rye, and barley, for these were the crops with which the migrant would have been most familiar.[11] Other observers found similar conditions. Thomas Graves, an engineer employed by the Massachusetts Bay Company, informed people contemplating migration that traditional agriculture produced unprecedented yields in New England. "Every thing that is heere eyther sowne or planted," he boasted, "prospereth far better then in old England: the increase of Corne is here farre beyond expectation."[12]

Graves and Higginson exaggerated America's potential bounty, but we know from other sources that English migrants successfully introduced Old World forms of agriculture into Massachusetts Bay. With the exception of Indian corn, the range of crops and livestock raised in the Bay Colony would have been familiar to any seventeenth-century husbandman from Yorkshire to Dorset. The point is simply that the movement to the New World did not require a major readjustment in the patterns of cultivation by which the settlers and their ancestors had supported themselves for generations.[13] Some men gave up positions in England's cloth industry to become farmers in Massachusetts, but even these people were acquainted with fields of wheat and oats. Even though they were skilled artisans by the standards of the time, they remained part of the agrarian rhythms that pervaded both city and town in the provinces. And those persons who had been full-time farmers in the old country prospered in Massachusetts, a clear indication that they were able to apply agricultural knowledge and techniques learned in England's local communities to their new environment.[14] Indeed, the records of many Massachusetts towns reveal that the founders established an open-field system of agriculture whose origins date from the Middle Ages, if not earlier.[15] These migrants were thus not forced by conditions beyond their control to experiment with strange crops such as rice, sugar, or tobacco, and because a father and his sons could cultivate enough land to support a family—even produce a little extra income from cash sales—there was no compulsion to recruit a large, cheap, subservient labor force. In fact, it was probably the transfer of cereal agriculture rather than an aversion to human bondage that kept the New Englanders from adopting slavery on a large scale. The contrast with Barbados, Carolina, and Virginia is obvious. In those colonies the cultivation of lucrative staple crops stimulated labor-intensive plantation agriculture. This type of economic structure was totally alien to the experience of most seventeenth-century English farmers, and so the move to one of these settlements inevitably involved greater cultural disorientation than did the transfer to Massachusetts Bay.[16] Had the men and women who sailed to New England during the 1630s accidentally found themselves in a lush environment full of exotic crops they might have become wealthy, but they probably would not have been able to replicate England's local communities. These villages assumed the existence of a relatively small, family-oriented agriculture.

The second factor is closely related to the first and while it may seem obvious, its importance cannot be easily dismissed. The relative barrenness of the New England environment—its lack of rare minerals, its inability to produce high-profit cash crops such as tobacco and sugar, its comparatively limited supply of pelts—contributed to the successful transfer of localism in several subtle ways. If the Bay colonists had stumbled upon natural resources for which there was a booming European market, they would have seen their tightly bound culture strained, perhaps even completely undermined, as men deserted the community to strike it rich on their own. Even before Winthrop's fleet arrived in America, however, thoughts of sudden wealth had been largely dispelled by the reports of earlier settlers and explorers. Unlike Virginia, this colony did not experience a gold rush. New England's rocky soil, about which local farmers have grumbled for three centuries, provided for the establishment of a healthy agricultural economy.[17] Few men became affluent before 1650, but by the same token, famine was virtually unknown in this region.

The successful reestablishment of Old World agricultural patterns meant in effect that the social structure of local English communities was not seriously challenged in America. The transfer to Massachusetts did not destroy traditional social relations, especially patterns of deference, and the colonists routinely accepted the right to rule of certain gentlemen like Winthrop. Moreover, because no noblemen bothered to move to New England, the distribution of wealth was probably more equitable than it had been in England. During the earliest decades of settlement, the distance between the richest man in a village and the average farmer was certainly not so pronounced as to create jealousies or tensions that might have destroyed corporate loyalties which were the foundations of New England localism.[18]

The Bay Colony's lack of lucrative natural resources assisted in the transfer of English local culture in another way that historians have not fully appreciated. Had the migrants discovered gold or produced large quantities of sugar, for example, they would have been forced to consider much more seriously than they ever did the possibility of assault by one of England's enemies. Ships loaded with valuable cargoes riding in Boston harbor would have presented tempting targets for a marauding Dutch, French, or Spanish fleet. The possibility of attack continuously threatened England's southern mainland and Caribbean colonies. The Dutch navy, for example, twice sailed up the James River, terrorizing Virginia planters and capturing merchant vessels filled with tobacco. Defense, particularly the construction of permanent sea forts, was very expensive, and the Bay Colony was fortunate to be spared this outlay. The fortifications that the settlers built during the early decades were small and ineffectual, and during the early decades of settlement, the colony's government did not demand taxes for foreign defense in an amount that strained the economies of the local communities.

The third major factor affecting the development of localism in New England was the absence of large numbers of hostile Indians along the Atlantic coast. An epidemic, probably smallpox carried over by the earliest explorers and settlers, swept through the Indian population on the eve of the Great Migration, destroying entire villages in eastern Massachusetts. The extent of the mortality among the Native Americans amazed the colonists who arrived with Winthrop in 1630, and because they did not understand the horrendous epidemiological consequences of intercultural contact, they attributed the clearing of the region of Indians to the workings of Providence.[19] Edward Johnson concluded that by means of contagious disease, Christ "not onely made roome for his people to plant; but also tamed the hard and cruell hearts of these barbarous Indians."[20] In his account of the country, Higginson noted that the Native Americans of the region "above twelve yeares since were swept away by a great & grievous Plague that was amongst them, so that there are verie few left to inhabite the Country."[21] In this plague, the Indians had obviously experienced a devastating culture shock that undermined the fabric of their society far more seriously than did the actual arrival of thousands of English immigrants. Winthrop believed that the Indians' calamity almost obliged colonists to fill the newly vacated territory. "As for the Natives in New England," he explained, "they inclose noe Land, neither have [they] any setled habytation, nor any tame Cattle to improve the Land by, and soe have noe other but a Naturall Right to those Countries. soe as if we leave them sufficient [land] for their use, we may lawfully take the rest." [22]

The destruction of the local Indian tribes meant that the Native Americans presented no immediate military threat. Those who lived close to the white settlements were constrained by the limitations of their numbers to maintain peaceful relations, and the only hostilities that occurred were far to the west, where the density of Indian population remained high. The New England experience, of course, contrasts sharply with that of Virginia. Captain John Smith and his colleagues landed by chance in the middle of one of eastern America's more powerful Indian confederations, and the struggling adventurers spent much valuable time battling Powhatan's warriors. The Indian menace dominated Virginia affairs for almost two decades, siphoning off human and material resources that were desperately needed for other purposes. In 1622, for instance, the local tribes launched a carefully coordinated attack on the English settlements and, within a matter of hours, killed more than 350 planters. [23] But in New England white-Indian relations were far more harmonious and certainly far less lethal. It was not until the 1670s when the scattered tribes regrouped under the leadership of King Philip or Metacom that the New England Indians became a serious military threat.

This forty-year period of relative peace with the Native Americans further encouraged the development of New England localism. [24] As a group, peasants and subsistence farmers throughout the world have had good reason to dread war, since during times of armed conflict their rulers—be they kings, emperors, or czars—inevitably demanded that farm families surrender their harvest as well as their sons to the army. These sacrifices peasants made only with the greatest reluctance, and not a few crowned heads of Europe have marched off to meet the enemy only to discover that their own subjects have risen in rebellion. The reasons are obvious. A rural agricultural economy is relatively inelastic and, therefore, unable to react quickly to a sudden change, especially one that requires a major redirection of income away from the local community in the form of taxes. In ordinary times, peasant farmers utilize as much land as they can, and their production in any given year is a function of the availability of labor, the size of their holdings, and the cooperation of nature. When the central government calls for new taxes to fund the war effort, the peasant cannot suddenly expand productivity. He is already operating at or near maximum efficiency, and if a son goes off to fight, the peasant may be forced to reduce the number of acres under cultivation. Each new tax, therefore, forces the peasant to take food and goods away from his family. For a short time he may bear this imposition, but if the war continues, the local community disintegrates and peasants become refugees.[25]

This type of severe dislocation occurred with discouraging frequency in early seventeenth-century Europe. Indeed, Charles's foolish and expensive military adventures in the late 1620s undermined the crown's authority among the common people as well as the gentry, and in heavily Puritan regions such as East Anglia, known to have produced a large number of New England migrants, the bitterness over forced billeting, press gangs, and transient Irish mercenaries sometimes sparked riots and mutinies.[26] The men and women who transferred to Massachusetts were happily liberated from bearing the costs of prolonged armed conflict. Epidemics among the Indians had removed the most serious potential enemy, and groups of settlers who might under other circumstances have found themselves serving as soldiers in New England immediately began to clear and cultivate the land. While their tax rates were sometimes substantial, the levied monies supported primarily local activities—construction of meetinghouses and schools, the minister's salary, the laying out of new village roads—and they were willing to pay these costs. What demands the colony-wide authorities made upon the local communities do not appear to have been onerous. Indeed, the records before 1675 contain few complaints about the cost of the central government. By the time the Indian tribes of New England threatened the colonists' security, requiring major expenditures for defense, the local communities were well established and certainly better prepared to deal with the costs of war than they had been in the 1630s. Moreover, in the 1670s, faced with King Philip's forces, the settlers saw the necessity of funding an army, something that Charles's subjects had not seen.[27]

The fourth element contributing to the vitality of New England localism was the longevity of the early settlers. The prospect of a longer life

was never one of the publicized attractions of this part of the world, and
the colonists themselves were probably unaware of the change in mortality rates. But it was a fact that men and women lived longer in Massachusetts than their peers in the mother country.[28] The New Englanders endured one particularly hard first winter during 1630,
although even during this short period the death and suffering they experienced scarcely compared with the horrors that greeted newcomers to
Barbados, Carolina, and Virginia. This factor cannot be overstated, for,
as historical demographers have learned, continuing high death rates
accompanied by widespread debilitating illnesses have a profoundly dis-
orienting impact upon a group's culture. It is almost impossible to reestablish the institutions of an Old World society when four out of five
migrants die within a year of their arrival. And yet that is exactly what
occurred in early Virginia and Maryland.[29] The Bay Colonists, however, were not haunted by a sense of dread that their work would be
swept away before completion, and without the problem of widespread
death and disease, they could immediately focus their attentions upon
the problems of creating new agricultural communities. Moreover, because of the improvement in life expectancy, New England's age structure was not unnaturally skewed toward youth. Middle-aged men such
as Winthrop and Johnson moved to Massachusetts and lived.[30] This
fact alone provided continuity between the local communities of England and those of America. These men became the patriarchs of the
New England villages, symbols of stability in an agrarian society.

The fifth element that eased the transfer of localism was the settlers'
homogeneity. There is no need to dwell on this point, for its importance should be obvious. The colonists spoke the same language, came
from the same mother country, and shared many cultural values. Moreover, they were Puritans who believed to a greater or lesser extent that
the Lord preferred congregationalism above all competing church poli-
ties. People who disagreed were free to move away, and many men and
women did just that. Those who remained, however, could assume that
while persons in neighboring villages might differ with them on details
such as where to run a boundary line, they concurred on fundamentals.
This common base created an atmosphere of mutual trust. The communities respected each other's autonomy, and when differences developed between towns, the inhabitants or their selectmen took the matter
to a colony court run by individuals like themselves. No one feared that
the farmers in one community would take up arms against another town

no matter how great the provocation. This situation presents a marked contrast with other seventeenth-century colonies such as Maryland, where Catholics periodically battled Protestants, or Virginia and South Carolina, where large numbers of unfree laborers threatened to disrupt the tranquillity of planter society.[31]

The last factor contributing to the strength of localism in the Bay Colony was quite different from those that we have already discussed, and it may be an outgrowth of those elements rather than an independent phenomenon. Almost as soon as they arrived in the New World, the migrants succeeded in constructing a physical embodiment of their commitment to localism. Each community built a meetinghouse that served both civil and ecclesiastical functions. It provided a central place where men and women regularly assembled to shape and define their society. They gathered here to pray and sometimes to argue over land divisions or unruly hogs, but the very act of meeting together became in itself a ritual act that reinforced the sense of community. The buildings took on a symbolic significance—much as cathedrals did in medieval towns or smaller churches still do in Latin American peasant villages— that is difficult for us to appreciate fully today. In early Virginia, where buildings often collapsed from neglect within a generation and where the planters dispersed along the rivers, there was no visible symbol of community analogous to the New England meetinghouse. In the eighteenth century, however, county courthouses began to serve some of the same functions.[32]

The successful transfer of English localism to the New World was a two-stage process. First, it involved an act of volition. The migrants like other Englishmen at the time wanted to preserve their local communities from external interference, and when other means to achieve that goal failed in the late 1620s and 1630s, they moved to the New World. But the mere intention to preserve a traditional culture was not sufficient to assure success. A series of other factors—several of them completely fortuitous—made it possible for them to replicate in large measure the culture they had known in England. It is important to stress that none of the six elements we have discussed would in itself have led to the establishment of the New England villages as we know them. The crown's sudden aggressive intervention in the affairs of England's local communities coupled with a growing uneasiness about the nation's spiritual health were major factors determining the eventual shape of Massachusetts society. New England's soil and climate that permitted the settlers to grow the same crops that they had cultivated in the mother country, the absence of extremely valuable natural resources, the decimation of the region's Indian population, the longevity of the founders, and the settlers' homogeneity, these conditions facilitated the transfer of localism. If one or two of these factors had been missing, the Bay Colony might not have been noticeably affected. If all of them were removed, however, it is doubtful that localism could have survived, much less flourished. What Governor Berkeley and other seventeenth-century planners perhaps failed to understand was that one cannot simply will a local community into existence.

V

War, Taxes,
and Political Brokers:
The Ordeal of Massachusetts Bay,
1675–1692

DECLENSION HAS LONG fascinated historians of late seventeenth-century Massachusetts Bay. The members of Winthrop's generation, we are told, came to the New World on a special mission, but their sons and daughters soon lost sight of the "city on a hill." Puritan divines obligingly recorded evidence of the children's loss of faith, a trend that threatened to unloose God's wrath upon New England. Public controversy was a particularly troublesome symptom of spiritual decline. The settlers clashed over a whole range of material concerns, selfish matters, forgetting apparently that the Lord expected them to "be knitt together in this worke as one man." Increase Mather, who monitored the colony's religious health, asked rhetorically in 1682, "Have not we been like foolish Birds, pecking at one another, until the great Kite be ready to come, and devour one as well as another?" Many modern historians share the minister's belief that institutional controversy—indeed, change of any sort—was somehow bound up with secularization.

With respect to Mather, I do not find this interpretation persuasive. It is true that within certain institutional settings the colonists forcefully, even truculently articulated their demands. They quarreled over taxes and asked embarrassing questions about what their rulers did with public funds. I argue in this chapter that dissension or perception of dissension was largely the product of extraordinary expenditures connected with war. It cost more to be a citizen of Massachusetts Bay in 1680 than it had in 1640, and one would expect villagers to challenge political leaders more frequently after King Philip's War than they had done in the earlier period. Ballooning levies strained relations between different levels of authority, especially local and colonial, and as time passed, the position of established political brokers in this society was seriously eroded. But while some individuals condemned these changes in the political culture and lamented the loss of the "old peaceable ruleable, genuine Spirit," I found little evidence that this period witnessed a widespread rejection of the founders' values.

I

On April 18, 1689, several hundred armed men toppled the Dominion of New England and jailed its governor, Sir Edmund Andros. The action occurred without bloodshed, and the orderliness of the proceedings made it easier for colonial pamphleteers later to describe the Glorious Revolution in Massachusetts Bay as a noble defense of property rights and individual liberties. Some witnesses to these events, however, did not record such lofty sentiments. They were particularly anxious about the sudden appearance of so many armed men in the streets of Boston. The spontaneous assembling of political rebels was unprecedented in the commonwealth and therefore not a little unnerving. According to one observer, when the members of the Boston militia companies took up positions along the roadways, there were at least a thousand more soldiers from inland villages waiting to enter the city on the "Charlestown side." "The country people," he reported, "came into the town, in the afternoon, in such rage and heat, that it made us all tremble to think what would follow."[1] Another colonist explained that an additional "six or 700 men marched down out of Middlesex to Charlestown . . . & there quartered the night."[2] Faced with overwhelming opposition, Andros and his small bodyguard wisely surrendered.

The "country people's" aggressive political behavior during this period cannot be explained simply as a protest against the inept policies of the Dominion government. To be sure, Andros and his cronies blatantly ignored due process when dealing with the colonists, but the Glorious Revolution in Massachusetts Bay also involved socioeconomic tensions that had been building for at least a decade before the governor's arrival in New England. Andros's expulsion provided a catalyst for social and political changes that some persons thought long overdue. Indeed, the popular rising of 1689 opened the way for political alterations in the Bay Colony that were as far-reaching as those which occurred in Virginia during Bacon's Rebellion and in New York during Leisler's Rebellion.[3]

The crisis of local authority in Massachusetts Bay between 1675 and 1692 involved two separate, though closely related developments. First, during this period one can discern a significant shift in the activities, functions, and recruitment of persons whom cultural anthropologists and political scientists sometimes label the "brokers." These individuals, present in all societies, mediate between various level of authority, justifying to members of local communities external policies and demands, while at the same time protecting village clients from outside pressures that threaten customary patterns of life. From time to time, unforeseen events such as a reorganization of national government or an outbreak of prolonged war erodes the brokers' effectiveness. Unprecedented external demands make it difficult for them to shield local clients from outside interference, and confronted with this collision of interests, brokers either adjust their activities to changing conditions or are replaced by new mediators capable of pleasing both constituencies.[4]

An analysis of the political culture of Massachusetts after 1675 provides a particularly dramatic example of the strains that war—and the debt that accompanied prolonged conflict—placed upon community brokers. Even in towns in which traditional corporate mediators survived, one finds severe political tensions, and in some villages these local leaders, many of them aging patriarchs, were replaced with younger, more aggressive figures who owed their standing in society less to religious orthodoxy, sober habits, and personal wealth than to an ability to manipulate outside power to the satisfaction of a distinct faction within the community. The challenge to established authority figures was certainly in progress well before the creation of the Dominion. The popular rising against Governor Andros simply gave the movement unexpected impetus. The story of these older mediators at a moment of crisis reveals much about the changing web of socio-economic relations and the texture of political life in Massachusetts following King Philip's War.[5]

A second, closely related element affecting the character of local authority was a shift in popular attitudes toward political participation. After 1675—and especially after 1689—an increasing number of people demanded a larger voice in the choice of leaders and the formulation of public policy. The forms of government which were already quite open by contemporary European standards did not become significantly more democratic than they had been at the time of the colony's founding. Rather, it was the way the men defined their role in politics that changed. In the period following King Philip's War, villagers questioned more frequently the decisions of town selectmen, particularly in financial matters, and by the time James II established the Dominion of New England, a growing number of colonists openly challenged local and colonial leaders. The bond of trust that had linked local brokers to village clients in the early decades of the colony's history gave way to skepticism. However much the older corporate mediators may have wanted to suppress the new popular demands, they could not do so, and their uneasiness about sharing power with hundreds of armed young men accounts in part for the near breakdown of civil government following the expulsion of Sir Edmund Andros.

Throughout this period war and taxes were driving engines of political change. Other elements undoubtedly influenced the process, the determination of English officials to regulate colonial commerce, the rise of powerful new merchant families within the province, the pressure of a growing population, and the secularization of values, just to name a few, but war and taxes were central, dynamic factors.[6] They spurred both a democratization of political affairs and a shift in village brokers. Expenditures connected with the Indian wars created a huge public debt which, in turn, forced colony rulers to levy taxes on a scale previously unknown in Massachusetts Bay. Concern about these rising expenses drew villagers increasingly into local and colonial politics. The longer hostilities continued—and conflict with the French and Native Americans became a continuing aspect of New England life during this period—the greater the strain between established mediators and obstreperous townsmen. Since the younger men of the colony resented the double burden of fighting and financing these wars, it is not surprising that they were among the first to support new village leaders.

II

For several decades after 1630, Massachusetts Bay remained a loose federation of corporate communities. The original migrants had journeyed to America in part to escape what they perceived as Charles I's unwarranted intervention into village affairs. In the New World they created small, homogeneous, relatively isolated farming communities that were often modeled upon those they had known in the mother country. By almost any standard of measurement, these early villages achieved remarkable stability. Because of the unexpected healthiness of New England, settlers lived longer in Massachusetts than they would have in England. The founding fathers became village patriarchs, surviving for decades after their arrival and providing reassuring symbols of community continuity. And while few people became fabulously wealthy in Massachusetts, most realized modest prosperity. Famine was virtually unknown in this region. Almost everyone received sufficient acreage to support a family, and though some men were richer than others, the distance between the richest and poorest was not as pronounced as it would have been in contemporary England. Certainly, early seventeenth-century New England towns were not plagued by a class of permanently impoverished men and women who might—as they did in Stuart England—have wandered from place to place spreading unrest and disease. Elections within the Bay communities for minister, selectmen, militia officers, and representatives to the colony's General Court reinforced the sense of local control throughout this society.[7]

When disputes over civil or ecclesiastical matters divided these newly settled communities, villagers often attempted to settle differences through loving mediation. Local arbitrators in Dedham counselled the parties to a disagreement to "live together in a way of neighborly love and do each other as they would have the other do themselves."[8] Dedham's procedure was not unusual. Townsmen tried to avoid genuinely divisive confrontations, and though feuds sometimes dragged on for years, they seldom undermined community stability. Only in extreme cases did villagers take their differences to colonial authorities whom they regarded not as "outsiders" but as legitimate spokesmen for corporate values. The courts of Massachusetts provided a legal means of resolving controversies, but colonial magistrates usually urged opposing sides to settle problems through local mediation.[9] As late as 1674, for example, a committee of the Massachusetts General Court reported that it had traveled to Mendon to discover what caused a "great dissatisfaction & differenc" among the inhabitants. The members of the committee explained that after full discussion of the issues, "there appeared reall remorse," and the townsmen reached an amicable settlement. The external authorities had not threatened coercion. They merely responded to a locally generated quarrel, offering a forum in which these particular villagers could reestablish harmony.[10]

Colonial rulers provided assistance in restoring community tranquillity, but during the early years of settlement, they did not ask for much in return. The financial demands of the Massachusetts government do not appear to have been burdensome. Because the colony was blessed with a long period of peace running roughly from 1637 to 1675, the General Court was spared the trouble of building expensive fortifications or maintaining hungry armies in the field, precisely the type of expenditures that sparked popular protest in mid-seventeenth-century Virginia. Except for a few months in 1637 when Massachusetts troops engaged in a one-sided war against the Pequots in Connecticut, the Bay Colonists avoided armed clashes with the Native Americans, and while colonial authorities assessed an annual tax on the towns, usually in the form of a single country rate, the villagers themselves levied significantly larger sums. The greatest outlay was the minister's salary. Townsmen also taxed themselves from time to time for the construction of a new meetinghouse or the completion of a special project of local importance.[11]

During the early years of settlement, citizens of the local communities assumed that colonial rulers represented the interests of the villages in which they resided. Each town elected deputies to the General Court. The voters trusted and respected these individuals. They were orthodox in their religious beliefs, somewhat more prosperous than their fellow townsmen, and frequently experienced in local civil and ecclesiastical affairs. Because the deputies generally lived in the communities which they represented, they understood—indeed, shared—their neighbors' concerns, and for the most part these men were ideal political brokers in a society which held localism in high regard.

The colonial assistants, members of the upper house of the Massachusetts legislature, were elected at large, but regardless of the procedures by which they obtained office, many voters apparently thought that every major town should have a magistrate of its own. When John Winthrop, Jr., an influential magistrate, decided to leave Ipswich for a new career in Connecticut, his friend Nathaniel Ward explained that Winthrop's local supporters "are in a misery for the want of you."[12] In fact, in 1638 the Massachusetts General Court recognized the magistrates' local ties by ordering "that every towne shall beare the charges of

their *owne magistrates.*"[13] While this community identification grew
weaker as time passed, the colony-wide leaders were still a source of
pride to the communities in which they lived. Their values were those
of the local voters, and since the demands of the central government
were relatively light, the colonial rulers seldom strained the bond of
trust that connected them to the local communities. Like the deputies,
these more prominent colonial rulers—men such as William Pynchon
and John Endecott—functioned well as mediators.[14]

III

Indian war set off a chain of events that profoundly altered the colony's
political culture. King Philip's War broke out in late June 1675, and it
marked among other things the beginning of a movement toward government centralization that changed the relation between town and colony authorities. For a time this process was all but imperceptible. To
the New Englanders' surprise, Metacom's warriors more than held their
own on the battlefield, and the death toll on both sides was dreadful.
The very nature of this exhausting war forced colonial leaders to make
unprecedented demands upon the local communities. Warrants were
dispatched from Boston to levy troops out of the village trainbands;
recalcitrants had to be pressed into uniform. Quartermasters required
animals and supplies, and men whose lives had previously revolved
around the conduct of local affairs found themselves suddenly coordi-
nating a major war effort.[15] Since the conflict dragged on far longer
than anyone expected, military officers frequently encountered harsh
criticism from persons who anticipated swift victories. The effect of military defeat on an individual's claim to deference is difficult to judge,
but some brokers who served ineffectually as officers apparently lost
their constituents' respect. Urian Oakes, one of New England's more
learned ministers, for example, exclaimed to the members of Boston's
elite artillery company in 1677, "I hope the Gentlemen-Souldiers
present will not blame any of us, if we cannot look upon their *Train-
ings,* and *Artillery-Exercises* with such an Eye as formerly before the
Warre."[16]

A more significant result of King Philip's War, at least as far as the
villagers were concerned, was the creation of a large colonial debt. One
estimate placed the colony's expenses at £150,000, and even if this fig-

ure represented an exaggeration, the war involved a colony-wide outlay on a scale previously unknown in Massachusetts.[17] And this financial obligation in turn was a major catalyst in changing the relation between colonial and local authorities. In villages throughout the Bay Colony after 1675, inhabitants began to pay a greater share of their taxes to the colony than they did to their own community. In 1672, for example, the residents of Dorchester assessed themselves £50 3s 8d for local purposes. That same year they paid colonial authorities £28 4s 4d. But by 1678 the colony's rates had increased to £111 10s 7d, while the town's tax amounted to £13 12s 10d.[18] In Salem the town rates for 1672 were a little more than seven pounds greater than were the colonial rates, but by 1679 the General Court requested £264 from Salem as opposed to the £121 19s which was required to support the town government.[19] In Dedham, Watertown, Wenham, and Woburn the trend seems to have been the same.[20]

The extraordinarily inequitable structure of colonial taxation exacerbated economic tensions. For as the levies increased, the state's demands upon the poorer members of society were proportionally greater than those made upon their more affluent neighbors.[21] The colony rates consisted of a poll as well as a property tax, so that each country rate (as single units of taxation were called) included a head tax of 1s 8d and a property tax of a penny on the pound. As long as Boston authorities requested only a single country rate, the usual level before 1675, a person in humble circumstances had little cause to complain. But as the country rates were doubled and redoubled, the head tax was duplicated, creating a much greater hardship for people of lower income than for those holding extensive properties. In order to finance the war effort, the colony government levied at least twenty-six separate country rates in 1675–76.[22] This demand placed a staggering burden on the villagers. In 1675 the inhabitants of Woburn paid the colony a little over £30, but during the fourteen-month period from June 1675 to August 1676, they sent a whopping £530 5s 9d to the colony's treasurer.[23] Admittedly, with a war raging colonists acceded to these rates without serious protest, but over the next decade the structure of taxation remained an irritant.

The defeat of Philip's warriors failed to restore colonial taxation to its pre-war level. In 1677 town constables received orders from the General Court to collect nine country rates. While Massachusetts allowed villagers to meet their obligation in "country pay," in other words, in

wheat, barley, or corn, two of the colony rates for 1677 had to be delivered in specie.[24] Even in the best of times, hard currency was in short
supply in Massachusetts, and for small farmers just recovering from a
debilitating war, this request must have seemed oppressive. While the
colony's revenue demands abated somewhat after 1677, Boston authorities in 1678 called for three rates; in 1679 they levied five more. Agents
dispatched to England to defend the colony's charter further drained the
treasury, and there were other new expenses. In 1680 the citizens were
confronted with four rates, two in specie and two in country pay. At no
time before the creation of the Dominion of New England did colony
taxes fall below two rates.[25]

Contemporaries who agreed about very little during this period concurred about the depressed state of the colony's post-war economy. Everywhere they looked, they encountered hardship. Daniel Gookin, a
strident defender of an independent religious commonwealth in
America, thought that the General Court should not bother to send
agents to lobby for the charter, because such representatives "will contract a very great charge & expences which the poore people are very
unable to stand under considering the great [?] . . . that wee have had
by warr, smal pox, fires, sea loses, Blastings & other publike loses."[26]
The political moderate Simon Bradstreet, on the other hand, was willing to accept closer ties with the crown; but in 1684 he warned a royal
placeman against "the sending over a Governor, which would be
chargeable, [for] the people here as you know are generally very poore."
To be sure, there were some wealthy men living in Boston, but even
these were not so affluent as it was rumored. According to Bradstreet,
"The warr with the Indians and late great fyres have much impoverished this Country, and the unproffitableness of trade every where doeth
much discourage."[27] Not surprisingly, just a few months after he
penned this letter, the selectmen of Mendon informed the General
Court that colony taxes were so high that the village could not even
continue "the maintaynance of the gospell."[28]

The colony's growing expenditures coupled with a decline in commerce hit small farming villages like Mendon particularly hard. The
rural agricultural economy was relatively inelastic, and therefore unable
to react to sudden change, especially one that required a major redirection of income away from the local community in the form of taxes.[29]
In Massachusetts Bay following King Philip's War, rising commodity
prices might have reduced such financial pressures. But in point of fact,

the conclusion of hostilities did not generate inflation in agricultural returns. [30] Since Bay farmers could not substantially increase productivity and since the return on agricultural commodities did not inflate as rapidly as did colonial taxation, the external demand for revenue obviously represented a major sacrifice for the great majority of the population. Not surprisingly, town records from this period reflect a growing attention on the local level to financial affairs. In the early decades of settlement, the allotment of land dominated village minutes, but after 1675 inhabitants spent an increasing amount of public meeting time discussing assessments, budgets, and appropriations. A rising load of paperwork inevitably accompanied the escalation of government expenditures. Indeed, the *ad hoc* accounting systems that apparently served well enough before King Philip's War seemed no longer adequate. Communities attempted to bring greater precision to their records; specific disbursements, for example, were spelled out in more detail than they had ever been before. [31] This change must have come as an unpleasant shock to persons accustomed to less demanding procedures. Village constables were charged with the collection of rates for colony, town, and minister, and even conscientious individuals found that their account books became confused. [32]

Matters involving the pocketbook inevitably stimulated popular participation in government affairs. Not only did villagers meet more frequently than they had done before the war, they also aggressively reassumed powers that earlier generations had delegated to town selectmen. In the early 1680s, for example, the residents of Watertown decided that they themselves would levy town taxes and oversee disbursements. [33] In 1681 the selectmen and townsmen of Wenham fought over expenditures, and after a particularly heated session, the records noted, "Also that the abovesaid Rate be made over againe by the Select men leaveing out the mony abovesaid which the towne agred to leave out." [34] In more prosperous times the villagers might have trusted their elected officials to handle such business, but as the economy weakened, local people challenged traditional authority.

In Charlestown this new assertiveness took an unexpected turn. In 1685 a controversy broke out between a large group of village residents and the town's proprietors over the use of the community commons. If this dispute had occurred in an earlier period of Massachusetts' history, it might have been settled through loving mediation. But the ninety angry men who petitioned the General Court about commons privileges were in no loving mood, and their protest revealed the extent to which some brokers had lost touch with their clients. The unhappy householders pointedly couched their arguments in terms of money and votes. "The deprived Inhabitants" explained that they considered themselves "to be the greatest pt of the Towne, and Likewise Suppose wee doe pay the greatest part of all rates and Taxes Levied in the Towne." It seemed unreasonable for a small number of proprietors to profit from control over the commons while the majority of townsmen desperately required access to this land. As the petitioners reminded the members of the General Court, apparently without irony, local affairs should "be ordered for the good of the Whole family."[35]

What gives this document special interest, however, is the aggrieved householders' sense of economic division within Charlestown. Hard times caused less affluent villagers to become increasingly sensitive about their status within the town, and they were willing to take their grievance all the way to London if that move would guarantee justice. The petitioners warned, "Some of us knowes what Priviledges England affords *all* the Inhabitants there, as Namely free commons to poore as well as Rich." If the threat of an English appeal were not sufficient to upset the colony's rulers, the Charlestown group noted "farther this honored Court may please to take notice that there are now Severall of the members of this Honored Court, greatly interested in the above said Propriety as Namely the Honored Deputy Governor Thomas Danforth, Samuel Nowell and James Russell Esqs, and Capt. Sprague and Capt. John Phillips." Humble petitioners who took pride merely in the fact that they could "all wright theaire own names" had directly challenged the integrity of several powerful magistrates.[36] In Charlestown, at least, economic inequalities had begun to erode the authority of established brokers, and though the parties in this dispute probably remembered a time when the Bay magistrates would have swiftly punished such impudence, both sides must have recognized that the colony's political culture had changed significantly since the time of Governor John Winthrop.

The Charlestown petition revealed the change taking place in broker-client relations. The war and charter defense forced corporate mediators to make unpopular demands. Indeed, economic factors largely beyond their control transformed colonial authorities from trusted agents into outsiders whom villagers increasingly identified with interests beyond the local community. The brokers naturally felt threatened by the spreading restiveness. Rude insinuations and crude majoritarianism alienated them from their clients, and it is not surprising that some of them openly criticized democratic procedures.[37] As one minister explained in this period, "In the beginning of times was occasioned much disadvantage to the government of the church by making it too popular; and no less to the civil government, by too much contriving to advance the liberties of the people."[38]

Just before the establishment of the Dominion of New England, not a few colonial leaders—men who bore the surnames of prominent founders—had lost confidence in their ability to rule. They looked to English authorities to bring greater order and stability to Massachusetts Bay. Joseph Dudley, son of the colony's second governor, eagerly sought after royal patronage during the 1680s, causing one crown official to observe acidly, if Dudley "finds things resolutely manniged, will cringe and bow to anything; *he hath his fortune to make in the world.*"[39] To a greater or lesser degree, William Stoughton, Wait Winthrop, and Peter Bulkeley marched to the same drummer. These men were not unlike brokers in some underdeveloped countries today who abandon the traditional culture of their fathers for the sophisticated culture of the outside world. As Dudley explained to William Blathwayt, secretary to the Lords of Trade, "[I] have in a great Measure lost my reputation with the people which yet I am not Concerned for, for that I am sure I have persued nothing more then their own best Interests which is to obtayn his Majesties favour."[40]

IV

In 1684 the Court of Chancery in London annulled the Massachusetts Charter. In its place James II established an administrative system called the Dominion of New England, in one stroke abolishing elective government in the Bay Colony. The King's appointed governor, Sir Edmund Andros, managed in only a few years to alienate almost everyone with whom he came in contact. Historians have catalogued the evils of the Dominion, but they have overlooked the fact that this centralization of authority did not represent so violent a break with the past as some pamphleteers writing after the Glorious Revolution claimed. The leaders of the Old Charter government put up only the mildest protest about the alteration of their constitution, and some men like Dudley welcomed the reorganization.[41] Edward Randolph, an imperial agent who lobbied hard for a royal governor in Massachusetts, marveled how little the character of the colony's leadership changed after the charter revocation. The same old faces reappeared. In July 1686 he wrote in frustration to the Lords of Trade and Plantations that "of over sixty officers of the Militia there are not above half a dozen who are not either Church-members [Congregationalists] or attenders at their meetings." But Randolph failed to realize that many of these people who seemed so provincial from the English perspective were actually as out of step with the villagers of Massachusetts Bay as was Randolph himself.[42]

The military and fiscal problems confronting Andros were similar to those which had plagued the Old Charter rulers. In the summer of 1688 war broke out along the New England frontier, and Indian warriors now allied with French troops destroyed several settlements in Maine. Andros raised an army of almost eight hundred men, the largest fighting force assembled in Massachusetts since King Philip's War. By this time, however, the populace thoroughly disliked the royal governor; they disliked chasing Indians in Maine even more. The soldiers pressed out of the local militia units failed to engage the enemy, much less defeat him, and in the process of marching back and forth across Maine, ran up expenditures so large that by 1690 the charge for their services remained unpaid.[43]

Andros discovered what his immediate predecessors had already learned, war and taxes drew people who might otherwise remain apathetic into a critical examination of public policy. Colonists wondered why the costs for defense were so high and why the enemy so successful. On January 8, 1689, Joshua Moodey, a Congregational minister, wrote to Increase Mather explaining, "There is a Presse for 200 more, what for, who can tell? There are no Indians to bee seen by them, nor any service to bee done (some to have strengthened the Garrisons might have done well). There are strange conjectures which I dare not write; but I very much fear a dreadfull, lengthy, wasting Indian war."[44] On March 27—just a few weeks before the country people toppled Andros—the Dominion Council anxiously debated "The raising of money for defreying the Charge of the Forces," and one councillor who later supported the governor's overthrow suggested new taxes "on Pole & Estates." The Dominion's most enduring legacy was an unresolved frontier war and a pile of unpaid bills.[45]

On April 18, 1689, Andros's rule abruptly ended, opening a floodgate for accumulated frustrations and demands. A Council of Safety composed of Old Charter magistrates and Boston merchants stepped forward, in the words of Cotton Mather, "to prevent the shedding of *Blood*." [46] These gentlemen expressed uneasiness about their position. They fretted about offending the new king, William III, or so they claimed. But the rank and file who overthrew the Dominion had little patience with foot-dragging. As one man reported, "two-thirds of the People were for reassuming their ancient Government." [47]

The majority obtained its goal only after months of haggling with the colony's old rulers. In May an assembly of delegates representing the various towns voted overwhelmingly to revive the Old Charter government, at least until such time that the king provided instructions to the contrary. The Council of Safety accepted this plan; insisting all the time that its action was only a temporary expedient. Simon Bradstreet, 86 years old and obviously feeble in mind and body, returned to the governorship. Other colonial leaders who had held office in 1686 took their places on the Court of Assistants.[48] But, despite their apparent willingness to compromise with the local communities, they refused to tackle difficult issues. Throughout the summer they procrastinated, waiting for William to recognize their political legitimacy, in other words, to provide them with constitutional authority based upon something more tangible than the voice of the people.[49]

Fear of the king's displeasure only in part explains the indecisiveness of the old corporate mediators. They sensed the impossibility of reestablishing the Old Charter government. The problems with this system had been evident to them before Andros arrived in New England. They had always regarded with apprehension the people's growing assertiveness in civil affairs. The Glorious Revolution exacerbated these fears, for rebellion poignantly demonstrated that "the Sword" lay "in every man's hands."[50] Armed men, suddenly made aware of their full political power, would not long remain silent in face of objectionable leaders and policies.

With war still raging along the eastern frontier, the Old Charter rulers were eventually compelled to make unpopular financial decisions. The army in Maine demanded large sums of money, and the only way to obtain these funds was through multiple country rates. Even if the people could have paid such high taxes, an unlikely proposition, they were less than enthusiastic about financing a war in Maine.

The French and Indians did not immediately threaten the security of most Massachusetts towns in 1689, and in any case, despite heavy expenditures for military operations under Andros, Bay troops had failed to defeat the enemy. The prospects for victory seemed little better than they had in 1688. The Bradstreet government postponed the inevitable confrontation with the villagers as long as possible. It appealed first for loans to support the soldiers, but finally the General Court issued warrants for six country rates "for paying of Soldiers and publique Charges that have arisen since the Revolution by reason of the War."[51]

Because of the continuing hostilities and rising government costs, the political revolution in Massachusetts did not stop with a restoration of the Old Charter government precisely as it had operated before 1686. While town representatives praised the former constitution, they also authorized a major expansion of the colonial franchise. In this way, rebellion ratified broad popular political participation. Before the creation of the Dominion, only adult males who were either church members in full communion or who owned a very large amount of property could vote in colony elections. The system favored the older, more substantial members of society. In fact, many of the armed young men who participated in the Glorious Revolution had been disfranchised under the Old Charter, and no sooner had they locked Andros in jail than they clamored for a voice in the provisional government established in 1689. As one pamphleteer announced after Andros's overthrow, "an *Election* or *Free Choice* in *Government* by the People . . . was one *main* thing aimed at in the Motion of the Army." The writer went on to explain ominously that if anyone attempted to stifle the popular desire "the whole Countrey will ly under unexpected dissapointments & such great dissatisfactions, that (it is to be feared) will have a very uncomfortable Issue."[52] A petition sent to the General Court at about the same time, though worded more diplomatically, noted that an expansion in the size of the electorate "will be an absolute meanes to Unite the hearts of this people Together in the bond of love which undoubtedly will conduce much to the preserving of the peace."[53]

On February 12, 1690, the General Court decided that henceforth adult males who possessed good character, who paid four shillings in a single country rate, and who owned a house or lands worth at least six pounds were eligible to become freemen.[54] This seemingly innocuous act opened a floodgate of political participation in Massachusetts Bay. Those records for March and April which have survived contain the names of at least 917 men who now enrolled as full citizens of the commonwealth for the first time.[55] Considering the probable loss of some freemen lists, the actual total must have been even higher.[56] Population figures for late seventeenth-century Massachusetts are rough estimates, but if the total of the colony's adult males in 1690 was approximately ten thousand—certainly a reasonable guess—then almost ten percent of the colony's adult males took advantage of this legislation within only sixty days.[57]

A new aggressive spirit soon surfaced in local politics. Villagers terminated selectmen who held office under the Dominion even though these people had a long history of community service. In 1689, for example, townsmen in Dedham purged eight selectmen who possessed considerable experience in running village affairs and in their place chose five younger residents who lacked administrative seasoning. The exact issues at stake in Dedham are unknown, but it would seem that the newcomers, impatient with the leadership of the older generation and caught up in the revolution, thrust an entire group of established local brokers aside.[58]

As might be expected, the villagers' assertiveness created the greatest turmoil in military elections. The post-Revolutionary ordering of the local trainbands released long suppressed generational tensions, as younger, less well-established men confronted with possibility of actual combat surged forward to select officers whom they could trust. Following Andros's overthrow, the Bradstreet government moved swiftly to establish control over the militia. The war against the French and Indians required fresh troops, and these soldiers in turn would be levied out of the individual trainbands. On June 14, 1689, the General Court ordered that commissioned officers in the various towns—captains, lieutenants, and ensigns—who had been in office on May 2, 1686, and who were not now either infirm or absent from the village to take their places at the head of their companies. If a vacancy had occurred since 1686, the "householders and soldiers" of the community were instructed to *nominate* a replacement. In order to qualify for a commission, a man had to be at least twenty-one years of age, not a servant, and acceptable to the members of the colonial legislature.[59]

But when it came time to fill vacancies, villagers throughout the Bay Colony misinterpreted the government's order. The "householders and soldiers" gathered not to *nominate* commission officers, but to *elect* them. Some towns may have made an honest mistake. In others, however, the inhabitants seem willfully to have ignored the colony rulers, and in these villages the selection of officers led to spirited contests. The elections certainly generated broad community participation. When the results of these meetings reached Boston in the summer of 1689, some anonymous clerk meticulously lined out the word "chose" and inserted "nominated" before the names of the new officers, a pretense that the villages had actually followed the procedures laid down by colony rulers. Such alterations in the records, however, could not obscure the critical battles for personal loyalty which took place in many Massachusetts towns.[60]

The military elections in Charlestown began a long nightmare in the life of Lawrence Hammond. Little in the background of this established corporate mediator prepared him for a bitter confrontation with his neighbors. Hammond was a strong-willed cooper who, among other things, possessed a sense of humor.[61] In 1689 he had almost a quarter century of public service behind him. Indeed, during the last decades of the Old Charter government, Hammond became a successful local broker, shuttling back and forth between Boston and Charlestown carrying news and explaining policies. The village freemen showed their trust by electing him to the House of Deputies several times, and in 1677 he received 589 votes for assistant. While this figure was not large enough to place him among the colony's magistrates, Hammond commanded respect outside Charlestown. In 1681 Edward Randolph lumped Hammond in with "the Popular" or Puritan party, a group which Randolph believed wanted to transform Massachusetts Bay into an independent commonwealth. Whether this charge was accurate is difficult to assess. Hammond became a full member of the Charlestown congregation, and at least once actively participated in the selection of a new minister.[62]

To be sure, Hammond picked up enemies along the way. He was a poor loser, and when his side failed to carry a major decision in the church, he refused to accept defeat gracefully. He even signed a document accusing his opponents of being "Too undeliberate, over-hasty and precipitate in their motives."[63] He also accepted a military commission from Andros.[64] Hammond had been a militia officer since 1668, and while he may privately have disagreed with Dominion policies, he saw nothing improper with remaining at the head of what he had come to regard in almost a proprietary sense as *his* trainband. If villagers resented his actions, they did not reveal their sentiments to

Hammond. On the eve of the Glorious Revolution, his diary contains no indication that his position within the local community was in jeopardy.[65]

Early on the morning of July 2, 1689, Captain Hammond learned just how many enemies he had made.[66] A letter signed by forty-two men in the Charlestown company explained that "being warned by beat of Drum," they assembled on the training field. Hammond asked why the meeting had been called, and a spokesman for the local soldiers informed him that they intended to carry out the Court's order concerning the selection of officers. The men were divided on how best to proceed. Some said that they "must chuse all their officers"; others insisted that the old leaders must be continued. When one person turned to Hammond for guidance, the Captain lost his temper, snapping "he was not made the interpreter of the Council order." When another soldier inquired whether Hammond held his commission from the Dominion or the Old Charter government, Hammond did not answer. He told the militiamen that such questions were "Impertinent." The challenge had taken him by surprise. He regarded himself as the rightful captain, but he refused to beg before the men he had so recently commanded. When several of the more forward members of the company declared "they would not be debarred of their Liberty," Hammond announced he would have no part in such illegal activities.[67]

Before he left the field, Hammond delivered a remarkable speech. His words revealed the hurt and confusion of a person suddenly rejected by a large segment of his community. Indeed, this was an epitaph for an Old Charter broker. By his own lights, he had always worked for the company's best interests. His "Fellow Souldiers," he recalled, had chosen him lieutenant in 1668, and while he had not sought the post, he accepted it out of affection for his friends and neighbors in Charlestown. According to Hammond, "My acceptance of that Charge soone (by the providence of God) devolved a greater [one] upon me." He became captain. Hammond doubted his ability "to discharge a Leader's place to a Company," but again the local militiamen persuaded him to shoulder the responsibility. And now faced with opposition, Hammond announced his willingness to step aside. "And," he continued, "as I have hitherto maintained a true Love & respect for you all, so shall it remaine & continue in my more private capacity wch shall at all times appear as occasion shall offer in any way within my power, except that of Command." The assembled soldiers should remember, "as we have for so long a time been united in Love, so it is my desire we may part in love Wishing you and your Officers may alwayes unite in Love." This was the rhetoric of a corporate mediator. Love may have been the source of community traquillity in the past, but in 1689, "a discontented, factious, Censorious, unreasonable & invidious Spirit [has] spread among us." What had happened to the "old peaceable ruleable, genuine Spirit" in his village, Hammond did not know.[68]

Militia elections generated a local crises in Northampton similar to that which had occurred in Charlestown. The inhabitants of this town in western Massachusetts not only thrust out of office a group of established corporate leaders, but also revealed in the process the inability of the colony rulers to mediate controversy on the village level. Not even the threat of Indian attack muted factionalism in Northampton. The trouble began when a segment of the trainband gathered on July 18 to select an entirely new slate of officers. These soldiers understood they were supposed to obey the captain, lieutenant, and ensign who had been in commission in 1686, and they therefore explained to the General Court in great detail why the incumbents could no longer exercise military authority in Northampton. Seventy-nine-year-old Captain Aaron Cooke not only had moved out of the village, but also had offended the company by accepting a commission from Governor Andros. Lieutenant Joseph Hawley, a local school teacher of imperious temperament, lost the militia's respect in 1686 by reneging on a promise he made to the soldiers. According to their claim, Hawley had pledged that they "should [have] Liberty to make choise of A man to be presented to the Court for Approbation to be their Lieut," but when it came time to poll the members of the trainband, he went back on his word. And Ensign Timothy Baker never formally accepted a commission at the head of the company.[69]

In 1689 the militiamen urged Hawley to hold an election so that they could drop those officers "so much disliked by them."[70] Such words hardly charmed the Lieutenant, who knew full well how unpopular he had become. When he procrastinated, calling the Court's order a "Ratle to plese fools," the local soldiers proceeded on their own.[71] Just as the men were about to cast their ballots, however, Cooke and Hawley appeared, warning the company that its actions were illegal. Their presence "discouraged 10 or 12 from Acting," but fifty individuals recorded their votes. As might be expected, Hawley received only two or three of them. According to one observer, the new officers—Captain Preserved

Clapp, Lieutenant John King, Senior, and Ensign Ebenezer Strong—were chosen "by a very full vote."[72] The Northampton trainband then sent these names to Boston for confirmation by the General Court. Cooke and Hawley did not surrender their offices without a fight. Cooke in particular took the offensive, labeling the soldiers' explanation of their behavior as irresponsible lies. He pointed out to the members of the General Court, for example, that he had only temporarily moved away from Northampton. He resided in Hadley with his new wife and her children, and as soon as her affairs were in order—she was a widow—he intended to return to his home in Northampton. In his absence, Cooke's sons had maintained his business interests, a sure sign that the father had not departed the community for good. These were facts which the Captain claimed were common knowledge in Northampton. He added also that despite what the men said about Hawley, the Lieutenant was a fine officer, a respected teacher, and even "preached on ocasion att the neighboringe towns."[73] But most important, Cooke regarded Hawley and himself as the community's rightful leaders. Long service and visible wealth, not familiarity with the common soldiers, made them the choice of "sober & considerate men."[74]

If Cooke can be believed, the newly elected officers were men of notoriously low character. It was unthinkable that the town would entrust Clapp with a position of leadership. According to Cooke, Clapp "is noe freeman and joyns to noe church but [is] a Companion with tiplers that would never submite to our holsome laws." Moreover, when Clapp had served as a sergeant, he had behaved "tumultously." King represented an even greater embarrassment to the community. He had a reputation as a heavy drinker, and on two occasions after becoming intoxicated on church wine, he almost killed himself, once in the snow and once in a fire.[75]

In late July, John Pynchon provided a more balanced account of the controversy in Northampton. Pynchon was the most prominent person in the upper Connecticut River Valley, and under the Old Charter government, he had functioned as a successful broker for the towns of western Massachusetts. Before the arrival of Andros, Pynchon would have been able to mediate a dispute such as the one that divided Northampton. Like other aging colonial leaders, however, he had seen his powers of arbitration slip away. He viewed the Northampton agitation with detachment, as if he sensed that an outsider from Springfield could no longer bring harmony to other local communities. "There is a Party at

Northampton," he explained to Governor Bradstreet, "who fal in with Serj King or rather that are stirred up by him, who does so blow up discontents against their former officers." King, a new factional broker, aimed at becoming the captain and enrolled his kinfolk in the effort to remove the present officers. Pynchon learned that "it hath so far prevailed that he is Nominated for Lieutenant having so many Relations, as I am informed about 32 in the Towne by Marriage & Blood who have helped it & are the Faction in the Busyness." During the Old Charter period this aggressive pursuit of self-interest would have been condemned, but in post-revolutionary Northampton King's unorthodox behavior found broad support.[76]

Pynchon urged the Provisional Government in Boston to straighten out the business, but it was no more successful than he had been. In August Pynchon again tried to settle the controversy. The effort failed disastrously, and in words similar to those of Lawrence Hammond, Pynchon reported that King had announced before the soldiers that Pynchon possessed no authority over the Northampton company. King and his friends added to Pynchon's humiliation by spreading a rumor that even the "Springfield men would not obey me." He closed his report with the sad admission that the Northampton rebels "bid defiance to the old commission officers, [to] such a height of Pride . . . that nothing would or could be done by . . . my orders & directions."[77]

As in Charlestown and Northampton, the Court's order regarding the militia split Woburn's inhabitants into factions and provided additional insight into the forces transforming the colony's political culture. As soon as it became known in Woburn that the commission officers of 1686 were to continue in office, a group of "householders and soldiers" penned a strongly-worded protest. They insisted upon dropping the aged John Carter from command, because in their estimation he was "altogether unfitt for the place of captaine." He was not only somewhat feeble, but also extremely hard of hearing. Carter's deafness apparently created serious problems in Woburn when it came time to press men for service in the colonial army. After a warrant for a certain number of men arrived from Boston, Carter's son read it to his father in such a loud voice "that it was herd in the streets by several upon which report the young men obsconded." The Captain further undermined his position in the community by holding a commission under the Dominion government. The fifty-one persons who petitioned the General Court about Carter in July also accused him of arbitrary acts "all which hath disaffected his souldiers and haveing this oppertunety [we] doe Ernestly desier Relefe."[78]

This petition drew a stinging response from Carter's friends. They regarded the popular challenge to the Captain's authority as nothing less then "A Mutiny" and assured the General Court that the majority of Woburn's soldiers supported the officers of 1686. The villagers, they explained, would have accepted Carter had it not been for Gershom Flagg, a would-be broker who went "from hous to hous to gitt hands on a paper of objections against Capt. Carter." Such unprecedented behavior smacked of rebellion. The counter-petition contained only four names, a fact which apparently worried the signers since they announced that they could have obtained more than sixty additional signatures "but we thought it would look mutinous."[79] The concept of majority rule clearly did not sit well with these men, but mutiny or no, they too found themselves counting heads. Carter himself seemed befuddled by the entire affair.[80] He held out for a month, but when local constables refused to carry out Carter's orders to press men for the army, the Court unceremoniously dropped him from commission. A few persons in Woburn "were troubled that their *good ould Captain* who had been in Millitary office more than 40 yeares" was so rudely thrust aside, but even they must have realized that Carter, like Hammond and Cooke, did not speak for a rising new constituency.[81]

Spreading local factionalism perturbed colony leaders. With hostilities continuing along the frontier, it seemed sensible that citizens should cooperate for the common good. In villages like Charlestown, Northampton, and Woburn, however, people who had not actively participated in the political process before 1686 now insisted upon a voice in governance, even if that demand shattered community harmony. Cotton Mather begged the colonists, "Pray, mind the Business of your own Station; Pull the *Ropes*, ply the *Oars*, and the *Sails*, as you are Commanded."[82] Mather's words fell on deaf ears. Established brokers could no longer count on their clients' reflexive deference. One might have thought that Governor Simon Bradstreet, a survivor of the Great Migration, would have become a powerful symbol shoring up traditional values in difficult times. But Bradstreet found himself unable to command the popular respect which previous Old Charter magistrates had received. One pamphleteer who understood the political shifts that were taking place poked fun at the members of the provisional government, "for they were like young conjurers, who had raised a Devil they could not govern."[83]

Just at the time when the fabric of society seemed to be unraveling, the war took a turn for the worse, and several ill-planned expeditions against the French in Canada left the people of Massachusetts Bay with the largest debt in their history. One merchant compared the colony's condition to that of Spain after 1588. Cotton Mather moaned about "the *Extream Debts* which [the] Country was now plunged into; there being *Forty Thousand* Pounds, more or less, now to be paid, and not a Penny in the Treasury to pay it withal."[84] Others agreed with Mather about the source of the colony's problem, but they estimated the debt at closer to £50,000.[85]

The government's responses to this staggering financial burden increased popular participation in the formulation of public policy, if only through vociferous criticism. Indeed, the immediate social effects of the Canadian expeditions were not dissimilar to those that followed King Philip's War, for as one Minister observed in December 1690, "the people cannot conceive what becomes of all the money taken from them."[86] The amount of colonial taxes levied after the military debacles skyrocketed. In November alone the General Court called for twenty single country rates, making a total of thirty-seven since Andros's overthrow.[87] These revenues did not begin to cover the colony's obligations. Rulers borrowed money from colonial merchants just to pay soldiers returning from Canada, and when private loans failed to solve the state's financial problems, it tried an unprecedented expedient, the issuance of paper money.[88] The government promised to redeem the notes at full value in specie when taxes came due later in the year.[89] Despite guarantees, however, the bills quickly depreciated, angering the soldiers who were forced to accept them as pay. In February 1691 one colonist reported in disgust, "The loss and waste, which we have suffered over the Canadian expedition, can hardly be repaired, whatever some men may say. We are stopping the mouths of soldiers and seamen by a new mint of paper-money. Not many will take it, and those that will scarce know what to do with it."[90]

The accumulating debt and inept military policy increasingly became matters for public debate. People openly discussed the merits of government decisions, frequently second-guessing elected colony leaders in ways they had not during the Old Charter period. In fact, the bond of trust between ruler and citizen, between broker and client had weakened to the point where men brazenly raised questions about conflict of interest within the Massachusetts government.[91] "All the *Taxes* hitherto raised have bin most advantageously Employed," one writer lectured defensively. "Our Present *Rulers*, have no personal benefit by them; They spend their time and care, and are at cost too, for all, in the *Contentment*, of the people." [92] And another author, probably Increase Mather, lashed out at the grumblers, " 'Tis true the *Taxes* are great and so is the *Cause*. The *Wars* (who ever began them) have Occasioned all this; Those in the Government have no personal Advantage by your *Taxes* . . . the Taxes are to save your *Lands* and *Lives* from the Common Enemies." [93] But troops who were stuck with the depreciated paper were less charitable toward those in political authority. Because of the inflated currency, "the poor *Soldier* is horribly injured, who have adventured their lives in the publick Service, and the *Government* made *contemptible* as not worthy to be trusted." [94]

By the end of 1690 the entire society seemed on the verge of anarchy. Various colonists expressed genuine fear about the "Rage and Fury of the People." [95] In April 1691, for example, one person wrote from Boston that since the Glorious Revolution, the state had spent £200,000 on war-related expenses, and he then added, "I much feare what is cominge on us for that theire great Cabalinge this weeke with a Resolution to make all accknowledge the govert & Power wch I am affraid will Create Trouble. I question whether wee shall live to see any more Happy Days." [96] This picture of impending chaos, no doubt, was overdrawn. Whatever optimism that may have accompanied the overthrow of Andros's government, however, had dissolved. An essayist writing about the new currency asked his contemporaries in 1691, "were not peoples Heads Idly bewhized with Conceits that we have no *Magistrates*, no *Government*, And by Consequence that we have no Security for any thing, which we call our own (a *Consequence* they will be Loth to allow, though they cannot help it, If once we are Reduced to *Hobs* his state of *Nature*, which (says he) is a *state of War*, and then the *strongest* must *sake* [*sic*] *all*)." [97] The Old Charter magistrates who staffed the provisional government could no longer rule. Like the village brokers dropped in the 1689 local civil and military elections, their ability to function effectively as leaders had ended. [98]

Even the most infamous event in New England history indirectly derives from the collapse of political authority. The impotence of the Bradstreet government, of course, does not reveal why people in Salem Village accused each other in 1692 of witchcraft, but it does help to explain why the fantasies of a few adolescent girls sparked mass hysteria. The external controls necessary to stop the executions had disintegrated.

The divisions within Salem Village, like those of Charlestown, Northampton, and Woburn, were fueled in part by general changes in the political culture of Massachusetts Bay.[99]

If the Massachusetts government had been able to defend the colonists from the French and Indians, the witch hunting episode might never have occurred, much less gotten out of hand. But following the Canadian expeditions, the Bay colony lay open to easy enemy attack. Without money and without reliable troops, colonial leaders could do little to aid exposed communities. Late in the fall of 1691 rumors circulated through the towns of Essex County, including Salem Village, that enemy soldiers were operating in the area.[100] The actual appearance of French and Indian forces combined with a knowledge of the inadequacies of the local defense system generated terror throughout the region, and it is not surprising that accusers often linked suspected witches not only to the devil, but also to the French and Indians. As Cotton Mather reported, "One who was Executed at Salem for Witchcraft had confessed That at their Cheef Witch-meetings, there had been present some French canadians, and some Indian Sagamores, to concert the methods of ruining New England."[101] The victims claimed that their tormentors in Salem Village even organized "a Company about 23 or 24 and they did Muster in Armes."[102] In a sense, the ferreting out of witches was a desperate final response to a powerful enemy whose successes only highlighted the weakness of the Massachusetts government.

In the spring of 1692 William Phips, the newly appointed royal governor of Massachusetts, landed in New England with a new charter. His arrival ended an unhappy period that the Reverend Samuel Willard described tersely as "the short *Anarchy* accompanying our late Revolution."[103] The central government acquired a legitimacy that it had obviously lacked after Andros's overthrow, and it reestablished a working relation between colonial and local authorities. The political culture of Massachusetts, however, did not return to what it had been before King Philip's War. The corporate mediators of the early Old Charter years now seemed quaint anachronisms. After 1692 frequent warfare against the French and Indians coupled with massive public expenditures necessary to support it in large part determined the character of politics, and eighteenth-century brokers found themselves caught between villagers aggressive in their pursuit of economic self-interest and royal appointees eager to defeat an enemy whatever the costs.[104]

VI

Looking Out for Number One: The Cultural Limits on Public Policy in Early Virginia

JAMESTOWN TODAY POSSESSES a desolate, unsettling quality. The ghosts of ancient failure and human suffering still haunt this place. A church tower is the only seventeenth-century structure that remains standing. A row of moldering brick foundations scattered along the river front is all that is left of the settlers' homes. Walking among these ruins, one senses that Jamestown was seldom a happy community. A colorful reconstruction of an early fort and paintings depicting the colonists at work fail to mask the horrors that confronted the first Jamestown adventurers. It was here that English migrants filled with dreams of riches in the New World died by the hundreds, perhaps by the thousands. Epidemic, mutiny, starvation, war, even cannibalism, these are terms that describe life in this early outpost.

Within this same area of Tidewater Virginia, a visitor can still see the splendid mansions of the eighteenth-century gentry. The juxtaposition of these great plantations with the desolation of Jamestown is striking. The gentry's homes give the impression of order, stability, and success. Everything is under control. Wandering about the grounds of William Byrd's Westover on a bright spring day, for example, one feels Byrd's self-confidence. There is no hint here of the grim struggle for survival that permeates the atmosphere at Jamestown. In fact, it is difficult to conceive how the society that created such impressive structures could possibly have had its origins in that earlier community. What influence could the Virginia of Captain John Smith and Sir Thomas Dale have had upon the world of William Byrd II, Robert "King" Carter, and William Fitzhugh?

Were the roughneck adventurers simply an embarrassing anomaly in Virginia history, a group of persons whose exploits left no lasting mark upon the colony's later cultural development? In this chapter about Virginia—and in all the others that appear later in the collection—I try to answer these questions. "Looking Out for Number One" explores in some detail the relation between values and institutions during the 1620s, and how, while many changes occurred in colonial Virginia, these values demonstrated remarkable persistence up to the era of the American Revolution.

I

Despite their common English background, the thousands of men and women who migrated to Barbados, Virginia, and New England during the seventeenth century created strikingly different societies in the New World. As historian Thomas J. Wertenbaker explained of Virginia, it ". . . developed a life of its own, a life not only unlike that of England, but unique and distinct."[1] Certainly, anyone analyzing the founding of these colonies must account for the appearance of diverse social forms.

This essay examines the development of a distinct culture in Virginia roughly between 1617 and 1630. Although early Virginians shared certain general ideas, attitudes and norms with other English migrants, their operative values were quite different from those that shaped social and institutional behavior in places such as Massachusetts Bay. Virginia's physical environment—its extensive network of navigable rivers, its rich soil, its ability to produce large quantities of marketable tobacco—powerfully reinforced values which the first settlers carried to America. The interplay between a particular variant of Jacobean culture and a specific New World setting determined the character of Virginia's institutions, habits of personal interaction, and patterns of group behavior that persisted long after the early adventurers had died or returned to the mother country.

To understand the relation between culture and behavior in early Virginia, one must pay close attention to the early values that the settlers transferred to the New World. Here a distinction that social anthropologists make between "dominant" and "variant" values is helpful.[2] The men and women who sailed for the Chesapeake Bay in the early seventeenth century were certainly part of a general English culture. They shared a set of views, customs, and expectations with other

Jacobeans, with New Englanders and Barbadians, with persons who remained in the mother country. Historians of colonial America have analyzed this common cultural background, and there is no need to recount their findings.

From such accounts one learns that the crucial formative values transferred to Virginia were religious and political. The colonists' constitutional heritage provided civil and legal imperatives; their religion a world view that structured their daily lives. Perry Miller insisted that Virginians were products of the English Reformation. Both Virginians and New Englanders, he argued, were ". . . recruited from the same type of Englishmen, pious, hard-working, middle-class, accepting literally and solemnly the tenets of Puritanism—original sin, predestination, and election—who could conceive of the society they were erecting in America *only* within a religious framework." Miller maintained that without knowledge of this theological system, the history of Virginia was no more than "a bare chronicle."[3] Other writers, without denying the importance of Calvinistic Protestantism, stressed the role of English legal and political precedents in shaping institutional behavior. Wesley Frank Craven explained that the Chesapeake migrants brought ". . . their identification with the traditions of the Common Law, a decentralized system of local administration, and parliamentary usages of government for the development of the colony's political institutions."[4]

Early Virginians undoubtedly subscribed to these general constitutional and religious values and whenever feasible, attempted to translate them into action. Anyone who reads the colony's history learns that the first settlers saw God's hand behind human affairs, marched to church to the beat of a drum, and formed a representative legislative body called the House of Burgesses. But this analysis does not carry one very far in understanding why Virginia society was unlike those formed by English migrants in other parts of the New World, or why, despite the presence of common dominant values, various groups of settlers created distinctive patterns of social and institutional behavior.

Such problems are reduced when we realize that the early settlers in Virginia were an unusual group of Jacobeans. They did not represent a random sample of seventeenth-century English society or a cross-section of English values. While little is known about the specific origins or backgrounds of the settlers, we do possess a fairly clear idea of the inducements that persuaded them to move to Virginia. The colony's promotional literature emphasized economic opportunity, usually quick and easy riches. In his "True Relation of the State of Virginia" written in 1616, for example, John Rolfe pitied England's hard-working farmers who barely managed to make ends meet. "What happiness might they enjoy in Virginia," Rolfe mused, "where they may have ground for nothing, more than they can manure, reap more fruits and profits with half the labour."[5] And in 1622 Peter Arundle, overlooking the colony's recent military setbacks at the hands of the Indians, assured English friends that " . . . any laborious honest man may in a shorte time become ritche in this Country."[6] It was a compelling dream, one which certain Englishmen were willing to accept as truth. Indeed, so many persons apparently risked life and possessions in the illusive search for the main chance that John Harvey, a future royal governor of Virginia, begged men of integrity on both sides of the Atlantic to control "the rumors of plenty to bee found at all time[s] in Virginia."[7]

The lure of great wealth easily obtained particularly appealed to a specific type of seventeenth-century Englishman, members of a distinct sub-culture within Jacobean society. By all accounts, early Virginians were ambitious, self-confident men who found themselves in a position to take advantage of an unusual economic opportunity. Whatever religious and political ideas they may have held in England, however much they revered common-law institutions and accepted the general tenets of Anglicanism, they flocked to the New World prepared to exploit their surroundings for quick profits. They were extraordinarily individualistic, fiercely competitive, and highly materialistic. Other Englishmen, of course, shared the adventurers' passion for material gain, but by establishing economic privatism as the colony's central value, the Virginia Company of London spawned an aberrant society, a sub-culture of excessively individualistic men who were no more representative of the world they left behind then were the rogues and vagrants who served in James's expeditionary forces.[8]

No one in London foresaw conflict between a well-ordered, cohesive community composed of independent adventurers and a society based upon the expectation of almost unlimited personal gain. English planners simply assumed that people eager for wealth would cooperate for the common good. Material ambition had to be tempered with religion, to be sure, but pious greed did not necessarily threaten the colony's stability. In a pamphlet prepared for the company in 1612, the author specifically advised the stockholders not to impede the Virginia planters "in growing religious, nor in gathering riches, two especiall bonds (whether severed or conjoined) to keepe them in obedience, the one for conscience sake, the other for feare of losing what they have gotten: without the first they are prophane, without the second desperate."[9]

II

The transfer of variant values, of course, only partially explains Virginia's cultural development. The attitudes, beliefs, and ideas that the founders brought with them to the New World interacted with specific environmental conditions. The settlers' value system would certainly have withered in a physical setting that offered no natural resources capable of giving plausibility to the adventurers' original expectations. If by chance the Virginians had landed in a cold, rocky, inhospitable country devoid of valuable marketable goods, then they would probably have given up the entire venture and like a defeated army straggled home. That is exactly what happened in 1607 to the unfortunate men who settled in Sagadohoc, Maine, a tiny outpost which failed to produce instant wealth.[10] Virginia almost went the way of Sagadohoc. The first decade of its history was filled with apathy and disappointment, and at several points, the entire enterprise seemed doomed. The privatistic values that the colonists had carried to Jamestown—their tough, greedy, competitive individualism—were dysfunctional—even counter-productive—in an environment which offered up neither spices nor gold, neither passages to China nor a subject population easily subdued and exploited. In fact, before 1617 this value system generated only political faction and petty personal violence, things that a people struggling for survival could ill afford.[11]

The successful cultivation of tobacco altered the course of Virginia's cultural development. Clearly, in an economic sense, the crop saved the colony. What is less obvious but no less true, is that the discovery of a lucrative export preserved the founders' privatistic orientation. Suddenly, after ten years of error and failure, the adventurers' transported values no longer were at odds with their physical environment. The settlers belatedly stumbled across the payoff; the forests once so foreboding, so unpromising, now could be exploited with reasonable expectation of quick return.

In 1617 Virginians sent their first cargo of tobacco to England. The selling price was generally high, and even though the quality of the American leaf left much to be desired, colonists reported, "All our riches for the present doe consiste in Tobacco." In 1619 John Pory, secretary of Virginia, explained that "one man by his owne labour hath in one yeare raised to himselfe to the value of £200 sterling; and another by the meanes of six servants hath cleared at one crop a thousand pound English." Pory admitted that these were unusual cases but nevertheless insisted that other persons could duplicate the results.[12] If the Virginians had discovered precious metals or short cuts to the Orient, their income would have been greater, but two hundred pounds sterling was quite enough to convert them to the new crop. As one planter noted, "the market-place, and the streets, and all other spare places [are] planted with Tobacco. . . ."[13]

If anyone during this period anticipated that Virginia's prosperity would generate social cohesion, they were mistaken. The tobacco boom unleashed a frenetic scramble for riches. Every man was out for himself.[14] As Sir Francis Wyatt, an able person who became governor of Virginia in 1621, explained, no colonist "can endure not to have the free use of his owen [sic]."[15] Old planters who had paid for their own transportation to the New World before 1616 and who managed somehow to survive the horrors of the first decade now rushed to make up for lost time. Newcomers schemed to strike it rich before disease or Indians struck them down.[16] And no one was too particular about the means employed to gain wealth.[17] The colony's appalling rate of mortality only exacerbated the unsettled quality of Virginia life. In this social environment, the toughest, luckiest, and most unscrupulous planters usually came out on top.

The Virginians' settlement pattern reflected their distinctive, highly individualistic system of values.[18] Once a European market for tobacco had been established, people fanned out along the James and York rivers. Whenever possible, they formed what directors of the Virginia Company called private hundreds, semi-autonomous plantations often five or more miles apart which investors developed for their own profit. By 1619 forty-four separate patents for these private plantations had been issued—Southampton, Berkeley Hundred, and Martin's Hundred were several of the more ambitious—and by the 1620s the dispersed settlement pattern characteristic of Virginia society throughout the colonial period was well entrenched.[19] In 1617 one planter who returned to Virginia after a short absence noted with surprise, "the Colonie [is] dispersed all about, planting *Tobacco.*"[20]

The distances between people may have been considerable. It was reported in 1618, for example, that the Indians murdered a group of settlers including several children "that dwelt a mile from the towne [Jamestown]."[21] One cannot convincingly attribute the dispersion of population to the cultivation of tobacco. Rather, the haphazard spread of men and women along the James River and its tributaries was a cultural phenomenon. As Governor Wyatt discovered when he arrived in the region, "most plantations were placed straglingly and scatteringly, as a choice veine of rich ground invited them, and *further from neighbours the better.*"[22] In other words, the early planters regarded space as private, and in contrast to the New Englanders, who clustered around shared public grounds, Virginians expressed their individualism through actual physical separation.

The scattering of men and women along the colony's waterways, their self-imposed isolation, reduced the kind of ongoing face-to-face contacts that one associates with the villages of seventeenth-century New England.[23] A migrant to Virginia tended to be highly competitive and to assume that other men would do unto him as he would do unto them—certainly an unpleasant prospect. Dispersion heightened suspicion. Because communication between private plantations was difficult, Virginians possessed no adequate means of distinguishing the truth about their neighbors from malicious rumor, and lacking towns and well-developed voluntary organizations, without shared rituals, ceremonies, even market days, they grew increasingly distrustful of whatever lay beyond the perimeter of their own estates.[24] Nor were these early private plantations a kind of small, self-contained community held together by a body of shared positive beliefs. The ratio of men to women was so imbalanced before 1630 that most of the young adult servants could not have formed families. They may have clung to fellow workers out of a common sense of fear or oppression, much as people in hospitals or prisons sometimes form temporary communities, but such relations in Virginia were ephemeral and frail. The poorer freemen and indentured servants had little meaningful contact with men like themselves living outside a private plantation.

The value system that Virginians transferred to the New World was also in large part responsible for the creation of a dependent labor force.

Indeed, the exploitation of other human beings for quick profits owed as much to the planters' privatistic perceptions of the world as to the booming tobacco economy, and by 1617 only two meaningful social categories existed in Virginia: a person was either free or dependent, either an exploiter or a resource. There was no middle ground in this highly competitive environment. Those men who held positions of political and commercial power viewed servants and slaves simply as necessary instruments in achieving economic success.[25] As a consequence of this materialistic outlook, life on the private plantations was often a degrading experience for thousands of immigrants who arrived in Virginia as dependent laborers. Whatever their expectations about the colony may have been before they migrated, the servants' reality consisted of poor food, meager clothing, hard work, and more often than not, early death.

Such unhappy conditions naturally depressed laborers who journeyed to America with high hopes of bettering their lives. Company propaganda led them to believe that the colony was over its time of troubles. But in fact, there was an immense disparity between the rhetoric and reality. It is almost impossible for a modern historian to calculate the psychological effect of such disappointment upon thousands of young people. The majority of them left no personal account of their impressions. Evidence from other sources, however, suggests that not a few lost the will to live. In December 1620 George Thorpe, a man respected for integrity, wrote that he was "perswaded that more doe die here of the disease of theire minde then of theire body by havinge this countrey['s] victualls over-praised unto them in England."[26] A few months later Captain Thomas Nuce informed Sir Edwin Sandys, head of the Virginia Company in London, that "the people lyve very barely for the most part. . . . I assure you the world goes hard with many even at this tyme. The labor is infynite."[27] This was not the type of report that Sandys wanted to hear, and it surely was not the kind of information that he passed on to prospective tenants. Once they arrived in Virginia under contract, of course, the servants were trapped. Someone had paid for their transportation, and the employer demanded his pound of flesh. By 1623 the situation had not noticeably improved. George Sandys, brother of Sir Edwin, observed acidly that new tenants were landing in Virginia so discouraged by the scene that greeted them "that most give themselves over, and die of Melancholye."[28]

Contemporaries admitted that Virginia planters treated servants more harshly than did English masters. In a description of the colony written in 1619, for example, John Rolfe observed that there had been many complaints—presumably to the Virginia Company—against "the Governors, Captaines, and Officers in *Virginia*: for buying and selling men and boies, or to bee set over from one to another for a yeerely rent." These innovations, he argued, were "in *England* a thing most intolerable." It was a scandal that "tenants or lawfull servants should be put from their places, or abridged their Covenants." Rolfe urged the immediate eradication of these illegal practices.[29] In the mid-1620s, Captain Smith stated that masters in Virginia should possess the same privileges over their servants as English masters did over theirs, "but to sell him or her for forty, fifty, or three-score pounds, whom the Company hath sent over for eight or ten pounds at most, without regard to how they shall be maintained . . . is odious."[30] In Virginia, however, such criticism fell upon deaf ears. Powerful planters seized upon all new sources of labor, and it was no coincidence that the first black slaves were sold in Jamestown at precisely this point in the colony's development.

But dependency has another side. In Virginia dominance went hand in hand with fear, for no matter how tractable, how despondent, the servants may have appeared, both masters and laborers recognized the potential for violence inherent in such relationships. In the early 1620s several worried planters complained that Captain John Martin, a long-standing trouble maker for the Virginia Company, " . . . hath made his owne Territory there a Receptacle, of Vagabonds and bankerupts & other disorderly persons."[31] Whether the rumors of Martin's activities were accurate is not the point. In such a society a gathering of "Vagabonds" represented a grave threat, a base from which the exploited could harrass their former masters. The anxiety resurfaced in 1624 when the Virginia Company lost its charter, and no one in the colony knew for certain who held legitimate authority. In shrill rhetoric that over the course of a century would become a regular feature of Virginia statute books, the colony's Assembly immediately ordered, " . . . no person within this Colonie upon the rumor of supposed change and alteratione [may] presume to be disobedient to the presente Government, nor servants to theire privatt officers, masters or overseers, at their uttmost perills."[32]

The distrust that permeated Virginia society poisoned political institutions. Few colonists seem to have believed that local rulers would on their own initiative work for the public good. Instead, they assumed that persons in authority used their offices for personal gain. One settler called Governor George Yeardley, a man who grew rich directing public affairs, " . . . the right worthy statesman for his own profit."[33] William Capps, described simply as an old planter, referred to the governor as an "old smoker" and claimed that this official had " . . . stood for a cypher whilst the Indians stood ripping open our guts."[34] Cynicism about the motives of the colony's leaders meant that few citizens willingly sacrificed for the good of the state. In fact, Virginia planters seem to have regarded government orders as a threat to their independence, almost as a personal affront. William Strachey, secretary of the colony, condemned what he labeled the general "want of government." He reported, " . . . every man over-valuing his owne worth, would be a Commander: every man underprizing anothers value, denied to be commanded."[35] Other colonists expressed agreement with Strachey's views. During the famous first meeting of the House of Burgesses in 1619, the representatives of the various plantations twice commented upon the weakness of Virginia's governing institutions. Toward the end of the session, they declared that whatever laws they passed in the future should go into immediate effect without special authorization from London, ". . . for otherwise this people . . . would in a shorte time growe so insolent, as they would shake off all government, and there would be no living among them."[36]

The colonists' achievements in education and religion were meager. From time to time, Virginians commented upon the importance of churches and schools in their society, but little was done to transform rhetoric into reality. Church buildings were in a perpetual state of decay; ministers were poorly supported by their parishioners. An ambitious plan for a college came to nothing, and schools for younger children seem to have been nonexistent. The large distances between plantations and the pressure to keep every able-bodied person working in the fields no doubt discouraged the development of local schools and parish churches, but the colony's dispersed settlement plan does not in itself explain the absence of these institutions.[37] A colony-wide boarding school—a Harvard of Virginia—could have been constructed in Jamestown, but the colony's planters were incapable of the sustained, cooperative effort that such a project would have required. They responded to general societal needs as individuals, not as groups. Later in the seventeenth century some successful planters sent their sons at great expense to universities in England and Scotland, but not until the end of the century did the colonists found a local college.[38]

III

An examination of Virginia's military policies between 1617 and 1630 provides the clearest link between cultural values and institutional behavior. During this important period, military affairs were far better recorded than were other social activities, and the historian can trace with a fair degree of confidence how particular military decisions reflected the colonists' value system. And second, in any society military efforts reveal a people's social priorities, their willingness to sacrifice for the common good, and their attitudes toward the allocation of community resources. Certainly, in early Virginia, maintaining a strong defense should have been a major requirement. Common sense alone seems to dictate that a group of settlers confronted with a powerful Indian confederation and foreign marauders would, in military matters at least, cooperate for their own safety.[39] But our common sense was not the rule of the seventeenth-century Virginian. The obsession with private profits was a more compelling force than was the desire to create a dependable system of self-defense. This destructive individualism disgusted John Pory, at one time the colony's secretary of state. In 1620 he reported that Governor Yeardley asked the men of Jamestown " . . . to contribute some labor to a bridge, and to certaine platformes to mounte greate ordinance upon, being both for the use and defense of the same Citty, and so of themselves; yet they repyned as much as if all their goods had bene taken from them."[40]

Virginians paid dearly for their failure to work together. On March 22, 1622, the Indians of the region launched a coordinated attack on the scattered, poorly defended white settlements, and before the colonists could react, 347 of them had been killed. The details of this disaster are well known.[41] The Massacre and the events of the months that followed provide rare insight into the workings of the Virginia culture. The shock of defeat called into question previous institutional policies—not just military ones—and some colonists even saw the setback as a mandate to reform society, to develop a new set of values.[42]

Virginia's vulnerability revealed to some men the need to transform the privatistic culture into a more tightly knit, cooperative venture. Local rulers bravely announced that "this Massacre will prove much to the speedie advancement of the Colony and much to the benifitt of all those that shall nowe come thither." [43] No longer would the planters live so far apart. Shortsighted dreams of tobacco fortunes would be laid aside, and the people would join together in the construction of genuine towns. And most important, the settlers would no longer evade their military responsibilities. As the members of the Virginia Council wrote only a month after the Massacre, "our first and princypall care should have beene for our safetie . . . yet its very necessarie for us yett at last, to laye a better and surer foundatione for the tyme to Come." [44] Indeed, the summer of 1622 was to be a turning point in the colony's development, a new beginning after several false starts. Captain Smith declared "upon this Anvill wee now beat our selves an Armour of proofe hereafter . . . [to] make us more circumspect." [45] The Virginia General Assembly proclaimed March 22 an annual holiday, a perpetual, solemn reminder to all men and women of their former errors. It was to be a public, ritual expression of contempt for the system of values that had left Virginia so defenseless. [46]

Governor Wyatt, apparently acting with the support of men like George Yeardley and George Sandys, decided that the Massacre necessitated a far-reaching restructuring of Virginia society. Wyatt was especially enthusiastic about the withdrawal from the scattered frontier farms. As he explained, the continued threat of violence had "enforced us to quitt many of our Plantacons, and to unite more neerly together in fewer places the better for to Strengthen and Defende our selve[s]." [47] In April the local rulers informed directors of the Virginia Company in London that a plan was under consideration whereby "wee may soe fortifie our selves, that neyther the Indyans may infest us (which they will continuallie endevor to doe) nor forraine enemy subvert us which wilbe the master peece of this great woorke." [48] The Virginia leaders also asked the company's permission to remove the colonists to an entirely new location.

While waiting for a response from England, Wyatt authorized an expedition to find the most promising site for the new community. On June 20 he commissioned former governor Yeardley to lead a group of colonists to the Eastern Shore. The argumentative character of this document suggests that it was not written so much for Yeardley as for company officials in London. Whatever the case may have been, the commission provides insight into the type of society that reformers wanted to establish. The preamble stated that Virginians had become "so dispersed" that they knew neither "friendly comerce and mutuall societie," nor "common safety." To guarantee that the colonists would not be "so straglingly seated" in the future, each man received only four acres of land "for his particular employment." While Wyatt did not elaborate, especially about the need for friendly commerce and mutual society, it appears that he envisioned a community composed of small freeholders. Certainly, a plan calling for four-acre plots would have precluded the development of large gangs of dependent laborers. Yeardley's commission also instructed him to set the buildings "in such forme" that even with the addition of more persons in the summer, the Eastern Shore community could be easily defended.[49]

George Sandys wrote rhapsodically about the proposed settlement. Not only would the people be "better governed"—after all who knew what the Virginians were up to on their isolated plantations—but they could also live in greater "Comfort and securitie." Within a short time after the colonists had drawn themselves "into a narrower Circuite," towns would spring up, "framed houses erected, Orchards planted, and grounds impailed for the keeping of Cattle, staple Comodities the better advanced, strenth, beautie, pleasure, riches and reputation added forthwith to the Collonie."[50] That people could resist the chance to make such a great leap forward seemded to Sandys positively perverse.

But they did. The Company discouraged relocation. And despite the death and destruction and the bold declarations about a new start, colonists proceeded to repeat the very activities that contemporary commentators agreed had originally left them so vulnerable to attack. Even though the Indians remained a grave threat to security throughout the 1620s the settlers continued to grumble about the burden of military service. Each person assessed the tragedy only in personal terms—how, in other words, the Indian Massacre had affected his ability to turn a profit. By the end of the summer of 1622, there were unmistakable signs that many people no longer regarded the defeat of the Indians as a community responsibility. Few men talked of the common good; fewer still seemed prepared to sacrifice their lives or immediate earning power in order to preserve the colony from a second disaster.

The military danger, although clearly perceived, scarcely eroded the colonists' privatism, their sense that if they were just left alone they might prosper, even strike it rich. How their neighbors fared was of little concern. Following the Indian attack, Wyatt ordered a general retreat, but "Master Gookins at Nuports newes, having thirtie five of all sorts with him refused that order, and made good his part against the Savages." Samuel Jordan, a representative at the first legislative assembly in Jamestown, gathered a group of men around him and fortified his residence, which was known as "Beggars Bush." Captain Crashaw also ignored Wyatt's command. The Captain "with five others fortified himselfe in despight of all the Savages, with the helpe of other Savages, and made offer to the Colonie, if they would send him a shallop with Armes, men and provision *for Trade*, that [at] the next Harvest he would provide them Corne sufficient, which then . . . was little to bee had in the Countrie." And "Mistris" Proctor about whom little is known "would have adventured the like, and did it for three weekes till the Officers (as some report) would no longer permit her."[51]

Other colonists returned to isolated frontier plantations as soon as possible. The Massacre did not deter the demand for fresh land. As the Virginia Council explained, "many forward Planters already want roome to seate on."[52] Sandys was amazed by what was happening. He attributed the spread of population to the colonists' greed. On the first anniversary of the Massacre, he grumbled that Virginians staked out ever larger possessions, "larger then 100 tymes their Nomber were able to Cultivate."[53] But Sandys was unable to reverse this seemingly self-destructive trend. Virginians were wedded to tobacco, and tobacco inevitably brought dispersion. "I protest for my owne part," he told an English correspondent, "if I knew how to defraie the expences of the yeare, I would not set one plant of Tobacco whilst I lived in this Countrie: so much [do] I loath it and onlie desire that I could subsist without it."[54] Throughout the colonial period, Virginians echoed Sandys's lament, and then, like him, set out thousands of tobacco plants.

The dispersion of fighting men, of course, invited another defeat. In a poignant letter to his parents in England, young servant Richard Frethorne captured the fear that permeated life on the private plantations. In the spring of 1623 rumors of Indian raids heightened Frethorne's dread. He and his fellow workers heard that the enemy had recently killed twenty-six English settlers and obtained a fresh stock of firearms, "so that they may now steale upon us and wee Cannot know them from English, till it is too late . . . and then there is no mercie." There was no way to verify such frightening intelligence. Each day Frethorne expected to be his last: "Our Leiftenant is dead, and his father, and his brother, and there was some 5 or 6 of the last yeares 20 of which there is but 3 left . . . [and] we are but 32 to fight against 2000 if they should come, and the nighest helpe that Wee have is ten miles of us, and when the rogues overcame this place [Martin's Hundred] last, they slew 80 Persons[,] how then shall wee doe for wee lye even in their teeth."[55] What is striking about Frethorne's letter is that it was composed just twelve months after the Massacre had supposedly revealed to all survivors the consequences of lying in the Indians' teeth.

By the mid-1620s the colonists were again scattered along the river banks, each planter pursuing his own private interests as if the Massacre had never occurred. Only persons unfamiliar with the culture of Virginia still bothered to advocate reform of settlement patterns. In 1624, after studying a map of the region, George Wyatt informed his son the governor that "your Plantation is d[r]awen out into longe, weake and skattered inhabitation with smale and unapt defences."[56] The senior Wyatt lived in Kent, England, and from the perspective of three thousand miles, his point made good sense. John Harvey decided after only a short visit "that by the dispersion of the Plantations the Savage hath the advantage in this warre and that theire suddaine assaultes that doe us more harme than wee doe them."[57] From a military point of view, these too were sound observations. What Harvey and the elder Wyatt did not understand was that the parameters of Virginia's defense had already been determined. Military policy—for better or worse—had to take into account the cultural fact of dispersion. As Governor Wyatt reported in 1626, the planters' "too much affection to their privat dividents" made it impossible "to prevent the suddaine incursions of the Salvages, nor secure any range for cattle."[58]

The Virginia Council protested to colonial administrators in England, "It is noe smale difficultie and griefe unto us to mantaine a warr by unwillinge people, who . . . Cyre out of the loss of Tyme against their Commanders, *in a warr where nothinge is to be gained.*"[59] By contrast, the village militia in Massachusetts Bay provided an effective fighting force precisely because the soldiers trusted those persons who remained at home. In theory, at least, most New Englanders defined their lives in terms of the total community, not in terms of private advancement, and the troops had no reason to believe that their friends and neighbors would try to profit from their sacrifice.[60] But in Virginia, long before the massive enslavement of black Africans, human relationships were regarded as a matter of pounds and pence, and each day one man chased the Indians through the wilderness or helped build a fortification, another man grew richer growing tobacco. When William Capps in 1623 attempted to organize a raiding party of forty men to go against the Indians, he was greeted with excuses and procrastination. Almost in disbelief, he informed an English correspondent of the planters' train of thought: "take away one of my men, there's 2000 Plantes gone, thats 500 waight of Tobacco, yea and what shall this man doe, runne after the Indians? . . . I have perhaps 10, perhaps 15, perhaps 20 men and am able to secure my owne Plantacion; how will they doe that are fewer? let them first be Crusht alitle, and then perhaps they will themselves make up the Nomber for theire own safetie." [61] Perhaps Frethorne's anxiety grew out of the knowledge that no one beyond Martin's Hundred really cared what the Indians might do to him and his comrades.

Such foot-dragging did nothing to promote colonial security. Regardless of the planters' behavior, however, Virginia's leaders felt compelled to deal with the Indians. After all, as appointed officials, they did not want to appear incompetent before the king and his councillors. But colonial rulers soon discovered that in the absence of public-spirited citizen-soldiers, their range of military responses was effectively reduced to three. The governor and his council could make the business of war so lucrative that Virginians would willingly leave the tobacco fields to fight, entrust private contractors with the responsibility of defending the entire population, or persuade the king to send English troops at his own expense to protect the colonists from their Indian enemies. Unfortunately, each alternative presented specific drawbacks that rendered it virtually useless as military policy.

The first option was to make the conditions of service so profitable that the planters or, in their place, the planters' servants would join in subduing the common enemy. In times of military crisis, such as the one following the Great Massacre, both Company and Crown officials tried their best to persuade the settlers that warfare was not all hardship and sacrifice—indeed, that for some men, presumably not themselves, Indian-fighting could be an economic opportunity. For the majority, however, such arguments rang hollow. The colonists had learned that local Indians made poor slaves, and in a spacious colony like Virginia, the offer of free land was an inadequate incentive for risking one's life. The promise of plunder drew few men away from the tobacco fields, and with typical candor, Captain John Smith announced in 1624, "I would not give twenty pound for all the pillage . . . to be got amongst the Salvages in twenty yeeres."[62]

A second possible solution for Virginia's military needs was to hire someone to defend the colonists. The merits of this approach seemed obvious. The state could simply transfer public funds to groups of enterprising individuals who in turn might construct forts along the rivers, build palisades to ward off Indian attacks, and even in some cases fight pitched battles along the frontier. Unlike the New Englanders, who generally regarded matters of defense as a community responsibility, much like providing churches and schools, Virginians accepted the notion that private contractors could serve as an adequate substitute for direct popular participation in military affairs.

In this belief the Virginians were mistaken. A stream of opportunists came forward with schemes that would compensate for the colony's unreliable militia. Without exception these plans not only drained the public treasury but also failed to produce lasting results. Indeed, Virginia's social values spawned a class of military adventurers—perhaps military profiteers would be a more accurate description—who did their best to transform warfare into a lucrative private business.

Some of the private military schemes of the 1620s were bizarre, others humorous, almost all misallocations of public revenues.[63] In the summer of 1622 a sea captain named Samuel Each, whose military qualifications remain obscure, offered to construct a fort of oyster shells to guard the mouth of the James River. Each's project seemed a convenient way to secure the colony's shipping from possible foreign harassment. For his work, the captain was promised a handsome reward, but as was so often to be the case in the history of seventeenth-century Virginia, the contractor disappointed the settlers' expectations. The proposed site for the fortification turned out to be under water at high tide and " . . . at lowe water with everie wynd washt over by the surges."[64] One colonist sardonically described Each's pile of sea shells as "a Castle in the aire" and suggested that the captain had wisely died on the job *"to save his Credit."*[65]

During the 1620s other adventurers followed, but their performance was no more impressive than Each's. These men sometimes couched their proposals in rhetoric about the common good. There was no question, however, about what considerations motivated the contractors. Certainly, Captain John Smith perceived Virginia's military problems as a personal opportunity, if not to enrich himself, then at least to obtain additional glory. Since his departure from Jamestown, he had dreamed of returning to Virginia, and as soon as word of the Massacre reached London, Smith came forward with a bold proposal. He argued before the Virginia Company that the settlers wasted their time in "watching and warding," for as reports from the New World made abundantly clear, they were "altogether unable to suppresse the Salvages." According to Smith, moreover, the colonists could never be expected to do better. Their values were all wrong. "Every man," the old veteran explained, "now being for himselfe will be unwilling to be drawne from their [sic] particular labours, to be made as pack-horses for all the rest, without any certainty of some better reward and preferment then I can understand any there can or will yet give them."

Smith offered to transport one hundred soldiers and thirty sailors to Virginia, to provide them with necessary supplies, and to drive the Indians from the area. The troops would form what Smith termed a "running Army," a highly mobile body of troops designed to terrorize enemy villages. Upon the return of peace, the mercenaries would settle "in some such convenient place," and become a permanent military garrison, "ready upon any occasion against the Salvages, or any other for the defence of the Countrey." Smith calculated that the king's customs supplemented by contributions from grateful planters would pay for the entire project. For himself, Smith requested only "the proper labour of the Salvages"—whatever that may have been. Company leaders residing in London listened politely to Smith's proposal, but at this point their finances were in desperate shape. Some directors concluded that a "running Army" sent from England would be too expensive; others pointed out—as well they might—that "the Planters should do that of themselves." [66]

Smith was not alone. Enterprising colonists also saw the public defense as a potential business opportunity. In 1628, for example, two of Virginia's more successful planters, Samuel Mathews and William Claiborne, presented the king of England with what they called "A Proposition Concerning the Winning of the Forest." They humbly informed Charles I that their plan grew "not out of any private respects, or intent to gaine to our selves, but because in our owne mindes wee perceive [?] our selves bound to expend both our lives and fortunes in so good a service for this Plantation." Skepticism about the extent of their anticipated personal sacrifice is justified, for in the next paragraph, the two Virginians demanded 1200 pounds "in readie monye" and 100 pounds sterling every year thereafter.[67] Governor Francis Wyatt gave the project grudging support. He explained that because of the colonists' unwillingness to alter their pattern of settlement in the interest of defense, Mathews and Clairborne should be encouraged to construct a fortified wall running six miles between the Charles and James rivers. The two men promised to build a palisade and staff it with their own armed servants.[68] There is no record of what happened to this particular plan, but if it had been accepted, the servants most likely would have spent their days planting tobacco for two men already quite wealthy.

The reliance on military adventurers held dangers of which the Virginians of the 1620s were only dimly aware. As long as the price of tobacco remained relatively high, the colonists ignored much of the waste and favoritism associated with lucrative military contracts. But high taxes caused grumbling, even serious social unrest. In the early 1620s the members of the Virginia Council reported that when it came time to reimburse Captain Each, there was "a generall unwillingnes (not to say an opposition) in all almost but ourselves."[69] As tobacco profits dropped over the course of the seventeenth century, small planters and landless freemen showed an increasing hostility to private military contractors, and a major precipitant of Bacon's Rebellion was Governor William Berkeley's expensive frontier forts which appeared to do little good except for a few of the Governor's friends engaged in the Indian trade.[70]

A second difficulty with the adventurers was only dimly perceived during the 1620s. The colony needed every able-bodied defender that could be found, and no one seems to have worried much about arming indentured servants and poor freemen. But in later years, Virginians would have cause to reconsider the wisdom of creating mercenary bodies composed largely of impoverished recruits. The leading planters discovered, in fact, that one could not systematically exploit other human beings for private profit and then expect those same people to risk their lives fighting to preserve the society that tolerated such oppressive conditions. As privatism became the way of life, the colony's leading planters were less and less certain whether internal or external enemies posed a greater threat to Virginia's security.[71]

A third possible solution to the settlement's early military needs was direct English assistance. During the 1620s Virginia's leaders frequently petitioned the mother country for arms, men, and supplies. In 1626—four years after the Massacre—the royal governor informed the

Privy Council that the security of Virginia required "no less n[u]mbers then five hundred soldiers to be yearly sent over for certen yeeres, with a full yeers provisione of victualls, appareil, armes, munitions, toole, & all necessaryes." On other occasions officials in Virginia admitted that as few as 50 or 100 troops would do, but however many men England provided, the colonists expected the king to pay the bill. Free protection would remove the necessity for high taxes.[72] Understandably, the English administrators never found the settlers' argument persuasive, and royal policy makers may well have wondered what several thousand colonists were doing to defend themselves.

Before the 1670s not a single English soldier was dispatched to Virginia. Nevertheless, despite repeated failures in gaining English assistance, the dream of acquiring a cheap, dependable military force remained strong. Had the colony's own citizens been more involved in Virginia's defense, more willing to live closer together, there would have been no reason to plead for outside support. But the spirit of excessive individualism ironically bred a habit of dependence upon the mother country, and as soon as internal problems threatened the peace, someone was sure to call for English regulars.[73]

Virginia's military preparedness was no more impressive in 1630 than it had been a decade earlier. The colony's rulers still complained that the planters " . . . utterly neglected eyther to stand uppon their guard or to keepe their Armes fitt." The Council admitted helplessly that "neyther proclamacions nor other strict orders have remedied the same."[74] The settlers were incorrigible. Forts remained unbuilt; the great palisade kept neither the colonists in nor the Indians out. And in 1644 the local tribes launched a second, even more deadly attack, revealing once again the fundamental weakness of Virginia's military system.[75]

IV

Virginia's extreme individualism was not an ephemeral phenomenon, something associated only with the colony's founding or a peculiar "boom town" atmosphere. Long after the 1620s, values originally brought to the New World by adventurers and opportunists influenced patterns of social and institutional behavior, and instead of providing Virginia with new direction or a new sense of mission, newcomers were assimilated into an established cultural system. Customs became statute law; habitual acts tradition.[76]

The long-term effects of these values upon society are examined in other sections of this volume. It should be noted here, however, that seventeenth-century Virginians never succeeded in forming a coherent society. Despite their apparent homogeneity, they lacked cohesive group identity; they generated no positive symbols, no historical myths strong enough to overcome individual differences. As one might expect, such a social system proved extremely fragile, and throughout the seventeenth century Virginians experienced social unrest, even open rebellion.[77]

Nor should the grand life style of the great eighteenth-century planters, the Byrds, the Carters, the Wormeleys, mislead one into thinking that their value system differed significantly from that of Virginia's earliest settlers. These "first families" of the early eighteenth century bore the same relationship to Captain John Smith and his generation as Cotton Mather and his contemporaries did to the founders of Massachusetts Bay. The apparent political tranquility of late colonial Virginia grew not out of a sense of community or new value-orientations, but of more effective forms of human exploitation. The mass of tobacco field laborers were now black slaves, men and women who by legal definition could never become fully part of the privatistic culture.[78] In Byrd's Virginia voluntaristic associations remained weak; education lagged, churches stagnated, and towns never developed. The isolation of plantation life continued, and the extended visits and the elaborate balls of the period may well have served to obscure the competition that underlay planter relationships. As one anthropologist reminds us, "in a society in which everyone outside the nuclear family is immediately suspect, in which one is at every moment believed to be vulnerable to the underhanded attacks of others, reliability and trust can never be taken for granted."[79] In the course of a century of cultural development, Virginians transformed an extreme form of individualism, a value system suited to soldiers and adventurers, into a set of regional virtues, a love of independence. an insistence upon personal liberty, a cult of manhood, and an uncompromising loyalty to family.[80]

VII

A Changing Labor Force
and Race Relations
in Virginia,
1660–1710

ONE SCHOLAR WHO reviewed the most recent literature on Early American society included me among the "Left Pastoralists." I am not entirely certain what this label means, but if it fits anything I have written, then surely it must be "A Changing Labor Force and Race Relations." Migrants by tens of thousands arrived in mid-century Virginia searching for what Governor William Berkeley aptly termed a chance "of bettering their condition in a Growing Country." Modern economic historians may tell us that these people had a fair opportunity to achieve upward mobility in the New World—at least, before 1670—but contemporary indentured servants, black slaves, and impoverished freemen seemed quite unaware of the favorable circumstances in which they found themselves. They claimed they were exploited at every turn, and in their anger and frustration, poor Virginians—black as well as white—joined in violent protest.

This chapter explores complex economic and social conditions that shaped race relations in the second half of the seventeenth century. For a brief period, some blacks and whites placed material interests before racial considerations and cooperated in challenging the authority of the great planters. During the 1680s, largely because of a major change in the colony's demographic structure, the "giddy multitude" dissolved. Virginia split along racial lines, and an opportunity to form a different kind of society was temporarily lost.

I

Seventeenth-century Virginians were an unruly lot. While New Englanders lived in relative peace with one another, Virginians rioted and rebelled; even in periods of apparent calm, they were haunted by the specter of social unrest.[1] These men witnessed a series of disorders between 1660 and 1683, most of which were local in character, some were only threats of violence, but a few involved several counties and one escalated into a colony-wide civil war.

Wealthy planters and political officeholders at the time offered a simple explanation for these events. In each case opportunists had played upon the hopes and fears of the "giddy multitude," an amalgam of indentured servants and slaves, of poor whites and blacks, of landless freemen and debtors.[2] Nathaniel Bacon was the most successful and therefore the most notorious of these agitators, but there were others. A gang of desperate "Oliverian Soldiers" supposedly organized the servant uprising of 1663, and high governing officials believed Robert Beverley, Sr., clerk of the House of Burgesses, had sparked the tobacco cutting riots of 1683. No one will ever know whether the mass of discontented workers fully supported, or even understood, the demands of a Bacon or Beverley. The "giddy multitude" may have taken advantage of divisions within the ruling class to express its anger over economic and social conditions beyond its control. Whatever its goals, control of this group preoccupied the Virginia gentry for nearly a quarter century.

During the 1680s Virginia's time of troubles drew to a close, and by the beginning of the eighteenth century the colony had achieved remarkable social stability. The Glorious Revolution in America which disrupted New York and Massachusetts in 1689 passed almost unnoticed in Virginia. To be sure, the tobacco planters were apprehensive about a band of black Maroons that harassed the settlers of the northern counties, but there was little talk of a general uprising of poor whites, indentured servants, and Negro slaves. The "giddy multitude" which a few years earlier had caused Governor William Berkeley to despair of ever controlling "a People wher six parts of seaven at least are Poore Endebted Discontented and Armed" had ceased to threaten the colony's internal peace.[3]

Many elements contributed to the transformation of Virginia society during the last half of the seventeenth century, but none seems more curious than the disappearance of the "giddy multitude."[4] This group of malcontents requires closer investigation, but unfortunately, the judicial records and tax lists from this period are incomplete, making it difficult to determine the precise identity of these people. The sources are rich enough, however, to provide substantial information about the general character of the "giddy multitude." By examining this material one begins to understand why the great planters regarded the lower classes as such a serious threat to Virginia's internal security. This analysis should also suggest how the changing composition of the colony's labor force between 1660 and 1710 affected Virginia's progress from chronic disorder to stability and more, how it fundamentally altered the relationship between blacks and whites.[5]

II

A pamphleteer writing about Virginia at mid-century observed the colony's earliest years had been marked by failure and disappointment. But those unhappy days, he argued, were gone forever, and Virginians could anticipate a new era of prosperity.[6] Evidence seemed to support his claims. The colonists had recently reduced the once powerful Powhatan Confederacy to impotence, pushing local Indians to the frontiers of white settlement. Planters rushed to develop the fertile tobacco-producing lands along the rivers north of the James, first the York and then the Rappahannock and Potomac. What Virginia needed—what it had always needed—was a large inexpensive labor force, workers who could perform the tedious tasks necessary to bring tobacco to market.[7]

In the middle of the seventeenth century, the solution to this problem was the importation of white indentured servants. Some historians have claimed that Virginia planters preferred white laborers to Negro slaves, but the argument is not persuasive. Before the mid-1680s, the mainland colonies did not possess a reliable, inexpensive source of blacks.[8] White Englishmen were available, however, in large numbers. Beginning in the 1650s, indentured servants flooded into Virginia at a faster rate than ever before, several thousand arriving annually.[9] Many came voluntarily. They were people who, in Governor Berkeley's words, arrived in America with a "hope of bettering their condition in a Growing Country."[10] Most signed their indentures while still in the mother country, promising to work for a stated number of years in exchange for the costs of transportation, food, clothes, and shelter in

Virginia. Almost nothing is known about the class of people who found this offer attractive, but many were probably middling sorts.[11]

Other servants found themselves in Virginia even though they had little or no desire to be there. Unscrupulous merchants called "spirits" took advantage of the labor boom, dumping over the years many English laborers onto the colonial market.[12] The "spirits" operated out of England's major port cities, preying upon the poor, young, and unsuspecting. Some victims were enticed to the New World with stories of quick riches; others were coerced.[13] One man testified before Parliament in 1660 that he had been sent "against his will to Virginia" by his sister's "cruell contrivance."[14] Once a vessel left England, the "spirited" servants reportedly received just enough food to stay alive. It was even rumored in the mother country that if a storm threatened the ship, the sailors were likely to throw an old person overboard as a suspected witch. That seventeenth-century Englishmen found such stories credible indicates that the servants' voyage to America could often be a terrible ordeal.[15] Since the "spirits" seldom kept records of their dealings, their share of the servant commerce is difficult to estimate. Historians minimize the extent of this illicit trade, but one author describing the colony in 1649 claimed that the "spirits" were the planters' chief source of indentured servants.[16]

Great Virginia planters expressed disappointment with the quality of their servants regardless of the means by which they had been recruited. The owners of large tobacco plantations wanted hard-working, honest, and obedient laborers, but the merchants seemed to be delivering "the very scum and off-scouring" of England.[17] The planters, no doubt, were guilty of hyperbole, combining poor and ignorant persons with a few known criminals into a single category of undesirables. Throughout Berkeley's administration, leaders complained about the "importacon of Newgateers" and "Jaylebirds" whom they regarded as a serious threat to the colony's security.[18] The gentry came to see the servants as a dangerous and untrustworthy group requiring constant surveillance. How much these attitudes affected relations between individual masters and servants is impossible to determine, but the planters' representation of the indentured workers as a bunch of "desperate villans" may have been a self-fulfilling description.[19]

Many servants were as disappointed with their masters as their masters were with them. As early as 1649, rumors circulated in England that "all those servants who are sent to Virginia are sold as slaves."[20]

Tales of harsh treatment were probably the source of such stories. One man who returned to the mother country reported that he had "served as a slave" in Virginia for nine years and had "endured greate hardshipp."[21] But the servants' unhappiness had deeper roots than hard labor and poor food. Many were not psychologically prepared for life in Virginia, and the frustrations they experienced led in time to bitterness and depression.[22] For a majority of servants the colony had represented a new start, an opportunity to achieve wealth and status denied them in England. Propagandists fed these hopes, depicting Virginia as a land of milk and honey. Indeed, one writer observed that servants about to emigrate spoke of the colony as "a place where food shall drop into their mouthes." Many expected free land at the end of their service.[23] The reality never matched the dreams. Virginia at mid-century burst inflated expectations and shocked all but the well-informed. William Bullock, a pamphleteer writing in 1649, understood this problem and warned planters about purchasing servants who "not finding what was promised, their courage abates, & their minds being dejected, their work is according."[24]

The servants' life did not necessarily improve when they reached the end of their contracts.[25] What the new freeman desired most was land, but no one in Virginia seemed willing to furnish it. Successful planters were not eager to establish commercial rivals. Indeed, contemporaries condemned the covetousness of those members of the Virginian gentry who engrossed "great Tracts of land" and deprived others of the means of achieving economic independence. In his account of Bacon's Rebellion, William Sherwood denounced the colony's "Land lopers" who claimed thousands of acres yet "never cultivated any part of itt . . . thereby preventing others seateing, soe that too many rather then to be Tennants, seate upon remote barren Land."[26] Since before 1680 remote lands meant constant danger from the Indians, many ex-servants chose to work for wages or rent land in secure areas rather than settle on the frontier. It has been estimated that no more than 6 percent of this group ever became independent planters. Landless laborers more often became overseers on the plantations, supervising servants and slaves whose condition differed little from their own.[27]

Freemen found themselves tied to an economic system over which they had little control. Fluctuations in the price of tobacco could reduce wage earners and small planters to abject poverty. It was not a question of work habits. According to an account in 1667, a man, on the average, could produce 1200 pounds of tobacco each year, which after taxes left him with approximately 50 shillings. It left so little, in fact, that the colony's secretary marvelled, "I can attribute it to nothing but the great mercy of God . . . that keeps them [the small planters] from mutiny and confusion."[28] In 1672 Governor Berkeley explained to the English Privy Council that single freemen could hardly maintain themselves by their own labor.[29] They fell into debt, unable to purchase necessary imported goods—especially clothing. Whatever hopes they once entertained of becoming prosperous planters gave way to anger. Their numbers swelled, and their disappointment must have discouraged those persons who were still indentured. Certainly, no one seemed surprised when the king's commissioners, investigating in 1677 the causes of Bacon's Rebellion, discovered a major part of the rebel army had been "Free men that had but lately crept out of the condition of Servants."[30]

Another component of the "giddy multitude" was Virginia's Negroes. Historians know relatively little about this group. Governor Berkeley thought there were some two thousand blacks in the colony in 1671, but recent scholarship regards that estimate as high. By the early 1680s, the Negro population had probably risen to three or four thousand.[31] A majority of the blacks in this period appear to have come to Virginia from the West Indies. Around the turn of the century, for example, it was reported on the authority of one planter that before 1680 "what negroes were brought to Virginia were imported generally from Barbados."[32] There is no way of ascertaining how long the blacks had lived on Barbados before transferring to the mainland, but it is doubtful Virginia planters would have invested what little capital they possessed in expensive "unseasoned" laborers who could easily die after a single summer in the tobacco fields. If the blacks had stayed a year or two on Barbados, they probably learned to speak some English. Morgan Godwyn, a minister who had visited the island colony in the 1670s, noted that many Negroes there not only spoke English, but did so "no worse than the natural born subjects of that Kingdom."[33] Their facility with the English language could have played an important part in Virginia's unrest, for it would have enabled blacks to communicate with indentured servants and poor whites.[34]

The status of black men in mid-seventeenth-century Virginia remains obscure; a few were free, some were indentured servants and most were probably slaves. After 1660 the Virginia legislature began to deprive black people of basic civil rights. Although the process of total debasement was not completed until the 1700s, it has generally been assumed that Negroes were a separate and subordinate group within Virginia as early as Governor Berkeley's second administration (1662–77).[35] The problem with this interpretation is that it relies too heavily upon statute law as opposed to social practice, and dismisses the fact that some whites and blacks cooperated—even conspired together—until the late 1670s.[36]

No one could deny that many whites saw Negroes as property to be exploited, and these men may have been responsible for shaping Virginia legislation. On the lowest levels of colonial society, however, race prejudice may have developed more slowly than it did among the successful planters. Black and white field hands could hardly have overlooked the things they had in common. For the Negroes the original trip from Africa to the West Indies had been a terrible ordeal. Few whites had experienced a psychological shock of this magnitude, but some of them had been forceably abducted and confined in foul quarters until a ship was prepared to sail, and were then transported to the New World under conditions vaguely similar to those endured by Africans.[37] Although little is known about the relative treatment of whites and blacks in Virginia before Bacon's Rebellion, it is doubtful that English servants fared better than Negroes. Evidence from Barbados at this time reveals that planters there regarded white servants as a short-term investment to be exploited ruthlessly and thus, "for the time the servants have the worser lives [than the Negroes], for they are put to very hard labour, ill lodging, and their dyet very sleight."[38] If such conditions prevailed on the mainland, it would help explain why some poor and indentured whites voluntarily joined with black men to challenge the planters' authority. One should understand, of course, that a willingness to cooperate under certain circumstances does not mean white laborers regarded Negroes as their equals. Indeed, such actions only indicate that economic grievances could sometimes outweigh race prejudice.

Between 1660 and 1685, members of the colony's labor force expressed their discontent in a variety of ways, some by isolated, spontaneous acts of violence, others by larger conspiratorial ventures. If an individual became desperate enough, he or she might strike a master.[39] Disaffected servants and slaves also ran away. The problem of fleeing bondsmen became quite serious in Berkeley's Virginia, and numerous colonial statutes tried to curb the practice. People often ran away in groups, fearing perhaps the Indians or the wilderness itself. Servants and slaves, eager for freedom and lured by rumors of a better life somewhere else, slipped away into the forests. Blacks and whites sometimes fled together, conscious that without cooperation their bid for freedom and escape might fail and bring instead immediate physical punishment and probably additional years of drudgery.[40] Whatever the terrors of flight, there were always persons desperate enough to take the chance. Some even plotted escape on shipboard before seeing America.[41] Planters assumed that the desire for freedom was contagious and that unless runaways were quickly suppressed, other men—black and white—would soon imitate them. When a group of fugitive slaves frustrated all attempts to retake them in 1672, the planters' greatest concern was that "other negroes, Indians or servants . . . [might] fly forth and joyne with them."[42]

Insurrection offered another means by which discontented workers expressed unhappiness with conditions in Virginia. While such organized disturbances were relatively infrequent, an occasional uprising reinforced the planters' fears and remained a source of uneasiness years after the violence had been quelled. During the early 1660s, servants upset the peace in several counties. The first disorder occurred in York and appears to have been sparked by complaints among indentured workers of "hard usage" and inadequate diet. Several conspirators, weary of "corne & water," demanded meat at least two or three times a week. The leader, an indentured servant named Isaac Friend, suggested that his followers petition the king for redress. This idea was dropped when someone pointed out that even if Charles II would listen, the group could never get a letter out of Virginia. Friend then decided that forty servants should band together and "get Armes & he would be the first & have them cry as they went along, 'who would be for Liberty, and free from bondage,' & that there would be enough come to them & they would goe through the Countrey and kill those that made any opposition, & that they would either be free or die for it." Someone apparently revealed the plans before Friend and the others began their freedom march through Virginia. When the commissioners of York questioned the leader about his actions, he admitted making seditious speeches, but protested that he never intended to put the scheme into operation. Despite Friend's assurance, York officials refused to regard the episode as a servant's prank. They ordered Friend's master to keep close watch over him and warned the heads of all families in the county to take note of "like dangerous discourses."[43]

Two years later officials in Gloucester County, a fast growing region north of York, discovered another conspiracy. The causes of this disturbance are difficult to reconstruct since most of the Gloucester records have been lost and the surviving testimony is inconsistent. In his history of Virginia published in 1705, Robert Beverley, Jr. claimed that veterans of Cromwell's army who had been transported to the colony as indentured servants stirred up "the poor People . . . [and] form'd a villanous Plot to destroy their Masters, and afterwards to set up for themselves." Presumably Beverley drew his information from old planters and local tradition, but the available contemporary documents do not mention "Oliverian Soldiers."[44] A Gloucester court in 1663 accused nine "Laborers" of conspiring to arm thirty persons to overthrow the government of Virginia. While extant depositions reveal nothing about the political ideas of this group, they do suggest that some participants regarded bondage as their primary grievance. For example, one member reported that the conspirators had secretly pledged to seize weapons, march on the colonial capital and "demand our freedome." If the royal governor denied this request, the rebels planned to leave Virginia.[45]

The reaction to the attempted servant uprising of 1663 appears excessive unless one considers it in the context of the strained relationship between the major tobacco planters and colonial laborers. After the organizers of the plot had been captured and several executed, the servant who had warned the planters received his freedom and £200. The day on which the conspirators were arrested became an annual holiday.[46] Virginia officials notified Charles II of the details of the insurrection in such exaggerated terms that the king immediately ordered the colonists to construct a fortress to protect the governor and his loyal officials.[47] As late as 1670, the memory of the servant plot could still unnerve the gentry of Gloucester, Middlesex, and York. Indeed, when it appeared that the mother country had allowed too many criminals and undesirables to emigrate to Virginia, the leading planters of these counties protested and reminded royal officials of "the horror yet remaining amongst us of the barbarous designe of those villaines in September 1663 who attempted at once the subversion of our Religion, Lawes, libertyes, rights and priviledges."[48]

During the 12 years preceding Bacon's Rebellion, fear of the labor force increasingly affected the character of Virginian society. Although no organized violence against the planters or the government occurred in this period, the laborers—black and white—constituted a subversive element. They were essential to the colony's economic well-being, but at the same time, no one trusted them. It was a foolish plantation owner who did not recognize the danger, for in a community in which so many men were unhappy, even seemingly contented workers might be potential conspirators. The tobacco gentry tried to regulate the lives of their bondsmen, and according to colonial statute, any servant who attended an unlawful meeting or travelled about the countryside without a pass risked arrest.[49] But these measures were insufficient to insure domestic tranquillity. Even if the behavior of the slaves and servants could have been closely controlled (a doubtful proposition at best), the poor freemen remained a threat.[50]

The extent of Virginia's social instability was revealed by events in 1676. Indian raids exacerbated long-standing grievances, and when a young planter named Nathaniel Bacon came forward as spokesman for the discontented, he sparked a civil war. Because Bacon's Rebellion was the most momentous event in seventeenth-century Virginia, it has been the object of intense investigation. Historians concerned chiefly with the behavior of the colony's elite have offered several interpretations of what motivated the leaders of this insurrection.[51] Such analysis is of little value in understanding the "giddy multitude," however, since whatever the aims of Bacon and his lieutenants, there is little evidence their goals were the same as those of their followers. Contemporaries, in fact, believed Bacon had aroused popular fears and frustrations to achieve his own private ends. The House of Burgesses concluded in 1677 that this rebellion, like others before it, resulted from "false Rumors, Infused by ill affected persons provoking an itching desire" in the common people.[52] Indeed, the loyal planters around Berkeley despised Bacon not so much because he was ambitious or even because he had led an unauthorized march against local Indians, but because he had carried his case to the populace. After Bacon had been captured in June 1676, the governor pardoned him; and even though the rebel leader had defied Berkeley's orders several times and slaughtered a village of friendly Occaneechee Indians, Berkeley believed Bacon's submission to be sincere.[53] But Bacon had already stirred forces beyond his control. His followers demanded action. Within two days of receiving his pardon, Bacon "heard what an incredible Number of the meanest of the

People were every where Armed to assist him and his cause."[54] He did not disappoint them. Had Bacon somehow confined the dispute to the upper class, he might have been forgiven for his erratic behavior, but once the servants, slaves, and poor freemen became involved, he had to be crushed.[55]

Participants on both sides of the conflict believed it had pitted the rich against the poor, the privileged against the oppressed or as Berkeley described it the "Rabble" against "the better sort people."[56] There is no reason to doubt the validity of this assessment. To many persons, the Rebellion must have seemed the type of class confrontation which Berkeley and his friends had long feared. "The poverty of the Country is such," Bacon declared, "that all the power and sway is got into the hands of the rich, who by extortious advantages, having the common people in their debt, have always curbed and oppressed them in all manner of wayes."[57] Although historians may discover the Virginian gentry was not as selfish as Bacon claimed, the leader's class rhetoric appealed to a large number of colonists.[58]

It would be interesting to identify these people, to know more about their social status, but the rebels have preserved their anonymity. Surviving records have yielded only a few names out of the hundreds who took up arms against the government. Contemporaries, however, insisted Bacon's troops had been recruited from the lowest ranks of Virginia society. They were the rabble, the disaffected, the vulgar, the indigent. In June 1676, loyalist William Sherwood reported "Now tag, rag, and bobtayle carry a high hand."[59] Philip Ludwell, another prominent colonial official, told an English correspondent that Bacon had raised five hundred soldiers "whose fortunes & Inclinations being equally desperate, were fit for the purpose there being not 20 in the whole Route, but what were Idle & will not worke, or such whose Debaucherie or Ill Husbandry has brought in Debt beyond hopes or thought of payment."[60] Another account described the rebel army as a body composed of three parts: "freemen, searvants, and slaves."[61]

The lower-class origins of Bacon's troops receives additional verification from a narrative written by an English sea captain, Thomas Grantham. This rough adventurer arrived in Virginia just as the Rebellion was ending. Bacon had already died, and groups of dispirited rebels throughout the colony were debating whether to surrender or carry on the fight. Grantham volunteered to serve as an intermediary between Berkeley and his enemies. The governor accepted the offer, and the captain set off in his thirty-gun ship, the *Concord*, in search of the rebel bands. At a fortified position called West Point, he persuaded Joseph Ingram and "about 250" soldiers to submit to the governor's authority in exchange for a full pardon. Grantham then travelled three miles more to the plantation of Colonel John West, the rebels' "Chiefe Garrison and Magazine." At West's home he encountered approximately four hundred "English and Negroes in Armes." In fact, he confronted the very sort of men that Berkeley's followers had often claimed supported Bacon.

The soldiers complained about Ingram's capitulation, and some urged shooting Grantham on the spot. But the captain knew how to talk himself out of difficult situations and brazenly informed "the negroes and Servants, that they were all pardoned and freed from their Slavery." With other such "faire promises" and a liberal supply of brandy, Grantham won most of the discouraged rebels over to the government, but "eighty Negroes and Twenty English . . . would not deliver their Armes." Perhaps these holdouts realized the captain had no power to grant bondsmen freedom; perhaps they believed fighting in a desperate cause better than returning to their masters. Whatever their reasoning, Grantham was one step ahead of the rebels. He tricked them onto a small boat by promising safe passage across the York River, and when the Negroes and servants were aboard, he threatened to blow them out of the water with the guns of the *Concord* unless they immediately surrendered. His account closes with the return of the captured "Negroes & Servants . . . to their Masters."[62]

The presence of so many black rebels at West's plantation provides evidence that many Virginians in Berkeley's time regarded economic status, not race, as the essential social distinction. Even the gentry seems to have viewed the blacks primarily as a component of the "giddy multitude." If the large tobacco planters could have played the white laborers off against the Negroes, they surely would have. The governor's supporters charged Bacon with many failings: atheism, hypocrisy, pride, avarice; but no one attacked the rebel leader for partiality toward black men.[63] One loyalist account of the Rebellion noted that Richard Lawrence, one of Bacon's advisers, had indulged in "the darke imbraces of a Blackamoore, his slave," but in the narrative literature of this period, such racial comments were rare.[64]

If the colonial gentry had been as worried about the danger of black insurrection in 1676 as they were in the eighteenth century, one would have expected some writer to have condemned Bacon's arming the slaves. The silence on this point is especially strange since it may have been illegal in Virginia for Negroes to bear arms.[65] Englishmen such as Captain Grantham appear to have been more conscious of the mixed racial character of Bacon's army than were the local planters.[66] Possibly the colonists had come to view the entire labor force, not just a part of it, as the threat to their safety. The absence of racial slurs does not indicate that Virginia leaders in 1676 felt no prejudice against Negroes. Rather, the planters may have taken for granted the cooperation of slaves, servants and poor freemen.

Bacon's Rebellion has often been described as a turning point in Virginia's history.[67] The settlement of the insurrection did bring about important political changes, especially in the colony's relationship to England; but it did almost nothing to allay the gentry's fear of the "giddy multitude." The social and economic conditions that had originally caused the labor force to participate in the disorder persisted after calm supposedly had been restored. In 1677, a small and relatively insignificant disturbance near Albemarle Sound in Carolina revealed the degree of the planters' uneasiness about maintaining order within their own colony. The disruption, known as Culpeper's Rebellion, grew out of several local grievances, the chief being the collection of a Parliamentary tax. What bothered the Virginians was not the rebels' specific demands, but the character of the rebels themselves. Observers in Carolina reported that Culpeper's force included the worst elements in colonial society. One person warned that if this band of impoverished whites and blacks succeeded in Carolina, it might soon "make Inroads and dayly Incursions" into Virginia.[68]

An even graver danger was the temptation which the Albemarle community presented to the poor laborers and bondsmen in other colonies. As one Carolinian explained, Virginia leaders hoped for a quick suppression of the rebels, "Being exceeding sensible of the dangerous consequences of this Rebellion, as that if they be not suddenly subdued hundreds of idle debtors, theeves, Negros, Indians and English servants will fly unto them." There is no evidence that Virginia workers actually ran to the Albemarle settlements. What is significant, however, is the fear of a lower-class exodus. The colony's elite assumed a coalition of "servants, Slaves & Debtors" would defy established authority if the opportunity arose, and since Virginia's economy had not improved following Bacon's Rebellion, no one knew when a confrontation might occur.[69]

In 1681, five years after Bacon's death, Virginia's leaders were still worried about the possibility of a general servant uprising. At one point they urged the king to allow the foot companies originally sent to Virginia in 1677 to remain so that the Redcoats could "prevent or suppress any Insurrection that may otherwise happen during the necessitous unsettled condition of the Colonie."[70] And Thomas Lord Culpeper, the colony's royal governor (no relation to the leader of the Carolina disorder), regarded the labor force as the chief threat to internal peace. In 1679 the king had instructed Culpeper to "take care that all Planters and Christian Servants be well and fitly provided with Arms." But after living in Virginia only a short time, the governor realized the crown's order was impractical, if not counterproductive. In 1681 Culpeper scribbled in the margin next to this instruction: "Masters have arms. Servants not trusted with."[71]

The lower classes once again turned to violence in the spring of 1682. The primary cause of this disturbance was chronic economic depression, although the political ambitions of Robert Beverley, Sr., clerk of the House of Burgesses, probably served as a catalyst for unrest. For several years, over-production of tobacco had brought hard times to everyone. In an effort to raise prices, some Virginians advocated the voluntary cessation of planting. Royal officials, however, discouraged these plans in the belief they would reduce customs revenue (a tax based on the volume of trade). When the colony's governor prorogued the Burgesses preventing any legislation on the issue, people in Gloucester took matters into their own hands.[72] Mobs marched from plantation to plantation, cutting tobacco plants as they went. Each victim immediately became a fervid "cutter," since once his crop had been destroyed, he wanted to ensure that his neighbors did not profit by his loss. The panic spread to other counties, and although Deputy Governor Henry Chicheley quickly dispatched cavalry units to apprehend the leading "mutineers" and to frustrate further "Insurrection and outrages," the rioting and "night mischiefs" continued for well over a month.[73]

III

After 1682 the character of social violence changed in Virginia. Never again would the "giddy multitude"—indentured servants, black slaves, and poor freemen—make common cause against the colony's ruling planters. In fact, the plant-cutting riots were the last major disturbance in which white laborers of any sort took part. Over the next two decades, white men came to regard blacks—and blacks alone—as the chief threat to Virginia's tranquillity.

The transformation came slowly; for several years colonial leaders were hardly aware of it. Late in the summer of 1682, Secretary Spencer predicted new disorders simply because it was the season when "All plantations [are] flowing with Syder." He even thought he detected a spirit of unrest that "Bacon's Rebellion left itching behind it." But no rebellion occurred.[74] In 1683, Governor Culpeper reported that all was calm in Virginia. "All hands are at worke," he wrote, "none excepted. And yet there is an evil spiritt at Worke, who governed in our Time of Anarchy." Again, no disorder followed.[75] Two years later, Governor Francis Effingham asked William Blathwayt, secretary of the Lords of Trade, for a special force of 20 men "in Case any disorder should accidenteally happen," but the governor undermined the urgency of his request by admitting "all things here are in a peaceable and Quiett Condition."[76] The lower-class whites, the common people, seemed interested in planting tobacco, settling frontier lands and raising families, and none showed much inclination toward organized violence. Not even the Glorious Revolution or rumors that hordes of Maryland Catholics planned to descend upon the colony could stir the "giddy multitude."[77] In 1697, the governor's council in Virginia reported: "The country is in peace and happiness."[78] By 1700, the general uprisings of whites, sometimes supported by a few Negroes, were no more than an unpleasant memory. The eighteenth-century Virginia gentry feared the blacks and the policies of certain aggressive royal governors, but no one expressed apprehension about the poor whites, the tenants, the indentured servants, or the debtors. The problem is to explain how this change came about.

Many elements contributed to the transformation of Virginia, but none was more important than the rise of tobacco prices after 1684. In Berkeley's time, the tobacco market had generally been poor. Some years were better than others, but prices never regained the level achieved in 1660. During the last two decades of the seventeenth century, economic conditions improved. The demand for Virginia crops expanded, and poor yields and natural disasters occurred often enough to prevent market saturation.[79] These were not boom years as the 1620s had been, but tobacco prices were high enough to raise the lower classes out of the poverty that had been so widespread before the 1680s.[80] Contemporaries appreciated the relationship between economic improvement and social tranquillity. Governor Culpeper informed crown officials in 1683 that "peace and quietness" would continue in Virginia "so long as tobacco bears a price." [81] The next year Spencer observed that the people had calmed down since they had begun working for a full harvest. [82]

While rising prices reduced social tensions, they did not in themselves bring about the disappearance of the "giddy multitude." The character of the labor force also changed during this period. Before Bacon's Rebellion, planters imported thousands of indentured servants; and because the demand for workers exceeded the supply, planters accepted whomever merchants delivered. After 1680, however, commercial developments outside Virginia altered the servant trade. English companies achieved the capacity to ship Negroes directly from Africa to the mainland colonies and during the last years of the seventeenth century, tobacco planters purchased slaves in increasingly larger numbers. This new source of labor was not only more economic than the indentured servants had been, but it also allowed planters greater selectivity in the choice of servants. William Fitzhugh, for example, one of the colony's major slave holders, refused to take "ordinary servants," warning a trader, "I would have a good one or none." [83]

A second element affecting the quality of indentured servants was England's crackdown on the "spirits." In 1682 Charles II issued a proclamation regulating the recuitment of servants. No indenture would be valid unless signed before a magistrate in the mother country, and no person under 14 years old could be shipped to America without parental consent. [84] The king's humanitarian act may in part have been an attempt to protect legitimate merchants from fraudulent suits by individuals claiming to have been abducted. In the early 1680s a group calling itself "the Principall Merchants of England traders to the Plantacions" protested that unnecessary prosecutions had so discouraged traders from carrying servants to the New World that some colonies would soon find themselves with "few white men to Governe & direct the Negroes." [85]

Whatever the causes, the number of indentured servants arriving in Virginia dwindled. Those who did immigrate, however, were of a higher social rank than those who flooded the colony at mid-century. Large planters wanted servants with special skills. In 1687 Fitzhugh advised an Englishman how to establish a plantation in Virginia: "the best methods to be pursued therein is, to get a Carpenter & Bricklayer Servants, & send them in here to serve 4 or five years, in which time of their Service they might reasonably build a substantial good house . . . & earn money enough besides in their said time, at spare times from your work . . . as will purchase plank, nails & other materials."[86] Of the seven indentured servants mentioned in Fitzhugh's will, one was a carpenter, one a glazier, and another the planter's own cousin.[87] Unlike the planters of Berkeley's time, Fitzhugh's contemporaries seldom complained that their servants were "desperate villans" recruited from the "very scum" of England. Conditions had changed. The indentured workers who emigrated after the mid-1680s escaped the crushing poverty and frustrations that so embittered the previous generation of servants. For these later arrivals Virginia may well have appeared a land of opportunity.

The poor freemen also became less disruptive in this period. Landless and indebted persons, many of them former servants, had once flocked to Bacon's standard. Yet, by the mid-1680s, no one seems to have regarded them as a serious threat to Virginia's internal security. These people benefited greatly from improved economic conditions. Few at the lowest levels of white society experienced the grinding poverty that a decade earlier had driven desperate men to violence. Food was abundant and clothes easier to obtain. Indeed, by the beginning of the eighteenth century, Virginians boasted of eradicating poverty. The planter-historian Robert Beverley, Jr. noted in 1705 that the colonists "live in so happy a Climate, and have so fertile a Soil that no body is poor enough to beg, or want Food, though they have abundance of People that are lazy enough to deserve it." Beverley concluded that compared to European nations, Virginia was "the best poor man's Country in the World."[88] Foreign visitors corroborated Beverley's observation. When a French Protestant, Francis Louis Michel, travelled through Virginia in 1702, he reported finding no poor people and wrote: "It is indeed said truthfully that there is no other country, where it is possible with so few means and so easily to make an honest living and be in easy circumstances." As tobacco prices improved, the less prosperous freemen found wealthier neighbors willing to advance credit. And if a person possessed a special skill or trade, he could command a good wage. "I have seen a common journeyman paid annually 30 lbs. sterling, including his board," one man wrote. "But I have heard of master workmen who receive above a guinea daily."[89]

As always, freemen wanted land. In Berkeley's time, hostile Indians along the frontier and "Land lopers" among the gentry frustrated this desire. After the mid-1680s, however, changes in Virginia reduced these obstructions—the colonists simply removed the Indians. A foreign traveller at the turn of the century discovered that Indians "have not come into the colony to inflict damage, because for one thing they are afraid of the English power, but especially because they are unable to flee from the cavalry." As early as 1687, Virginians counselled prospective colonists that Indians "are not greatly to be feared."[90]

Often the colony's most influential planters, such as William Byrd, William Fitzhugh, and Ralph Wormeley, claimed the vacated Indian lands. One means of obtaining large tracts in the west was to lead the militia in a successful march against the Indians. "The colonels of these troops," a Frenchman explained, "claimed the plantations of the savages & had them surveyed, so that at the present time [1687] there are large tracts of very good land for sale in Virginia."[91] Some of these men held on to the land, building the vast estates that became an integral part of the Virginia aristocracy in the eighteenth century, but much of the acreage was sold. Several Virginians, in fact, became speculators and showed no desire to discourage small farmers from settling the newly secured territory. Fitzhugh, one of the colony's largest landowners, urged an English associate to promote the planter's Virginia lands, for any transfer "will be doubly advantageous to me first by meeting with an opportunity to serve you through your friends, & secondly, by profitably either selling or tenementing my Land, which till so done, is rather a charge than profit."[92] Easy and flexible terms were offered to interested buyers. Ralph Wormeley, for example, was willing to sell "ten thousand acres of ground he owned . . . for one ecu an acre."[93]

If landless freemen could not afford acreage in Virginia, they could move to Carolina or Pennsylvania, areas largely inaccessible before 1680. This practice was fairly common. In 1695, Governor Francis Nicholson complained "many families, but especially young men" were leaving Virginia and Maryland for Pennsylvania where land could be purchased at a lower rate.[94] A visitor to Virginia in 1702 "heard many good reports about Pennsylvania and that some people from Virginia moved there."[95] Whichever option the ex-servant chose—buying land in Virginia or moving—he could anticipate becoming an independent planter. Although relatively few advanced to the highest ranks of society, the freeman's horizons were broader in 1700 than they had been in 1670.[96]

After the 1680s the experience of the blacks in Virginia was increasingly different from that of other colonists. Improved tobacco prices raised white laborers out of poverty, making their servitude endurable and their freemanship secure. But the same economic conditions brought large numbers of Negroes into the colony as slaves. No one knows exactly how rapidly the black population grew after 1680. There seem to have been about four thousand slaves at the time of the tobacco-cutting riots. Estimates of the size of the Negro population in 1700 range as high as twenty thousand. Even if this figure is excessive, the number of Africans arriving in Virginia expanded substantially in the last two decades of the seventeenth century.[97]

The leading tobacco planters required no encouragement to make the transition from white to black labor. The wealthiest among them had accumulated enough capital to purchase and maintain large gangs of Negroes. For the first time in the century, English trading companies were able to supply blacks on a reasonably regular basis. The colonists bought all the Negroes the slavers could transport and then demanded more.[98] In 1696, a group of Chesapeake planters and merchants petitioned Parliament to lift restrictions on the African trade, since the company holding the monopoly (the Royal African Company) could not meet the escalating demand for blacks in Maryland and Virginia.[99]

The changes in the slave community were more complex than population statistics alone reveal. In fact, the sheer growth in numbers only partially explains why whites no longer joined with blacks to threaten planter society. An equally important element in understanding race relations in this period was the Negroes' experience before arriving in Virginia. With each passing year an increasing proportion of slaves came directly from Africa.[100] These immigrants had no stopover in Barbados to learn English or to adjust either physically or mentally to an alien culture. They were simply dumped on the wharves of the river plantations in a state of shock, barely alive after the ocean crossing. Conditions on the slave ships were terrible. One vessel from Guinea unloaded 230 blacks, but reported that a hundred more had died at sea.[101] No white servant in this period, no matter how poor, how bitter or badly treated, could identify with these frightened Africans. The terrors they had so recently faced were beyond comprehension. The sale of the blacks emphasized the difference between races. "The negroes are brought annually in large numbers," a visitor to Virginia recounted at the turn of the century. "They can be selected according to pleasure, young and old, men and women. They are entirely naked when they arrive, having only corals of different colors around their necks and arms." These strange, helpless blacks repulsed the writer who noted that even the Indians seemed preferable to these "animal-like people." [102] His reactions, no doubt, were shared by many white Virginians. In 1699, members of the House of Burgesses described the blacks in a manner unknown in Berkeley's time, claiming it unnecessary to expose slaves to Christianity, since "the gross barbarity and rudeness of their manners, the variety and strangeness of their languages and the weakness and shallowness of their minds rendered it in a manner impossible to attain to any progress in their conversion." [103]

Language became a major barrier between white laborers and the thousands of new black immigrants. [104] Before the 1690s, no one recorded any problem in communicating with Negroes. Indeed, it is difficult to comprehend how servants and slaves could have conspired to run away or rebel had they been unable to understand one another. The flood of Africans directly into Virginia not only made it difficult for whites to deal with blacks, but also hindered communications between blacks. [105] The colonists apparently regarded the great variety of African tongues as a protection against black insurrection. Early in the eighteenth century, Governor Alexander Spotswood, convinced of the need for stricter controls over the labor force, warned Virginians that the slaves' "Babel of Languages" offered no real security, since "freedom Wears a Cap which can without a Tongue, Call Together all Those who long to Shake off the fetters of Slavery." [106]

The blacks hated their status. They ran away whenever possible, and on at least one occasion, formed a small band that terrorized the colonists of Rappahannock County. [107] Rumors of Negro plots made the planters uneasy, with good reason. A group of slaves could easily have seized a plantation and murdered the master and his family before troops could have been summoned. [108] But there was little chance that the blacks at this time could have overrun the colony; without the support of poorer whites and indentured servants, they were badly outnumbered. The white cavalry that hunted down the Indians could have done the same to the slaves. [109] The changes in Virginia society after the mid-1680s had set whites against blacks, the armed, organized forces of the planters against the small, isolated groups of slaves. In Berkeley's time the militia had been regarded as a means of protecting the elite from the entire labor force, but the early eighteenth-century historian Hugh Jones reported that "in each county is a great number of disciplined and armed militia, ready in case of any sudden irruption of Indians or insurrection of Negroes."[110] The labor force was still the major threat to internal security in Virginia, but now the laborers were predominantly black.

Like the Barbadians, the seventeenth-century Virginians exchanged white servants for Negro slaves, and in so doing exchanged a fear of the "giddy multitude" for a fear of slave rebellion. By 1700, whites had achieved a sense of race solidarity at the expense of blacks. Negroes were set apart as objects of contempt and ridicule. The whites, even the meanest among them, always knew there was a class of men permanently below them. But the story of Virginia's labor force between 1660 and 1710 was more than a dreary narrative of suffering and oppression. For a few decades, it had been possible to overlook racial differences, a time when a common experience of desperate poverty and broken dreams brought some whites and blacks together. Such conditions were present in the American South during the 1890s, and it is not unlikely that they will appear again.

VIII

Horses and Gentlemen:
The Cultural Significance
of Gambling
Among the Gentry of Virginia

THIS ESSAY INVESTIGATES the cultural implications of social and demographic change for Virginia's great planters. In the previous chapter I explained that during the last quarter of the seventeenth century the character of the colony's labor force became more African and less free. It was during this same period that the members of the Virginia gentry began to organize quarter-horse races, wild sprints on which the planters waged extraordinary sums of money. These two occurrences, I contend, were not unrelated. Indeed, powerful gentlemen evolved a new form in which to express old values. As I explained in the volume's general introduction, change and persistence were closely interconnected, and the horse race provides surprising insights into the ways that the great planters maintained dominance in an expanding, biracial society.

I

In the fall of 1686 Durand of Dauphiné, a French Huguenot, visited the capital of colonial Virginia. Durand regularly recorded in a journal what he saw and heard, providing one of the few firsthand accounts of late seventeenth-century Virginia society that have survived to the present day. When he arrived in Jamestown the House of Burgesses was in session. "I saw there fine-looking men," he noted, "sitting in judgment booted and with belted sword." But to Durand's surprise, several of these Virginia gentlemen "started gambling" soon after dinner, and it was not until midnight that one of the players noticed the Frenchman patiently waiting for the contest to end. The Virginian—obviously a veteran of long nights at the gaming table—advised Durand to go to bed. "'For,' said he, 'it is quite possible that we shall be here all night,' and in truth I found them still playing the next morning."[1]

The event Durand witnessed was not unusual. In late seventeenth- and early eighteenth-century Virginia, gentlemen spent a good deal of time gambling. During this period, in fact, competitive gaming involving high stakes became a distinguishing characteristic of gentry culture. Whenever the great planters congregated, someone inevitably produced a deck of cards, a pair of dice, or a backgammon board; and quarter-horse racing was a regular event throughout the colony. Indeed, these men hazarded money and tobacco on almost any proposition in which there was an element of chance. Robert Beverley, a member of one of Virginia's most prominent families, made a wager "with the gentlemen of the country" that if he could produce seven hundred gallons of wine on his own plantation, they would pay him the handsome sum of one thousand guineas. Another leading planter offered six-to-one odds that Alexander Spotswood could not procure a commission as the colony's governor. And in 1671 one disgruntled gentleman asked a court of law to award him his winnings from a bet concerning "a Servant maid."[2] The case of this suspicious-sounding wager—unfortunately not described in greater detail—dragged on until the colony's highest court ordered the loser to pay the victor a thousand pounds of tobacco.

The great planters' passion for gambling, especially on quarter-horse racing, coincided with a period of far-reaching social change in Virginia.[3] Before the mid-1680s constant political unrest, servant risings both real and threatened, plant-cutting riots, and even a full-scale civil war had plagued the colony.[4] But by the end of the century Virginia had achieved internal peace.[5] Several elements contributed to the growth of social tranquility. First, by 1700 the ruling gentry were united as they had never been before. The great planters of the seventeenth century had been for the most part aggressive English immigrants. They fought among themselves for political and social dominance, and during Bacon's Rebellion in 1676 various factions within the gentry attempted to settle their differences on the battlefield. By the end of the century, however, a sizable percentage of the Virginia gentry, perhaps a majority, had been born in the colony. The members of this native-born elite—one historian calls them a "creole elite"—cooperated more frequently in political affairs than had their immigrant fathers. They found it necessary to unite in resistance against a series of interfering royal governors such as Thomas Lord Culpeper, Francis Nicholson, and Alexander Spotswood. After Bacon's Rebellion the leading planters—the kind of men whom Durand watched gamble the night away—successfully consolidated their control over Virginia's civil, military, and ecclesiastical institutions. They monopolized the most important offices; they patented the best lands.[6]

A second and even more far-reaching element in the creation of this remarkable solidarity among the gentry was the shifting racial composition of the plantation labor force. Before the 1680s the planters had relied on large numbers of white indentured servants to cultivate Virginia's sole export crop, tobacco. These impoverished, often desperate servants disputed their masters' authority and on several occasions resisted colonial rulers with force of arms. In part because of their dissatisfaction with the indenture system, and in part because changes in the international slave trade made it easier and cheaper for Virginians to purchase black laborers, the major planters increasingly turned to Africans. The blacks' cultural disorientation made them less difficult to control than the white servants. Large-scale collective violence such as Bacon's Rebellion and the 1682 plant-cutting riots consequently declined markedly. By the beginning of the eighteenth century Virginia had been transformed into a relatively peaceful, biracial society in which a few planters exercised almost unchallenged hegemony over both their slaves and their poorer white neighbors.[7]

The growth of gambling among the great planters during a period of significant social change raises important questions not only about gentry values but also about the social structure of late seventeenth-century Virginia. Why did gambling, involving high stakes, become so popular among the gentlemen at precisely this time? Did it reflect gentry values or have symbolic connotations for the people living in this society? Did this activity serve a social function, contributing in some manner to the maintenance of group cohesion? Why did quarter-horse racing, in particular, become a gentry sport? And finally, did public displays such as this somehow reinforce the great planters' social and political dominance?

In part, of course, gentlemen laid wagers on women and horses simply because they enjoyed the excitement of competition. Gambling was a recreation, like a good meal among friends or a leisurely hunt in the woods—a pleasant pastime when hard-working planters got together. Another equally acceptable explanation for the gentry's fondness for gambling might be the transplanting of English social mores. Certainly, the upper classes in the mother country loved betting for high stakes, and it is possible that the all-night card games and the frequent horse races were staged attempts by a provincial gentry to transform itself into a genuine landed aristocracy.[8] While both views possess merit, neither is entirely satisfactory. The great planters of Virginia presumably could have favored less risky forms of competition. Moreover, even though several planters deliberately emulated English social styles, the widespread popularity of gambling among the gentry indicates that this type of behavior may have had deeper, more complex cultural roots than either of these explanations would suggest.[9]

In many societies competitive gaming is a device by which the participants transform abstract cultural values into observable social behavior. In his now-classic analysis of the Balinese cockfight Clifford Geertz describes contests for extremely high stakes as intense social dramas. These battles not only involve the honor of important villagers and their kin groups but also reflect in symbolic form the entire Balinese social structure. Far from being a simple pastime, betting on cocks turns out to be an expression of the way the Balinese perceive social reality. The rules of the fight, the patterns of wagering, the reactions of winners and losers—all these elements help us to understand more profoundly the totality of Balinese culture.[10]

The Virginia case is analogous to the Balinese. When the great planter staked his money and tobacco on a favorite horse or spurred a sprinter to victory, he displayed some of the central elements of gentry culture—its competitiveness, individualism, and materialism. In fact, competitive gaming was for many gentlemen a means of translating a particular set of values into action, a mechanism for expressing a loose but deeply felt bundle of ideas and assumptions about the nature of society. The quarter-horse races of Virginia were intense contests involving personal honor, elaborate rules, heavy betting, and wide community interest; and just as the cockfight opens up hidden dimensions of Balinese culture, gentry gambling offers an opportunity to improve our understanding of the complex interplay between cultural values and social behavior in Virginia.

II

Gambling reflected core elements of late seventeenth- and early eighteenth-century gentry values. From diaries, letters, and travel accounts we discover that despite their occasional cooperation in political affairs, Virginia gentlemen placed extreme emphasis upon personal independence. This concern may in part have been the product of the colony's peculiar settlement patterns. The great planters required immense tracts of fresh land for their tobacco. Often thousands of acres in size, their plantations were scattered over a broad area from the Potomac River to the James. The dispersed planters lived in their "Great Houses" with their families and slaves, and though they saw friends from time to time, they led for the most part isolated, routine lives.[11] An English visitor in 1686 noted with obvious disapproval that "their Plantations run over vast Tracts of Ground . . . whereby the Country is thinly inhabited; the Living solitary and unsociable." Some planters were uncomfortably aware of the problems created by physical isolation.[12] William Fitzhugh, for example, admitted to a correspondent in the mother country, "Society that is good and ingenious is very scarce, and seldom to be come at except in books."[13]

Yet despite such apparent cultural privation, Fitzhugh and his contemporaries refused to alter their life styles in any way that might compromise their freedom of action. They assumed it their right to give commands, and in the ordering of daily plantation affairs they rarely tolerated outside interference.[14] Some of these planters even saw themselves as lawgivers out of the Old Testament. In 1726 William Byrd II explained that "like one of the Patriarchs, I have my Flocks and my Herds, my Bond-men and Bond-women, and every Soart of Trade amongst my own Servants, so that I live in a kind of Independence on every one but Providence."[15] Perhaps Byrd exaggerated for literary effect, but forty years earlier Durand had observed, "There are no lords [in Virginia], but each is sovereign in his own plantation."[16] Whatever the origins of this independent spirit, it bred excessive individualism in a wide range of social activities. While these powerful gentlemen sometimes worked together to achieve specific political and economic ends, they bristled at the least hint of constraint.[17] Andrew Burnaby later noted that "the public or political character of the Virginians corresponds with their private one: they are haughty and jealous of their liberties, impatient of restraint, and can scarcely bear the thought of being controuled by any superior power."[18]

The gentry expressed this uncompromising individualism in aggressive competitiveness, engaging in a constant struggle against real and imagined rivals to obtain more lands, additional patronage, and high tobacco prices. Indeed, competition was a major factor shaping the character of face-to-face relationships among the colony's gentlemen, and when the stakes were high the planters were not particular about the methods they employed to gain victory.[19] In large part, the goal of the competition within the gentry group was to improve social position by increasing wealth.

Some gentlemen believed that personal honor was at stake as well. Robert "King" Carter, by all accounts the most successful planter of his generation, expressed his anxiety about losing out to another Virginian in a competitive market situation. "In discourse with Colonel Byrd, Mr. Armistead, and a great many others," he explained, "I understand you [an English merchant] had sold their tobaccos in round parcels and at good rates. I cannot allow myself to come behind any of these gentlemen in the planter's trade."[20] Carter's pain arose not so much from the lower price he had received as from the public knowledge that he had been bested by respected peers. He believed he had lost face. This kind of intense competition was sparked, especially among the less affluent members of the gentry, by a dread of slipping into the ranks of what one eighteenth-century Virginia historian called the "common Planters."[21] Governor Francis Nicholson, an acerbic English placeman, declared that the "ordinary sort of planters" knew full well "from whence these mighty dons derive their originals."[22] The governor touched a nerve; the efforts of "these mighty dons" to outdo one another were almost certainly motivated by a desire to disguise their "originals," to demonstrate anew through competitive encounters that they could legitimately claim gentility.

Another facet of Virginia gentry culture was materialism. This certainly does not mean that the great planters lacked spiritual concerns. Religion played a vital role in the lives of men like Robert Carter and William Byrd II. Nevertheless, piety was largely a private matter. In public these men determined social standing not by a man's religiosity or philosophic knowledge but by his visible estate—his lands, slaves, buildings, even by the quality of his garments. When John Bartram, one of America's first botanists, set off in 1737 to visit two of Virginia's most influential planters, a London friend advised him to purchase a new set of clothes, "for though I should not esteem thee less, to come to me in what dress thou will,—yet these Virginians are a very gentle, well-dressed people—and look, perhaps, more at a man's outside than his inside."[23] This perception of gentry values was accurate. Fitzhugh's desire to maintain outward appearances drove him to collect a stock of monogrammed silver plate and to import at great expense a well-crafted, though not very practical, English carriage.[24] One even finds hints that the difficulty of preserving the image of material success weighed heavily upon some planters. When he described local Indian customs in 1705, Robert Beverley noted that Native Americans lived an easy, happy existence "without toiling and perplexing their mind for Riches, which other people often trouble themselves to provide for uncertain and ungrateful Heirs."[25]

The gentry were acutely sensitive to the element of chance in human affairs, and this sensitivity influenced their attitudes toward other men and society. Virginians knew from bitter experience that despite the best-laid plans, nothing in their lives was certain. Slaves suddenly sickened and died. English patrons forgot to help their American friends. Tobacco prices fell without warning. Cargo ships sank. Storms and droughts ruined the crops. The list was endless. Fitzhugh warned an English correspondent to think twice before allowing a son to become a Virginia planter, for even "if the best husbandry and the greatest forecast and skill were used, yet ill luck at Sea, a fall of a Market, or twenty other accidents may ruin and overthrow the best Industry."[26] Other planters, even those who had risen to the top of colonial society, longed for greater security. "I could wish," declared William Byrd I in 1685, "wee had Some more certain Commodity [than tobacco] to rely on but see no hopes of itt."[27] However desirable such certainty may have appeared, the planters always put their labor and money into tobacco, hoping for a run of luck. One simply learned to live with chance. In 1710 William Byrd II confided in his secret diary: "I dreamed last night . . . that I won a tun full of money and might win more if I had ventured."[28]

Gaming relationships reflected these strands of gentry culture. In fact, gambling in Virginia was a ritual activity. It was a form of repetitive, patterned behavior that not only corresponded closely to the gentry's values and assumptions but also symbolized the realities of everyday planter life. This congruence between actions and belief, between form and experience, helps to account for the popularity of betting contests. The wager, whether over cards or horses, brought together in a single, focused act the great planters' competitiveness, independence, and materialism, as well as the element of chance.[29] It represented a social agreement in which each individual was free to determine how he would play, and the gentleman who accepted a challenge risked losing his material possessions as well as his personal honor.[30]

III

The favorite household or tavern contests during this period included cards, backgammon, billiards, nine-pins, and dice. The great planters preferred card games that demanded skill as well as luck. Put, piquet, and whist provided the necessary challenge, and Virginia gentlemen— Durand's hosts, for example—regularly played these games for small sums of money and tobacco.[31] These activities brought men together, stimulated conversation, and furnished a harmless outlet for aggressive drives. They did not, however, become for the gentry a form of intense, symbolic play such as the cockfight in Bali.[32] William Byrd II once cheated his wife in a game of piquet, something he would never have dared to do among his peers at Williamsburg. By and large, he showed little emotional involvement in these types of household gambling. The exception here proves the rule. After an unusually large loss at the gaming tables of Williamsburg, Byrd drew a pointed finger in the margin of his secret diary and swore a "solemn resolution never at once to lose more than 50 shillings and to spend less time in gaming, and I beg the God Almighty to give me grace to keep so good a resolution. . . ." Byrd's reformation was short-lived, for within a few days he dispassionately noted losing another four pounds at piquet.[33]

Horse racing generated far greater interest among the gentry than did the household games.[34] Indeed, for the great planters and the many others who came to watch, these contests were preeminently a social drama. To appreciate the importance of racing in seventeenth-century Virginia, we must understand the cultural significance of horses. By the turn of the century possession of one of these animals had become a social necessity. Without a horse, a planter felt despised, an object of ridicule. Owning even a slow-footed saddle horse made the common

planter more of a man in his own eyes as well as in those of his neighbors; he was reluctant to venture forth on foot for fear of making an ad-
verse impression. As the Reverend Hugh Jones explained in 1724, "almost every ordinary Person keeps a Horse; and I have known some
spend the Morning in ranging several Miles in the Woods to find and
catch their Horses only to ride two or three Miles to Church, to the
Court House, or to a Horse-Race, where they generally appoint to meet
upon Business."[35] Such behavior seems a waste of time and energy
only to one who does not comprehend the symbolic importance which
the Virginians attached to their horses. A horse was an extension of its
owner; indeed, a man was only as good as his horse. Because of the
horse's cultural significance, the gentry attempted to set its
horsemanship apart from that of the common planters. Gentlemen took
better care of their animals, and according to John Clayton, who visited
Virginia in 1688, they developed a distinctive riding style. "They ride
pretty sharply," Clayton reported; "a Planter's Pace is a Proverb, which
is a good sharp hand-Gallop."[36] A fast-rising cloud of dust far down a
Virginia road probably alerted the common planter that he was about to
encounter a social superior.

The contest that generated the greatest interest among the gentry was
the quarter-horse race, an all-out sprint by two horses over a quarter-
mile dirt track.[37] The great planters dominated these events. In the
records of the county courts—our most important source of information
about specific races—we find the names of some of the colony's most
prominent planter families—Randolph, Eppes, Jefferson, Swan, Kenner, Hardiman, Parker, Cocke, Batte, Harwick (Hardidge), Youle (Yowell), and Washington. Members of the House of Burgesses, including
its powerful speaker William Randolph, were frequently mentioned in
the contests that came before the courts.[38] On at least one occasion the
Reverend James Blair, Virginia's most eminent clergyman and a
founder of the College of William and Mary, gave testimony in a suit
arising from a race run between Captain William Soane and Robert
Napier.[39] The tenacity with which the gentry pursued these cases, almost continuations of the race itself, suggests that victory was no less
sweet when it was gained in court.

Many elements contributed to the exclusion of lower social groups
from these contests. Because of the sheer size of wagers, poor freemen
and common planters could not have participated regularly. Certainly,
the members of the Accomack County Court were embarrassed to dis-

cover that one Thomas Davis, "a very poore Man," had lost 500 pounds of tobacco or a cow and calf in a horse race with an adolescent named Mr. John Andrews. Recognizing that Davis bore "a great charge of wife and Children," the justices withheld final judgment until the governor had an opportunity to rule on the legality of the wager. The Accomack court noted somewhat gratuitously that if the governor declared the action unlawful, it would fine Davis five days' work on a public bridge.[40] In such cases county justices ordinarily made no comment upon a plaintiff's or defendant's financial condition, assuming, no doubt, that most people involved in racing were capable of meeting their gaming obligations.

The gentry actively enforced its exclusive control over quarter-horse racing. When James Bullocke, a York County tailor, challenged Mr. Mathew Slader to a race in 1674, the county court informed Bullocke that it was "contrary to Law for a Labourer to make a race being a Sport for Gentlemen" and fined the presumptuous tailor two hundred pounds of tobacco and cask.[41] Additional evidence of exclusiveness is found in early eighteenth-century Hanover County. In one of the earliest issues of the colony's first newspaper, the *Virginia Gazette*, an advertisement appeared announcing that "some merry-dispos'd gentlemen" in Hanover planned to celebrate St. Andrew's Day with a race for quarter-milers. The Hanover gentlemen explained in a later, fuller description that "all Persons resorting there are desir'd to behave themselves with Decency and Sobriety, the Subscribers being resolv'd to discountenance all Immorality with the utmost Rigour." The purpose of these contests was to furnish the county's "considerable Number of Gentlemen, Merchants, and credible Planters" an opportunity for "cultivating Friendship."[42] Less affluent persons apparently were welcome to watch the proceedings provided they acted like gentlemen.

In most match races the planter rode his own horse, and the exclusiveness of these contests meant that racing created intensely competitive confrontations. There were two ways to set up a challenge. The first was a regularly scheduled affair usually held on Saturday afternoon. By 1700 there were at least a dozen tracks, important enough to be known by name, scattered through the counties of the Northern Neck and the James River valley. The records are filled with references to contests held at such places as Smith's Field, Coan Race Course, Devil's Field, Yeocomico, and Varina.[43] No doubt, many races also occurred on nameless country roads or convenient pastures. On the appointed day the planter simply appeared at the race track and waited for a likely challenge. We know from a dispute heard before the Westmoreland County Court in 1693 that John Gardner boldly "Challeng'd all the horses then upon the ground to run with any of them for a thousand pounds of Tobo and twenty shillings in money."[44] A second type of contest was a more spontaneous challenge. When gentlemen congregated over a jug of hard cider or peach brandy, the talk frequently turned to horses. The owners presumably bragged about the superior speed of their animals, and if one planter called another's bluff, the men cried out "done, and done," marched to the nearest field, and there discovered whose horse was in fact the swifter.[45]

Regardless of the outcome, quarter-horse races in Virginia were exciting spectacles. The crowds of onlookers seem often to have been fairly large, as common planters, even servants, flocked to the tracks to watch the gentry challenge one another for what must have seemed immense amounts of money and tobacco. One witness before a Westmoreland County Court reported in 1674 that Mr. Stone and Mr. Youle had run a challenge for £10 sterling "in sight of many people."[46] Attendance at race days was sizable enough to support a brisk trade in cider and brandy. In 1714 the Richmond County Court fined several men for peddling liquors "by Retaile in the Race Ground."[47] Judging from the popularity of horses throughout planter society, it seems probable that the people who attended these events dreamed of one day riding a local champion such as Prince or Smoaker.

The magnitude of gentry betting indicates that racing must have deeply involved the planter's self-esteem. Wagering took place on two levels. The contestants themselves made a wager on the outcome, a main bet usually described in a written statement. In addition, side wagers were sometimes negotiated between spectators or between a contestant and spectator.[48] Of the two, the main bet was far the more significant. From accounts of disputed races reaching the county courts we know that gentlemen frequently risked very large sums. The most extravagant contest of the period was a race run between John Baker and John Haynie in Northumberland County in 1693, in which the two men wagered 4000 pounds of tobacco and forty shillings sterling on the speed of their sprinters Prince and Smoaker.[49] Some races involved only twenty or thirty shillings, but a substantial number were run for several pounds sterling and hundreds of pounds of tobacco. While few, if any, of the seventeenth-century gentlemen were what we would call gambling addicts, their betting habits seemed irrational even by the more prudential standards of their own day: in conducting normal business transactions, for example, they would never have placed so much money in such jeopardy.

To appreciate the large size of these bets we must interpret them within the context of Virginia's economy. Between 1660 and 1720 a planter could anticipate receiving about ten shillings per hundredweight of tobacco. Since the average grower seldom harvested more than 1500 pounds of tobacco a year per man, he probably never enjoyed an annual income from tobacco in excess of eight pounds sterling.[50] For most Virginians the conversion of tobacco into sterling occurred only in the neat columns of account books. They themselves seldom had coins in their pockets. Specie was extremely scarce, and planters ordinarily paid their taxes and conducted business transactions with tobacco notes—written promises to deliver to the bearer a designated amount of tobacco.[51] The great preponderance of seventeenth-century planters were quite poor, and even the great planters estimated their income in hundreds, not thousands, of pounds sterling.[52] Fitzhugh, one of the wealthier men of his generation, described his financial situation in detail. "Thus I have given you some particulars," he wrote in 1686, "which I thus deduce, the yearly Crops of corn and Tobo, together with the surplusage of meat more than will serve the family's use, will amount annually to 60000 lb. Tobo wch. at 10 shillings per Ct. is 300 £ annum."[53] These facts reveal that the Baker-Haynie bet—to take a notable example—amounted to approximately £22 sterling, more than 7 percent of Fitzhugh's annual cash return. It is therefore not surprising that the common planters seldom took part in quarter-horse racing: this wager alone amounted to approximately three times the income they could expect to receive in a good year. Even a modest wager of a pound or two sterling represented a substantial risk.

Gentlemen sealed these gaming relationships with a formal agreement, either a written statement laying out the terms of the contest or a declaration before a disinterested third party of the nature of the wager. In either case the participants carefully stipulated what rules would be in effect. Sometimes the written agreements were quite elaborate. In 1698, for example, Richard Ward and John Steward, Jr. "Covenanted and agreed" to race at a quarter-mile track in Henrico County known as Ware. Ward's mount was to enjoy a ten-yard handicap, and if it crossed the finish line within five lengths of Steward's horse, Ward would win five pounds sterling; if Steward's obviously superior animal won by a greater distance, Ward promised to pay six pounds sterling.[54] In another contest William Eppes and Stephen Cocke asked William Randolph to witness an agreement for a ten-shilling race: "each horse was to keep his path, they not being to crosse unlesse Stephen Cocke could gett the other Riders Path at the start at two or three Jumps."[55]

Virginia's county courts treated race covenants as binding legal contracts.[56] If a gentleman failed to fulfill the agreement, the other party had legitimate grounds to sue; and the county justices' first consideration during a trial was whether the planters had properly recorded their agreement.[57] The Henrico court summarily dismissed one gambling suit because "noe Money was stacked down nor Contract in Writing made[,] one of wch in such cases is by the law required."[58] Because any race might generate legal proceedings, it was necessary to have a number of people present at the track not only to assist in the running of the contest but also to act as witnesses if anything went wrong. The two riders normally appointed an official starter, several judges, and someone to hold the stakes.

Almost all of the agreements included a promise to ride a fair race. Thus two men in 1698 insisted upon "fair Rideing"; another pair pledged "they would run fair horseman's play."[59] By such agreements the planters waived their customary right to jostle, whip, or knee an opponent, or to attempt to unseat him.[60] During the last decades of the seventeenth century the gentry apparently attempted to substitute riding skill and strategy for physical violence. The demand for "fair Rideing" also suggests that the earliest races in Virginia were wild, no-holds-barred affairs that afforded contestants ample opportunity to vent their aggressions.

The intense desire to win sometimes undermined a gentleman's written promise to run a fair race. When the stakes were large, emotions ran high. One man complained in a York County court that an opponent had interfered with his horse in the middle of the race, "by meanes whereof the s[ai]d Plaintiff lost the said Race."[61] Joseph Humphrey told a Northumberland County court that he would surely have come in first in a challenge for 1500 pounds of tobacco had not Captain Rodham Kenner (a future member of the House of Burgesses) "held the defendt horses bridle in running his race."[62] Other riders testified that they had been "Josselled" while the race was in progress. An unusual case of interference grew out of a 1694 race which Rodham Kenner

rode against John Hartly for one pound sterling and 575 pounds of
tobacco. In a Westmoreland County court Hartly explained that after a
fair start and without using "whipp or Spurr" he found himself "a great
distance" in front of Kenner. But as Hartly neared the finish line, Kenner's brother Richard suddenly jumped onto the track and "did hollow
and shout and wave his hat over his head in the plts [plaintiff's] horse's
face." The animal panicked, ran outside the posts marking the finish
line, and lost the race. After a lengthy trial a Westmoreland jury decided that Richard Kenner "did no foule play in his hollowing and
waveing his hatt."[63] What exactly occurred during this race remains a
mystery, but since no one denied that Richard acted very strangely, it
seems likely that the Kenner brothers were persuasive as well as powerful.

Planters who lost large wagers because an opponent jostled or "hol-
lowed" them off the track were understandably angry. Yet instead of
challenging the other party to a duel or allowing gaming relationships to
degenerate into blood feuds, the disappointed horsemen invariably took
their complaints to the courts.[64] Such behavior indicates not only that
the gentlemen trusted the colony's formal legal system—after all,
members of their group controlled it—but also that they were willing to
place institutional limitations on their own competitiveness. Gentlemen
who felt they had been cheated or abused at the track immediately
collected witnesses and brought suit before the nearest county court.
The legal machinery available to the aggrieved gambler was complex;
and no matter how unhappy he may have been with the final verdict,
he could rarely claim that the system had denied due process.

The plaintiff brought charges before a group of justices of the peace
sitting as a county court; if these men found sufficient grounds for a
suit, the parties—in the language of seventeenth-century Virginia—
could "put themselves upon the country."[65] In other words, they could
ask that a jury of twelve substantial freeholders hear the evidence and
decide whether the race had in fact been fairly run. If the sums involved
were high enough, either party could appeal a local decision to the colony's general court, a body consisting of the governor and his council.
Several men who hotly insisted that they had been wronged followed
this path. For example, Joseph Humphrey, loser in a race for 1500
pounds of tobacco, stamped out of a Northumberland County court,
demanding a stop to "farther proceedings in the Common Law till a
hearing in Chancery."[66] Since most of the General Court records for

the seventeenth century were destroyed during the Civil War, it is impossible to follow these cases beyond the county level. It is apparent
from the existing documents, however, that all the men involved in
these race controversies took their responsibilities seriously, and there is
no indication that the gentry regarded the resolution of a gambling
dispute as less important than proving a will or punishing a criminal.[67]
It seems unlikely that the colony's courts would have adopted such an
indulgent attitude toward racing had these contests not in some way
served a significant social function for the gentry.

IV

Competitive activities such as quarter-horse racing served social as well
as symbolic functions. As we have seen, gambling reflected core elements of the culture of late seventeenth-century Virginia. Indeed, if it
had not done so, horse racing would not have become so popular
among the colony's gentlemen. These contests also helped the gentry to
maintain group cohesion during a period of rapid social change. After
1680 the great planters do not appear to have become significantly less
competitive, less individualistic, or less materialistic than their predecessors had been.[68] But while the values persisted, the forms in which they
were expressed changed. During the last decades of the century unprecedented external pressures, both political and economic, coupled with a
major shift in the composition of the colony's labor force, caused the
Virginia gentry to communicate these values in ways that would not
lead to deadly physical violence or spark an eruption of blood feuding.
The members of the native-born elite, anxious to preserve their autonomy over local affairs, sought to avoid the kinds of divisions within
their ranks that had contributed to the outbreak of Bacon's Rebellion.
They found it increasingly necessary to cooperate against meddling
royal governors. Moreover, such earlier unrest among the colony's plantation workers as Bacon's Rebellion and the plant-cutting riots had
impressed upon the great planters the need to present a common face to
their dependent laborers, especially to the growing number of black
slaves who seemed more and more menacing as the years passed.

Gaming relationships were one of several ways by which the planters,
no doubt unconsciously, preserved class cohesion.[69] By wagering on
cards and horses they openly expressed their extreme competitiveness,

winning temporary emblematic victories over their rivals without thereby threatening the social tranquility of Virginia. These non-lethal competitive devices, similar in form to what social anthropologists have termed "joking relationships," were a kind of functional alliance developed by the participants themselves to reduce dangerous, but often inevitable, social tensions.[70]

Without rigid social stratification racing would have lost much of its significance for the gentry. Participation in these contests publicly identified a person as a member of an elite group. Great planters raced against their social peers. They certainly had no interest in competing with social inferiors, for in this kind of relationship victory carried no positive meaning: the winner gained neither honor nor respect. By the same token, defeat by someone like James Bullocke, the tailor from York, was painful, and to avoid such incidents gentlemen rarely allowed poorer whites to enter their gaming relationships—particularly the heavy betting on quarter horses. The common planters certainly gambled among themselves. Even the slaves may have laid wagers. But when the gentry competed for high stakes, they kept their inferiors at a distance, as spectators but never players.

The exclusiveness of horse racing strengthened the gentry's cultural dominance. By promoting these public displays the great planters legitimized the cultural values which racing symbolized—materialism, individualism, and competitiveness. These colorful, exclusive contests helped persuade subordinate white groups that gentry culture was desirable, something worth emulating; and it is not surprising that people who conceded the superiority of this culture readily accepted the gentry's right to rule. The wild sprint down a dirt track served the interests of Virginia's gentlemen better than they imagined.

IX

Of Time and Nature: A Study of Persistent Values in Colonial Virginia

WHILE READING THE major writers of colonial Virginia—John Smith, Robert Beverley, William Byrd, and Thomas Jefferson—I was struck by similarities in the structure of their ideas. Despite changes that had occurred in the colony, each man asked his audience essentially the same question. Why had Virginians—men and women blessed with such a marvelous environment—not made better progress in creating a proper society? This query forced Virginians to review their own past, and what they saw disturbed them greatly. People had abused nature, taken its bounty for granted. It was clearly time for a new start. With different values, Virginians could in a very short time correct their mistakes. The message seldom varied, the same diagnosis, the same prescription, all of which suggested that the founders' value system persisted much longer than Early American historians have thought.

I

If one were to ask where to start a history of colonial Virginia, the answer would appear self-evident: begin at the beginning. In the case of Virginia, however, such common-sense advice provides little assistance, since it begs the question: which beginning? And to this query, there are numerous plausible responses. People have argued that the colony's development commenced with Sir Walter Raleigh's lost expedition at Roanoke, with the settlement of Jamestown in 1607, with the creation of the House of Burgesses, with the Indian Massacre of 1622, with the establishment of a royal colony out of the financial ruins of the Virginia Company, with the arrival of ambitious young men at mid-century bearing surnames that would later become synonymous with the Virginia gentry, with Bacon's Rebellion, with the dramatic shift after 1680 from a labor force consisting largely of white indentured servants to one that was predominantly black and enslaved, with the establishment of a native-born elite, or with a period of peace and prosperity in the eighteenth century known as Virginia's golden age. Some historians, I suspect, would just as soon forget the entire colonial experience and commence the story of Virginia with the achievements of George Washington and Thomas Jefferson.

It appears from this list that one starting point is as valid as any other. The history of Virginia, in fact, is analogous to the severed rattlesnake that became a popular symbol during the American Revolution. Somehow the pieces fit together, forming a healthy reptile, or in this case, a coherent history, but efforts to join the parts have been singularly unsuccessful. Discontinuities punctuate the colony's development. Each generation of Virginians seems to have started anew, paying little attention to what had preceded it, and the world of Captain John Smith appears to bear only a tenuous connection to that of William Byrd II, let alone that of Thomas Jefferson.

The history of colonial Massachusetts contrasts strikingly with that of Virginia.[1] As everyone knows, the Bay Colony began with the arrival of Governor John Winthrop and thousands of Puritan migrants. To suggest alternative starting points seems ridiculous, for such a claim contravenes not only what the colonists said about their own origins, but also what recent scholars have written. Historians from Cotton Mather to Perry Miller have assumed that the first Bay settlers planted ideas and institutions that persisted over time. Massachusetts society changed between Winthrop's death and the American Revolution, to be sure, but the colony's development involved no sharp breaks with the past, at least none of which contemporaries were aware. They took for granted a rich local heritage that originated with the founding generation.[2]

One could offer many examples of the Bay colonists' sense of a coherent history, but one will suffice. In 1786 John Adams was asked how

Virginia might be transformed into a New England. Adams's formula was simple enough. The southern colonists should establish town meetings, military training days, local schools, and village churches. He believed that the "Meeting house, the School house and Training Field are the Sceanes where New England men were formed." Like so many historians of the Bay Colony, Adams found it impossible to discuss these institutions without reflecting on their past. "Can it now be ascertained," he mused, "whether Norton, Cotton, Wilson, Winthrop, Winslow, Saltonstall, or who, was the Author of the Plan of Town Schools, Townships, Militia Laws, Meeting houses and Ministers &c?"[3] The question was rhetorical. What was significant was the undoubted link between past and present, the continuity over almost two centuries.

A comparison of our perception of the histories of these two colonies is instructive on another level. When historians of Massachusetts write of continuities, they refer for the most part to a persistent local culture, an enduring bundle of ideas, norms, and attitudes that supposedly shaped patterns of public behavior not only in Winthrop's time but in Cotton Mather's and Jonathan Edwards's as well. Of course, the Bay Colony experienced a number of Indian attacks and political disruptions, but no one seriously contends that these events—King Philip's War or the Glorious Revolution for example—destroyed the colony's cultural coherence. Tradition was woven into the fabric of daily life, providing members of this society with a strong sense of identity and purpose. It is no longer fashionable to refer to this persistent mental structure as "the New England Mind," but whatever we call these particular ideas and values, they remain crucial to an understanding of the history of colonial New England.[4]

Efforts to provide colonial Virginians with a "mind" of their own have met with limited success. Certainly, no one has discerned a persistent set of deep values, nothing at any rate capable of giving coherence to the colony's cultural development. Some enterprising historians attempted to transform planters into Puritans, arguing that, appearances to the contrary not withstanding, Virginians and New Englanders were Calvinists. Virginians marched to the same drummer that set the pace for Winthrop and his friends. While this interpretation possesses a certain plausibility, it fails to explain obvious cultural differences between the two regions. The claim that the Puritan Ethic had taken root in colonial Virginia prompted C. Vann Woodward, a southerner as well as a historian, to observe, "One cannot help wondering at times how some of those Southern mavericks, sinners that they were, might have reacted to being branded with the Puritan iron. It might have brought out the recalcitrance, or laziness, or orneriness in them—or whatever it was that was Southern and not Puritan."[5]

Other scholars, perhaps uneasy about the taint of Puritanism and defensive about the apparent lack of intellectual activities in pre-Revolutionary Virginia, praised the planters for reproducing a genteel English culture in the New World.[6] There are several problems with this interpretation, not the least of which is that it leaves Virginia culture with virtually no structure of its own. From this perspective, it was merely a chameleon-like reflection of British taste and behavior, and one suspects that while some leading members of the gentry were inordinately fond of English ways, Virginians developed values that set them apart from their counterparts in the mother country.

A third approach perceives Virginia culture as a potpourri of pragmatism and hedonism, an extended celebration of the good life in which horse flesh and Bumbo swilling were as significant as theological abstractions. The Virginians galloped about the countryside, while New England Puritans worried about predestination. The shallowness of this view should be obvious. Virginia culture involved more than transient pleasure-seeking. None of these three interpretations, in fact, offers substantial insight in developing a sophisticated comprehension of Virginia's colonial culture, and it is not surprising that university libraries are filled with monographs exploring every aspect of New England thought, while Virginia studies have languished.

Perceptions of Virginia's culture and history are not unrelated. The discontinuities in the colony's development were a function of its apparent inability to produce a persistent value system. If one established the existence of an indigenous *mentalité*, a coherent set of ideas and attitudes that shaped the way Virginians regarded themselves within a particular social and physical environment, then one might discover that the sharp breaks in the colony's history were in fact recurrent expressions of a deeply-rooted mental structure. The nature of the problem must be precisely stated. We are not concerned solely with the colonists' formal intellectual life, with the books they read, the colleges they attended, the poets they knew and the like. Our goal is broader. We are attempting to reconstruct as best we can specific core values that actually shaped social behavior. The fit between values and behavior, of course, is never neat; everyone can think of an exception to a particular generalization. Nevertheless, insights into a *mentalité* help us to see parallels between quite different kinds of activities, between economic calculations and leisure habits, between political decisions and religious custom.

One window into the colonists' mental structure—though certainly not the only one—is time. We are not dealing specifically with the small segments of time that divide our days either into units of work or leisure, nor are we discussing time as a cosmic abstraction, a linear or cyclical movement through eternity. Rather we are concerned more narrowly with man's perceptions—in this case the colonial Virginians' perceptions—of the limits that time places upon human actions. Our focus in this essay, therefore, is on what I shall call "temporal horizons."[7]

A temporal horizon affects the ways in which men and women interact with each other and with the environment in which they find themselves. Horizons vary from society to society; they change within a single society over the course of centuries. In some groups the past is such a burden, the present generation so encumbered with binding customs, traditions, and precedents, that the present involves only the maintenance of old ways, and for members of such societies the future represents simply a continuation of established patterns. For other groups, man's temporal field is circumscribed by a continuing present in which neither the future nor the past have significant motivational impact upon day-to-day activities. There is little to preserve and therefore no incentive to make firm plans for the distant future.[8] The essential point is that perceptions of the proper range of human action in time are cultural phenomena, and overly broad generalizations about the nature of time in pre-industrial societies miss subtle differences between contemporary subcultures. Neighboring agricultural societies like New England and Virginia, for example, developed separate and distinctive notions about temporal limits. The challenge for us is to discover how the members of specific societies sorted out "conceptions of the Past, the Present, and the Future."[9]

Colonial Virginians left us a remarkable record of their preferential ordering of time. Almost without exception, the past for them possessed little interest. Indeed, those Virginians who bothered to write down their views revealed an extraordinarily impoverished sense of local tradition. What former generations achieved in the region generated neither

heroes nor myths, neither pride nor curiosity. The past in itself legiti-
mated no particular course of action, nor for that matter did it validate a
continuing institutional structure.[10] Whenever possible Virginians focused their attentions on what they called the colony's "present state," a
dynamic present flowing continuously into a future that bore no necessary resemblance to the past.[11] This rejection—one is tempted to term it
a radical rejection—of local history would have received an un-
comprehending reception not only in colonial New England where
Puritans regarded the past as a golden age of piety and the future as an
opportunity to restore the religiosity of former times, but also in the
nineteenth-century South with its burden of frustration, failure, and
defeat. Certainly, the characters of post-Civil War Southern novels who
searched for what Woodward calls "the past in the present" would have
questioned the judgment of someone who declared, "I like dreams of
the future better than the history of the past." Imagine their surprise on
discovering that this particular dreamer was Thomas Jefferson, who
among other things was a Southerner.[12]

The colonial Virginians' contempt for their own past betrayed a great
deal about a persistent turn of mind. The recurrent escape from local
history was an aspect of the colonists' sense of self in time, a self constantly interacting with what the Virginians themselves regarded as an
unusually rich agricultural environment. Nature itself became a symbol
of futurity. And in part because the rich soil and warm climate seemed
so supportive of human endeavors, Virginians assumed that they could
start anew at any point, that their actions could overcome previous error
no matter how embarrassing it might have become, that by rational
calculations they could force nature to yield up the treasure that they
knew was there, and that the proper goal of these efforts and reforms
was general prosperity, not in some distant time or for children yet un-
born, but for the present generation. In Virginia everyone could start
again; the past could never become a burden so long as nature's bounty
sustained future dreams. This complex bundle of assumptions about
man-in-nature shaped Jefferson's perceptions of time as powerfully as it
did Captain Smith's. The apparent discontinuities in Virginia history
were in some measure a reflection of a deeply rooted, indigenous *mentalité* that stressed innovation over tradition.

The relation between behavior, environment, and values is obviously
of critical importance to the interpretation being advanced here.
Virginia's natural abundance reinforced certain values, lending credibil-

ity to the nation that man could escape the past. But values were not merely dependent variables. Because they affected the way an individual perceived his or her range of choices at any given time, they possessed what one anthropologist termed "singular sociological consequence."[13] The particular mental structure that evolved in Virginia placed narrow limits on the colonists' temporal horizon. If one were going to achieve wealth, one had to do it quickly, probably within a very short span of years.

As a consequence of this temporal limitation, Virginians frequently demanded instant returns on physical and monetary investment, and perhaps because of this outlook, their economic activities sometimes appeared not only ill-conceived but also frenetic. The founders, for example, looked for gold and passages to China, but when tobacco promised sudden riches, they exploited that staple for all it was worth, assuring each other that the boom would last forever. Later Virginians advocated a silk industry, iron manufacturing, towns filled with artisans, just to name a few, and if these overly ambitious schemes failed to achieve the intended results, they at least help us to understand why the colonial Virginian so often appears to have been something of a hustler.[14] Despite past setbacks, he remained confident that a fresh plan would generate the big pay-off. And in politics, especially during the Revolutionary years, the rejection of the past coupled with a deep-seated belief in man's ability to reshape his environment may have made it easier for Jefferson and his contemporaries to contemplate major alterations in the laws governing land tenure and established religion.

A word is required about the sources employed in this study. We shall analyze the writings of major planters such as Robert Beverley, William Byrd II, William Fitzhugh, and Thomas Jefferson. These men were hardly the common folk of colonial Virginia. Although we would like to possess other sustained insights into the *mentalité* of white Virginians, few exist, and we are necessarily compelled to rely on the material that has survived.[15]

II

During the last decades of the sixteenth century, energetic propagandists such as Richard Hakluyt the younger convinced an English reading public that Virginia could produce great wealth. Hakluyt's enthusiasm for the "Western Planting" was contagious, especially for Englishmen who coveted the fabulous treasure that Spaniards supposedly carted back from the New World. According to Hakluyt, lucky Virginia adventurers might come across a short route to the Orient. Others would certainly discover exotic crops and scarce metals. Enterprising persons who seized this opportunity would find "wine, oiles, oranges, lymons, figges &c. . . . all which moche more is hoped."[16] Hakluyt made the process of tapping America's natural abundance sound so easy. And there was the rub. The sole responsibility for success or failure in Hakluyt's Virginia lay with the colonists. If they planned carefully and financed the project fully, then they would realize their dreams in a very short time. If they stumbled in paradise, however, they would have only themselves to blame.

By the time James replaced Elizabeth as England's monarch, Virginia had become synonymous with extraordinary natural abundance. The popular London play "Eastward Hoe" (1605) depicted the region as a paradise that would make even a Spaniard jealous. One character, Captain Seagull, asserted, "I tell thee, golde is more plentifull there then copper is with us." The Captain claimed on the basis of allegedly firsthand intelligence that whenever the natives of Virginia desired rubies and diamonds, "they goe forth on holydayes and gather 'hem by the sea-shore."[17] People in the audience recognized the exaggerated aspects of Seagull's report. Nevertheless, inclusion of such fanciful material by successful playwrights reveals the currency of rumors about Virginia's bounty. The Virginia Company never guaranteed its subscribers rubies by the cupful, but the author of one promotional tract assured men and women interested in moving to Virginia that "the place will make them rich."[18]

Inflated expectations led to frustration. No sooner had settlers landed in Jamestown than they engaged in pathological activities that made it virtually impossible for anyone to become rich. The miseries of these early adventurers have been recounted many times, and their unhappy tale does not need repeating. What is remarkable from our perspective is that despite the colonists' bitter disappointments, few persons in England or America questioned Virginia's natural fecundity. In 1610 one man boasted that the region was "One of the goodliest countries under the sunne," and he asked in words that would be echoed in the writings of later Virginians, "Why should not the rich harvest of our hopes be seasonably expected?"[19]

Why indeed? The answer was painfully obvious to persons who thought themselves knowledgeable about Virginia affairs. Had healthy, honest adventurers been dispatched to Jamestown instead of irresponsible idlers, the colony's short existence would have been much happier. As Robert Johnson explained in 1612, the enterprise began well enough, but "numbers of irregular persons" undermined well-conceived plans. In a short time, ambition, sloth, and greed made a fatal appearance, and although these vices brought the colony to the verge of extinction, Johnson confidently proclaimed "the New Life of Virginea." An adjustment in the Company's recruitment policies would erase previous errors. The immediate future looked bright, after all "Nature hath already seated there, the soile and climate . . . for the use of mankind and trade of merchandise."[20] Even at this early point in Virginia's development, men were already bent upon escaping the past.

Judging from Captain John Smith's account of Virginia published in 1624, Johnson's optimism appears to have been premature. Smith, of course, generated controversy not only as the colony's leader but also as its historian. Some readers found the Captain's expansive ego offensive; others questioned his veracity. While recent scholarship has not made a case for Smith's humility, it has sustained the accuracy of his observations.[21] Thomas Jefferson certainly would have agreed with this assessment. He concluded from his own research into Virginia history that Smith was "honest, sensible, and well informed," but Jefferson quickly added that the Captain's "style is barbarous and uncouth."[22] Smith never attained the legendary status accorded to William Bradford and John Winthrop, and for that failure, Smith probably has Virginia's ignoble early history to blame. It simply was not a place that produced heroes.

Smith provided a thorough analysis of the experiences of the early adventurers. Theirs was not an attractive tale, as Smith knew all too well, but he insisted that unless one carefully examined the history of the settlement, one could not understand why Virginians had repeatedly failed to create a prosperous, cohesive society. "It might well be thought," he wrote in his *Generall Historie* (1624), "a Countrie so faire (as *Virginia* is) . . . would long ere this have beene quietly possessed, to the satisfaction of the adventurers, and the eternizing of the memory of those that effected it." Smith promised to answer the question no doubt on the minds of everyone associated with the venture: how did it come "to

passe [that] there was no better speed and successe in those proceedings?" [23]

Despite his personal involvement in Virginia affairs, Smith apparently tried to be objective. He recounted the difficulties that had
confronted the first colonists: a powerful and hostile Indian confederation, a poorly selected site for Jamestown, and an unreliable food supply
from the Virginia Company in London. Ultimately, however, Smith
condemned the colonists themselves for Virginia's brief but troubled
history. They had been too greedy, too lazy, too short-sighted to establish the kind of society that he for one believed should have been
created. And because the values of the settlers had not changed significantly after 1610, Virginia's economy had stagnated. In fact, it produced little of worth except "private mens [sic] Tobacco, and faire
promises." [24] Smith looked to the future, to a new beginning that would
enable men to transform fair promises into tangible success.

Like his predecessors, Smith assumed that the Lord had blessed
Virginia with unusual natural abundance. However unpolished the
Captain's style may have appeared to Jefferson, Smith possessed an eye
for beauty. His *Historie* contained lyrical descriptions of the colony's
edenic qualities. "The mildnesse of the ayre, the fertilitie of the soyle,
and the situation of the rivers are so propitious to the nature and use of
man," he declared, "as no place is more convenient for pleasure, profit,
and mans sustenance." In another passage, he marvelled that "heaven
and earth never agreed better to frame a place for mans habitation." [25]
Smith's high opinion of Virginia was the product of observation, and
his readers must have believed that he knew what he was writing about.
Be that as it may, his vision of the colony's rich potential was not strikingly different from that of Richard Hakluyt, a man who never ventured
west of England. Smith held out the same assurance of instant prosperity that had originally drawn adventurers to Jamestown, and it never occurred to him that his seductive prose might spawn a new generation of
idle, selfish trouble-makers.

A few, relatively minor adjustments in the governance of Virginia
would set the colony on a proper course and preserve it from a recur-
rence of past miseries, at least that was what Smith claimed. If English
authorities sent better settlers to America, raised the price of corn and
thus discouraged the cultivation of tobacco, appointed less mercenary
governors, and funded an army to clear the frontier of Indians, then

Virginia would begin to produce the bounty that had so long been anticipated. Smith modestly nominated himself to lead the military expedition, and while his self-promotion was heavy-handed, it revealed his convictions that Virginia was at a turning point. In a few years, everyone would forget about the past, and quite predictably he wanted to play a major role in any effort that would bring glory to the king, the colonists, and of course Captain Smith.[26]

By the late 1630s Virginia's survival was no longer in doubt. Despite significant gains, however, George Donne found no evidence of new life in the colony. In fact, the famous poet's second son—a royal officeholder in Virginia—angrily denounced the Virginians in 1638 for their failure to develop the region's full economic potential. After his return to England, Donne presented Charles I with a rambling essay entitled "Virginia Reviewed." In this piece he observed in language similar to Smith's, "Strannge it may appeare to all Men[,] to some wonderfull, That in A country soe long by the English possessed, there should bee now but a beginning for a setled Government."[27]

The sources of the colony's chronic problems were clear to Donne, and he ticked off no less than two dozen specific errors that his predecessors had made. He accused them of ignorance, negligence, cruelty, riot, sloth, and a host of other equally unattractive practices. He even upbraided them for treachery in dealing with the natives, a charge that would have surprised Smith and a good many planters who thought the Indians had a monopoly on duplicity. From Donne's perspective, the efforts of a quarter century had come to nothing. Not even the dissolution of the Virginia Company in 1624 and the establishment of a royal government in the colony had made a significant impact. According to the essayist, these events had not diminished the colonists' fierce avarice. He reported that "till of very late daies every mans owne particular profitt hath bene more earnestly pursued then the comodity [profit] of the Country it selfe."[28]

But like Smith, Donne believed that Virginia was about to turn the corner. Descriptions of the colony's extraordinary resources apparently had become so commonplace in London by the late 1630s that Donne was reluctant to spend his time recounting the region's natural abundance. "It is not anye of myne," he told the king, "after soe manye Printed Intelligences to reiterate the generall and particular comodities and profitts of this land, the quallities of the Ayre[,] the fertility of the Soyle, the abundance of the Sea and Rivers." The primary goal of the essay was to convince Charles that Virginia would become a truly bountiful paradise as soon as a better class of person settled there. No more "ragges and Scumme" need be sent. Indeed, Donne advocated a radical change in policy, a root-and-branch approach, for even a few disruptive, idle individuals might upset the entire venture. Although Donne did not use the word, the problem in Virginia was socialization. He warned, "The disposition, the habitt of Myndes and Manners corruptlie affected not onelie distill into the race issueing from them, but are taught to immitate the like, and are alike instructed by them in every probabillitye." A fresh start depended upon "Men of understanding and honestye," upon less "greedie" persons.[29] We shall never know what the Virginians of this period thought of Donne's specific charges, for even if they despised the man, they did not bother to publish a different, more flattering version of the colony's past. They too looked to the future.

The passage of time neither dulled enthusiasm for Virginia's natural abundance nor moderated contempt for its past. At midcentury a group of pamphlets appeared in London reaffirming the colony's immense economic potential. One anonymous writer who provided his readers with "a full and true Relation of the present State of the Plantation" bragged of the "fat rich Soile" waiting for skilled cultivators. "The land in *Virginia*," he explained, "is most fruitfull, and produceth with very great increase, whatsoever is committed into the Bowels of it, Planted, Sowed."[30] In another piece attributed only to "E. W. Gent.," the author asserted that anyone who questioned Virginia's fecundity was clearly "distrustfull of God's providence." To be sure, the Colony's past represented a chronicle of misery. The Indians—apparently not the ones that Donne had seen—treacherously crushed the early settlements, but by 1650 Virginia "hath raised her dejected head."[31] William Bullock called for a new system of governance, new crops, and a new settlement pattern to speed the recovery. Had Virginians built their homes closer together and concentrated their attentions on something other than tobacco, "they might have been in this time a great and flourishing people."[32]

In 1656 John Hammond, a tobacco planter, produced a small guide for English people interested in moving to the Chesapeake. At the beginning of his pamphlet entitled *Leah and Rachell, or the two fruitfull Sisters, Virginia and Mary-Land: Their Present Condition, Impartially Stated and Related*, he promised to be objective. Unlike other writers, Hammond denied any intention to describe Virginia as a New World paradise. The colony had faults, and an honest reporter had to lay "down the former state of *Virginia*, in its Infancy and filth." Anyone who knew anything about the colony's history realized that during the first decades of settlement, the region had attracted an unusually large number of "Rogues, whores, and desolute and rooking persons." The "avarice and inhumanity" of these coupled with persistent rumors of the intolerable labor demanded in the Chesapeake colonies gave the "Sisters" a bad name. [33]

Unfortunately, these stories possessed a foundation in fact. According to Hammond, "At the first settling and many years after, it [Virginia] deserved most of those aspersions (nor were they then aspersions but truths)." The embarrassments were not confined to the earliest years. As recently as 1644 the Indians had massacred Chesapeake planters. While Hammond noted that some "honest and vertuous inhabitants" could be found in the colony, he treated its history as a tale of scandal, and in this respect his candor hardly set him apart from other people who had written about Virginia. One can almost hear Hammond's sigh of relief when he at last arrived at his "main subject," the colony's "present Condition and Happiness." The two fruitful sisters, he assured his readers, were capable of exporting a broad range of lucrative crops; indeed, the area "is become a place of pleasure and plenty." [34] Half a century after Smith's *Generall Historie* was published, Hammond's Virginia was about to overcome its sordid past. The people would soon form a prosperous, cohesive community.

Lionel Gatford, an English merchant familiar with Chesapeake affairs, contributed another essay to the growing literature on Virginia's "Present Sad State." While Gatford admitted in his *Publick Good Without Private Interest* (1657) that he had not visited the New World, he explained how he had diligently collected reports about Virginia and therefore felt qualified to discuss its past as well as its future. However he may have gathered his information, he produced an argument remarkably similar to that of persons who had actually lived in America. Gatford stated his opinions with surprising vehemence. He declared in no uncertain terms that Virginia had brought "shame and dishonour" upon England. It seemed obvious that "a Colonie, Planted in such a Country 60 yeares since or more, and that by Christians, and those of the same Nation and Profession of faith with us" should have achieved better results. Failure was one thing, but failure by English Protestants was unacceptable.

Gatford recounted the many "Errors, miscarriages, & crimes" that Virginians had committed over the years. His list rivaled Donne's. No one escaped criticism; magistrates and merchants, planters and preachers, none of these self-seeking people accomplished anything of merit. The settlers even drank too much. As a result of this unhappy legacy, Virginia was now in his words about "to give up the Ghost." The only hope at this point was to take advantage of the colony's impressive natural resources. As one might expect, Gatford had a plan. Recruit honest workers, trained ministers, and skilled rulers, place these people in towns instead of allowing them to disperse over the countryside, and the future might not turn out so badly after all.[35]

The assumption running through Gatford's analysis as well as Hammond's and Donne's was that newcomers to Virginia could successfully tap the colony's economic potential, that they could in fact obtain prosperity within their own lifetime, without repeating the mistakes of the past. For half a century the colonists had located where they pleased, fought the Indians when it was convenient to do so, cultivated tobacco to their heart's content, and resisted the blandishments of London investors and royal governors to change their ways. In large measure, therefore, their aggressive attempts to realize Virginia's full promise for the present generation accounted for their "Errors, miscarriages, & crimes," for if everyone worked for one's "Private Interest," no one sacrificed for the "Publick Good." Certainly, if immediate gain was the goal of human activity, then long-term projects like the construction of towns possessed little popular appeal.[36]

Few Virginians—and this includes Thomas Jefferson—worked as energetically as did Governor William Berkeley to liberate the colonists from their own past. This talented man who dominated Virginia political life for more than three decades dreamed of launching the colony on a fresh start. Moreover, because of his broad experience and powerful contacts, he was in a remarkably strong position to bring it about. Berkeley not only was popular in Virginia, he also understood the intricacies of imperial affairs. With the Restoration of Charles II in 1660, the governor lobbied for changes in England's colonial policy, especially in manners affecting American commerce.[37] Yet, while Berkeley confronted an unprecedented set of economic problems, he viewed the colony's past, its resources, and its immediate future from a cultural perspective that placed him in a tradition dating back to Captain John Smith's time.

In 1663 Berkeley published a short essay, A *Discourse and View of Virginia*, designed to convince English leaders of the colony's crucial importance within an expanding mercantile system. The governor reminded his readers of Virginia's great natural advantages, and this observation compelled him to ask several difficult, though predictable questions: why if the colony enjoyed such a full measure of the Lord's blessings had its inhabitants failed to develop them? Why had it taken the planters so long to see these opportunities?

Berkeley's response was imaginative. In a remarkable piece of casuistry he simply lopped off the earliest years of Virginia history, claiming that one could not legitimately consider them part of the colony's permanent development. The first settlers arrived in 1607, but they met with such "insuperable difficulties" that they made virtually no progress toward the establishment of a flourishing plantation. Berkeley was even reluctant to begin the colony's story in the 1620s, "for many years after this, the danger and scarcity of the Inhabitants was so famed through *England*, that none but such as were forced could be induced to plant or defend the place." Indeed, of those poor souls who did migrate to the New World, thirty out of every thirty-one were men, and as Berkeley noted with mock seriousness, "*Populus virorum* is of no long duration any where." Conditions in Virginia improved sometime in the 1630s. Thus, contrary to what some persons believed, Virginia was not sixty years old. The actual figure was more like twenty, and it seemed churlish to fault the colonists for having accomplished so little in such a short period.

Berkeley admitted the existence of genuine problems in Virginia. The quality of its servants, for example, left a good deal to be desired. The concentration on tobacco weakened the economy. Like many other colonial Virginians, Berkeley detested this staple. He declared that during the colony's early history, "our Governours by reason of the corruption of those times they lived in, laid the Foundation of our wealth and industry on the vices of men; for about the time of our first seating of the Country, did this vicious habit of taking *Tobacco* possesse the English Nation." The governor saw no reason to saddle the present generation with past mistakes. The region could easily produce other, more useful goods: silk, flax, hemp, tar, pitch, iron, masts, timber, and potash. These exports would free England from a dependence upon commercial rivals, but more important, they would invigorate Chesapeake society. What made Berkeley's plan particularly appealing was his assurance that the transition from Tobacco to other commodities would take only seven years. Almost everyone involved in this experiment would be around to enjoy the profits.[38]

The careers of William Fitzhugh and other late-seventeenth-century planters provide eloquent testimony to Berkeley's inability to cure Virginia of the tobacco habit. These men succeeded where others had failed, and although their estates were modest by the standards of Robert "King" Carter and William Byrd II, Fitzhugh's contemporaries built what they called "great" houses, placed impressive bets on the quarter horses, and conducted themselves in public with as much ceremony as their income would allow. Fitzhugh is particularly interesting for our study not only because he was an articulate planter, but also because he wrote a "History of Virginia." His views about time and nature allow us to examine the Virginia *mentalité* during a period of far-reaching social change. Following Bacon's Rebellion a group of powerful local families—the Carters, Byrds, Beverleys, and Wormeleys, just to name a few—consolidated its dominance over Virginia's political and economic life. Improvements in the colony's mortality meant that members of these families lived longer than had earlier migrants. In fact, it was during these years that native-born planters began to outnumber immigrants in the House of Burgesses and other high ruling councils. But the most significant change at the end of the century was the transformation of the colony's labor force from one composed largely of white indentured servants to one that was black and enslaved.[39] Although these demographic shifts profoundly altered the social structure, they did not noticeably affect the way colonists perceived of their place in time and nature.

Actually, no copy of Fitzhugh's work survived the colonial period. What we know of his study, we learn through his letters. In 1687 Fitzhugh explained to his English correspondent Nicholas Hayward that "I have had it in my thoughts to write a small treatise, or History of Virginia." But as Fitzhugh's prospectus made clear, he was not even curious about the colony's past. He went Berkeley one better and ignored his predecessors altogether. This planter proposed describing Virginia's "Scituation, Temperature, & fertility, nature of its present inhabitants, with their method & manner of living, the plenty of Iron Mines, almost everywhere in the Country, & probable conjectures of the Discovery of others." The "History" would inform readers about "the easie & profitable living" available in Virginia as well as the "easie & even Government." If Fitzhugh's book sounds more like a promotional tract than a formal study of the past, that is exactly what he intended. The purpose of setting down his impressions was "the persuading Inhabitants hither." Fitzhugh perceived of the colony's development in personal terms. Indeed, his vision of the future apparently extended little further than the sale of his own western lands to eager new colonists.[40]

Fitzhugh's apparent apathy about Virginia's past raises an important question: was the attitude of Fitzhugh and his contemporaries toward time a function of their inability to obtain sources of historical information or was it rather an expression of a mental structure in which the future ranked higher than the past? Certainly, a colonist in the late seventeenth century who took an interest in Virginia history would have found it difficult to construct an accurate account of events between the founding of Jamestown and the Glorious Revolution. Virginia possessed no professional group comparable to the Congregational ministers of New England who maintained an ongoing chronicle of provincial affairs. The Anglican church in Virginia was weak, so too was the colony's educational system. Even if a significant number of adults acquired minimal literacy—an unlikely proposition—there was no local press to produce items for them to read. Governor Berkeley actively discouraged printing, and in 1671 he informed the Lords Commissioners of Foreign Plantations, "I thank God, there *are no free schools* nor *printing,* and I hope we shall not have [either for a] hundred years; for *learning* has brought disobedience, and heresy, and sects into the world, and *printing* has devulged them."[41] In 1682 another royal governor, Lord Thomas Culpeper, prohibited printing "anything" in Virginia until the king's pleasure be known, and it was not until 1733 that a printer established a regular business in Williamsburg.[42]

To make matters worse for the rare Virginian with an historical turn of mind, documents concerning past events were often lost or misfiled. The House of Burgesses complained before the end of the seventeenth century that its records were in such disarray that lawmakers could not even ascertain which statutes were still in force. By 1747 the situation had not significantly improved. William Stith, a minister who attempted to write a history of the colony, grumbled that many records pertaining to the early development of Virginia had perished, "and those, which have survived the Flames and Injuries of Time, have been so carelessly kept, are so broken, interrupted, and deficient, have been so mangled by Moths and Worms, and lie in such a confused and jumbled State" as to be virtually useless.[43]

But the lack of historical sources does not explain the widespread lack of interest in Virginia history. In peasant societies throughout the world the absence of written evidence helps to sustain elaborate myths about the past. They are handed down from generation to generation through face-to-face contacts, each teller modifying or embellishing the story to fit changing social conditions. Virginia was in part an oral society.[44] Many colonial "paisans"—as one French visitor called them—were untouched by the written or printed word. When a traveler asked people about Virginia's past, he perceived a weakly developed sense of local tradition. The colonists not only confused basic chronology, they also possessed no heroes whose past deeds might have impressed a curious outsider. The Huguenot Durand of Dauphiné learned only that "Maryland was discovered before Virginia, in the reign of Queen Mary . . . [and] Virginia was discovered sometime later, under Queen Elizabeth, & is called Virginia for this Queen who never married."[45] A few years later, Francis Louis Michel, another French-speaking visitor, inquired about the history of Virginia, and the account he received was no more accurate or complex than the one recorded by Durand.[46] Both men, however, included in their journals long, glowing descriptions of the colony's natural abundance. They adopted, in effect, the temporal horizons of their hosts. The colony's immediate future was filled with such rich opportunities that the past became irrelevant.

In 1697 three Virginia residents, Henry Hartwell, James Blair, and Edward Chilton, collaborated on a small book entitled *The Present State of Virginia and the College*. Of this group, Blair was the most prominent and probably wrote a lion's share of the manuscript. This testy Scottish minister became president of the College of William and Mary and a major force in Virginia political life. As several royal governors learned, Blair was a man of strong opinions, and he never backed away from a fight. *The Present State* reflected the contentious atmosphere that surrounded the college in its early days. Beyond the immediate battles between the president and his enemies, the book also tells us a good deal about persistent values in Virginia. In many significant ways, the structure of the argument paralleled that of other works we have already examined.

The three authors presented their readers with a puzzle. How was it that Virginia was at once the best and worst place in the world? The answer, of course, depended upon what aspects of the colony one examined. The soil and climate, the wondrous network of rivers and the vast stands of timber, these elements made Virginia a New World paradise. But the marvelous resources had not been developed. The colonists had abused their natural gifts through greed and mismanagement. As the writers explained, "For the most general true Character of *Virginia* is this, That as to all the Natural Advantages of a Country, it is one of the best, but as to the Improved Ones, one of the worst of all the *English* Plantations in *America*." Impartial observers at the turn of the century would have expected to find ports and markets, certainly well-established towns, but instead Virginia—and one suspects that Blair penned this section—"looks all like a wild Desart; the High-Lands overgrown with Trees, and the Low-Lands sunk with Water, Marsh, and Swamp: The few Plantations and clear'd Grounds bearing no Proportion to the rough and uncultivated." In fact, the authors concluded that the colony was "one of the poorest, miserablest, and worst Countries in all *America*, that is inhabited by Christians." Not only had generations of Virginians failed to exploit obvious economic opportunities, they also stood as a blot on Christian tradition.[47]

Blair and his friends generously gave the Virginians another chance. It was true that "the Obstinacy of the People" and the "narrow, selfish Ends of most of their Governors" had doomed long-range, expensive projects like the founding of market towns. Nevertheless, natural abundance could erase past errors, and the process of redemption need not take a long time. Rational planning would create a flourishing silk and iron industry; well-governed people would support the construction of villages. Everyone would prosper. "It is impossible," the authors claimed, "to reckon up all the Improvements which might be made in such a Country, where many useful Inventions would present themselves to the Industrious."[48] With a little luck and good governors, Blair's generation might witness the long awaited new beginning.

Francis Makemie agreed with Blair about the importance of towns. This Anglican minister published a short essay in 1705, A *Plain & Friendly Perswasive*, in which he described village life as a panacea for Virginia's many problems. Makemie's pamphlet reflected the tendency of colonists to reach out for instant solutions, to ignore inconvenient obstacles that hindered reform. But operating within narrow temporal horizons, men like Makemie were compelled to advocate plans that would benefit the present generation. Public policy designed for instant success was a little like placing an extravagant wager on a quarter-horse race: if the sprinter came home first, the planter won a bundle of money, but if the horse lost, the better seemed extraordinarily improvident. The comparison is not far-fetched. The great planters of Makemie's time raced their horses for very high stakes, and the minister may well have reasoned they would respond favorably to a long-shot on the future of Virginia.

Makemie found nothing in the colonists' past that merited praise. They had simply survived from year to year "with a kind of stupid satisfaction." The time had at last arrived, Makemie believed, for Virginians to throw off their bad habits. "After so long and unaccountable a neglect of our greatest Interest, for which the Eyes and Censures of the World have been upon you," they should now join together, "and look upon this as the happy Juncture and Period, for Commencing the Happiness of *Virginia*." Towns were the key to this renaissance. They would stimulate employment, education, and religion. With market centers, prices for imported goods would be lower and honesty more pervasive. Makemie insisted that Virginia possessed sufficient natural resources to put this plan into effect. "I dare assure you," he reminded his readers, "here is a Country Capable of a superlative Improvement, beyond many Countries in the World." A Virginia with towns would undoubtedly free itself from the "Scandalous Imputations" of the past.[49]

In 1705 Robert Beverley published a long essay similar to the one William Fitzhugh had proposed some years earlier. Beverley never saw the other man's work. The resemblance reflected common cultural roots, a shared set of assumptions about Virginia society. Both writers were successful planters; both speculated in western lands. But whereas Fitzhugh's manuscript was lost in London, Beverley's *History and Present State of Virginia* appeared as a handsome book, and the author's witty, sometimes sardonic style makes it as readable today as it was in the eighteenth century.[50]

Beverley possessed only marginal interest in the colony's past. In fact, the title of his book was quite misleading, for it contained merely a superficial account of Virginia history. For the most part, Beverley's examination of the events of the previous century appears to have depressed him. The period before 1675 received relatively scant attention. Like Captain John Smith from whom he liberally borrowed, Beverley held most of the founders in low regard. After listing the tragedies that had befallen the settlers during the first two decades, he decided that the leaders of the Virginia Company in London and the colonists in America brought these miseries upon themselves. Both groups succumbed to greed, constantly demanding instant returns when they should have laid the foundations of long-term prosperity. As Beverley explained, "the chief Design of all Parties concern'd was to fetch away the Treasure from thence, aiming more at sudden Gain, than to form a regular Colony."[51]

It is not clear from Beverley's account when if ever, Virginia acquired regular form. After the downfall of the Virginia Company, the colonists continued to make grave mistakes, and to compound their problems, the king sent to Virginia a series of corrupt, self-seeking governors. Beverley relished documenting the indiscretions of recent royal appointees, especially those of his *bête noire*, Governor Francis Nicholson. From Beverley's perspective, the past involved no more than a chronicle of disappointment and failure.[52] In such a story there were no genuine heroes, certainly no myths capable of providing the present generation with a compelling sense of common purpose.

Beverley took particular pains to dissociate himself from the colony's past. In the introduction to *The History and Present State*, he announced, "I am an *Indian*." This surprising self-identification was a more complex literary device than it may at first appear. Of course, he wanted to distinguish his writing style from that of contemporary English authors. Beverley depicted himself as an American, as an innocent from the New World, and as we all know, this particular self-image served provincials such as Benjamin Franklin quite well when they visited London. But for Beverley, the Indian was also a private symbol of Virginia's ignoble past. It was the Native Americans, not the Virginians, who possessed a coherent culture. As Beverley explained in a long anthropological section of his book, the Indians found social meaning within a web of traditions; they were products of history in a way that the planters had never been.[53] On quite another personal level, the Indian reminded Beverley of the colonists' errors. The settlers, for example, had stubbornly refused to intermarry with local tribes when such a decision might have speeded Virginia's economic development. In short, to be an Indian in 1705 was not to be a Virginian. By radically divorcing himself from the colony's past, Beverley could pose as an ideal architect for Virginia's new beginning.

In the second section of his book, Beverley moved from Virginia's history to its natural resources, and his spirits improved substantially. He concentrated on what he termed the colony's "Unimproved State Before the English Went Thither." Since at the time of Beverley's writing the English had lived in Virginia for a century, one may well wonder how he reconstructed the colony's original nature. The answer is that Beverley simply observed the world around him. Nothing had changed substantially since Captain John Smith's arrival; he emphatically found no evidence of "improvements."[54]

Even an undeveloped Virginia inspired intense admiration. It possessed boundless potential: the safest coast "in the universe," many "commodious" rivers, rich soils "fitted to every sort of plant," an "abundance" of indigenous fruits, luxurious vegetation, an amazing variety of fish as well as a "multitude" of wild fowl and game. "This and a great deal more," Beverley exclaimed, "was the natural production of that country, which the native Indians enjoyed without the course of industry." The colonists had taken paradise for granted. "Indeed," he argued, "all that the English have done since their going thither has been only to make some of these native pleasures more scarce by an inordinate and unseasonable use of them, hardly making improvements equivalent to that damage."[55]

Beverley was no more willing than previous writers had been to drum the Virginians out of Eden. The colonists faced a serious challenge, but if they met it constructively, paradise might be regained. First of all, they needed to realize that unimproved nature was a dangerous temptation, a serpent that had lured their predecessors into deadly economic sins. In the past, the "Liberality of Nature" dulled people's enthusiasm for hard labor. Beverley complained that colonists preferred to "Spunge upon the Blessings of a warm Sun, and a fruitful Soil, and almost grutch [begrudge] the Pains of gathering in the Bounties of the Earth." If Virginians wanted to escape the unpleasant legacy of their own past, however, and develop the natural resources that surrounded them, they had to be up and doing. Beverley intended to "rouse them out of their Lethargy, and [to] excite them to make the most out of those happy Advantages which Nature had given them."[56]

Other men had attempted to shame Virginians into reform with no discernible success. Beverley, however, was optimistic about the colony's immediate future. Surely, rational planters would come to understand the foolishness of relying upon tobacco, an unpredictable commodity, when they could easily switch to more reliable products such as flax, hemp, cotton, silk, wool, and naval stores, just to name a few items on Beverley's list. His book suggested that the transformation could take place immediately.[57] Virginia's next generation could harvest the colony's full bounty, and if foreigners who read this account wanted to participate in the new start, Beverley just happened to have some land of his own for sale.[58]

Hugh Jones tried his hand at depicting Virginia society in 1724. On the title page of his book *The Present State of Virginia*, Jones identified himself as the "Chaplain to the Honourable Assembly, and lately Minister to *James-town*, &c. in *Virginia*." The minister completed his manuscript at the height of Virginia's so-called Golden Age. Royal governors and ambitious planters had recently discovered that their interests were not as dissimilar as they may have appeared during the seventeenth century. Tobacco prices were on the rise. And yet, while Jones must have been conscious of these positive developments, he could muster no more enthusiasm for the colony's history than had Beverley and Fitzhugh. He compressed the story of the development of Virginia into four pages. Jones clearly did not bother himself with original research, and what little information he provided of the first two decades, he seems to have taken from Smith's account. The brevity of Jones's historical section reflected his conviction that nothing of importance had occurred in Virginia before the beginning of the eighteenth century. He observed in the introduction that "this Country is altered wonderfully, and far more advanced and improved in all Respects of late Years, since the beginning of Colonel *Spotswood's* Lieutenancy, than in the whole Century before his Government."[59]

The Reverend Jones anticipated that the colony's future would even be brighter. His mind hummed with various projects to improve Virginia, and for Jones improvement meant economic prosperity. He was so swept up in plans to develop Virginia's natural resources that he found it difficult to understand people whose perceptions of time and nature differed from his own. He was astounded, for example, to discover that the local Indians "have no Notion of providing for Futurity." The Native Americans ate "Night and Day" while the supply of food lasted, giving not the slightest thought to tomorrow's hunger. One wonders what the Indians would have thought of Jones's temporal horizons. His obsessive futurity would probably have seemed as alien to them as their recording time by the migrations of "wild Geese" appeared to Jones.[60]

With an eye cocked to the future, Jones packed *The Present State* with "Schemes and Propositions for the better Promotion of Learning, Religion, Invention, Manufactures, and Trade in *Virginia*." For him, the colony's resources were boundless. Without question Virginia equaled or surpassed England's other New World possessions "in Goodness of Climate, Soil, Health, Rivers, Plenty, and all Necessaries, and Conveniencies of Life." Sometimes the minister allowed fantasies to get the better of good sense. In fact, in some sections of the book he sounded suspiciously like Captain Seagull. That authority reported rubies by the cupful, but according to Jones, "In the Rocks up *James* River, as in other Places is a Stone resembling a Diamond. . . . [and] There has been formerly discovered a Sand taken for Gold Dust." If he had read Smith's history more carefully, Jones would have learned that Virginia had already endured one gold rush, and it is doubtful that the planters of the early eighteenth century wanted to repeat that experience.[61]

Jones believed that by recruiting a large new labor force the colony could reach its full potential. He was uneasy, however, about increasing the number of black workers in the Chesapeake area. It made more sense to him to populate Virginia with England's vagrants, beggars, and rogues. If highwaymen were sent to the tobacco colonies, they might be "kept to Business, and getting Money in an honest Way."[62] This panacea was no more realistic than had been the plan to construct market towns on every river. And one suspects that colonists familiar with servant unrest during the seventeenth century, especially Bacon's Rebellion, may have grimaced when they heard of this particular scheme.[63]

William Byrd II—perhaps more than any other pre-Revolutionary planter—provides us with insights into the *mentalité* of colonial Virginians. It is difficult, however, to know exactly where to place him in a chronological discussion. Over the first four decades of the eighteenth century, he turned out a number of essays and travel accounts, the most famous being the *History of the Dividing Line*. He also produced a remarkable series of dairies that recorded his daily life in intimate detail. He recounted his dreams, his frustrations, his prejudices, and of course his many sexual adventures. But at no time did Byrd write a sustained analysis of the present state of Virginia. His assumptions about time and nature were scattered through various publications, and only by viewing these works as a group can we appreciate how fully he subscribed to values that by mid-century had become a signature of Virginia culture.[64]

Byrd was only marginally interested in the colony's past. Unlike the outspoken pamphleteers of the previous century, he saw no need to excoriate the founders for their miscalculations. His tone was indifferent, even irrelevant, as if the present in which he existed bore only a tenuous relation to the decisions of his own father's generation. In an essay published in 1701, Byrd lamented that Virginians had accomplished so little in the New World. "I say," he explained, "it is a very melancholy Consideration, that so great a part of the World, by Nature so rich and improvable, should lie almost wholly rude, and uncultivated for want of People." Byrd's predecessors had failed to develop the colony's natural resources, but they had not all been fools. Some "worthy good men" had migrated to Virginia in search of wealth, but for complex reasons "most, if not all of them, were disappointed in their Hopes."[65] Neither villains nor heroes appeared in Byrd's piece. The history of Virginia involved missed opportunities and false starts, but not gross errors.

Nor had Byrd's opinion changed much by the time he wrote the *History of the Line* more than three decades later. He noted that without Captain John Smith the earliest settlers would surely have destroyed themselves. The Captain forced the idlers to work, and while that was no mean achievement, Smith was not thereby transformed into a figure of major historical importance. Indeed, Virginia survived almost in spite of the people who inhabited it. As Byrd explained, "This Settlement stood its ground from that time forward in spite of all the Blunders and Disagreements of the first Adventurers, and the many Calamities that befel the Colony afterwards."[66] Byrd agreed with Robert Beverley that the colonists should have intermarried with the local Indians, for as Byrd observed somewhat irreverantly, "Morals and all considered, I cant think the Indians were much greater Heathens than [were] the first Adventurers."[67] The quality of later Virginians improved, to be sure, but they were hardly worthy of veneration. In fact, the New Englanders of the seventeenth century had done a far better job of developing America's natural resources. The northern colonists, it seems, were frugal and industrious, "By which excellent Qualities they had much the Advantage of the Southern Colony, who thought their being Members of the Establish'd Church sufficient to Sanctifie very loose and Profligate Morals."[68]

Natural abundance, Byrd believed, could nullify the errors of the past. This view liberated Virginians from history. The members of the present generation need not worry about former miscalculations so long as the colony's rich natural resources held out the possibility of a new start. And about Virginia's potential, Byrd possessed not the slightest doubt. He thought that it rivaled paradise in every respect. The area was fruitful and healthy, full of "Beasts, Birds, and Fruits," and blessed with excellent rivers teeming with fish.[69] Byrd's enthusiasm was effusive. In 1731 he informed an English correspondent that Virginia "differs but a very few degrees from that of Paradise. The sun that imparts life, growth and motion to the animal and vegetable world, looks upon us every day in the year. . . . Heaven pours out its horn of plenty upon us, and furnishes us even to luxuary."[70] The recipient of this letter may well have asked how a person living in such a marvelous environment could ask for anything more.

And there was the problem. Byrd had no intention of promoting an uncritical satisfaction with the present state of Virginia. The colony's promise lay in the future, and to Byrd it seemed self-evident that men like himself could improve on paradise. Surely the Lord did not want the colonists to leave nature "almost wholly rude."[71] This point echoes through the pages of Byrd's *History of the Dividing Line*. The lazy North Carolinians were quite content with the fruits of an unimproved nature, and if the Virginians of Byrd's time were not careful, they would find themselves unwittingly transformed into "Porcivorous" Carolinians. The danger was quite genuine. A few Virginians had already turned their backs on industry and frugality. "I am sorry to say it," Byrd confessed, "but Idleness is the general character of the men in the Southern Parts of this Colony as well as in North Carolina. The Air is so mild, and the Soil so fruitful, that very little Labour is requir'd to fill their Bellies."[72]

Byrd devised a plan for Virginia that took these problems into account. He avoided seventeenth-century panaceas. Productive silk worms and populous market towns, however desirable they may have been, were not in themselves capable of fulfilling the promise of Chesapeake society. Byrd's immediate schemes for the future were centered in a large tract of western land which he appropriately called "Eden."[73] In this fertile territory, he proposed quite literally to sponsor a new start. He explained that "a Colony of 1000 families might, with the help of Moderate Industry, pass their time very happily there." These yeomen farmers, men and women freed from the institutions and traditions of Virginia, would soon be producing the very goods that Virginians had so long ignored: silk, hemp, flax, cotton, and rice. They would even raise "Orange, Lemon, and Olive Trees." Anything was possible in Eden, if one found the right people to settle there.[74] Byrd did not pin his hopes upon the Virginians. He turned instead to French and Swiss Protestants, diligent migrants who might succeed where Virginians had failed. As one might expect, Byrd stood to profit from the experiment. He offered pieces of paradise to newcomers at a fair market price, and if his calculations were correct, he would reap the returns from Virginia's newest beginning within a very short time.

Not until the middle of the eighteenth century did a Virginian attempt to write a book concerned solely with the colony's past. While serving as minister for Henrico Parish, William Stith completed his *History of the First Discovery and Settlement of Virginia,* and the lengthy manuscript was published in Williamsburg in 1747. Stith explained in the introduction that he had produced the work for several different reasons. First, his position as minister allowed him the leisure to pursue scholarship. Second, his uncle John Randolph had started an account of the colony's early settlement, and Stith was apparently persuaded to finish it. But most of all, he was convinced that a history would be "a great Satisfaction, and even Ornament, to our Country."[75]

Despite such patriotic declarations, however, Stith's heart does not seem to have been in the project from the very beginning. Like a young scholar forced to write a term paper, he complained every step of the way. He originally expected to draw upon convenient published histories of the colony, but everything he found turned out to be "empty and unsatisfactory." This unhappy discovery forced Stith to examine old records, a task he grew to despise. "And I can further declare," he explained, "with great Truth, that had any thing of Consequence been done in our History, I could most willingly have saved myself the Trouble, of conning over our old dusty Records, and of studying, connecting, and reconciling the jarring and disjointed Writings and Relations of different Men and different Parties." Judging by the results of his labors, one wonders whether Stith should even have bothered attempting to make sense out of documents "mangled by Moths and Worms."[76] He slogged his way through the colony's early years, and if a mid-century Virginian had possessed even a spark of curiosity about the past, Stith's plodding style would have quickly extinguished that interest. Jefferson refused to recommend the book. Stith, he observed, "was a man of classical learning, and very exact, but of no taste in style. He is inelegant, therefore, and his details often too minute to be tolerable, even to a native of the country, whose history he writes."[77]

Stith felt ambivalent about the colony's past. The founders of Virginia received praise for establishing a representative form of government. By creating the House of Burgesses, Stith explained, they had defied that "puny Monarch,"[78] James I, and "From this Time [1619] therefore, we may most properly date the Original of our present Constitution."[79] But Stith was in no sense a hagiographer. Unlike George Washington's inventive biographer, Parson Mason Weems, Stith made no sustained attempt to transform the colony's founders into mythic figures. After the Stuarts dissolved the Virginia Company in 1624, Stith lost interest in the story of Virginia. He too felt that somehow his predecessors had failed, that the colony had not attained its true potential.

Virginia's lack of prosperity, he believed, could be traced to the practice of "transporting loose and dissolute Persons to *Virginia*, as a Place of Punishment and Disgrace." In a statement that echoed—no doubt unconsciously—George Donne's essay, Stith confessed that unsavory migrants "Laid one of the finest Countries in *British America*, under the unjust Scandal of being a mere Hell upon Earth, another *Siberia*." If different, more intelligent policies had been adopted along the way, Virginia's history might well have been happier. Certainly, anyone could see that the younger "Northern Colonies" had consistently drawn a better sort of person and had "accordingly profited thereby. From this one Cause, . . . they have outstripped us so much, in the Number of their Inhabitants, and in the Goodness and Frequency of their Cities and Towns."[80] Stith had come full circle. He set out to write a history, but by the time he finished the project, he found himself dreaming of a brighter future in which no one would mistake Virginia for Siberia.

Local history meant little more to the leaders of Revolutionary Virginia than it had to men like Smith, Beverley, and Byrd. The colonists' attacks on Parliament and the ministers of George III contained only casual reference to Virginia's past. One searches in vain through the *Virginia Gazette*, the colony's only newspaper, for evidence that Virginians possessed any history whatsoever, let alone one that might have helped them through a period of economic and political disruption. Pamphleteers such as Richard Bland did not evoke the memory of noble sacrifice and high ideals. They recognized, of course, that Virginians had long ago established the principle of no taxation without representation, but surprisingly this achievement inspired little pride and almost no curiosity.[81] No Revolutionary Virginian traced the origins of representative government to specific founders, and by almost any standard of measure, the Virginia heritage seemed shallow and uninteresting when compared to that of contemporary New England.[82]

Thomas Jefferson articulated more fully than did any other Virginian at this time a deeply rooted set of assumptions about time and nature. Unless one understands the remarkable persistence of certain local values, one could easily interpret Jefferson's attitudes toward the past, present, and future as a reflection of his peculiar genius, an idiosyncratic turn of mind that separated him from the world of the late-eighteenth-century planters. But upon closer inspection, his views seem quite orthodox, for like the pre-Revolutionary Virginians, he took for granted man's ability to escape the past and perfect the future simply by putting his mind to the task.[83]

Jefferson found Virginia history boring. He had acquired a general familiarity with the colony's past, but in all his readings he came across nothing that possessed more than antiquarian interest. In his *Notes on the State of Virginia*, Jefferson attempted to sidestep the topic altogether. He described the region's natural resources, its people, its commerce—subjects that excited his mind—and only in the last chapter did he turn reluctantly to local history. He listed Virginians who had discussed the colony's development, Smith, Stith, and Beverley, but Jefferson found these works so poorly crafted that he could not in good faith recommend them to his own readers. If a "foreigner" insisted upon learning about early Virginia history, he could examine a short book by Sir William Keith—an Englishman no less—for according to Jefferson, Keith was "agreeable enough in style, and passes over events of little importance." Jefferson provided no interpretation of his own. In fact, *Notes on Virginia* closed with a "chronological catalogue of American state-papers" from 1496 to 1768, a rather clumsy device for someone who made a point about style.[84]

Jefferson realized, of course, that the past consisted of more than a list of events. It was also a culture, a bundle of institutions and traditions handed down from generation to generation, and when Jefferson thought of history as a heritage rather than a chronicle, his indifference turned to anger. The customs of pre-Revolutionary Virginians, he argued, should not be accepted as a blueprint for present behavior simply because they were old. Indeed, Jefferson believed that much of the past should be destroyed root and branch, and in some of his writings, he sounded like a French *philosophe* flaying the Ancient Regime. Colonial lawmakers, for example, had been so eager to gain royal favor that they lost sight of Virginia's true interests. "Our minds," Jefferson explained, "were circumscribed within narrow limits by an habitual belief that it was our duty to be subordinate to the mother country in all matters of government. . . . The difficulties with our representatives were of habit and despair, not of reflection and conviction." [85] Tradition had saddled Revolutionary Virginians with bigoted clergymen who ignored their "pastoral functions." It was responsible for slavery and a dependence upon tobacco. [86] It had even affected the character of the colonists themselves. As Jefferson informed the Marquise De Chastellux, "I have thought them [the Virginians], as you have found them, aristocratical, pompous, clannish, indolent, hospitable, and I should have added . . . thoughtless in their expenses and in all their transactions of business." [87] These people seemed strikingly similar to Byrd's North Carolinians, and it is understandable why Jefferson was no more eager than Byrd to write the history of Virginia.

Jefferson perceived the Revolution as a new beginning. It gave Virginians not only political independence, but also an opportunity to liberate themselves from the errors of the past. Jefferson was acutely aware of his own role in this reformation, and in some writings he described himself as part of "a new generation," a group of men with sufficient wisdom and courage to transform Virginia society. [88] From our vantage point, Jefferson's plans to redesign political, ecclesiastical, and educational institutions seems extraordinarily ambitious. How could he and his contemporaries brush aside institutions and procedures that originated in the seventeenth century? But Jefferson's vision of what Virginians could accomplish was not limited by precedent. In one of his most quoted statements, he insisted that "The earth belongs always to the living generation. They may manage it then, and what proceeds from it, as they please. . . . They are masters too of their own persons, and consequently may govern themselves as they please." [89] This radical definition of temporal horizons would not have shocked the pre-Revolutionary Virginians that we have discussed. They too believed that the present population could shape its own future, even if that meant totally abandoning the past, and while Jefferson did not think that towns, or

silk, or honest immigrants were capable in themselves of ensuring freedom and prosperity, he did share the earlier Virginians' faith in the possibility of new beginnings.

Virginia's extraordinarily rich environment sustained Jefferson's optimism. The world in which the Revolutionaries lived overflowed with
natural resources waiting to be developed. It is difficult to read *Notes on
Virginia* without being overwhelmed by the author's confidence in nature. While his tone was both more secular and scientific than that of
earlier Virginians, his list of the state's natural advantages rivaled those
of the most enthusiastic promoters. Jefferson praised Virginia's rivers,
which now included the Mississippi and the Missouri as well as the
James and the York, its variety of minerals and plants, its unusually
large animals, and its climate, which he believed was becoming milder
all the time. Without these blessings, Jefferson's vision of a virtuous society composed of yeomen farmers would have appeared shallow and
unrealistic. But Virginia did in fact possess "an immensity of land," and
even though the cultivation of tobacco had declined precipitously in
recent years, Jefferson predicted that wheat and horses would more than
compensate for the loss of that "wretched" crop. The near future looked
bright.[90] As long as nature smiled on Virginia, anything was possible.

How many of Jefferson's contemporaries shared his assumptions
about time and nature is difficult to estimate, but the number probably
was not small. We know that Revolutionary Virginians showed little enthusiasm for defending institutions and customs that had developed during the colonial period. They abandoned the Anglican church, dropped
primogeniture and entail, and left off tobacco cultivation with scarcely a
whimper of protest. None of these things had acquired symbolic importance in Virginia; they certainly were not widely perceived as crucial
props to the social order.

Virginians less well known than Jefferson looked forward to the future, confident that it would bring fresh opportunities. In 1772, for example, one planter named Roger Atkinson bragged to an English merchant, "Sir it is with great Pleasure I acq't you that we have now got
another staple of late years, as it were created, viz: Wheat, w'ch will I
believe in a little time be equal if not superior to Tob'o—is more certain
& of w'ch we shall in a few years make more in Virg'ia than all the
Province of Pennsylvania put together."[91] And Mrs. Robert Carter,
the wife of one of Virginia's richer planters, contemplated with apparent
equanimity the creation of a free labor force to replace black slaves.
"How much greater," she informed a northern writer, ". . . must be

the value of an Estate here if these poor enslaved Africans were all in their native desired Country, & in their Room industrious Tenants, who being born in freedom, by a laudable care, would not only inrich their Landlords, but would raise a hardy Offspring to be the Strength & the honour of the Country."[92] Carter and Atkinson were not unusual persons. Virginians of their turn of mind discussed major breaks with the customary past without guilt or fear. If their plans failed—and of course many did—they could always try again.

The pervasiveness of the Virginia *mentalité* became dramatically evident during a series of confrontations between Jefferson and Edmund Pendleton. With good reason Jefferson regarded Pendleton as one of the ablest politicians in Virginia. During the period when Jefferson attempted to restructure Virginia society, Pendleton often led the opposition. He resisted the efforts to abolish entail and primogeniture, and he was an outspoken defender of the Anglican church. As Jefferson noted tersely, Pendleton "was zealously attached to ancient establishments."[93] In other words, he was a genuine conservative, a person whose temporal horizons were quite different from those of his radical contemporaries.

But then the leaders of the young state government turned their attentions to drawing up a new code of laws. After achieving independence from England, Virginia obviously required a code that reflected its republican character. A committee composed of Pendleton, Jefferson, and three other men met to compose a draft. "The first question," Jefferson reported, "was, whether we should propose to abolish the whole existing system of laws, and prepare a new and complete Institute, or preserve the general system, and only modify it to the present state of things." Pendleton's views were predictable, or so Jefferson thought. The conservative would fight to maintain traditional forms. But in fact, "Mr. Pendleton, contrary to his usual disposition in favor of ancient things, was for the former proposition. . . . To this it was objected, that to abrogate our whole system would be a bold measure, and probably far beyond the views of the legislature."[94] With conservatives like Pendleton, Virginia needed no radicals.

III

In the early nineteenth century, Virginians created a rich local past that contained among other elements dashing Cavalier exiles. Why writers in this period felt compelled to develop an elaborate origin myth for their society is not entirely clear, and the question takes us far beyond the scope of this book. One modern historian has suggested that the Virginians' romantic reinterpretation of their own past "probably owed as much to the novels of Sir Walter Scott as to any other influence."[95] No doubt, rising sectional tensions in the United States coupled with an outpouring of self-gratulatory northern histories put the Virginians on the defensive, and the Cavaliers can therefore be regarded in part as a response to the mythical Pilgrims and other New England folk heroes. One suspects, however, that the shift in the Virginians' temporal horizons betrayed even deeper cultural factors. The vision of a bounteous nature filled with untapped opportunities, in other words, the vision that sustained Jeffersonian optimism, lost much of its credibility in Virginia in the antebellum period. The state was no longer the center of economic growth. Its future lay in the past—in a Golden Age—and Virginians flocked west in search of the nature that their own state had once promised but no longer possessed.

Notes

I. Persistent Localism

1. See Perry Miller's remarks in the preface to the paperback edition of *The New England Mind: From Colony to Province* (Boston, 1961). See also Edmund S. Morgan, "Perry Miller and the Historians," *Harvard Review*, II (1964), 54.
2. Edmund S. Morgan discusses some of the problems in "The Historians of Early New England," in Ray Allen Billington, ed., *The Reinterpretation of Early American History: Essays in Honor of John Edwin Pomfret* (San Marino, Calif., 1966), 41–60.
3. The most recent literature has been reviewed at length by John M. Murrin in his "Review Essay," *History and Theory*, XI (1972), 226–75. See also Michael McGiffert, "American Puritan Studies in the 1960's," *William and Mary Quarterly*, 3rd ser., XXVII (1970), 36–67.
4. Some exceptions to the generalization should be noted: John Shy, "The American Military Experience: History and Learning," *Journal of Interdisciplinary History*, I (1970-71), 205–28; John J. Waters, "Hingham, Massachusetts, 1631-1661: An East Anglian Oligarchy in the New World," *Journal of Social History*, I (1967–68), 351–70; and Sumner Chilton Powell, *Puritan Village: The Formation of a New England Town* (Middletown, Conn., 1963).
5. Carl Bridenbaugh, *Vexed and Troubled Englishmen, 1590–1642* (New

York, 1968), 47. For a description of one such village see W. G. Hoskins, *The Midland Peasants: The Economic and Social History of a Leicestershire Village* (London, 1957), 185–94.

6. Alan Everitt, *Change in the Provinces: The Seventeenth Century*, Department of English Local History, Occasional Papers, 2nd ser., I (Leicester, Eng., 1969), 6–48. For more on local institutional diversity see George Lee Haskins, *Law and Authority in Early Massachusetts: A Study in Tradition and Design* (New York, 1960), 163–68.

7. Everitt, *Change in the Provinces*, 10; Alan Everitt, "The Peers and the Provinces," *Agricultural History Review*, XVI (1968), 66.

8. Lawrence Stone, "The English Revolution," in Robert Forster and Jack P. Greene, eds., *Preconditions of Revolution in Early Modern Europe* (Baltimore, 1970), 71.

9. Peter Laslett, *The World We Have Lost* (New York, 1965), 64; Bridenbaugh, *Vexed and Troubled Englishmen*, 243–45.

10. John Browne, *History of Congregationalism and Memorials of the Churches in Norfolk and Suffolk* (London, 1877), 79; Paul S. Seaver, *The Puritan Lectureships: The Politics of Religious Dissent, 1560–1662* (Stanford, Calif., 1970), 88–117.

11. Pishey Thompson, *The History and Antiquities of Boston (Boston, Eng., 1856)*, 70.

12. Patrick Collinson, *The Elizabethan Puritan Movement* (Berkeley and Los Angeles, 1967), 466.

13. Patrick Collinson, "The Godly: Aspects of Popular Protestantism in Elizabethan England" (paper presented to the *Past and Present* Conference on Popular Religon, July 7, 1966), 22.

14. *Ibid.*, 3. William Ames (1576–1633), a Puritan theologian exiled in Holland, wrote at length about a kind of semi-secret, locally organized congregationalism that developed within the Church of England during this period, a congregationalism that he called "Parish-omnipotency." It was this type of popular religious expression that Laud later attempted to suppress, and in so doing drove many respected local ministers of congregational persuasion to New England. See Keith L. Sprunger, *The Learned Doctor William Ames: Dutch Backgrounds of English and American Puritanism* (Urbana, Ill., 1972), 194–99.

15. Chapter III.

16. J. H. Elliott, "Revolution and Continuity in Early Modern Europe," *Past and Present*, No. 42 (1969), 50–51; Lawrence Stone, *The Causes of the English Revolution, 1529–1642* (London, 1972), 30, 63–64, 106–108, quotation on p. 64; Peter Laslett, "The Gentry of Kent in 1640," *Cambridge Historical Journal*, IX (1948), 148–64; Everitt, *Change in the Provinces*, 25–48; R. W. Ketton-Cremer, *Norfolk in the Civil War: A Portrait*

of a Society in Conflict (London, 1969), 20–28; Alan Everitt, "Social Mobility in Early Modern England," *Past and Present*, No. 33 (1966), 59–62.

17. Stone, "English Revolution," in Forster and Greene, eds., *Preconditions of Revolution*, 102; Brian Manning, "The Nobles, the People, and the Constitution," *Past and Present*, No. 9 (1956), 56–59.

18. Thomas Garden Barnes, *Somerset 1625–1640: A County's Government During the "Personal Rule"* (Cambridge, Mass., 1961), 172; Bridenbaugh, *Vexed and Troubled Englishmen*, 270–73; Stone, *Causes of the English Revolution*, 118.

19. J. R. Tanner, *English Constitutional Conflicts of the Seventeenth Century, 1630–1689* (Cambridge, 1962), 54–79; Barnes, *Somerset*, 203–43.

20. *Acts of the Privy Council of England, 1629 May–1630 May* (London, 1960), 4–5; B. E. Supple, *Commercial Crisis and Change in England, 1600–1642: A Study in the Instability of a Mercantile Economy* (Cambridge, 1959), 102–12.

21. Thomas Birch, *The Court and Times of Charles the First*, ed. Robert Folkestone Williams, II (London, 1848), 17.

22. E. M. Leonard, *The Early History of English Poor Relief* (Cambridge, 1900), 150–54; Barnes, *Somerset*, 172–202; Supple, *Commercial Crisis*, 234. Charles's other attempts to regulate the economy were equally irritating. See Joan Thirsk, ed., *The Agrarian History of England and Wales, IV: 1500–1640* (Cambridge, 1967), 237, and Stone, *Causes of the English Revolution*, 126.

23. Alexander Leighton, *An Appeal to the Parliament, or, Sion's Plea against the Prelacie . . .* (London, 1629), A3; William Prynne, *The Church of England's Old Antithesis to new Arminianisme . . .* (London, 1629); John F. H. New, *Anglican and Puritan: The Basis of Their Opposition, 1558–1640* (Stanford, Calif., 1964), 13–16; Paul A. Welsby, *Lancelot Andrewes, 1555–1626* (London, 1958); H. R. Trevor-Roper, *Archbishop Laud, 1573–1645* (London, 1940).

24. Cited in Bridenbaugh, *Vexed and Troubled Englishmen*, 305. See also Ketton-Cremer, *Norfolk in the Civil War*, 54–67, and John T. Horton, "Two Bishops and the Holy Brood: A Fresh Look at a Familiar Fact," *New England Quarterly*, XL (1967), 339–63.

25. Seaver, *Puritan Lectureships*, 293. In a superb essay dealing with religious change in Catholic Europe, John Bossy describes the process by which the Counter-Reformation forced popular, voluntary religious associations into parochial conformity. Although Bossy concentrates on the rural population of France and Italy, his comments on the "collapse of popular religion" help to explain contemporary New Englanders' fierce defense of local autonomy in religious affairs. "The Counter-Reformation and the People of Catholic Europe," *Past and Present*, No. 47 (1970), 51–70.

26. Samuel R. Gardiner, *The Personal Government of Charles I*, I (London, 1877), 218.

27. The best account is Linsay Boynton, *The Elizabethan Militia, 1558–1638* (London, 1967), 244–97. See also Chapter II, and Barnes, *Somerset*, 244–80. In France the military similarly disrupted local communities. See Georges Duby and Robert Mandrou, *A History of French Civilization*, trans. James Blakeley Atkinson (New York, 1964), 217–18.

28. Henry Manship, *The History of Great Yarmouth*, ed. Charles J. Palmer (Great Yarmouth, Eng., 1854), 371–72; Ketton-Cremer, *Norfolk in the Civil War*, 33–35.

29. Barnes, *Somerset*, 143–280; H. R. Trevor-Roper, "The General Crisis of the Seventeenth Century," in Trevor Aston, ed., *Crisis in Europe, 1560–1660* (New York, 1965), 90–91; Stone, *Causes of the English Revolution*, 124, 133.

30. MS. *Firth, c. 4, fos. 442–43*, Bodleian Library, Oxford University.

31. An excellent discussion of these social strains can be found in Ivan Roots, "The Central Government and the Local Community," in E. W. Ives, ed., *The English Revolution 1600–1660* (London, 1968), 34–46. See also Eric Kerridge, "The Revolts in Wiltshire Against Charles I," *Wiltshire Archaeological and Natural History Magazine*, LVII (1958), 72. Christopher Hill provides evidence of "the tendency of churchwardens to voice the views of their community, and oppose the wishes of the hierarchy." *Society and Puritanism in Pre-Revolutionary England* (New York, 1964), 441.

32. J. H. Plumb, "The Growth of the Electorate in England from 1600 to 1715," *Past and Present*, No. 45 (1969), 98–103; Evangeline de Villiers, "Parliamentary Boroughs Restored by the House of Commons, 1621–41," *English Historical Review*, LXVII (1952), 175–202.

33. Henry Swinden, *The History and Antiquities of The Ancient Burgh of Great Yarmouth* (Norwich, Eng., 1772), 478–515; Nathaniel Bacon, *The Annalls of Ipswiche, The Lawes Customs and Government of the Same*, ed. William H. Richardson (Ipswich, Eng., 1884), 498–99; Thompson, *History of Boston*, 79; *History and Antiquities of the County of Norfolk*, X (Norwich, Eng., 1781), 160.

34. See Chapter III.

35. Despite angry protests about ship money, for example, the king's finances were in a remarkably healthy state as late as 1638. G. E. Aylmer, *The Struggle for the Constitution, 1603–1689: England in the Seventeenth Century* (London, 1963), 84–85.

36. Elliott, "Revolution and Continuity," *Past and Present*, No. 42 (1969), 44; Hill, *Society and Puritanism*, 483–500.

37. Thirsk, ed., *Agrarian History*, 461.

38. Everitt, "Peers and the Provinces," *Ag. Hist. Rev.*, XVI (1968), 66; Everitt,

Change in the Provinces, 10; Roots, "Central Government," in Ives, ed., *English Revolution*, 42–46.

39. This type of migration and its effects on New World society are discussed at length in Josef J. Barton, *Peasants and Strangers: Italians, Rumanians, and Slovaks in an American City, 1890–1950* (Cambridge, Mass., 1975). For a greater appreciation of what happened in New England one should compare the social institutions that developed in regions to which immigration was largely an individual enterprise. See Edmund S. Morgan, "The First American Boom: Virginia 1618 to 1630," *WMQ*, 3rd ser., XXVIII (1971), 169–98, and Irene W. D. Hecht, "The Virginia Muster of 1624/5 as a Source for Demographic History," *ibid.*, XXX (1973), 65–92.

40. The idea that colonization involves a separation of specific cultural "fragments" from a mother country was first suggested to me by Louis Hartz, *The Founding of New Societies: Studies in the History of the United States, Latin America, South Africa, Canada, and Australia* (New York, 1964), 3–65. See also Haskins, *Law and Authority*, 60, 94–95.

41. See Stanley Elkins and Eric McKitrick, "A Meaning for Turner's Frontier, Part II: The Southwest Frontier and New England," *Political Science Quarterly*, LXIX (1954), 565–602. Although my interpretation of the development of early New England society differs somewhat from the one advanced by Elkins and McKitrick, I found their discussion of localism extremely valuable in preparing this essay.

42. The best discussion of Winthrop's actions is Edmund S. Morgan, *The Puritan Dilemma: The Story of John Winthrop* (Boston, 1958), 84–100.

43. My comments are based on Philip J. Greven, Jr., *Four Generations: Population, Land, and Family in Colonial Andover, Massachusetts* (Ithaca, N.Y., 1970); Powell, *Puritan Village*; Darrett B. Rutman, *Winthrop's Boston: Portrait of a Puritan Town, 1630–1649* (Chapel Hill, N.C., 1965); John Demos, *A Little Commonwealth: Family Life in Plymouth Colony* (New York, 1970); and Waters, "Hingham, Mass.," *Jour. Soc. Hist.*, I (1967–68), 351–70.

44. Rutman, *Winthrop's Boston*, 25–28, 280–83.

45. J. Franklin Jameson, ed., *Johnson's Wonder-Working Providence, 1628–1651*, Original Narratives of Early American History (New York, 1910), 110, 99, 100.

46. The term "outlivers" comes from Richard L. Bushman, *From Puritan to Yankee: Character and the Social Order in Connecticut, 1690–1765* (Cambridge, Mass., 1967), 54–72.

47. A good discussion of one town covenant can be found in Kenneth A. Lockridge, *A New England Town, The First Hundred Years: Dedham, Massachusetts, 1636–1736* (New York, 1970), 3–22.

48. Haskins, *Law and Authority*, 70–73.

49. Timothy H. Breen and Stephen Foster, "The Puritans' Greatest Achievement: A Study of Social Cohesion in Seventeenth-Century Massachusetts," *Journal of American History*, LX (1973), 5–22.

50. Edmund S. Morgan, "New England Puritanism: Another Approach," *WMQ*, 3rd ser., XVIII (1961), 236–242; Kenneth A. Lockridge, "The History of a Puritan Church, 1637–1736," *NEQ*, XL (1967), 399–424.

51. Williston Walker, ed., *The Creeds and Platforms of Congregationalism* (New York, 1893), 229–30.

52. Thomas Lechford, *Plain Dealing: Or, Newes from New-England . . .* (1642), Massachusetts Historical Society, *Collections*, 3rd. ser., III (1833), 74–75.

53. David D. Hall, *The Faithful Shepherd: A History of the New England Ministry in the Seventeenth Century* (Chapel Hill, N.C., 1972), 212–14; Walker, ed., *Creeds and Platforms*, 137, 159–61.

54. Hall, *Faithful Shepherd*, 85.

55. See the remarks on the English background *ibid.*, 85, 96–99.

56. See Chapter II and Rutman, *Winthrop's Boston*, 215.

57. James Kendall Hosmer, ed., *Winthrop's Journal, "History of New England, 1630–1649,"* Original Narratives of Early American History (New York, 1908), I, 79.

58. Mass. Hist. Soc., *Winthrop Papers*, III (Boston, 1943), 503.

59. John Winthrop, Jr., to Henry Oldenburg, Nov. 12, 1668, Mass. Hist. Soc., *Colls.*, 5th ser., VIII (1882), 133.

60. Edmund S. Morgan, ed., *Puritan Political Ideas, 1558–1794* (Indianapolis, 1965), xv-xliv; Haskins, *Law and Authority*, 25–84; T. H. Breen, *The Character of the Good Ruler: A Study of Puritan Political Ideas in New England, 1630–1730* (New Haven, Conn., 1970), 35–86.

61. Morgan, *Puritan Dilemma*, 3–33. For an examination of the relationship between one English "country community" and the leadership of early Virginia, see Laslett, "Gentry of Kent," *Cambridge Hist. Jour.*, IX (1948), 148–64.

62. Breen, *Character of the Good Ruler*, 58–69.

63. Hosmer, ed., *Winthrop's Journal*, I, 74.

64. *Ibid.*, 74–75. On the Watertown petition see Morgan, *Puritan Dilemma*, 107–10, and Haskins, *Law and Authority*, 29–30.

65. Nathaniel B. Shurtleff, ed., *Records of the Governor and Company of the Massachusetts Bay in New England*, I (Boston, 1853), 118, italics mine.

66. Mass. Hist. Soc., *Proceedings*, XLVIII (1915), 47–48. For other examples of the division between the county and community interests, see Hosmer, ed., *Winthrop's Journal*, I, 362–64, II, 204. A new interpretation of these disputes has been offered by Robert Emmett Wall, Jr., *Massachusetts Bay: The Crucial Decade, 1640–1650* (New Haven, Conn., 1972). Wall regards

the deputies of the 1640s as more representative of the "local elite" than of "the mass of freemen" (p. 26). But regardless of whom the deputies represented, it is clear that the major political divisions of this decade were sparked by the conflict between local and colony-wide interests.

67. Hosmer, ed., *Winthrop's Journal*, II, 229–30; Wall, *Massachusetts Bay*, 93–120; Waters, "Hingham, Mass.," *Jour. Soc. Hist.*, I (1967–68), 352, 365–66; John Coolidge, "Hingham Builds a Meetinghouse," *NEQ*, XXXIV (1961), 435–40.

68. Lockridge, *New England Town*, 19. Philip J. Greven, Jr. makes a similar point in "Historical Demography and Colonial America: A Review Article," *WMQ*, 3rd ser., XXIV (1967), 453. See also Richard S. Dunn, "The Social History of Early New England," *American Quarterly*, XXIV (1972), 669.

II. THE COVENANTED MILITIA

1. Works that carefully work out the English background are Sumner C. Powell, *Puritan Village; The Formation of a New England Town* (Middletown, Conn., 1963); and Edmund S. Morgan, "The Labor Problem at Jamestown, 1607–18," *American Hist. Rev.*, LXXVI (1971), 595–611; John J. Waters, "Hingham, Massachusetts, 1631–1661: An East Anglian Oligarchy in the New World," *Journal of Social History*, I (1967–68), 351–70. Also see Lawrence Stone, "English and United States Local History," *Daedalus* (Winter 1971), 128–32.

2. J. H. Hexter, *Reappraisals in History* (New York, 1961), 194–95.

3. For example, Samuel Eliot Morison, *Builders of the Bay Colony* (Boston, 1958), 146–47; and Herbert L. Osgood, *The American Colonies in the Seventeenth Century*, 3 vols. (New York, 1904–7), I, 497–503. For a better analysis of the trainbands see John Shy, "A New Look at the Colonial Militia," *William and Mary Quarterly*, 3rd ser., XX (1963), 175–84; and David R. Millar, "The Militia, the Army and Independency in Colonial Massachusetts" (Cornell University Ph.D. diss., 1967).

4. See Perry Miller, "Thomas Hooker and the Democracy of Connecticut," in his *Errand into the Wilderness* (New York, 1964), 16–47; Edmund S. Morgan, *The Puritan Dilemma, The Story of John Winthrop* (Boston, 1958), 84–100; T. H. Breen, *The Character of the Good Ruler, A Study of Puritan Political Ideas in New England, 1630–1730* (New Haven, 1970), 35–86.

5. Twenty-five years ago, Morrison Sharp, a student of the New England militia, published an article analyzing the relationship between Puritan society and the village trainbands. His work was useful in preparing this essay, but I do not share Sharp's belief that the history of New England institu-

tions should be written in terms of a conflict between "aristocrats" and "common men." Sharp's interpretation can be found in "Leadership and Democracy in the Early New England System of Defense," *American Hist. Rev.*, L (1945), 244–60.

6. Gladys Scott Thomson, *Lords Lieutenants in the Sixteenth Century: A Study in Tudor Local Administration* (London, 1923); Lawrence Stone, *The Crisis of the Aristocracy, 1558–1641*, abr. edn. (London, 1967), 96–100; J. H. Hexter, "Storm Over the Gentry," in his *Reappraisals in History*, 146–47; *The Montagu Musters Book, 1602–1623*, ed. Joan Wake (Northamptonshire Rec. Soc., VII, 1935), xvii–lxi; C. G. Cruickshank, *Elizabeth's Army* (Oxford, 1946); Lindsay Boynton, *The Elizabethan Militia, 1558–1638* (London, 1967); J. C. Sainty, *Lieutenants of Counties, 1585–1642* (London Univ. Institute of Historical Research, Bulletin, Special Supplement No. 8, May 1970); Conrad Russell, *The Crisis of Parliament* (London, 1971), 160–63.

7. *State Papers Relating to Musters, Beacons, Shipmoney, &c. in Norfolk, 1626–1637*, ed. W. Rye (Norwich, 1907), 4–6; *Montagu*, ed. Wake, xxix–xxx; A. Clark, "The Essex Territorial Force in 1608," *Essex Review*, XVII (1909), 105–6; Thomson, *Lords Lieutenants*, 87–88.

8. Bodl. Lib., MS. Firth c. 4, fo. 103.

9. *Montagu*, ed. Wake, pp. l–lxi; *State Papers in Norfolk*, ed. Rye, 3; Thomson, *Lords Lieutenants*, 80; William B. Willcox, *Gloucestershire; A Study in Local Government, 1590–1640* (New Haven, 1940), 38, 73–75.

10. T. G. Barnes, *Somerset, 1625–1640: A County's Government During the "Personal Rule"* (Cambridge, Mass., 1961), 98–102; *Montagu*, ed. Wake, lxi; *The Twysden Lieutenancy Papers, 1583–1668*, ed. G. S. Thomson (Kent, Arch. Soc. Rec. Branch, X, 1926), 9.

11. Barnes, *Somerset*, 119–20, 248; *Montagu*, ed. Wake, xxxvi; B. W. Quintrell, "The Government of the County of Essex, 1603–1642" (London University, Ph. D. diss., 1965), pp. 231–33; Brit. Mus., King's MS. 265, fo. 618.

12. *Montagu*, ed. Wake, lxi.

13. Boynton, *Elizabethan Militia*, 240–50; *State Papers in Norfolk*, ed. Rye, vi–vii, 7; *Musters, Beacons and Subsidies in the County of Northampton, 1586–1623*, ed. J. Wake (Northamptonshire Rec. Soc., III, 1926); Bodl. Lib., MS. Firth c. 4, fo. 220.

14. *State Papers in Norfolk*, ed. Rye, vii, 16–17; Boynton, *Elizabethan Militia*, 246–50; Bodl. Lib., MS. Firth c. 4, fos. 270–72.

15. See Lindsay Boynton, "Martial Law and the Petition of Right," *Eng. Hist. Rev.*, LXXIX (1964), 279.

16. Stephen J. Stearns, "Conscription and English Society in the 1620s," *Journal of British Studies*, XL (1972), 4–5.

17. HMC, Cowper MSS., 12th Report, Appendix, pt. I, v. 1, 362–63.

18. Charles Dalton, *Life and Times of General Sir Edward Cecil* (2 vols., London, 1885), II, 85.
19. Brit. Mus., Add. MS. 21922, fo. 96A.
20. Carl Bridenbaugh, *Vexed and Troubled Englishmen, 1590–1642* (New York, 1968), 267; *State Papers in Norfolk*, ed. Rye, 78–79; HMC, Cowper MSS., 12th Report, Appendix, pt. I, v. 1, 298.
21. See Sir John Eliot's vivid description of the men returning to Plymouth after the Cadiz expedition in Harold Hulme, *The Life of Sir John Eliot, 1592 to 1632* (New York 1957), 99–100; Wilcox, *Gloucestershire*, 98–100.
22. HMC, 10th Report, Appendix, pt. VI, 115.
23. Cited in Willcox, *Gloucestershire*, 100; Dalton, *Sir Edward Cecil*, II, 76–77.
24. *The Victoria History of the County of Essex*, 5 vols., ed. William Page (London, 1907), II, pp. 224–29; Willcox, *Gloucestershire*, 116–17; Barnes, *Somerset*, 107–9; Bodl. Lib., MS. Firth c. 4, fo. 246.
25. Barnes, *Somerset*, 109; *Montagu*, ed. Wake, xxxv–xxxvi.
26. John Rushworth, *Historical Collection*, 8 vols. (London, 1659), I, 419; Willcox, *Gloucestershire*, 100–101; Barnes, *Somerset*, 109; *State Papers in Norfolk*, ed. Rye, 57–58; Bodl. Lib., MS. Firth c. 4, fo. 296; Brit. Mus., Add. MS. 21922, fo. 77.
27. Boynton, *Elizabethan Militia*, 272; Bodl. Lib., MS. Firth c. 4, fo. 296; *ibid.*, Tanner MS. 72, fo. 322; "Debates and Proceedings in the House of Commons, 1628–1629," Yale University, Massachusetts Hist. Soc. MSS. (hereafter cited as Massachusetts MSS.), fos. 94–95.
28. *Calendar of State Papers, Domestic, 1627–1628*, 522; *Acts of the Privy Council, September 1627–June 1628*, 292–93.
29. Willcox, *Gloucestershire*, 98–99. In the parliament of 1628 Sir Walter Earle explained, "In my Countrie under colour of placeing some soldiers there came 20 in a troope to take sheepe, they distrube marketts and faires, Rob men on the high way, Ravish women breaking houses in the night, and enforseing men to ransome them selves, killing men that have assisted Constables that have come to keepe the peace . . ." (Massachusetts MSS., fo. 94). See Lindsay Boynton, "Billeting: The Example of the Isle of Wight," *Eng. Hist. Rev.*, LXXIV (1959), 23–40.
30. Massachusetts MSS., fo. 94. The Council blamed the lawlessness of the troops upon the people for not welcoming the soldiers into their homes (Bodl. Lib., MS. Firth c. 4, fo. 437). And Edward Cecil claimed: "There are many vagabonds that in the name of soldiers do outrages and thefts . . ." (*HMC*, Cowper MSS., 12th Report, Appendix, pt. 1, v. 1, 297). Regardless of who was to blame, the presence of large numbers of troops on English soil created what contemporaries perceived as an unprecedented level of social disorder.
31. Massachusetts MSS., fo. 71.

32. Rushworth, *Historical Collections*, I, p. 419; *The Court and Times of Charles the First*, 2 vols., ed. Thomas Birch (London, 1849), I, 208; *The Constitutional Documents of the Puritan Revolution, 1625–1660*, ed. Samuel Rawson Gardiner (Oxford, 1906), xix; Boynton, "Martial Law," 255–84; Brit. Mus., Harleian MS. 390, fo. 277. The Deputy Lieutenants worried about the legality of their acts. Some in Norfolk begged the Privy Council ". . . to prescribe some such certayne course to us who be Deputye Lieutenants as may free us from pursute in Law or in Parlamt by the offenders [those who refused to train or arm properly], if any thinge we should doe by ways of Coertion; that by Law directly is not warranted": *State Papers in Norfolk*, ed. Rye, p. 17.

33. Brit. Mus., Harl. MS. 980, fo. 320; Massachusetts MSS., fo. 95.

34. Bodl. Lib., MS. Firth c. 4, fos. 441–43. See Court of Quarter Sessions of Peace, Essex, Sessions Roll, 261a, 264.

35. *State Papers in Norfolk*, ed. Rye, viii–ix.

36. *Ibid.*, 122–23; *The Court of Charles*, ed. Birch, I, 331; *Journals of the House of Lords*, 1620–28, III, 700. G. E. Aylmer details the events leading up to the Witham violence in his "St. Patrick's Day 1628 in Witham, Essex," *Past and Present*, No. 61 (1973), 139–40.

37. Bodl. Lib., MS. Firth c. 4, fos. 442–43.

38. Early in the parliament of 1628 the Commons "ordered that a special committee of some Soldiers and lawyers shall meet about the penning of the law for soldiers and for regulating the power of the Deputy Lieutenants and finding of arms and of the manner of levying of soldiers": Massachusetts MSS., fo. 14. Historians of this period have underestimated the significance of the complaints about Charles's military system. A reading of the debates reveals, however, that the members of parliament regarded this issue as crucial, as important to many members as was religious reform.

39. Massachusetts MSS., fo. 72.

40. Barnes, *Somerset*, 258, 270–76; Boynton, *Elizabethan Militia*, 275–93; Bodl. Lib., Rawlinson MS. 674, fos. 48–49.

41. See John Shy, *Toward Lexington: The Role of the British Army in the Coming of the American Revolution* (Princeton, 1965), 3–7; Darrett Rutman, "A Militant New World, 1607–1640" (University of Virginia Ph.D. diss., 1959); *The Records of the Governor and Company of the Massachusetts Bay in New England*, 5 vols. in 6, ed. Nathaniel B. Shurtleff (Boston, 1853–54) (hereafter cited as *Mass. Records*), I, 26, 29, 30, 31, 75, 83, 97, 237, 385, 390–91, 392–93.

42. *Winthrop Papers*, 5 vols. (Massachusetts Hist. Soc., 1929–47), III, 87.

43. Oliver A. Roberts, *History of the . . . Ancient and Honorable Artillery Company of Massachusetts, 1637–1888*, 4 vols. (Boston, 1895), I, 1–3; *Mass. Records*, I, 75, 77; John Winthrop, *History of New England*, 2 vols.,

ed. James K. Hosmer (New York, 1908) (hereafter cited as Winthrop, *History*), I, 78; II, 153–54.

44. L. Effingham DeForest and A. L. DeForest, *Captain John Underhill: Gentleman, Soldier of Fortune* (New York, 1934), 6–7, 28; Winthrop, *History*, I, 91–92, 240, 275–77, 308–9; II, 12–14, 41–42.

45. See Sharp, "Leadership and Democracy," 244–45; Osgood, *American Colonies*, I, 512–26; Jack S. Radabaugh, "The Militia of Colonial Massachusetts," *Military Affairs*, XVIII (1954), 1–18; *Mass. Records*, I, 84, 85, 117.

46. In Dorchester the townsmen attempted to make military service the least burden possible. The villagers ordered that anyone selected "to goe for a souldier" could "nominate" a friend to do his normal work at the wages usually given fighting men. Anyone who refused to assist the soldier could be fined. *Fourth Report of the Record Commissioners of the City of Boston . . . Dorchester Town Records* (Boston, 1883), 23–24.

47. Thomas Hooker, *A Survey of the Summe of Church Discipline* (London, 1648), pt. I, 47.

48. Massachusetts Archives, LXVII, fo. 51. On New England towns, see Kenneth A. Lockridge, *A New England Town: The First Hundred Years* (New York, 1970), 46; and T. H. Breen, "Who Governs: The Town Franchise in Seventeenth-Century Massachusetts," *William and Mary Quarterly*, 3rd ser., XXVII (1970), 461–62.

49. Winthrop, *History*, I, 79.

50. *Ibid.*, I, 74–75; Morgan, *Puritan Dilemma*, 108–14.

51. Winthrop, *History*, I, 125; *Mass. Records*, I, 187, 188; Sharp, "Leadership and Democracy," 256–58; Darrett Rutman, *Winthrop's Boston, Portrait of a Puritan Town, 1630–1649* (Chapel Hill, 1965), 160.

52. Edward Johnson, *The Wonder-Working Providence of Sions Savior in New England*, ed. J. F. Jameson (New York, 1910), 231.

53. *Winthrop Papers*, III, 503–4.

54. *Ibid.*, IV, 106 (my italics). Also Mass. Records, I, 221, 231.

55. *Mass. Records*, II, 49–50, 117, 191. See *ibid.*, I, 115–16, 354, for the text of the Residents Oath or the Oath of Fidelity. For an interesting parallel to the New England development, see the Leveller tract, *An Agreement of the Free People of England*, published in May 1649. The authors of this statement, bitter about the excesses of Cromwell's army, warned that "nothing threateneth greater danger to the Common-wealth, then that the Military power should by any means come to be superior to the Civil Authority." The Levellers, therefore, demanded that military officers, excepting only the general and his staff, be chosen by the citizens and removed "as they shall see cause." *Leveller Manifestoes of the Puritan Revolution*, ed. Don. M. Wolfe (New York, 1944), 409. There is no evidence that John Lilburne

and his friends were influenced by New England practice. It is striking, however, that the American colonists established open military procedures with relatively little opposition, while the Leveller demands were viewed by many English Puritans as radical and dangerous.

56. Edward Winslow, *New-Englands Salamander . . .* (London, 1647) in *Collections* (Massachusetts Hist. Soc., 3rd ser., II, 1830), 114–15, 121. Also E. Winslow, *Good Newes from New-England* (London, 1648) in *Collections* (Massachusetts Hist. Soc., 4th ser., I, 1852), 209.

57. *Mass. Records*, III, 268, 397. The only evidence is Daniel Gookin, Richard Russell, Thomas Savage, Francis Norton, and Roger Clap to the General Court: Massachusetts Archives, X, fo. 399, State House, Boston.

58. Winthrop, *History*, II, 229–31; *Mass. Records*, III, 17–23; John Child, *New-Englands Jonas Cast up at London . . .* (London, 1647) in *Tracts and Other Papers*, 4 vols., ed. Peter Force (Washington, 1846), IV, 5–6. In 1648, after tempers had cooled, the soldiers of Hingham petitioned the General Court, asking "this libertie as the rest of our naibours have: which we take to be our due, to chouse our owne officers, which if graunted, it will bee a great refreshment . . .": Massachusetts Archives, LXVIII, 42. See John J. Waters, "Hingham, Massachusetts, 1631–1661: An East Anglican Oligarchy in the New World," *Journal of Social History*, I (1968), 365–69. Also *Winthrop Papers*, V, 77–78; *Mass. Records*, II, 59, 133, 146.

59. See *Mass. Records*, III, 268; Millar, "The Militia," 66; Sharp, "Leadership and Democracy," 256, 258; Ellen E. Brennan, "The Massachusetts Council of the Magistrates," *New England Quarterly*, IV (1931), 58–73; Richard H. Marcus, "The Militia of Colonial Connecticut, 1639–1775: An Institutional Study" (University of Colorado Ph.D. diss., 1965), 46.

60. Winthrop, *History*, I, 260.

61. *Mass. Records*, II, 110–12; Winthrop, *History*, II, 254.

62. This analysis is only a rough estimate of military personnel in the Massachusetts General Court. New Englanders employed titles in an irregular manner, and modern scholars have little idea what elements governed their use. See Norman H. Dawes, "Titles as Symbols of Prestige in Seventeenth-Century New England," *William and Mary Quarterly*, 3rd ser., VI (1949), 69–84.

63. *Winthrop Papers*, IV, 360.

64. Winthrop, *History*, II, 323–24.

65. John J. Currier, *History of Newbury, Massachusetts* (Boston, 1902), 494–96; *Mass. Records*, III, 161, 229, 240.

66. Massachusetts Archives, LXVII, fos. 11–16.

67. *Records of Essex County*, III, 116.

68. *Mass. Records*, III, 264, 265.

69. Massachusetts Archives, CXII, fo. 112.

70. Massachusetts Archives, X, fo. 339 (punctuation added).

71. *Mass. Records*, III, 397.

72. "Narrative and Deposition of Captain Breedon," *Documents Relative to the Colonial History of the State of New-York*, 15 vols., ed. John R. Brodhead (Albany, 1853), III, 39–41.

73. *Ibid.*, III, 60.

74. For an account of the Commissioners' problems, see Charles M. Andrews, *The Colonial Period of American History*, 4 vols. (New Haven, 1934–38), III, 59–68.

75. *Mass. Records*, IV, pt. 2, 368, 422. As early as 1663, the General Court created a committee of Captain Daniel Gookin, Major Symon Willard, Major General John Leverett, Captain Francis Norton, and Captain Roger Clap to consider the problems of the militia, "for the rectifying what is amisse & the better settling of the same": *ibid.*, IV, pt. 2, 74. The law of 1668 may be the product of this committee.

76. Massachusetts Archives, LXVII, fo. 39a; *Mass. Records*, IV, pt. 2, 368. See Millar, "The Militia," 80–81.

77. People at the time apparently recognized this trend. A petition from the militia officers of Norfolk County, dated 31 May 1671, noted that the new militia law only affected the choice of officers "formerly chosen by a mixt multitude in private companies, & not of such as are chosen according to our pattent (if we mistake not) wholly by the vote & voice of freemen whos libertyes & privileges this court hath been, & is, sedulously carefull to preserve & mayntayn . . . .": Massachusetts Archives, LXVII, fo. 56.

78. Massachusetts Archives, LXVII, fo. 51.

79. *Mass. Records*, V, 30. On militia committees, see *ibid.*, IV, pt. I, 87.

80. John Winthrop, "A Modell of Christian Charity," in *The Founding of Massachusetts*, ed. Edmund S. Morgan (Indianapolis, 1964), 203.

81. See T. H. Breen and Stephen Foster, "The Puritans' Greatest Achievement: A Study of Social Cohesion in Seventeenth-Century Massachusetts," *Journal of American History*, LX (1973), 5–22.

82. *Mass. Records*, IV, pt. 2, 44.

83. Edmund S. Morgan, *The Puritan Family: Religion and Domestic Relations in Seventeenth-Century New England* (New York, 1966), 186.

84. Joshua Coffin, *A Sketch of the History of Newbury* (Boston, 1845), 87; "Correspondence of John Woodbridge, Jr. and Richard Baxter," ed. Raymond P. Stearns, *New England Quarterly*, X (1937), 574, 576.

85. Breen, "Who Governs," 472–74; Robert Wall, "The Decline of the Massachusetts Franchise, 1647–1666," *Journal of American History*, LIX (1972), 303–10; Kenneth A. Lockridge, *A New England Town*, 47–48, 80–83. Compare the experience of Massachusetts Bay with that of other seventeenth-century societies: see W. J. Eccles, "The Social, Economic,

and Political Significance of the Military Establishment in New France,"
Canadian Hist. Rev., LII (1971), 1–21; L. P. Wright, "The Military
Orders in Sixteenth- and Seventeenth-Century Spanish Society," *Past and
Present*, No. 43 (May 1969), 34–70. For an intriguing comparison see
Pater Clark and Paul Slack, eds., *Crisis and Order in English Towns
1500–1700. Essays in Urban History* (London, 1972). In their introduction
(pp. 21–25) the editors argue that the sixteenth and seventeenth centuries
witnessed a steady erosion of popular participation in town affairs. No one
has explored the possible relationship between local English institutions
and those of New England in the period after 1640; perhaps a broader investigation would reveal that the development of Massachusetts society paralleled that of the mother country.

86. The "Anglicization" of New England institutions is analyzed in John M.
Murrin, "Anglicizing an American Colony: The Transformation of Provincial Massachusetts" (Yale University Ph.D. diss., 1966).

III. Moving to the New World

1. For a detailed account of Great Migration historiography, see John T. Hor-
ton, "Two Bishops and the Holy Brood: A Fresh Look at a Familiar Fact,"
New England Quarterly, XL (1967), 339–46. Since Horton's article, the
New England migration has come in for a fresh look as part of a general interpretation of English migration in Carl Bridenbaugh, *Vexed and Troubled
Englishmen, 1590–1642* (New York, 1968). The most thorough study of
the English origins of the New England migration remains unpublished:
Norman C. P. Tyack, "Migration from East Anglia to New England before
1660" (Ph.D. diss., University of London, 1951). Tyack's approach is open
minded and well balanced, but his emphasis generally falls on the social
and economic discontents of the migrants. Also, R. D. Brown, "Devonians
and New England Settlement Before 1650," *Transactions of the Devonshire
Association for the Advancement of Science, Literature and Art*, XCV
(1963), 219–43.

2. The pioneering study here is Mildred Campbell, "Social Origins of Some
Early Americans," in James Morton Smith, ed., *Seventeenth-Century
America: Essays in Colonial History* (Chapel Hill, N. C., 1959), 63–89.
Campbell based her analysis on two lists of indentured servants who sailed
to America from Bristol and London in the latter half of the 17th century.
These sources do not reveal much about the character of the New England
migration of 1630 to 1642 nor even much about subsequent emigration to
this area. The New England colonies were such notoriously bad markets for
indentured servants that something under 2 percent of the individuals on

the two lists bothered to go there. Abbot Emerson Smith, *Colonists in Bondage: White Servitude and Convict Labor in America, 1607–1776* (Chapel Hill, N. C., 1946), 29, 308–9, 337.

3. The most important local studies are full-length accounts of Andover, Dedham, Sudbury, and Boston, and an analysis of family life in Plymouth Colony: Philip J. Greven, Jr., *Four Generations: Population, Land, and Family in Colonial Andover, Massachusetts* (Ithaca, N. Y., 1970); Kenneth A. Lockridge, *A New England Town: The First Hundred Years, Dedham, Massachusetts, 1636–1736* (New York, 1970); Sumner Chilton Powell, *Puritan Village: The Formation of a New England Town* (Middletown, Conn., 1963); Darrett B. Rutman, *Winthrop's Boston: Portrait of a Puritan Town, 1630–1649* (Chapel Hill, N. C., 1965); John Demos, *A Little Commonwealth: Family Life in Plymouth Colony* (New York, 1970).

4. One study which does focus on people rather than location is Julian Cornwall, "Evidence of Population Mobility in the Seventeenth Century," *Bulletin of the Institute of Historical Research*, XL (1967), 143–52.

5. The origin and significance of the registers is discussed in Charles Boardman Jewson, ed., *Transcript of Three Registers of Passengers from Great Yarmouth to Holland and New England, 1637–1639*. Norfolk Record Society, *Publications*, XXV (1954), 6–7, hereafter cited as Jewson, ed., *Transcript of Passengers to New England*.

6. John Camden Hotten, ed., *The Original Lists of Persons of Quality . . . and Others Who Went from Great Britain to the American Plantations, 1600–1700* (London, 1874); Charles Edward Banks, *The Planters of the Commonwealth: A Study of the Emigrants and Emigration in Colonial Times . . . 1620–1640* (Boston, 1930). Banks made some shrewd guesses when he placed servants with their likely masters or assigned ships and places of settlement to obscure individuals, but he also made some conjectural assignments unsupported by explicit evidence.

7. Banks, *Planters of the Commonwealth*, 13–14.

8. Tyack, "Migration from East Anglia," 76.

9. Hotten, ed., *Original Lists*, xxx–xxxi. In this respect Horton's attempt to distinguish between Leicestershire and Norfolk emigrants places more weight on Banks's statistics than their compiler himself thought they could bear. Horton, "Bishops and the Holy Brood," *NEQ*, XL (1967), 340–41, and Banks, *Planters of the Commonwealth*, 13–14. Charles Edward Banks's *Topographical Dictionary of 2885 English Emigrants to New England, 1620–1650*, 3rd ed. (Baltimore, 1963), although left unfinished at its author's death, covers a wider variety of sources and consequently does more justice to the North and West Country. The work is still biased in favor of East Anglia, however, by the pattern of surviving port records: an East Anglian migrant from a well-recorded port has far more chance of being

detected than a North or West Country man whose existence is known only from his accidental appearance in other, less systematic records.

10. We owe this example to Tyack, "Migration from East Anglia," 57–59.

11. These lists have often been reprinted, but the fullest and most accurate transcriptions are in Jewson, ed., *Transcript of Passengers to New England*, 20–23, 29–30, and "Two Early Passenger Lists, 1635–1637," *New England Historical and Genealogical Register*, LXXV (1921), 221–26. The latter list supersedes the inaccurate abstract in William Boys, *Collections for an History of Sandwich in Kent: With Notices of the Other Cinque Ports and Members, and of Richborough* (Canterbury, 1792), 750–52. Several of the Yarmouth certificates are so mutilated that the total of 193 is only an approximation: we have counted certificate number 56 as a party of seven (an anonymous cordwainer, his wife, four children, and one servant) and certificate number 149, the party of Benjamin Cooper, as listing only four children (the certificate speaks of five but only names four). The individual named in certificate 157, "Augesten Cal-," is Austin Kelham of Dedham, Mass. Jewson, ed., *Transcript of Passengers to New England*, 21, 29, 30.

12. We should add a further caution: systematic analysis in this study will be confined to adult males. Women will have a part in the story when it is possible to bring them in, but we cannot trace them with anything like the same exactitude as the men, who are far better recorded and who did not change their names with marriage. Nor is there much meaning in discussing either motivation for settlement or the effects of the migration on social relationships in dealing with children. They had less choice than the adults in their decision to move and no occupation to change at the time of their removal. Intergenerational social mobility would certainly have been worth investigating, but we cannot find enough detailed information about the adult migrants' incomes while in England (see below, n. 27) and therefore cannot compare one generation with the other. Deducting women, children, and a few doubtful cases leaves 81 men, masters and servants, who had taken a calling before moving to New England.

13. Edmund S. Morgan, *The Puritan Family: Religion and Domestic Relations in Seventeenth-Century New England* (rev. ed., New York, 1966), 145. Tyack, "Migration from East Anglia," 50. The total of 193 passengers from Great Yarmouth is made by the addition of one son-in-law (certificate number 149) and one grandchild (number 148); Jewson, ed., *Transcript of Passengers to New England*, 29. A few of the single people and some of the servants bore the same names as heads of households listed elsewhere on the same register, but even if they were related, the number of such circumstances is not large enough to modify these generalizations in any significant way.

14. Edmund S. Morgan, "The First American Boom: Virginia 1618 to 1630,"

William and Mary Quarterly, 3rd ser., XXVIII (1971), 179–80. We have discussed this point at greater length in T. H. Breen and Stephen Foster, "The Puritans' Greatest Achievement: A Study of Social Cohesion in Seventeenth-Century Massachusetts," *Journal of American History*, LX (1973), 5–22. See also Herbert Moller, "Sex Composition and Correlated Culture Patterns of Colonial America," *WMQ*, 3rd ser., II (1945), 115–18. Moller notes a moderate preponderance of males among the 1,637 migrants, but this is largely the product of his reliance on Banks (rather than Hotten) and his classification of a large portion of the women as of undetermined sex because of their apparently "unfeminine" names.

15. The ages of the women servants are more varied, but all except one were under thirty in 1637. We do not have similar information for the Sandwich migrants, but, as most nonservants were married, they were unlikely to have been very young. See Peter Laslett, *The World We Have Lost* (New York, 1965), 82–106.

16. Carucar's will was entered in court on Sept. 9, 1641, and proved on Oct. 30, 1643, under the name Richard Carver. "Abstracts of the Earliest Wills upon Record in the County of Suffolk, MS.," *New Eng. Hist. and Gen. Reg.*, II (1848), 262. Paine's will was brought into court in Dec. 1642. G. F. Dow, ed., *The Probate Records of Essex County, Massachusetts* (Salem, Mass., 1916–20), I, 37. However, both men had made their wills in 1638 and probably died soon after. Cooper's estate is mentioned as early as Sept. 27, 1637, while a letter of John Endecott to John Winthrop, Sr., dated Aug. 15, 1637, indicates that Cooper died at sea and that Endecott intended to take over the guardianship of his younger daughter. Three years later in 1640 Rebecca Cooper was still residing in Endecott's household. "Abstracts of Wills of the Early Settlers of New England," *New Eng. Hist. and Gen. Reg.*, VII (1853), 29; Endecott to Winthrop, Aug. 15, 1637, *Winthrop Papers*, Massachusetts Historical Society Publications (Boston, 1929–47), III, 483–84; Endecott to Winthrop, Feb. 12, 1641, *ibid.*, IV, 321.

17. For the comparable statistics for one town, Andover, see Greven, *Four Generations*, 25–27.

18. See Banks, *Planters of the Commonwealth*, 9.

19. The following description relies heavily on Joan Thirsk, ed., *The Agrarian History of England and Wales*, IV (Cambridge, 1967), 40–49, 56–57, and C. W. Chalkin, *Seventeenth-Century Kent: A Social and Economic History* (London, 1965), chaps. 1, 3–6, 14–16.

20. D. C. Coleman has recently reemphasized the importance of "the Protestant diaspora" in his "An Innovation and its Diffusion: the 'New Draperies,'" *Economic History Review*, 2nd ser., XXII (1969), 426–29. See also Chalkin, *Seventeenth-Century Kent*, 123–26; K. J. Allison, "The

Norfolk Worsted Industry in the Sixteenth and Seventeenth Centuries," *Yorkshire Bulletin of Economic and Social Research*, XII (1961), 61–65; William Page, ed., *The Victoria History of the Counties of England: A History of Kent*, III (London, 1932), 409.

21. In addition to the sources in n. 19 above, see also Eric Kerridge, *The Agricultural Revolution* (London, 1967), 270–72, 295–96, and Peter Clark and Paul Slack, eds., *Crisis and Order in English Towns, 1500–1700* (London, 1972), 6.

22. Campbell, "Origins of Early Americans," in Smith, ed., *Seventeenth-Century America*, 71–73.

23. A cordwainer is a worker in leather, a joiner is a specialized carpenter who works on lighter and more ornamental kinds of wood, and a calender presses cloth. The names of the freemen are taken from J. M. Cowper, ed., *The Roll of the Freemen of the City of Canterbury from A.D. 1392 to 1800* (Canterbury, 1903); Percy Millican, ed., *The Registers of the Freemen of Norwich, 1548–1713* (Norwich, 1934); *Calendar of the Freemen of Great Yarmouth, 1429–1800 . . .* (Norwich, 1910). The total number of men who actually were freemen is probably much higher since Norwich accounts for all but 3 of the 13, and it is also the only one of the three cities whose records are more or less complete. Cowper, ed., *Canterbury Freemen*, x, and *Yarmouth Freemen*, i.

24. Indeed the life style of the typical Canterbury craftsman was probably just a cut above that of a Kentish farm laborer, that is, just above bare subsistence. See Chalkin, *Seventeenth-Century Kent*, 261–62. Conditions in contemporary Exeter were no better: W. B. Stephens, *Seventeenth-Century Exeter: A Study of Commercial Development, 1625–1688* (Exeter, 1958), 4–42. There is no comparable study of Norfolk for the same period, but for the city of Norwich at a somewhat earlier date see J. F. Pound, "The Social and Trade Structure of Norwich, 1525–1575," *Past and Present*, No. 34 (July 1966), 46–69.

25. This apparently odd situation of a town dweller holding substantial amounts of land in the countryside actually occurred rather frequently in Kent because of the almost universal predominance of freeholds and smallholding and the Kentish practice of partible inheritance. The majority of Kentish landlords were small freeholders who nonetheless leased all or most of their land to others. For Johnson's English estate, see his will reprinted in Edward Johnson, *Wonder-Working Providence of Sions Saviour in New England*, ed. William Frederick Poole (Andover, Mass., 1867), cxxxvi; for the contemporary Kentish situation, see Chalkin, *Seventeenth-Century Kent*, 232–33, 232n.

26. The relevant sections of Wren's indictment are reprinted in John Browne, *History of Congregationalism, and Memorials of the Churches in Norfolk*

and Suffolk (London, 1877), 89; the bishop's rebuttal is in Sir Christopher Wren, *Parentalia, or Memoirs of the Family of the Wrens . . .* (London, 1750), 101–2. The Norwich municipal poor rate for 1633–34, however, gives a different ranking: Busby paid two pence, Metcalfe a penny and a half, and Lawes a penny. Walter Rye, ed., *The Norwich Rate Book from Easter 1633 to Easter 1634* (London, 1903), 63, 73, 75. The list, however, is of questionable value; see n. 27 below.

27. We cannot be more systematic about the migrants' financial positions on the eve of their departure because of an almost complete lack of tax records. The sole exception is the Norwich poor rate book for 1633–34, which (as Bishop Wren's respective judgments about Busby and Metcalfe indicate) at best is a rather blunt instrument for reconstructing social structure. The rate book lists weekly and monthly contributions without distinction, and it is based entirely on the assessed value of houses in the town, a notoriously inaccurate gauge of either income or wealth. Rye, ed., *Norwich Rate Book*, 3–4. No less a person than Archbishop Laud complained of this method of raising money in the city: "The City of Norwich containing 34 parishes, the boundes of the severall parishes are but narrow, and much wast ground is within the City, and the houses yield but a very small rent, specialy in comparison with London." S.P. 16/378/259r, Public Record Office.

28. There is an interesting nineteenth-century parallel to this process in Stephan Thernstrom, *Poverty and Progress: Social Mobility in a Nineteenth Century City* (Cambridge, Mass., 1964), 87–89.

29. On the disruption of the cloth trade, see B. E. Supple, *Commercial Crisis and Change in England, 1600–1642: A Study in the Instability of a Mercantile Economy* (Cambridge, 1959), 102–12, 120–25; Tyack, "Migration from East Anglia," 220-30. On the plague, see *ibid.*, 169–70; Wren, *Parentalia*, 101-2; Walter Rye, ed., *State Papers Relating to Musters, Beacons, Ship Money . . . in Norfolk, from 1626 chiefly to the Beginning of the Civil War* (Norwich, 1907), 216; Boys, *History of Sandwich*, 707–8, 708n. There is a vivid account of the effect of plague on urban commerce in Stephens, *Seventeenth-Century Exeter*, 13–14.

30. See n. 26 above. The latest study of Norfolk in this period accepts the figure of 3,000 exiles as approximately correct. R. W. Ketton-Cremer, *Norfolk in the Civil War: A Portrait of a Society in Conflict* (London, 1969), 76–79.

31. For Wren and his clergy, see *ibid.*, 62–88. Ketton-Cremer, however, has overlooked several suspended ministers. The seven who went to New England were Thomas Allen, Robert Peck, John Allen, John Phillips, George Burdett, Thomas Walker, and Edmund Browne. William Bridge and John Ward left Norwich for Holland where they were joined by another Norfolk refugee minister, Jeremiah Burroughs of Tivetshall. The city of Norwich

alone lost eight Puritan ministers in Wren's crackdown. See Kenneth Wayne Shipps, "Lay Patronage of East Anglian Puritan Clerics in Pre-Revolutionary England" (Ph.D. diss., Yale University, 1971), 267–99. We are indebted to Prof. Shipps for his help and suggestions on the handling of the East Anglian material.

32. Shipps, "Lay Patronage of East Anglian Puritan Clerics," 216–99; W. E. Layton, "Ecclesiastical Disturbances in Ipswich During the Reign of Charles I," *East Anglian*, N.S., II (1887–88), 209, 257, 315, 373, 405.

33. On the background and strength of the Puritan movement in Kent, see Patrick Collinson, *The Elizabethan Puritan Movement* (Berkeley and Los Angeles, 1967), 96, 140–41, 252–55, 258–59; Chalkin, *Seventeenth-Century Kent*, 223, 224–28. The Laudian regime in the shire is described in Alan Everitt, *The Community of Kent and the Great Rebellion, 1640–1660* (Leicester, 1966), 56–60. In 1640 Sir Edward Dering was complaining of the political power of the "puritanical that are separatists and lovers of separation." Quoted in J. H. Plumb, "The Growth of the Electorate in England from 1600 to 1715," *Past and Present*, No. 45 (Nov. 1969), 105.

   The Weald rather than East Kent is usually considered the shire's center of Puritan activity, but the latter region did not lack either nonconformists or outright Separatists. In his metropolitical report of 1634 Laud complained that "the Dutch Churches in Canterbury and Sandwich are great nurseries of Inconformity in those Parts," and in Jan. 1637 he noted that "there have been heretofore many in *Canterbury*, that were not conformable to Church Discipline, and would not kneel at communion," and then added with characteristic grimness, "but they are all now very conformable, as I hear expresly by my officers." George Wharton, ed., *The History of the Troubles and Tryal of . . . William Laud, Lord Archbishop of Canterbury* (London, 1695), 529, 539. See also Richard Culmer, Jr., *A Parish Looking-Glasse for Persecutors of Ministers, or the Persecuted Ministers apologie . . .* (London, 1657), 3; Robert Coachman, *The Cry of a Stone, or a Treatise; shewing what is the Right Matter, Forme, and Government of the visible Church of Christ . . . Together with a just reproofe of . . . such as are commonly called Brownists* (London, 1642), 36. "Robert Coachman" is Robert Cushman of Canterbury and New Plymouth. See Stephen Foster, "The Faith of a Separatist Layman: The Authorship, Context, and Significance of *The Cry of a Stone*," *WMQ*, 3rd ser., XXXIV (1977), 375–403.

34. To a remarkable extent the controversy over motivation has retained the terms set by James Truslow Adams and Samuel Eliot Morison over 30 years ago; see Adams, *The Founding of New England* (Boston, 1921), 121, 122, and Morison, *Builders of the Bay Colony* (Boston, 1930), 340–46. For an account of the controversy see Edmund S. Morgan, "The Historians of Early New England," in Ray Allen Billington, ed., *The Reinterpretation of*

Early American History: Essays in Honor of John Edwin Pomfret (San Marino, Calif., 1966), 45–52. It is worth noting that the study which treats the migrants in the greatest detail also discovers the most complexity in assessing the problem of motivation: Tyack, "Migration from East Anglia," ii, 77–78, 235, 347.

35. Nonconformity was notoriously strong in industrial and urban areas, partly on account of their receptivity to foreign influence and partly on account of the congruence of Puritan and urban outlooks. See George C. Homans, "The Puritans and the Clothing Industry in England," *NEQ*, XIII (1940), 519–29; Perez Zagorin, *The Court and the Country: The Beginning of the English Revolution* (London, 1969), 185–87, 185n; Gerald Strauss, "Protestant Dogma and City Government: The Case of Nuremberg," *Past and Present*, No. 36 (Apr. 1967), 38–58; C. H. Wilson, "Trade, Society, and the State," in E. E. Rich and C. H. Wilson, eds., *The Economy of Expanding Europe in the Sixteenth and Seventeenth Centuries* in *The Cambridge Economic History of Europe*, IV (Cambridge, 1967), 488–89. Moreover, the episcopal authorities under Charles I were particularly alarmed over the spread of Puritanism in the parliamentary boroughs and made special efforts to enforce conformity in these areas. Paul Seaver, *The Puritan Lectureships: The Politics of Religious Dissent, 1560–1662* (Stanford, Calif., 1970), chap. 4.

36. Ludkin's parish is given in Rye, ed., *The Norwich Rate Book*, 74. For Thomas Allen of St. Edmund's, see Wren, *Parentalia*, 95, and Ketton-Cremer, *Norfolk in the Civil War*, 80. Ludkin took his apprenticeship under one Christopher Ludkin of the parish of St. Peter Mancroft, who (along with virtually all the rest of that parish) was in trouble at Richard Corbett's episcopal visitation of 1633; see n. 37 below. Christopher may have been a relative of William but was definitely not his father (the latter was also named William). Millican, ed., *The Freemen of Norwich*, 232.

37. We cannot be more definite about Ludkin's religious tastes in part because of the gaps in the Norwich diocesan records. We have examined the following manuscripts, however, all at the Norfolk and Norwich Record Office, City Library, Norwich: VIS/7 (episcopal visitation book of 1636); SUN/4 (sundry orders, deprivations, excommunications, 1637–40); Norwich Archdeaconry verdicts and comperta books, Case 33, Shelf G, Box 8b (Yarmouth Comperta, 1637–40). None of these sources covers the period of the migration adequately, and VIS/7, the record of Wren's famous visitation of 1636, is particularly disappointing, lacking any account of the bishop or his visitors in Norwich, or the deaneries of Flegge (which includes Yarmouth) and Hingham. VIS/6 (the episcopal visitation of Richard Corbett in 1633) is somewhat fuller but the absence of a man's name is no indication of conformity: the records may be incomplete, the officials of the

archdeacons' courts may have declined to cite him at the visitation, or he may simply have managed to avoid being reported in any court. For what it is worth, then, VIS/6 definitely shows three Norwich emigrants of 1637 cited before the bishop in 1633: Michael Metcalfe and Thomas and Mary Oliver, all of St. Edmund's Parish. Additionally, a John Pears is cited in this parish and a John Baker in both the parishes of St. George Tombland and St. Peter Mancroft (William Ludkin's ex-master Christopher is also cited in the latter parish), and these may well be the emigrants of 1637.

38. For Metcalfe, see n. 37 above. His description of his troubles in 1636 (in vivid detail) is published in "Michael Metcalfe," *New Eng. Hist. and Gen. Reg.*, XVI (1862), 280–88.

39. Henry Dade to Archbishop Laud, Feb. 4, 1633/4. S.P. 16/260/35r.

40. The most determined effort to discriminate between the various cloth-producing areas is W. B. Stephens, "The Cloth Exports of the Provincial Ports, 1600–1640," *Econ. Hist. Rev.*, 2nd ser., XXII (1969), 228–43. However, Stephen's work excludes Yarmouth, and his essentially explor-atory study is too tentative to be incorporated in this chapter.

41. In addition to the sources cited in n. 20 above, see E. Lipson, *The History of the Woollen and Worsted Industries* (London, 1921), chaps. 1 and 2, and Charles Wilson, "Cloth Production and International Competition in the Seventeenth Century," in his *Economic History and the Historian* (London, 1969), 94–113. The situation becomes clearer by comparison with Exeter in the West Country: after a severe depression from 1625 to 1631, the city partially recouped its fortunes between 1632 and 1638 by transfer-ring from French into Dutch markets and by turning from broadcloth to the export of a mixed drapery, the new "Spanish Cloth"; that is, Exeter sur-vived by attempting with some success to become another Norwich in both its export and its export market, a trend strengthened, if anything, by the events of the 1640s. Stephens, *Seventeenth-Century Exeter*, 25–32, 66. W. D. Ramsay, *The Wiltshire Woolen Industry in the Sixteenth and Seven-teenth Centuries* (Oxford, 1943), chap. 7. We must stress, however, that we are not denying the existence of strains in the Norfolk and Kentish econo-mies, only trying to place them in their proper historical and geographical perspective.

42. Quoted in Browne, *A History of Congregationalism*, 101–2. Bishop Wren's views were similar. In replying to his impeachment, it was in his interest to emphasize economic disruptions, but while he claimed that the "meaner sort" emigrated "chiefly for Gaines and Means of life," he thought the "abler sort" had a second motive, "and that was the utter Dislike of all Church Government and of the Doctrine and Discipline by Law here es-tablished." Wren, *Parentalia*, 101–2.

43. For Oliver's connection with Metcalfe, see n. 37 above. John and Joseph

Batchellor came from Canterbury, and Henry from Dover, but all three were probably brothers. "Early Passenger Lists," *New Eng. Hist. and Gen. Reg.*, LXXV (1921), 223.

44. Wilson, "Cloth Production and Competition," in his *Economic History*, 108–9, 109n; Wilson, "Taxation and the Decline of Empires, an Unfashionable Theme," *ibid.*, 116–19; Wren, *Parentalia*, 101–2; Sir John Coke to William Boswell, Feb. 15, 1632/3, S.P. 84/146/66v–67r; Bridenbaugh, *Vexed and Troubled Englishmen*, 466–67.

45. Jewson, ed., *Transcript of Passengers to New England*, 5, 9–14. A substantial minority of the Englishmen going to the Netherlands from Yarmouth intended to serve in the Dutch army or its allied English contingents, and many others claimed they only intended to stay for a short time. But at least 109 announced their intention to settle permanently, and many others did not actually return to England for years, if at all.

46. Simeon Ashe and William Rathband, *A Letter of Many Ministers in Old England, Requesting the judgement of their Reverend Brethren in New England Concerning Nine Positions . . .* (London, 1643). Archbishop Laud also took an interest in religious developments in New England: W. Noel Sainsbury, ed., *Calendar of State Papers, Colonial Series, 1574–1660, preserved in the State Paper Department of Her Majesty's Public Record Office*, I (London, 1860), 194–259.

47. ——— to John Winthrop, ca. May 1637, *Winthrop Papers*, III, 398.

48. The evolution of the requirements for church membership in New England is treated in Edmund S. Morgan, *Visible Saints: The History of a Puritan Idea* (New York, 1963), 87–104. Thirty-seven of the eighty-one adult male migrants definitely joined a church, and one other was clearly a freeman of the Massachusetts Bay Colony and so presumably a church member. The remaining forty migrants include twenty persons so obscure that nothing is known about them, as well as several individuals who died soon after arriving in New England and several more who lived in towns such as Ipswich, where the early church records have been lost.

49. For Mary Oliver, see n. 37 above; Joseph B. Felt, *Annals of Salem*, 2nd ed. (Salem, Mass., 1845–49), II, 457–576; John Winthrop, *The History of New England from 1630 to 1649*, ed. James Savage, I (Boston, 1825), 281–82. Goodens is on Yarmouth Separatist lists for both 1628 and 1630. S.P. 16/124/162r; Champlin Burrage, *The Early English Dissenters in the Light of Recent Research, 1550–1641*, II (Cambridge, 1912), 309–12; Jewson, ed., *Transcript of Passengers to New England*, 22; John Russell Bartlett, ed., *Records of the Colony of Rhode Island and Providence Plantations in New England*, I (Providence, R. I., 1856), 24, 31. One other 1637 emigrant is on these Yarmouth Separatist lists, Margaret Neave, who also settled in Salem, a town which may have had a Separatist church for a

time. Jewson, ed., *Transcript of Passengers to New England*, 29, and Morgan, *Visible Saints*, 85–87, 103–4. At least four other migrants eventually found themselves in trouble in New England for an excess of religious zeal: Henry and Martha Batchellor, William Gault, and William Nickerson; all were originally church members. George Francis Dow, ed., *Records and Files of the Quarterly Courts of Essex County, Massachusetts* (Salem, Mass., 1911–21), I, 49, 305; II, 249; Charles F. Swift, *History of Old Yarmouth . . . from the Settlement . . . to 1794 . . .* (Yarmouth Port, Mass., 1884), 39.

50. John Cotton, *The Way of the Congregational Churches Cleared: In Two Treatises . . .* (London, 1648), 102.

51. The population of Canterbury fluctuated between 4,000 and 7,000; Norwich stood at about 15,000, while Boston did not reach 6,000 inhabitants until about 1700. Chalkin, *Seventeenth-Century Kent*, 30–32; Zagorin, *Court and Country*, 121n; Carl Bridenbaugh, *Cities in the Wilderness: The First Century of Urban Life in America, 1625–1742* (New York, 1938), 6; Evarts B. Greene and Virginia D. Harrington, *American Population Before the Federal Census of 1790* (New York, 1932), 19–21.

52. Much more research is needed on the relationship between the immigrant's place of origin in England and his subsequent experience in New England as divisions within the colonies may have owed much to divergences between the various regions of the mother country. Two pioneering studies in this respect are Powell, *Puritan Village*, and John J. Waters, "Hingham, Massachusetts, 1631–1661: An East Anglian Oligarchy in the New World," *Journal of Social History*, I (1967–68), 351–70.

53. For geographic mobility in early modern England, see E. E. Rich, "The Population of Elizabethan England," *Econ. Hist. Rev.*, 2nd ser., II (1949), 247–65; Peter Laslett and John Harrison, "Clayworth and Cogenhoe," in H. E. Bell and R. L. Ollard, eds., *Historical Essays, 1660–1750: Presented to David Ogg* (London, 1963), 183; W. G. Hoskins, *Provincial England: Essays in Social and Economic History* (London, 1963), 76, 190–208; Peter Clark, "The Migrant in Kentish Towns, 1580–1640," in Clark and Slack, eds., *Crisis and Order*, 117–54.

54. Joseph Dow, *History of the Town of Hampton, New Hampshire: From its Settlement in 1638, to the Autumn of 1892*, I (Salem, Mass., 1893), 19, 33, 568–69; Richard Frothingham, Jr., *The History of Charlestown, Massachusetts* (Boston, 1845), 88; "Lists of Baptisms," *New Eng. Hist. and Gen. Reg.*, IX (1855), 358; J. Wickham Case, ed., *Southold Town Records, Copied, and Explanatory Notes Added*, I (New York, 1882), 1–3, 219, 308; "Ancient Burial-Grounds of Long Island, N. Y.," *New Eng. Hist. and Gen. Reg.*, LIII (1899), 81; Lockridge, *New England Town*, 63–64.

55. John Demos finds comparable spatial mobility in Plymouth Colony: *Little*

Commonwealth, 9–10. But cf. Kenneth Lockridge's findings for Dedham, "The Population of Dedham, Massachusetts, 1636–1736," *Econ. Hist. Rev.*, 2nd ser., XIX (1966), 320–24.

56. Firmin was complaining about a conditional grant of land from Ipswich designed to force him to stay in the town. Firmin to John Winthrop, Dec. 26, 1639, *Winthrop Papers*, IV, 164.

57. S. B. Doggett, *A History of the Doggett-Daggett Family* (Boston, 1894), 325–42; "Early Records of Boston: A Register of the Births and Burials in Concord," *New Eng. Hist. and Gen. Reg.*, IV (1850), 271; "Marriages from the Early Records of Marshfield, Massachusetts," *ibid.*, VI (1852), 347; "Abstracts from the Earliest Wills on File in the County of Suffolk, Mass.," *ibid.*, VIII (1854), 228–29.

58. W. P. Upham and M. O. Howes, eds., *Town Records of Salem*, I (Salem, Mass., 1868), 53, 63, 94, 106, 110, 121, 133, 136, 160, 180.

59. Swift, *History of Yarmouth*, 24, 33, 37, 42–43, 61, 93, 94; W. C. Smith, *A History of Chatham, Massachusetts, formerly the Constablewick or Village of Monomoit* (Hyannis, Mass., 1909), 59, 60–62, 66–67, 77, 83, 93, 94; "Abstracts of Earliest Wills, Suffolk," *New Eng. Hist. and Gen. Reg.*, VIII (1854), 278–79; "Nathaniel Woodward of Boston, and Some of his Descendants," *ibid.*, LI (1897), 171.

60. Don G. Hill, ed., *The Early Records of the Town of Dedham . . . 1630–1845* (Dedham, Mass., 1886–99), III, 33, 83; *Report of the Record Commissioners of the City of Boston* (Boston, 1877–1906), III, 75, 77, 109, 140, hereafter cited as *Report of Boston Commissioners*; Henry S. Nourse, ed., *Early Records of Lancaster, Massachusetts, 1643–1725* (Lancaster, Mass., 1884), 39, 77, 282.

61. Upham and Howes, eds., *Salem Records*, 54; George A. Schofield, ed., *Ancient Records of Ipswich*, I (Ipswich, Mass., 1899), 45; Charles H. Bell, *History of the Town of Exeter, New Hampshire* (Exeter, N. H., 1888), 45, 47, 48; J. Dow, *History of Hampton*, 18; G. F. Dow, ed., *Essex Probate Records*, I, 11; G. F. Dow, ed., *Essex County Court Records*, I, 166; II, 378; Nathaniel B. Shurtleff, ed., *The Records of the Governor and Company of the Massachusetts Bay in New England, 1642–1649*, II (Boston, 1853), 148, hereafter cited as *Mass. Bay Records*; V. C. Sanborn, "The Grantees and Settlement of Hampton, N. H.," *Essex Institute Historical Collections*, LIII (1917), 242.

62. "Early Passenger Lists," *New Eng. Hist. and Gen. Reg.*, LXXV (1921), 221; *Report of Boston Commissioners*, IV, 93, 235, 250; *Records of the First Church at Dorchester, in New England, 1636–1734* (Boston, 1891), 5; Edward Pierce Hamilton, *A History of Milton* (Milton, Mass., 1957), 66, 128; Suffolk County Probate Books, Suffolk County Court House, Boston, XII, 282.

63. *History of the Town of Hingham, Massachusetts* (Hingham, Mass., 1893), III, 47; "Daniel Cushing's Record," *New Eng. Hist. and Gen. Reg.*, XV (1861), 270; *Report of Boston Commissioners*, II, 108; Suffolk County Probate Books, II, 51.

64. Joshua Coffin, A *Sketch of the History of Newbury, Newburyport, and West Newbury from 1635 to 1845* (Boston, 1845), 24; *Watertown Records*, I (Watertown, Mass., 1894), 5, 9, 14, 50–51; James Savage, A *Genealogical Dictionary of the First Settlers of New England, showing Generations of Those who came before May, 1692 on the Basis of Farmers' Register* (Boston, 1860–62), I, 316; Suffolk County Probate Records, III, 88.

65. Smith, *History of Chatham*, 93; *Mass. Bay Records*, 51; *Watertown Records*, 50; Inventory of John Pearce, Middlesex County Probate Books, II, 2, Middlesex County Court House, Cambridge, Mass.

66. Ezekiel Rogers to William Sykes, Dec. 2, 1646, Add. MSS., 4276, fo. 105, British Museum, quoted in Amos Everett Jewett and Emily Mabel Adams Jewett, *Rowley, Massachusetts: "Mr. Ezechi Rogers Plantation," 1639–1850* (Rowley, Mass., 1946), 33, and verified against the original manuscript. Another copy is in "Letters Written by Rev. Ezekiel Rogers of Rowley . . . ," *Essex Collections*, LIII (1917), 219–21. See Bernard Bailyn, *The New England Merchants in the Seventeenth Century* (Cambridge, Mass., 1955), 71–74, for an account of the failure of the weaving effort in New England. Systematic analysis of the relevant English port books for London and the outports confirms clothing was the most valuable and most common item in English cargos bound for New England, 1630 to 1650; Norman C. P. Tyack, "New England's Life Line: Shipping and Traffic to New England, 1630–1650," manuscript article kindly communicated by the author.

67. Coleman, "An Innovation and its Diffusion," *Econ. Hist. Rev.*, 2nd ser., XXII (1969), 423; D. C. Coleman, "Labour in the English Economy of the Seventeenth Century," *ibid.*, VIII (1955–56), 280–95; Wilson, "Taxation and the Decline of Empires," in his *Economic History*, 122–23.

68. See n. 66 above.

69. For Toppan's inventory, see G. F. Dow, ed., *Essex County Court Records*, V, 161. His 21 sheep were valued at £10, his 4 oxen by contrast at £20, his 8 cows at £28, and his single heifer at £2. Another migrant, Joseph Batchellor of Canterbury, possessed one cow and one heifer valued at £5 15s. total, but no sheep at all, while Edmund Towne, who came over as the apprentice of Henry Skerry of Great Yarmouth, owned at his death oxen and cattle valued at £17 17s., swine valued at £8, and sheep and lambs valued at only £6. *Ibid.*, I, 252–53; III, 235. An analysis of the first volume of the *Essex County Probate Records* shows sheep mentioned 59

times and lambs 39 as against 119 references to calves, 83 to cattle, 101 to steers, 118 to heifers, and 243 to other sorts of cows, as well as 213 references to various sorts of pigs and swine.

70. Thirsk, ed., *Agrarian History of England*, 40–49.

71. This generalization is based on an examination of the relevant town records and county probate files, printed and manuscript, for those individuals who can be traced. The change from an urban to a rural form of existence and from artisan to farmer stands in marked contrast with later patterns of migration in New England. The movement of population in Revolutionary Boston, for example, was chiefly from the outlying villages and towns to the city. Allan Kulikoff, "The Progress of Inequality in Revolutionary Boston," *WMQ*, 3rd ser., XXVIII (1971), 400–401; Stephan Thernstrom and Peter R. Knights, "Men in Motion: Some Data and Speculations about Urban Population Mobility in Nineteenth-Century America," in Tamara K. Hareven, ed., *Anonymous Americans: Explorations in Nineteenth-Century Social History* (Englewood Cliffs, N. J., 1971), 17–41.

72. Richard Carucar, husbandman of Scratby, Norfolk, brought three servants with him; Benjamin Cooper, who modestly styled himself a "husbandman" of Brampton, Suffolk, brought two servants and an estate of £1,014; Samuel Hall, yeoman of Canterbury, had three servants and left an estate valued at £144; Thomas Starr, yeoman of Canterbury, was less impressive, bringing no servants and leaving an estate inventoried at only £49 6s. 9d. in 1641. Jewson, ed., *Transcript of Passengers to New England*, 22, 29; "Will Abstracts, Suffolk County," *New Eng. Hist. and Gen. Reg.*, II (1848), 262; "Will Abstracts, New England Settlers," *ibid.*, VII (1853), 29–30; "Early Passenger Lists," *ibid.*, LXXV (1921), 221, 222; *Mass. Bay Records*, I, 314.

73. For Butler, see Charles Edward Banks, *The History of Martha's Vineyard, Dukes County, Massachusetts* (Boston, 1911–25), I, 132, 133; II, 55, 56. Butler styled himself "gent." on a deed of 1652. W. B. Trask, ed., *Suffolk Deeds*, I (Boston, 1880), 196–97. For Smith, see William S. Tilden, *History of the Town of Medfield, Massachusetts, 1650–1886* (Boston, 1887), 55, 63, 67, 479–80. For Henry Dow, John Moutlon, and Robert Page of Hampton, see Savage, *Genealogical Dictionary*, II, 63; III, 248, 331; J. Dow, *History of Hampton*, I, 17, 19, 33, 568–69; Sanborn, "Settlement of Hampton," *Essex Collections*, LIII (1917), 242; Thomas Amory Lee, "The Lee Family of Marblehead," *ibid.*, 282; "The Page Family," *New Eng. Hist. and Gen. Reg.*, XXVI (1872), 75–76. Thomas Call of Faversham, Kent, and Malden, Mass., left an estate of only £213, but he served his town as selectman in 1651. D. P. Corey, *History of Malden, Massachusetts, 1633–1785* (Malden, Mass., 1899), Pt. I, 107, 114; Middlesex County Probate Books, IV, 244. William Eaton of Staple, Kent, and Read-

ing, Mass., did not hold important town offices, but he ranked thirteenth out of fifty-five in the ministerial rate of 1666. Lilley Eaton, *Genealogical History of the Town of Reading* (Boston, 1874), 19–20, 281.

74. Arguably, some of the artisans could have come from farming families, but they would have begun their seven- or eight-year apprenticeships in their adolescence and, given their ages in 1637, would have been practicing their crafts in an urban setting for many years before arriving in New England. For example, eleven Norwich freemen completed their apprenticeships and attained their freedom between 1617 and 1632. Counting his apprenticeship, the youngest of them, Samuel Greenfield, would have been pursuing his vocation for a minimum of twelve years (since the age of fifteen at the latest) when he sailed for New England in 1637. Greenfield, in any case, was the son of a tailor, and of the three other Norwich freemen whose fathers' vocations are known, only one came from an agricultural background: the weaver Francis Lawes was the son of a husbandman, but he had begun a seven-year apprenticeship in 1608 and taken his freedom in 1617. In 1637 Lawes was at least twenty-nine years removed from any experience of farming. Millican, ed., *Freemen of Norwich*, 163, 231.

75. "Gleanings," *New Eng. Hist. and Gen. Reg.*, XV (1861), 331, and "The Ayres and Ayer Families," *ibid.*, XVII (1862), 308. See also *Mass. Bay Records*, II, 87, 192; III, 108; George Francis Dow, ed., *Town Records of Topsfield, Massachusetts, 1659–1739*, I (Topsfield, Mass., 1917), 6, 7, 44.

76. A Richard Jenkins is listed as "deceased abroad" in the Prerogative Court of Canterbury records for 1641. John and George F. Matthews, eds., *"Year Book of Probates": Abstracts of Probates and Sentences in the Prerogative Court of Canterbury, 1620–40*, III (London 1905), 119. Thomas Holmes is mentioned as deceased in the will of his brother in 1649; "Abstracts of the Earliest Wills in the Probate Office, Plymouth," *New Eng. Hist. and Gen. Reg.*, V, (1851), 386, "Wills, Suffolk, Mass.," *ibid.*, VII (1853), 230. A third servant, John Hook, may have been the apprentice killed by the Sandwich tailor Marmaduke Peerce in 1639. Winthrop, *History of New England*, 384.

77. William Bradford, *History of Plymouth Plantation, 1620–1647*, Massachusetts Historical Society Publications, II (Boston, 1912), 401–12. The authors are indebted to Kenneth Lockridge for bringing this list to their attention.

78. John Noble, ed., *Records of the Court of Assistants of the Colony of Massachusetts Bay*, II (Boston, 1901–28), 92, 135.

79. *Ibid.*, 95; Middlesex County Court Records, I, 95, 150, 158, Middlesex County Court House, Cambridge, Mass.

80. James N. Granger, *Launcelot Granger of Newbury, Mass., and Suffield, Conn.: A Genealogical History* (Hartford, Conn., 1893), 21; Bradford, *His-*

tory of Plymouth, 328; Charles Henry Pope, *The Pioneers of Massachusetts: A Descriptive List, drawn from Records of the Colonies, Towns, and Churches and other Contemporaneous Documents* (Boston, 1900), 196. Similarly, the sole surviving record of John Bucke, servant to Henry Batchellor, is his sentence for stealing in 1650. *Essex County Court Records,* I, 88.

81. Moulton married his master's daughter and left an estate of £478. For the Moulton family see n. 73 above, and for the Lincoln clan at Hingham see *History of Hingham,* II, 448ff.

82. For Johnson see n. 25 above, and J. M. Cowper, ed., *The Register Booke of the Parish of St. George the Martyr within the Citie of Canterburie of Christenings, Marriages and Burials* (Canterbury, 1891), 18. For Gedney see n. 58 above and Jewson, ed., *Transcript of Passengers to New England,* 30. For Butler, see n. 73 above and "Early Passenger Lists," *New Eng. Hist. and Gen. Reg.,* LXXV (1921), 221.

83. See notes 26 and 38 above. Hill, ed., *Dedham Records,* III, 75, 140; Suffolk County Probate Books, I, 497; II, 124, IV, 214. Metcalfe's inventory may be deceptive since it does not include any of the property of his wife. Moreover, he had an unusually large number of children and had already given away substantial property before his death. One son, Michael, Jr., who predeceased him, was worth £164, and another son, Nicholas, was forced to flee Norwich with his father, but did not come to America; eight children, however, did.

84. Only one of the migrants, the Rev. John Yonge, was a minister and none of them was then or at any later date an officer of the Massachusetts Bay Company. In fact, only one of the 81 adult males ever achieved major colony office, Capt. Edward Johnson, speaker of the lower house of the Massachusetts General Court.

85. *A Remonstrance on the State of the Kingdom* (1641) quoted in Mildred Campbell, " 'Of People either too Few or too Many': The Conflict of Opinion on Population and its Relation to Emigration," in William Appleton Aiken and Basil Duke Henning, eds., *Conflict in Stuart England: Essays in Honour of Wallace Notestein* (New York, 1960), 183. Unfortunately, we have not been able to find a copy of the original tract, but for a summary of contemporary fears see *ibid.,* 182–83. See also the warning of William, Lord Maynard, to Archbishop Laud in 1638. Sainsbury, ed., *Calendar of State Papers,* 1574–1660, 266.

86. Pope, *Pioneers of Mass.,* 523–24. Sixty-two of the 91 explicitly designated themselves as weavers. Another 168 men called themselves carpenters, joiners, or housewrights; 115 gave their profession as tailors, 81 as shoemakers and cordwainers, and 54 as coopers.

87. Powell's *Puritan Village* is still the most detailed study of the creation of the

New England agricultural system, and it is therefore of interest to note (206–12) that the roll of the earliest Sudbury settlers includes at least one weaver, two tailors, a malster, a clothworker's son, and a large proportion of migrants from the drapery centers of Sutton-Mandeville in Wiltshire and Sudbury, Suffolk.

88. Edward Johnson, *Wonder-Working Providence of Sions Saviour in New England*, ed. J. Franklin Jameson, *Original Narratives of Early American History* (New York, 1910), 36. Apart from Johnson, Joseph and Henry Batchellor originated in the parish while Nathaniel Ovel and (probably) Nicholas Butler were married there. "Early Passenger Lists," *New Eng. Hist. and Gen. Reg.*, LXXV (1921), 223–26; Cowper, ed., *The Parish of St. George*, 107, 111. Several parishes in the city of Norwich similarly account for a disproportionately large number of the migrants who sailed from Yarmouth; see Tyack, "Migration from East Anglia," 49–50. Patrick Collinson has also recently drawn attention to the importance of the existing religious associations in the recruiting of the Great Migration; see Collinson, "The Godly: Aspects of Popular Protestantism in Elizabethan England" (paper presented July 7, 1966, to the *Past and Present* conference on Popular Religion), 18.

IV. Transfer of Culture

1. Wilcomb E. Washburn, "Governor Berkeley and King Philip's War," *New England Quarterly*, XXX (1957), 363–77.

2. Throughout the seventeenth century Virginians discussed the need for towns, criticized each other for the failure to establish them, and persisted in isolating themselves on scattered farms and plantations along the colony's waterways. For descriptions of the early efforts to create village life, see Wesley Frank Craven, *The Southern Colonies in the Seventeenth Century, 1607–1689* (Baton Rouge, 1949), 129–32. In 1662 the Privy Council reminded Governor Berkeley of the economic prosperity of his "neighbours of New England" and instructed the Virginia government to build a town on every river (*ibid.*, 312). Henry Hartwell, James Blair, and Edward Chilton, *The Present State of Virginia, and the College*, ed. by Hunter D. Farish (Williamsburg, 1940), 10–11; Edmund S. Morgan, *American Slavery, American Freedom: The Ordeal of Colonial Virginia* (New York, 1975), 188–91, 287–88; John C. Rainbolt, "The Absence of Towns in Seventeenth-Century Virginia," *Journal of Southern History*, XXXV (1969), 343–60; Edward M. Riley, "The Town Acts of Colonial Virginia," *ibid.*, XVI (1950): 306–23; Sister Joan de Lourdes Leonard, "Operation Checkmate: The Birth and Death of a Virginia Blueprint for Progress, 1660–1676," *William and Mary Quarterly*, 3rd ser., XXIV (1967), 44–74.

The rulers of New France also envied New England's towns; see the instructions for Governor Chevalier De Callieres (25 May 1699) in *Collection
De Manuscrits . . . . A La Nouvelle France* (Quebec, 1884), II, 325.

3. I have discussed the character and structure of English society on the eve of
colonization more fully in Chapter I. That chapter concentrates on the dramatic shift after 1625 in the relationship between central and local government in England. I argue there, as I do here, that this change directly influenced the shape of civil, ecclesiastical, and military institutions in
Massachusetts Bay. However, I overlooked certain nonvolitional elements,
climatic and growing conditions in New England and the density of the
Native American population, for example, which cultural historians have
generally ignored but which in fact greatly facilitated the transfer of a particular European subculture to the New World. For more information on
early seventeenth-century English society, see Alan Everitt, *Change in the
Provinces: The Seventeenth Century*, Department of English Local History,
Occasional Papers, 2nd ser. (Leicester, Eng., 1969), I, 6–48; Thomas Garden Barnes, *Somerset 1625–1640: A County's Government During the
"Personal Rule"* (Cambridge, Mass., 1961), *passim*; David Grayson Allen,
"In English Ways: The Movement of Societies and the Transferal of English Local Law and Custom to Massachusetts Bay, 1600–1690" (Ph.D.
diss., University of Wisconsin, 1974), 9–19, 25–386.

4. The phrase appears in Nicholas Tyacke, "Puritanism, Arminianism and
Counter-Revolution," in Conrad Russell, ed., *The Origins of the English
Civil War* (New York, 1973), 132.

5. A full and provocative discussion of the tensions created on all levels of English society by Charles's blundering policies can be found in Russell, ed.,
Origins of the English Civil War. Especially relevant to the argument advanced here are Russell's own splendid Introduction, 1–31; Michael Haw-
kins, "The Government: Its Role and Its Aims," 35–65; L. M. Hill,
"County Government in Caroline England 1625–1640," 66–90; and J. H.
Elliott, "England and Europe: A Common Malady?" 246–57. Elliott observes of the essays in the Russell collection, "No reader of this volume can
fail to be struck by the constant return to a common theme—that innovation (or what passed for innovation), and even in some fields revolution,
came in the first instance from the court" (249). And in an important study
of electoral behavior in early Stuart England, Derek Hirst has demonstrated
that increasingly after 1624 voters throughout the country (their numbers
were far greater than previous historians working in this period realized)
were swayed by national issues, particularly by the religious and economic
policies of court. Hirst notes, "the reaction [of the electorate] was often
localist resentment at the impact of national policies, and it may be that the
truly novel change was the existence in the 1630s of a central government

willing to intervene dynamically and one which was (unlike the interventions of the government in the economic crises of the early 1620s) reluctant to consult the local leaders." *The Representative of the People? Voters and Voting in England Under the Early Stuarts* (Cambridge, Eng., 1975), 153 and *passim*.

6. See Chapter I. I am not suggesting, of course, that Charles's innovative policies were the *sole* motive for migrating to Massachusetts Bay during the 1630s. Individual men and women sailed to America for a variety of personal reasons: kinship ties, the persuasiveness of a local Puritan minister, economic ambition, bad marriage, just to name a few. But whatever the specific, often idiosyncratic causes for emigration may have been, we know that Englishmen of all sorts (but especially those of strong Puritan sympathies) resisted the spread of political and ecclesiastical centralization. The general threat to the independence of the local communities affected the colonists' institutional perceptions regardless of their personal backgrounds. As J. H. Elliott explains, "intervention in local affairs by the central government was looked upon as an alien intrusion, which automatically called forth a conservative response." Russell, ed., *Origins of the English Civil War*, 254.

7. Darrett B. Rutman, *Winthrop's Boston, Portrait of a Puritan Town, 1630–1649* (Chapel Hill, 1965), 135–201.

8. Kenneth A. Lockridge, *A New England Town: The First Hundred Years* (New York, 1970), 18–19; John J. Waters, "The Traditional World of the New England Peasants: A View from Seventeenth-Century Barnstable," *New Eng. Hist. and Gen. Reg.*, CXXX (1976), 3–21.

9. Josef Barton provides a detailed description of this process in two recent essays, "Leadership in Eastern and Southern European Ethnic Communities, 1870–1950," in John Higham, ed., *The Leadership of American Ethnic Groups* (Baltimore, 1977), 217–45; "Catholicism and Cultural Change in Czech Immigrant Communities, 1850–1920," in Randall Miller and Thomas Marzik, eds., *Immigration and Religion in American Cities* (Philadelphia, 1977), 1–22.

10. Francis Higginson, "New-Englands Plantation or, A Short and True Description . . . of that Country," in Edmund S. Morgan, ed., *The Founding of Massachusetts* (Indianapolis, 1964), 141, 144.

11. Joan Thirsk, ed., *The Agrarian History of England and Wales*, IV, 1500–1640 (Cambridge, 1967), 40–49; Eric Kerridge, *The Farmers of Old England* (London, 1973), 17–39 and *passim*.

12. "A Letter sent from New-England, by Master Graves . . . ," in Morgan, ed., *Founding*, 150.

13. Darrett B. Rutman, *Husbandmen of Plymouth: Farms and Villages in the Old Colony, 1620–1692* (Boston, 1967), 3–65; Robert Walcott, "Hus-

bandry in Colonial New England," *NEQ*, IX (1936), 218–52; Darret B. Rutman, "Governor Winthrop's Garden Crop: The Significance of Agriculture in the Early Commerce of Massachusetts Bay," *WMQ*, 3rd ser., XX (1963), 396–415; Percy W. Bidwell and John I. Falconer, *History of Agriculture in the Northern United States, 1620–1860* (New York, 1941), 5–32; Douglas R. McManis, *Colonial New England: A Historical Geography* (New York, 1975), 86–102.

Colonial American historians have not analyzed the complex cultural relation between peasants (farmers) and the crops that these settlers grew. For some suggestive insights into this relationship, see Thayer Scudder, "The Human Ecology of Big Projects: River Basin Development and Resettlement," in Bernard Siegel et al., eds., *Annual Review of Anthropology* (Palo Alto, 1973), II, 45–55; Harold C. Conklin, "Lexicographical Treatment of Folk Taxonomies," and Brent Berlin, Dennis E. Breedlove, and Peter H. Raven, "Folk Taxonomies and Biological Classifications," in Stephen A. Tayler, ed., *Cognitive Anthropology* (New York, 1969), 41–57, 60–65.

14. See Chapter III.

15. Philip J. Greven, Jr., *Four Generations: Population, Land, and Family in Colonial Andover, Massachusetts* (Ithaca, N. Y., 1970), 49–55; Sumner Chilton Powell, *Puritan Village: The Formation of a New England Town* (Middletown, Conn., 1963), 1–24, 104.

16. For the agricultural experiences of English men and women who traveled to other parts of North America during the seventeenth century, see Peter Wood, *Black Majority: Negroes in Colonial South Carolina, from 1670 through the Stono Rebellion* (New York, 1974), 35–62; Richard S. Dunn, *Sugar and Slaves: The Rise of the Planter Class in the English West Indies, 1624–1713* (Chapel Hill, 1972), chap. 6 and *passim*; Edmund S. Morgan, "The Labor Problem at Jamestown, 1607–18," *American Historical Review*, LXXVI (1971), 595–611.

17. Bernard Bailyn, *The New England Merchants in the Seventeenth Century* (New York, 1964, pb. ed.), 1–74; Rutman, "Governor Winthrop's Garden Crop," 393–415.

18. Lockridge, *A New England Town*, 73; Richard P. Gildrie, *Salem Massachusetts, 1626–1683: A Covenanted Community* (Charlottesville, 1975), 56–74; Gloria L. Main, "Inequality in Early America: The Evidence from Probate Records of Massachusetts and Maryland," *Journal of Interdisciplinary History*, VII (1977), 559–81; Stephen Foster, *Their Solitary Way: The Puritan Social Ethic in the First Century of Settlement in New England* (New Haven, 1971), *passim*, esp. chap. 4.

19. Francis Jennings, *The Invasion of America: Indians, Colonialism, and the Cant of Conquest* (New York, 1976, pb. ed.), 24–31, 207–8; McManis, *Colonial New England*, 22; Calvin Martin, "The European Impact on the

Culture of a Northeastern Algonquian Tribe: An Ecological Interpretation," *WMQ*, 3rd ser., XXXI (1974), 3–26; Alden T. Vaughan, *The New England Frontier: Puritans and Indians, 1620–1675* (Boston, 1965), 21–22, 28–29, 52–55, 103–4.

20. Jameson, ed., *Johnson's Wonder-Working Providence*, 40–41, 78–80.

21. Higginson, "New-Englands Plantation," in Morgan, ed., *Founding*, 147.

22. John Winthrop, "Reasons to be Considered, and Objections with Answers," in *ibid.*, 178.

23. Alden T. Vaughan, *American Genesis: Captain John Smith and the Founding of Virginia* (Boston, 1975), *passim*; Morgan, *American Slavery, American Freedom*, 44–70, 98–100; Wesley Frank Craven, *White, Red, and Black: The Seventeenth-Century Virginian* (Charlottesville, 1971), 39–67.

24. For example, William Hubbard, seventeenth-century Massachusetts historian, noted in his *A Narrative of the Indian Wars* (Norwich, 1777 (orig. pub. 1677)) that ". . . ever since the suppressing of the Pequods [*sic*] in the year 1637, until the year 1675, there was always in appearance amity and good correspondence on all sides, scarce an Englishman was ever known to be assaulted or hurt by any of them" (46).

25. Gabriel Ardant, "Financial Policy and Economic Infrastructure of Modern States and Nations," in Charles Tilly, ed., *The Formation of National States in Western Europe* (Princeton, 1975), 164–242.

26. See Chapter II. On war in seventeenth-century Europe, Theodore K. Rabb, *The Struggle for Stability in Early Modern Europe* (New York, 1975), 116–45.

27. Douglas Edward Leach, *Flintlock and Tomahawk: New England in King Philip's War* (New York, 1958), 103–11. The war effort left the colonists heavily indebted, and over the next decade the mounting costs for defense created serious dissensions on all levels of society. See Chapter V.

28. Kenneth Lockridge, "The Population of Dedham, Massachusetts, 1636–1736," *Economic History Review*, XIX (1966), 318–44; Greven, *Four Generations*, 24–30; Daniel Scott Smith, "The Demographic History of Colonial New England," *Journal of Economic History*, XXXII (1972), 165–83; Maris A. Vinovskis, "Mortality Rates and Trends in Massachusetts before 1860," *ibid.*, 184–213.

29. Morgan, *American Slavery, American Freedom*, 108–30; Irene D. W. Hecht, "The Virginia Muster of 1624/5 as a Source for Demographic History," *WMQ*, 3rd ser., XXX (1973), 65–92; Lorena S. Walsh and Russell R. Menard, "Death in the Chesapeake: Two Life Tables for Men in Early Colonial Maryland," *Maryland Historical Magazine*, LXIX (1974), 211–27.

30. See Chapter III; Greven, *Four Generations*, 24–30 and *passim*.

31. T. H. Breen and Stephen Foster, "The Puritans' Greatest Achievement: A Study of Social Cohesion in Seventeenth-Century Massachusetts," *Journal of American History*, LX (1973), 5–22.

32. John Coolidge, "Hingham Builds a Meetinghouse," *NEQ*, XXXIV (1961), 435–40; Ola Winslow, *Meetinghouse Hill* (New York, 1952), 6–65; Anthony Garvan, "The New England Plain Style," *Comparative Studies in Society and History*, III (1960), 106–22. On Virginia, Rhys Isaac, "Evangelical Revolt," *WMQ*, 3rd ser., XXXI (1974), 348–53.

V. War, Taxes, and Political Brokers

1. Cited in Thomas Hutchinson, *The History of the Colony and Province of Massachusetts-Bay*, ed. Lawrence S. Mayo, 3 vols. (Boston, 1936), I, 319–20.

2. Lawrence Hammond Diary, MS., Massachusetts Historical Society, 11. Also Nathanial Byfield, *An Account of the Late Revolution* (London, 1689), 6.

3. For a general account of the Glorious Revolution in Massachusetts and New York, see David S. Lovejoy, *The Glorious Revolution in America* (New York, 1972). Also T. H. Breen, *The Character of the Good Ruler: Puritan Political Ideas in New England, 1630–1730* (New Haven, 1970), chap. IV; Lois G. Carr and David W. Jordan, *Maryland's Revolution of Government, 1689–1692* (Ithaca, 1974). The best comparative study of political unrest in colonial America during this period is Bernard Bailyn, "Politics and Social Structure in Virginia," in James Morton Smith, ed., *Seventeenth-Century America: Essays in Colonial History* (Chapel Hill, 1959), 90–115. A thoughtful examination of political tensions in the Bay Colony is provided by Theodore B. Lewis, Jr. in his "Massachusetts and the Glorious Revolution, 1660–1692" (Ph.D. diss., University of Wisconsin, 1967).

4. Eric R. Wolf, "Aspects of Group Relations in a Complex Society: Mexico," *American Anthropologist*, LVIII (1956), 1075–76; Jerome Blum, "The Internal Structure and Polity of the European Village Community From the Fifteenth to the Nineteenth Century," *Journal of Modern History*, XLIII (1971), 541–76; Merilee Serrill Gringle, *Bureaucrats, Politicians, and Peasants in Mexico: A Case Study in Public Policy* (Berkeley, 1977); Arturo Valenzuela, *Political Brokers in Chile: Local Government in a Centralized Polity* (Durham, 1977); Sidney Tarrow, *Between Center and Periphery: Grassroots Politicians in Italy and France* (New Haven, 1977); G. Harry Stopp, Jr., "Cultural Brokers and Social Change in an American Peasant Community," *Peasant Studies*, V (1976), 18–22.

5. For a study of a similar development in another New England colony, one

should read Sydney V. James's "Colonial Rhode Island and the Beginnings of the Liberal Rationalized State" (paper delivered at the meeting of the Organization of American Historians, Chicago, April, 1967). Also David Grayson Allen, "In English Ways: The Movement of Societies and the Transferal of English Local Law and Custom to Massachusetts Bay, 1600–1690," (Ph.D. diss., University of Wisconsin, 1974), chap. XII.

6. The literature on commercial, demographic, and religious change in late seventeenth-century New England is immense. Anyone interested in these themes should read Michael G. Hall, *Edward Randolph and the American Colonies, 1676–1703* (Chapel Hill, 1960); Bernard Bailyn, *The New England Merchants in the Seventeenth Century* (Cambridge, Mass., 1955); Richard S. Dunn, *Puritans and Yankees, The Winthrop Dynasty of New England, 1630–1717* (Princeton, 1962); Perry Miller, *The New England Mind, from Colony to Province* (Cambridge, Mass., 1953); Philip J. Greven, Jr., *Four Generations: Population, Land, and Family in Colonial Andover, Massachusetts* (Ithaca, 1970). On war and taxation in France, see Llewain Scott Van Doren, "War Taxation, Institutional Change, and Social Conflict in Provincial France—The Royal *Taille* in Dauphine, 1494–1559," *Proceedings of the American Philosophical Society*, CXXI (1977), 70–96.

7. See Chapters I and IV; Kenneth A. Lockridge, *A New England Town: The First Hundred Years* (New York, 1970); Greven, *Four Generations*; A. L. Beier, "Vagrants and the Social Order in Elizabethan England," *Past and Present*, No. 64 (1974), 3–29.

8. Lockridge, *New England Town*, 13; Edward M. Cook, Jr., "Social Behavior and Changing Values in Dedham, Massachusetts, 1700–1775," *WMQ*, 3rd ser., XXVII (1970), 573–74.

9. George Lee Haskins, *Law and Authority in Early Massachusetts: A Study in Tradition and Design* (New York, 1960), chap. V.

10. Nathaniel B. Shurtleff, ed., *Records of the Governor and Company of the Massachusetts Bay in New England*, 5 vols. in 6 (Boston, 1853–54), V, 25–26.

11. Anne C. Sampson, "The Structure of Inequality: Taxation in Massachusetts Bay, 1630–1684" (master's essay, Northwestern University, 1977), 6–47.

12. Nathaniel Ward to John Winthrop, Jr., *4 Collections*, MHS, VII (1867), 25.

13. *Mass. Records*, I, 228; II, 47.

14. Breen, *Good Ruler*, chap. II.

15. The fullest discussion of the war and the social problems it created is Douglas Edward Leach, *Flintlock and Tomahawk: New England in King Philip's War* (New York, 1966, pb. ed.). On the general relation between

war and bureaucratic development, see Charles Tilly, ed., *The Formation of National States in Western Europe* (Princeton, 1975), intro., esp. 54–55.

16. Urian Oakes, *The Sovereign Efficacy of Divine Providence* (Boston, 1682), 27.

17. E. B. O'Callaghan and Berthold Fernow, eds., *Documents Relative to the Colonial History of the State of New York*, 15 vols. (Albany, 1856–87), III, 243–44.

18. Figures cited in Leach, *Flintlock and Tomahawk*, 110.

19. *Town Records of Salem*, 3 vols. (Salem, 1868–1934), II, 148, 154, 172, 209, 213–14, 275–76, 306.

20. Lockridge, *New England Town*, 136; Samuel Sewall, *History of Woburn* (Boston, 1868), 109–11; *Wenham Town Records, 1642–1706* (Salem, 1930), 42–45; *Watertown Records*, 8 vols. (Watertown, 1894–1939), II, 8–14; Sampson, "The Structure of Inequality," chap. 3.

21. Considering the importance of this problem, it is surprising that colonial historians have generally ignored the structure of taxation in seventeenth-century Massachusetts Bay. An unsatisfactory early study is Charles H. J. Douglas, "Financial History of Massachusetts: From the Organization of the Massachusetts Bay Colony to the American Revolution," *Studies in History, Economics and Public Law* (New York, 1897), I, 13–55. Darrett B. Rutman provides a helpful, though brief description of colonial and local levies in *Winthrop's Boston: A Portrait of a Puritan Town, 1630–1649* (Chapel Hill, 1965), 208–14. The tax system favored merchants or anyone in possession of hard currency. Persons who paid levies in "money" received as much as a 25–33 percent abatement on the country rate. The General Court also experienced difficulty assessing the property of "men of ability" whose estates lay outside the reach of Massachusetts law, presumably cargoes and ships at sea (*Mass. Records*, V, 16, 124–25, 139).

22. *Ibid.*, 16, 44–45, 55, 71, 81, 120–21, 124–25, 139, 156.

23. Sewall, *History of Woburn*, 109–11. Also James R. Trumbull, *History of Northampton, Massachusetts* (2 vols., Northampton, 1898), I, 289.

24. *Mass. Records*, V, 139, 156.

25. *Ibid.*, 195, 220, 245, 296, 324, 376–77, 398, 417, 454, 505. On the problem of keeping hard currency in Massachusetts, see Bailyn, *The New England Merchants*, 182–89.

26. Daniel Gookin, Senior, to a Committee of the General Court, February 14, 1686, Prince MSS., Massachusetts Historical Society, Document 34. Also Leach, *Flintlock and Tomahawk*, 244; *Mass. Records*, V, 124–25.

27. Simon Bradstreet to Edward Randolph, December 8, 1684, *4 Collections*, MHS, VIII (1868), 532–33.

28. Massachusetts Archives, CXII, 367–68, 420.

29. Gabriel Ardant, "Financial Policy and Economic Infrastructure of Modern States and Nations," in Tilly, ed., *Formation of National States*, 164–242.

30. Terry Lee Anderson, *The Economic Growth of Seventeenth-Century New England: A Measurement of Regional Income* (New York, 1975), 150.

31. The Salem town records reflect this growing financial complexity. The work load of the village constables increased immensely after King Philip's War. Indeed, the total levy for Salem in 1676 was two and a half times larger than the entire colony-wide assessment for 1645 (*Salem Records*, II, 213–14; Massachusetts Archives, C, 4). Also Kenneth A. Lockridge and Alan Kreider, "The Evolution of Massachusetts Town Government, 1640 to 1740," *WMQ*, 3rd ser., XXIII (1966), 559.

32. *Wenham Town Records*, 59, 79. The colony government experienced similar problems. Since Massachusetts did not spend a great amount of money before 1676, not much effort was required to keep track of income and expenditures. The responsibility could easily be handled by a magistrate familiar with commerce. After the war, however, the job became more difficult. The informal, probably idiosyncratic records kept by the colony's treasurer during the war, Richard Russell, took years and countless committee meetings to straighten out after Russell's sudden death (*Mass. Records*, V, 83, 128–29, 429, 434–46).

33. Lockridge and Kreider, "Evolution of Town Government," 559.

34. *Wenham Town Records*, 58–59.

35. Massachusetts Archives, CXII, 386.

36. *Ibid.* The dispute apparently flared up again in 1686 and 1687 (*ibid.*, 118–19; CXXVII, 78). The tensions generated by special privilege, or what was perceived as such, surfaced in Lynn. In a petition written in May 1685, village inhabitants "whoe were Soldiers Impressed & sent forth for the Service of the Countrey; In the warr: that was with the Indians" petitioned the General Court for new land. They explained, "that [their] Service was noe whitt to our particular outward advantage, but to the Contrary even much to our disadvantage; Had wee had the liberty of tarrying at home as our neighbours had Though wee had paid double rates, it would have been to our advantage as Indeed wee did pay our proportions by our estates in the Publique Rates to the utmost bounds. Notwithstanding all yet wee humbly conceive that by the Suppression of the Enemy . . . wee poore Souldiers and Servants to the Countrey were Instruments to procure much land . . ." (Massachusetts Archives, CXII, 398). The Lynn soldiers were correct about the land, but other, more powerful colonists had their eye on it. On the growing speculation in land by members of the colony's most prominent families, see Theodore B. Lewis, "Land Speculation and the Dudley Council of 1686," *WMQ*, 3rd ser., XXXI (1974), 255–72.

37. Massachusetts Archives, LXVII, 51. See Chapter II; Breen, "Who Governs:

The Town Franchise in Seventeenth-Century Massachusetts," *WMQ*, 3rd ser., XXVII (1970), 461–74.

38. William Hubbard, *A General History of New England* (Boston, 1848), 184; Perry Miller, *The New England Mind: From Colony to Province* (Boston, 1966, pb. ed.), chap. X.

39. Robert N. Toppan and Alfred T. S. Goodrick, eds., *Edward Randolph: Including His Letters and Official Papers . . . 1676–1703*, 7 vols. (Boston, 1898–1909), III, 145.

40. Blathwayt Papers, IV, Dudley to Blathwayt, May 4, 1684 (microfilm, Colonial Williamsburg, Inc.). See Clifford Geertz, "The Javanese Kijaji: The Changing Role of a Cultural Broker," *Comparative Studies in Society and History*, II (1960), 228–49.

41. Breen, *Good Ruler*, 134–50.

42. *Calendar of State Papers, Colonial Series, 1685–1688*, 222. I examine an analogous political division in Virginia during Bacon's Rebellion in Chapter VII.

43. Hutchinson, *History of the Colony*, I, 314–15, 337.

44. *4 Collections*, MHS, VIII (1868), 369–70.

45. Jeffries, MSS., MHS, I, fo. 146. Governor John Talcott of Connecticut wrote to Governor Andros on December 5, 1687, observing that if a general war with the French and Indians broke out, New Englanders could expect "great expences, a devastation of our plantations, and the effusion of much Christian blood, and the Country brought into poverty, as was our case in the last Indian war. . . ." In any case, Talcott was reluctant to fight unnecessarily "for the inriching of a few mercenary spirited men" engaged in the fur trade (misc. Bound MSS., MHS, vol. 1679–87).

46. Cotton Mather, *Decennium Luctuosum* (Boston, 1699), 27–28.

47. Robert Calef, *More Wonders of the Invisible World* (Boston, 1700), cited in Paul Boyer and Stephen Nissenbaum, eds., *Salem-Village Witchcraft: A Documentary Record of Local Conflict in Colonial New England* (Belmont, Cal., 1972), 101; Massachusetts Archives, CVII, 87.

48. Hutchinson, *History of the Colony*, I, 324–29.

49. Massachusetts Archives, XXXV, 104.

50. A. B., *An Account of the Late Revolutions in New-England* (London, 1689) in *The Andros Tracts*, 3 vols. (Boston, 1869), II, 199.

51. Massachusetts Archives, XXXV, 77; CVII, 271a, 288a, 296b.

52. "The COUNTREY-MAN's Answer to a Gentleman in BOSTON, Mr. N. N.'s LETTER to a Friend in the Countrey," in Richard C. Simmons, "The Massachusetts Revolution of 1689: Three Early American Political Broadsides," *Journal of American Studies*, II (1968), 11–12.

53. Massachusetts Archives, XXXV, 154.

54. *Ibid.*, XXXVI, 20. On June 10, 1689, the Deputies voted "that all are not

freemen in the present government, either Magistrates or Representatives may now be made free" (*ibid.*, CVII, 99). The colony rulers could not convincingly hold the line against franchise reform when some of them obviously could not meet the Old Charter standards.

55. *Ibid.*, XXXV, 349–60; XXXVI, 14, 20–27, 60–62, 91, 103–4, 255, 256; XXXVII, 9–12.

56. On the problem of unrecorded names, see Stephen Foster, "The Massachusetts Franchise in the Seventeenth Century," *WMQ*, 3rd ser., XXIV (1967), 613–23.

57. J. Potter, "The Growth of Population in America, 1700–1860," in D. V. Glass, ed., *Population in History: Essays in Historical Demography* (London, 1965), 638; Robert P. Thomas and Terry L. Anderson, "White Population, Labor Force and Extensive Growth of the New England Economy in the Seventeenth Century," *Journal of Economic History*, XXXIII (1973), 655.

58. Lockridge and Kreider, "Massachusetts Town Government," 569; Lockridge, *New England Town*, 88; John M. Murrin, "Review Essay," *History and Theory*, XI (1972), 260.

59. Massachusetts Archives, CVII, 113, 152, 154a, 156, 157a.

60. *Ibid.*, 124–46, 193a; see Chapter II.

61. At least, he recorded several jokes in his diary (Lawrence Hammond Diary, 9).

62. *Mass. Records*, V, 41, 57, 77, 83, 94–96, 210, 222, 231, 308; Photostats 1665–69, MHS, April 29, 1668; Photostats 1677, MHS, April 10, 1677; Richard Frothingham, *History of Charlestown, Massachusetts* (Boston, 1845), 235–36.

63. 3 *Collections*, MHS, I (1825), 248–64.

64. Massachusetts Archives, CVII, 180.

65. On April 18, 1689, he recorded in his diary some of the charges against the Dominion government and offered no defense for Andros's policies (Diary, 11).

66. As late as May 21, 1689, Hammond appears to have been in control of his company of the Charlestown militia (Massachusetts Archives, CVII, 50a).

67. *Ibid.*, 180–81.

68. *Ibid.*, 163–64; XXXV, 35b, 48b, 75b, 249; XXXVI, 239, 239a; CVII, 165, 180–81, 196–197a, 200, 297, 298.

69. *Ibid.*, CVII, 212, 213. See Trumbull, *History of Northampton*, I, 403–18.

70. Massachusetts Archives, CVII, 212.

71. *Ibid.*

72. *Ibid.*

73. *Ibid.*, 214.

74. *Ibid.*, 239.

75. *Ibid.*, 214.

76. *Ibid.*, 239–40. On Pynchon's social and economic standing see Stephen Innes, "Land Tenancy and Social Order in Springfield, Massachusetts, 1652 to 1702," *WMQ*, 3rd ser., XXXV (1978), 33–56.

77. Massachusetts Archives, CVII, 258–59, also 214; XXXVI, 242, 243, 414. A similar militia election controversy involving Pynchon occurred in Enfield, a village not far from Northampton. On July 5, 1689, the Enfield selectmen urged the General Court to settle the leadership of the local trainband, since "without an officer we are exposed to danger & when persons esteem them selves all as equalls every one's readie to command few will obey" (*ibid.*, 232).

78. *Ibid.*, 185.

79. *Ibid.*, 201.

80. *Ibid.*, 159.

81. *Ibid.*, XXXV, 329; CVII, 209; XXXVI, 1. On July 15, 1689, a group of Sherburn inhabitants complained that when they met to settle the village militia "the younger souldiers in an inconsiderate way made choice of 3 men for capt. Ltt. & Ensigne whereas according to the Judgments of the more settled sort of men amongst us a Ltt was high enough for us considering our state and condition" (*ibid.*, CVII, 209). Salisbury also divided over the choice of officers (*ibid.*, 223a, 223b, 304).

82. Cotton Mather, *The Present State of New-England* (Boston, 1690), 43.

83. "A Particular Account of the Late Revolution, 1689" in Charles M. Andrews, ed., *Narratives of the Insurrections, 1675–1690* (New York, 1915), 205. See also Hutchinson, *History of the Colony*, I, 329.

84. Cotton Mather, *Magnalia Christi Americana* (London, 1702), Bk. II, 51; Gay Transcripts, MHS, I (Phips Papers), 84–85.

85. *Calendar of State Papers, Colonial Series, 1689–1692*, 338.

86. *Ibid.*, 369.

87. Massachusetts Archives, XXXVI, 222b; Gay Transcripts, MHS, I (Phips Papers), 107 (Joseph Dudley to William Blathwayt, February 5, 1691).

88. Massachusetts Archives, XXXVI, 221, 261.

89. Andrew Davis, ed., *Colonial Currency Reprints, 1682–1751*, 4 vols. (Boston, 1910), I, 21–28.

90. *Calendar of State Papers, Colonial Series, 1689–1692*, 385; Hutchinson, *History of the Colony*, I, 340–41; Andrew Davis, "Currency and Banking in the Province of the Massachusetts Bay," *Publications of the American Economic Association*, 3rd ser., no. 4 (1900), 9–11.

91. *Some Additional Considerations Addressed Unto the Worshipful Elisha Hutchinson* (Boston, 1691) in Davis, ed., *Colonial Currency Reprints*, I, 197–204; Gay Transcripts, MHS, I (Phips Papers), 83.

92. *Some Additional Considerations* in Davis, ed., *Colonial Currency Reprints*, I, 198–99.

93. [Increase Mather], A *Vindication of New-England* in *The Andros Tracts*, II, 60.

94. *Some Additional Considerations* in Davis, ed., *Colonial Currency Reprints*, I, 194.

95. Gay Transcripts, MHS, I (Phips Papers), 75; Richard C. Simmons, "The Massachusetts Charter of 1691" in H. C. Allen and Roger Thompson, eds., *Contrast and Connection: Bicentennial Essays in Anglo-American History* (London, 1976), 81–82.

96. Blathwayt Papers, IV, Benjamin Davis to Francis Nicholson, April 17, 1691.

97. *Some Considerations on the Bills of Credit Now Passing in New-England* (Boston, 1691) in Davis, ed., *Colonial Currency Reprints*, I, 191–92.

98. Blathwayt Papers, IV, Brattle to Blathwayt, March 25, 1691. See Richard L. Bowen, "The 1690 Tax Revolt of Plymouth Colony Towns," *New England Historical and Genealogical Register*, CXII (1958), 4–14.

99. Paul Boyer and Stephen Nissenbaum provide the fullest account of the connection between the witch trials and the "conflicts and tensions generated within this small agricultural settlement" (eds., *Salem-Village Witchcraft*, xi). They develop the internalist interpretation, especially the psychological dimensions of community relations, in their *Salem Possessed: The Social Origins of Witchcraft* (Cambridge, Mass., 1974). However, neither they nor John Demos explains adequately why the Salem Village accusations sparked such widespread hysteria. This was not the first time that New Englanders had persecuted witches, but it was the only occasion when the proceedings got out of hand (see John Demos, "Underlying Themes in the Witchcraft of Seventeenth-Century New England," *American Historical Review*, LXXV (1970), 1311–26). Also John M. Murrin, "Revolution and Social Hysteria in England and the Colonies 1675–1692" (paper delivered at the Convention of the American Historical Association, 1968).

100. Massachusetts Archives, XXXVII, 88–89, 206.

101. Cotton Mather, A *Brand Pluck'd Out* (Boston, 1693) in George Lincoln Burr, ed., *Narratives of the Witchcraft Cases, 1648–1706* (New York, 1914), 282.

102. Deodat Lawson, A *Brief and True Narrative* (Boston, 1692) in *ibid.*, 163. Also Calef, *More Wonders of the Invisible World* (London, 1700), 98–99, 117; Hutchinson, *History of the Colony*, II, 36–37.

103. Samuel Willard, *Character of a Good Ruler* (Boston, 1694), 3.

104. Lockridge, *New England Town*, ch. VII; Murrin, "Review Essay," 240–44; Cook, "Social Behavior and Changing Values," 574–75.

VI. LOOKING OUT FOR NUMBER ONE

1. Thomas J. Wertenbaker, *The Planters of Colonial Virginia* (Princeton, 1922), 29. Also Wesley Frank Craven, *The Southern Colonies in the Seventeenth Century, 1607–1689* (Baton Rouge, 1964), 171.

2. Social anthropologists recognize that men and women living in a complex society such as colonial Virginia identify to a greater or lesser degree with separate, but overlapping cultures. On the one hand, they see themselves as representatives of a dominant culture, a general set of values which they share with a large number of people scattered throughout a nation or empire. On the other hand, membership in a smaller sub- or variant culture, a fragment of the dominant culture comprising persons living in a particular region, often influences local patterns of social behavior. The distinction between dominant and variant value systems is an important one for historians, for if the difference is not clearly kept in mind, they may find themselves clumsily attempting to relate dominant cultural values to variant social and institutional behavior. Such behavior, of course, is frequently the product of value-orientations peculiar to a certain subculture. As two authorities on the structure of values have explained, ". . . in most of the analyses of the common value element in cultural patterning, the *dominant* values of people have been overstressed and *variant* values ignored." Florence R. Kluckhohn and Fred L. Strodtbeck, *Variations in Value Orientations: A Theory Tested in Five Cultures* (Evanston, Ill., 1961), 3; Clyde Kluckhohn, ed., *Culture and Behavior* (Glencoe, Ill., 1962), 35–44; Evon Z. Vogt, "American Subcultural Continua as Exemplified by the Mormons and Texans," *American Anthropologist*, LVII (1955), 1168, 1170–71. Robert Redfield seems to be making a similar distinction when he describes the "great tradition and little tradition" of peasant society (*Peasant Society and Culture* (Chicago, 1965, pb. ed.), chap. III).

3. Perry Miller, "Religion and Society in the Early Literature of Virginia," in *Errand into the Wilderness* (New York, 1964, pb. ed.), 100, 108 (emphasis added). C. Vann Woodward accepts Miller's argument, but then noting how very different the culture of Virginia was from that of New England, concludes that "something . . . happened to them [the early Virginians] after they arrived" ("The Southern Ethic in a Puritan World," *William and Mary Quarterly*, 3rd ser., XXV (1968), 343–70).

4. Wesley Frank Craven, *White, Red, and Black: The Seventeenth-Century Virginian* (Charlottesville, 1971), 2.

5. *Historical Manuscripts Commission*, 8th Report, Appendix, Part II, 31.

6. Susan M. Kingsbury, ed., *The Records of the Virginia Company of London* (4 vols., Washington, 1906–35), III, 589.

7. *4 Collections*, Massachusetts Historical Society, IX, 73 (Aspinwall Papers).

On the expectation of quick wealth see David Bertelson, *The Lazy South* (New York, 1967), 19–27.

8. See C. G. Cruickshank, *Elizabeth's Army* (London, 1966), chap. II; Stephen J. Stearns, "Conscription and English Society in the 1620s," *Journal of British Studies*, XL (1972), 1–23.

9. [Robert Johnson], *The New Life of Virginea . . . Being a Second Part of Nova Britannia* [1612] in Peter Force, ed., *Tracts* (4 vols., Washington, D. C., 1836–46), I, No. 7, 17. See Richard L. Morton, *Colonial Virginia* (2 vols., Chapel Hill, 1960), I, 19–32; Sigmund Diamond, "From Organization to Society: Virginia in the Seventeenth Century," *American Journal of Sociology*, LXIII (1958), 457–75; Wertenbaker, *Planters of Colonial Virginia*, 32–33. Irene W. D. Hecht provides a general demographic analysis in "The Virginia Muster of 1624/25 as a Source for Demographic History," *WMQ*, 3rd ser., XXX (1973), 65–92. The early Virginia records do not allow the kind of close examination of the settlers' lives and backgrounds that has been done for the colonists of seventeenth-century New England. See, for example, Chapter III.

10. Charles M. Andrews, *The Colonial Period of American History* (4 vols., New Haven, 1934–38), I, 78–97.

11. The best account of these years remains John Smith, *Travels and Works*, eds., Edward Arber and A. G. Bradley (2 vols., Edinburgh, 1910), I, 47–227.

12. Lyon G. Tyler, ed., *Narratives of Early Virginia, 1606–1625* (New York, 1946), 284–85. Also Wertenbaker, *Planters of Colonial Virginia*, 64–65.

13. Smith, *Travels and Works*, II, 535.

14. See Edmund S. Morgan, "The First American Boom: Virginia 1618 to 1630," *WMQ*, 3rd ser., XXVIII (1971), 169–98.

15. *Ibid.*, 2nd ser., VI (1926), 116–17; *Records of the Virginia Company*, IV, 38–39.

16. See Karen Ordahl Kupperman, "Apathy and Death in Early Jamestown," *Journal of American History*, LXVI (1979), 22–40.

17. Smith, *Travels and Works*, II, 562.

18. There are dangers inherent in treating the Virginians in this period as a monolithic group. No doubt, within the immigrant population descernible subcultures existed (see, for example, Alden T. Vaughan, "Blacks in Virginia: A Note on the First Decade," *WMQ*, 3rd ser., XXIX (1972), 469–78). I have not found significant evidence, however, that the indentured servants, most of them young, white, English males, possessed a system of values strikingly different from that of their masters. Both planters and servants wanted to cash in on the boom economy and to return to England as quickly as possible. Later in the century the racial composition of Virginia's labor force changed radically, and certainly by 1680, it would be

erroneous to write of a single Virginia culture (see Allan Kulikoff, "The Beginnings of the Afro-American Family in Maryland," in Aubrey C. Land, Lois Green Carr, and Edward C. Papenfuse, eds., *Law, Society, and Politics in Early Maryland* (Baltimore, 1977), 171–96).

19. Wesley Frank Craven, *Dissolution of the Virginia Company* (New York, 1932), 59–63. On settlement patterns, see Evon Z. Vogt and Ethel M. Albert, eds., *People of Rimrock: A Study of Values in Five Cultures* (Cambridge, Mass., 1966), 163–70. Also Evon Z. Vogt and Thomas F. O'Dea, "A Comparative Study of the Role of Values in Social Action in Two Southwestern Communities," *American Sociological Review*, XVIII (1953), 645–51.

20. Smith, *Travels and Works*, II, 535.

21. *Ibid.*, 538.

22. *Ibid.*, 573 (emphasis added). The same statement appeared in Edward Waterhouse's pamphlet, "A Declaration of the State of the Colony [1622]," *Records of the Virginia Company*, III, 550.

23. On this point, see Bertelson, *The Lazy South*, 38–42. This is an imaginative, provocative study of the culture of early Virginia. It deserves much closer attention than it has received from recent colonial historians. For a comparison of seventeenth-century New England, Philip J. Greven, Jr., *Four Generations: Population, Land, and Family in Colonial Andover, Massachusetts* (Ithaca, 1970); Kenneth A. Lockridge, *A New England Town: The First Hundred Years, Dedham, Massachusetts 1636–1736* (New York, 1970); John Demos, *A Little Commonwealth: Family Life in Plymouth Colony* (New York, 1970).

24. See Philip A. Bruce, *Economic History of Virginia in the Seventeenth Century* (2 vols., New York, 1907), II, 522–24, 568. William Capps wrote from Virginia that the typical planter's attitude could be summed up in this statement: "I will forsweare ever bending my mind for the publique good, and betake me to my owne profit with some halfe a score of men of my owne, and live rooteinge in the earth like a hog, and reckon Tobacco ad unquem by hundredthes, and quarters" (*Records of the Virginia Company*, IV, 38).

25. The fullest account of the servants' lives in early Virginia is Edmund S. Morgan's "The First American Boom," 169–98. The competition for laborers was intense and sometimes got out of hand. Successful planters apparently viewed their rivals' servants as fair game. Such practices did little to foster a spirit of community in Virginia, and in 1619 the members of the assembly were forced to pass a law against "the inticing awaye the Tenants or Servants of any particular plantation from the place where they are seatted." The Governor and Council decided, however, that the workers were as much to blame as were their masters in fueling the competition and

therefore vowed to punish both "the seducers and the seduced" (*Records of the Virginia Company*, III, 167).

26. *Ibid.*, III, 417.

27. *Ibid.*, III, 455.

28. *Ibid.*, IV, 74.

29. Smith, *Travels and Works*, II, 542, 562. Robert C. Johnson, "The Transportation of Vagrant Children from London to Virginia, 1618–1622," in Howard S. Reinmuth, Jr., ed., *Early Stuart Studies: Essays in Honor of David Harris Williams* (Minneapolis, 1970), 137–51.

30. Tyler, ed., *Narratives*, 403.

31. *Records of the Virginia Company*, II, 42. For more on the problems with Captain Martin, see Tyler, ed., *Narratives*, 247–78.

32. *Records of the Virginia Company*, IV, 584.

33. *Historical Manuscripts Commission*, 8th Report, Appendix, Part II, 39. Also Robert Beverley, *The History and Present State of Virginia*, ed., Louis B. Wright (Charlottesville, 1968), 44.

34. *Historical Manuscripts Commission*, 8th Report, Appendix, Part II, 39.

35. William Strachey, "A True Reportory of the Wracke," in Samuel Purchas, *Hakluytus Posthumus or Purchas His Pilgrimes* (20 vols., Glasgow, 1906), XIX, 67.

36. Tyler, ed., *Narratives*, 277–78.

37. Philip A. Bruce, *Social Life in Old Virginia*, ed., Harvey Wish (New York, 1965, pb. ed.), 56, 293–94; Craven, *Southern Colonies* 132, 142–43.

38. Louis B. Wright, *The First Gentlemen of Virginia* (Charlottesville, 1964, pb. ed.), 95–113; Beverley, *Present State of Virginia*, chap. VIII.

39. See Louis M. Terrell, "Societal Stress, Political Instability, and Levels of Military Effort," *Journal of Conflict Resolution*, XV (1971), 329–46. Morgan offers some suggestions about the relationship between the need to look after "self-preservation" and the desire to profit from "the present crop" in his article "The First American Boom," 181. On the Character of Virginia's Indians in this period, see Craven, *White, Red, and Black*, 39–67.

40. *Records of the Virginia Company*, III, 302.

41. A full account is in Morton, *Colonial Virginia*, I, 72–85.

42. On the colonists' immediate reactions, see William S. Powell, "Aftermath of the Massacre: The First Indian War, 1622–1632," *Virginia Magazine of History and Biography*, LXVI (1958), 44–75; John Smith, *Travels and Works*, II, 584: *Records of the Virginia Company*, III, 612.

43. *Records of the Virginia Company*, II, 116. Also *ibid.*, 96. John Smith, *Travels and Works*, II, 579. In July 1622 James I heard about the Virginia disaster. The king "with great indignacion apprehended the cause thereof to be the same that their lordships did vizt that the Planters in Virginia at-

tended more their present proffitt rather than their safety and pleasing their humors and fancies by Lyvinge so scatteringly and dispersedly . . ." (*Records of the Virginia Company*, II, 96).

44. *Ibid.*, III, 613. See also *ibid.*, IV, 65–66. On the colony's former lax ways, *ibid.*, III, 71, 161, 302; IV, 10, 22–25. On the loose defense system before 1622 read Craven, *Dissolution*, 195–203, and Darrett B. Rutman, "A Militant New World, 1607–1640" (Ph.D. diss., University of Virginia, 1959), 243.

45. Smith, *Travels and Works*, II, 579.

46. William W. Hening, ed., *The Statutes at Large* (13 vols., Richmond, 1819–23), I, 123, 177, 202, 263. Also Powell, "Aftermath of the Massacre," 44–75.

47. *Records of the Virginia Company*, III, 612.

48. *Ibid.*, 612–13.

49. *Ibid.*, III, 656–57.

50. *Ibid.*, IV, 66.

51. Purchas, *Hakluytus*, XIX, 169–70 (emphasis added). George Sandys maintained that Virginians "throughout this wild Countrye, planted dispersedlie in small familyes, far from Neighbours . . . [and] lyve like Libertines out of the eye of the Magistrate, not able to secure themselves, nor to bee relieved by others, upon anie occasion" (*Records of the Virginia Company*, IV, 70).

52. *Ibid.*, II, 487.

53. *Ibid.*, IV, 66, 70.

54. *Ibid.*, IV, 65.

55. *Ibid.*, IV, 58–61.

56. Jon Kukla of the Virginia State Library originally brought this letter to my attention. See J. Frederick Fausz and Jon Kukla, "A Letter of Advice to the Governor of Virginia, 1624," *WMQ*, 3rd ser., XXXIV (1977), 104–12, 118.

57. *4 Collections*, MHS, IX, 71.

58. *WMQ*, 2nd ser., VIII (1928), 164.

59. *Ibid.*, IV, 451 (emphasis added); *WMQ*, 2nd ser., VIII (1927), 210. Also Wesley Frank Craven, "Indian Policy in Early Virginia," *ibid.*, 3rd ser., I (1944), 73.

60. See Chapter II; Breen and Foster, "The Puritans' Greatest Achievement," 5–22. The fullest discussion of the New Englanders' attitudes toward the pursuit of wealth and its relationship to community life is Richard L. Bushman's *From Puritan to Yankee, Character and the Social Order in Connecticut, 1690–1765* (Cambridge, Mass., 1967).

61. *Records of the Virginia Company*, IV, 38–39; John Smith, *Travels and Works*, II, 588. Also *Acts of the Privy Council, 1628 July–1629 April*, 88.

Vogt and O'Dea report a fascinating parallel in their study of Mormon and Texan subcultures in New Mexico. Like the seventeenth-century Virginians, the Texans either could not or would not cooperate with their neighbors in any general project for the common good such as paving roads or building a high school gymnasium. The authors quote one typical Texan speech, "I've got to look after my own farm and my own family first; I can't be up here in town building a gymnasium." The Mormons responded to the same common problems as a group, volunteering their time and energy for the good of the entire community ("Comparative Study of the Role of Values," 650).

62. John Smith, *Travels and Works*, II, 590. The settlers, of course, desperately needed food after the disaster. But even faced with such a general problem, the governor had to warn Virginia troops against private trading with the enemy unless they had received their commander's authorization (*Records of the Virginia Company*, III, 655). On the value of land in relation to the labor force and on the quality of Virginia's rulers during the 1620s, see Morgan, "First American Boom." Some of the colony's most prominent planters received military commissions during this decade, but it is interesting to note that a law of 1629 gave them fairly broad discretion in the use of their power. Indeed, "if there shall be cause that the commander in person cannot attend these services, then in such cases, and in his absence he is to appoint his deputie" (H. R. McIlwaine, ed., *Journals of the House of Burgesses of Virginia 1619–1658/9* (Richmond, 1915), 52).

63. Captain Roger Smith in 1623; *WMQ*, 2nd ser., VIII (1928), 52; *Records of the Virginia Company*, IV, 229; William Capps in 1623; *ibid.*, IV, 37; Captain Bargrave in 1623, "Lord Sackville's Papers Respecting Virginia, 1613–1631," *American Historical Review*, XXVII (1921–22), 493–538, 733–65; Samuel Mathews in 1630; William W. Hening, ed., *The Statutes at Large* (13 vols., Richmond, 1819–23), I, 150, 175.

64. *Records of the Virginia Company*, IV, 74.

65. *Ibid.*, Philip A. Bruce, *Institutional History of Virginia in the Seventeenth Century* (2 vols., New York, 1910), II, 129–30.

66. Smith, *Travels and Works*, II, 588–90.

67. Colonial Office Papers, Class I, Vol. 4, No. 10, Public Record Office, London, microfilm, Yale University Library.

68. *WMQ*, 2nd ser., VIII (1928), 164. Captain Thomas Yong's Voyage to Virginia (1634), 4 *Collections*, MHS, IX, III.

69. *Records of the Virginia Company*, VI, 454; also, *WMQ*, 2nd ser., VI (1926), 118; *Virginia Magazine of History and Biography*, XVI (1908), 37. In December 1622 Captain Martin was appointed Master of Ordinance in Virginia, ". . . with the like fees and Proffitts as are accustomed to the like place here in England. . . ." The Company almost immediately began to

receive complaints about such high salaries (*Records of the Virginia Company*, II, 169).

70. John W. Shy, *Toward Lexington: The Role of the British Army in the Coming of the American Revolution* (Princeton, 1965), 8. Governor Berkeley seems to have been concerned about protecting the Indian trade, and in any case, whatever his motivations may have been, is defensive forts required heavy special taxation (see Craven, *Southern Colonies*, 374–79). Wilcomb E. Washburn defends Governor Berkeley from charges of allowing profits from the Indian trade to affect government policy, but Washburn admits that the colonists had good reason to question Berkeley's motives, (*The Governor and the Rebel, A History of Bacon's Rebellion in Virginia* (Chapel Hill, 1957), 28–29).

71. Edmund Morgan describes several military schemes involving debtors and landless freemen which were advanced by leading planters after Bacon's Rebellion (see "Slavery and Freedom: The American Paradox," *Journal of American History*, LIX [1972], 5–29). Also Chapter VII.

72. *Records of the Virginia Company*, IV, 572; CO 1/4, 1:CP 1/5, 22; WMQ, 2nd ser., VI (1927), 118; VIII (1928), 165.

73. On the contrast between New England and Virginia, see John W. Shy, "A New Look at Colonial Militia," *WMQ*, 3rd ser., XX (1963), 175–79. When the English finally did send an army to Virginia, the results were not exactly what the leading planters expected (see Washburn, *Governor and Rebel*, 92–113).

74. H. R. McIlwaine, ed., *Minutes of the Council and General Court of Colonial Virginia* (Richmond, 1924), 184.

75. Morton, *Colonial Virginia*, I, 152–56; Craven, *Southern Colonies*, 362–63; Craven, *White, Red, and Black*, 55–67.

76. See Sigmund Diamond, "Values as an Obstacle to Economic Growth: The American Colonies," *Journal of Economic History*, XXVII (1967), 573.

77. See Chapter VII; Morgan, "Slavery and Freedom"; and T. H. Breen and Stephen Foster, "The Puritans' Greatest Achievement: A Study of Social Cohesion in Seventeenth-Century Massachusetts," *Journal of American History*, LX (1973), 5–22.

78. Morgan, "Slavery and Freedom," and John C. Rainbolt, "The Alteration in the Relationship between Leadership and Constituents in Virginia, 1660 to 1720," *WMQ*, 3rd ser., XXVII (1970), 411–34.

79. Stanley H. Brandes, "Social Structure and Interpersonal Relations in Navanogal (Spain)," *American Anthropologist*, LXXV (1973), 759. Also Edmund S. Morgan, *Virginians at Home: Family Life in the Eighteenth Century* (Williamsburg, 1952), 73–85. I have explored the changing forms of competition in late seventeenth-century Virginia in Chapter VIII.

80. See Bruce, *Economic History*, II, 568–69, 579.

VII. A Changing Labor Force

1. See T. H. Breen and Stephen Foster, "The Puritans' Greatest Achievement: A Study of Social Cohesion in Seventeenth-Century Massachusetts," *Journal of American History*, LX (1973), 5–22 (hereafter cited as JAH).

2. The House of Burgesses used the term to describe the followers of Nathaniel Bacon (H. R. McIlwaine, ed., *Journals of the House of Burgesses of Virginia 1659/60–1693* (Richmond, 1914), 73). Similar phrases were common in the 1670s. The last example I have found was a proclamation of 1685 referring to "the Giddy headed multitude." (H. R. McIlwaine, ed., *Executive Journals of the Council of Colonial Virginia* (Richmond, 1925), I, 75).

3. William Berkeley to "Mr. Secretary" [Thomas Ludwell], July, 1676, in the Henry Coventry Papers at Longleat, estate of the Marquis of Bath (microfilm, Library of Congress), LXXVII, fo. 145.

4. The disappearance of the "giddy multitude" was only one of several factors affecting Virginia in the last half of the seventeenth century. Equally important were changes in the character of the colony's ruling class. Between 1650 and 1720, the elite was transformed from a body of factious, socially insecure immigrants into a self-confident, unified provincial aristocracy. The behavior of these wealthy planters has been the object of careful examination and much is known about their role in events such as Bacon's Rebellion. The danger for the historian is not in overlooking the gentry, but in crediting it with too large a responsibility in bringing about social change. On the transformation of the Virginia gentry, see Bernard Bailyn, "Politics and Social Structure in Virginia," in James Morton Smith, ed., *Seventeenth-Century America: Essays in Colonial History* (Chapel Hill, 1959), 90–115; John C. Rainbolt, "The Alteration in the Relationship between Leadership and Constituents in Virginia, 1660 to 1720," *William and Mary Quarterly*, 3rd ser., XXVII (1970), 411–34 (hereafter cited as WMQ).

5. Professor Edmund S. Morgan has discussed the character of Virginia's labor force in the late seventeenth century, analyzing how the transition from a predominantly white, indentured labor force to one composed almost entirely of Negro slaves affected the character of colonial Virginia society and how this process later shaped the manner in which the Founding Fathers defined liberty, freedom and equality. Although Morgan was primarily concerned with the development of the institution of slavery, as opposed to changing race relations, his work was extremely valuable in the preparation of this piece. See "Slavery and Freedom: The American Paradox," *JAH*, LIX (1972), 5–29. George M. Fredrickson carries this discussion forward into the ninteenth century and borrowing a term from the

sociologist Pierre L. van den Berghe, describes southern society as an "Her-renvolk democracy"—democracy for the master race, but tyranny for subordinate groups. See *The Black Image in the White Mind: The Debate on Afro-American Character and Destiny, 1817–1914* (New York, 1972, pb. ed.), 58–110.

6. John Hammond, *Leah and Rachel, or, the Two Fruitful Sisters Virginia, and Mary-Land* . . . (London, 1656) reprinted in Peter Force, *Tracts and Other Papers* (Washington, 1844), III, 7–9.

7. See Edmund S. Morgan, "The First American Boom: Virginia, 1618 to 1630." *WMQ*, 3rd ser., XXVIII (1971), 618–30; Wesley Frank Craven, *The Southern Colonies in the Seventeenth Century, 1607–1689* (Baton Rouge, 1949), 214–15.

8. John Spencer Bassett, ed., *The Writings of "Colonel William Byrd"* (New York, 1901), xi; Craven, *Southern Colonies*, 214–15; K. G. Davies, *The Royal African Company* (London, 1957), 38–44.

9. Wesley Frank Craven, *White, Red, and Black: The Seventeenth-Century Virginia* (Charlottesville, 1971), 5, 14–15.

10. Colonial Office Papers, Class I, Vol. 26, No. 77, Public Record Office, London, microfilm, Yale University Library (hereafter cited as CO).

11. See Katheryne Hunlocke to her daughter, August 3, 1648, *WMQ*, 1st ser., IV (1895), 174. On the social origins of persons coming to the New World at this time, see Craven, *White, Red, and Black*, 5, 7–9; Mildred Campbell, "Social Origins of Some Early Americans," in J. M. Smith, ed., *Seventeenth-Century America*, 63–89.

12. See George Donne's unpublished essay "Virginia Reviewed," British Museum, Harleian MSS. 7021, 11A–12.

13. Abbot Emerson Smith, *Colonists in Bondage, White Servitude and Convict Labor in America, 1607–1776* (New York, 1971, pb. ed.), 67–74.

14. Leo F. Stock, ed., *Proceedings and Debates of the British Parliaments Respecting North America, 1542–1739* (Washington, 1924–37), I, 269.

15. [Lionel Gatford], *Publick Good Without Private Interest* . . . (London, 1657), 9–12.

16. Craven, *White, Red, and Black*, 6–7; [Gatford], *Publick Good*, 5; William Bullock, *Virginia Impartially Examined* . . . (London, 1649), 14; *Calendar of State Papers Colonial, 1661–1668*, 98 (hereafter cited as *CSP Colonial*).

17. [Gatford], *Publick Good*, 4.

18. CO 1/25, nos. 26, 28; CO 1/27, no. 9. Although the number of convicts coming to Virginia at this time was small, the colonists may have employed words such as "Newgateers" as general terms to describe lower-class immigrants. On the actual criminals, see A. E. Smith, *Colonists in Bondage*, 89–135.

19. CO 1/25, no. 28.

20. Bullock, *Virginia Impartially Examined*, 13–14.

21. Stock, ed., *Proceedings and Debates*, I, 269; CO 1/49, no. 11; Alexander Moray to Sir Robert Moray, June 12, 1665, *WMQ*, 2nd ser., II (1922), 159–60. See Oscar and Mary F. Handlin, "Origins of the Southern Labor System," *WMQ*, 3rd ser., VII (1950), 202–5.

22. For a general discussion of psychological adjustment to an unfamiliar environment in the colonial period, see Jack P. Greene, "Search for Identity: An Interpretation of the Meaning of Selected Patterns of Social Response in Eighteenth-Century America," and David F. Musto, "On 'Search for Identity': A Comment," *Journal of Social History*, III (1970), 189–224. The problem of psychological adjustment to New World conditions is a topic that deserves closer attention than it has so far received.

23. Bullock, *Virginia Impartially Examined*, 2–8, 14; Hammond, *Leah and Rachel*, 12–19. One Englishman captured the servants' attitudes in a conversation before departure to the New World: "There was little discourse amongst them, but of the pleasantness of the soyl of that Continent we were designed for . . . the temperature of the Air, the plenty of Fowl and Fish of all sorts; the little labour that is performed or expected having so little trouble in it, that it rather may be accounted a pastime than anything of punishment" (cited in A. E. Smith, *Colonist in Bondage*, 70).

24. Bullock, *Virginia Impartially Examined*, 14. The servants' anger is vividly described in an anonymous pamphlet *The Vain Prodigal Life, and Tragical Penitent Death of Thomas Hellier . . .* (London, 1680). In his rage Hellier, a servant recruited for Virginia by false promises, murdered three people in Charles City County.

25. William W. Hening, *The Statutes at Large: Being a Collection of All The Lawes of Virginia . . .* (Richmond, 1819–23), II, 388; *WMQ*, 1st ser., XII (1902), 36.

26. William Sherwood, "Virginias Deploured Condition . . ." [1676]; *4 Collections*, Massachusetts Historical Society, IX (1871), 164; [Gatford], *Publick Good*, 9.

27. Thomas J. Wertenbaker, *The Planters of Colonial Virginia* (Princeton, 1922), ch. V; Philip A. Bruce, *Economic History of Virginia in the Seventeenth Century* (New York, 1896), II, 47; Morgan, "Slavery and Freedom," 20.

28. Thomas Ludwell to Lord John Berkeley, CO 1/21.

29. *Virginia Magazine of History and Biography*, XX (1912), 136–37 (hereafter cited as *VMHB*).

30. John Berry and Francis Maryson, "A True Narrative of the Rise, Progresse, and Cessation of the Late Rebellion in Virginia . . . ," *VMHB*, IV (1897), 127. For the fullest and most recent discussion of the planters' fear

of the landless and impoverished freemen, see Morgan, "Slavery and Freedom," 20–24.

31. A. E. Smith, *Colonists in Bondage*, 328; Craven, *White, Red, and Black*, 98; CO 1/47, no. 106.

32. Elizabeth Donnan, ed., *Documents Illustrative of the History of the Slave Trade to America* (Washington, 1930–35), IV, 89; Craven, *White, Red, and Black*, 93–94; Bruce, *Economic History*, II, 84–86; Philip D. Curtin, *The Atlantic Slave Trade* (Madison, 1969), 57–58, 118–19.

33. Craven, *White, Red, and Black*, 94–95; Morgan Godwyn, *The Negro's and Indians Advocate* (London, 1680), 101.

34. I have found no evidence in the colonial statutes or private correspondence to indicate that language was a barrier dividing whites and blacks before the 1680s.

35. O. and M. Handlin, "Southern Labor System," 204, 209–13; Carl Degler, "Slavery and the Genesis of Race Prejudice," *Comparative Studies in Society & History*, II (1959–60), 51–57; Winthrop Jordan, *White Over Black: American Attitudes Toward the Negro, 1550–1812* (Chapel Hill, 1968), 71–75; D. B. Davis, *The Problem of Slavery in Western Culture* (Ithaca, 1966), 245–47; Craven, *White, Red, and Black*, 75–76; Richard R. Beeman, "Labor Forces and Race Relations: A Comparative View of the Colonization of Brazil and Virginia," *Political Science Quarterly*, LXXXV (1971), 632–35.

36. See below, especially the discussion of Bacon's Rebellion. Also T. H. Breen and Stephen Innes, *"Myne Owne Ground": Race and Freedom on Virginia's Eastern Shore, 1640–1676* (New York, 1980).

37. See A. E. Smith, *Colonists in Bondage*, 67–74; Kenneth M. Stampp, *The Peculiar Institution: Slavery in the Ante-Bellum South* (New York, 1956), 21–22.

38. Richard Ligon, *A True and Exact History of the Island of Barbados* (London, 1657), 43–44; Carl and Roberta Bridenbaugh, *No Peace Beyond the Line: The English in the Caribbean, 1624–1690* (New York, 1972), 24–26, 103–8, 168; A. O. Exquemelin, *The Buccaneers of America*, trans., A. Brown (Baltimore, 1969), 64–66; V. T. Harlow, *A History of Barbados* (Oxford, 1926), 302–6.

39. Hening, *Statutes*, I, 538.

40. *Ibid.*, II, 26, 35; B. Fleet, *Virginia Colonial Abstracts, Charles City County Court Orders, 1664–1665* (vol. XIII), 37; H. R. McIlwaine, ed., *Minutes of the Council and General Court of Colonial Virginia* (Richmond, 1924), 467; Jordan, *White Over Black*, 75.

41. Hening, *Statutes*, II, 273; *VMHB*, XX (1912), 137; Bruce, *Economic History*, II, 19–29; Susie M. Ames, *Studies of the Virginia Eastern Shore in the Seventeenth Century* (Richmond, 1940), 88–89.

42. Hening, *Statutes*, II, 35, 299.

43. "Records of the York County Court," *WMQ*, 1st ser., XI (1902), 34–37: "York County in the Seventeenth Century," *Tyler's Magazine of History and Biography*, I (1920), 266.

44. Robert Beverley, *The History and Present State of Virginia* [1705], ed., Louis B. Wright (Chapel Hill, 1947), 69.

45. "The Servants' Plot of 1663," *VMHB*, XV (1908), 38–41.

46. Beverley, *History of Virginia*, 69.

47. *Ibid.*, 70.

48. CO 1/25, nos. 26, 28.

49. Hening, *Statutes*, II, 187–88, 195; J. C. Ballagh, *White Servitude in the Colony of Virginia: A Study of the System of Indentured Labor in the American Colonies*, Johns Hopkins University Studies, XIII (Baltimore, 1895), 318; Craven, *Southern Colonies*, 215–17.

50. See "Surry County Court Records, September, 1672," *VMHB*, VII (1900), 314.

51. For a review of the historiography on Bacon's Rebellion, see Wesley Frank Craven, *The Colonies in Transition*, 1660–1713 (New York, 1968), 137–56. Also Bailyn, "Politics and Social Structure," 105–15; Wilcomb E. Washburn, *The Governor and The Rebel: A History of Bacon's Rebellion in Virginia* (Chapel Hill, 1957).

52. McIlwaine, ed., *Journals of Burgesses*, 73. See also Richard Lee's comments in *Coventry Papers*, LXXVII, fo. 161.

53. Washburn, *Governor and Rebel*, 51–52.

54. *Coventry Papers*, LXXVII, fo. 144.

55. *Ibid.*, 91, 92. For example, in the mid-1670s Giles Bland, the king's collector of customs in Virginia and the son-in-law of a powerful English official, kept his conflicts confined to the colony's ruling class and thus, escaped with fines and censures. When he later joined Bacon's forces, however, Bland was executed (Washburn, *Governor and Rebel*, 92–93).

56. *Coventry Papers*, LXXVII, fo. 144.

57. CO 5/1371, 241; Coventry Papers, LXXVII, fo. 442.

58. The Burgesses believed Bacon's class rhetoric had wide appeal. They claimed Bacon gathered an army by arousing "the people with Liberty and free estate from Bondage, and that he would make the meanest of them equall with or in better Condition then those that ruled over them" (McIlwaine, ed., *Journals of Burgesses*, 74).

59. William Sherwood to Secretary Joseph Williamson, June 28, 1676, CO 1/37, no. 17; also no. 1.

60. Philip Ludwell to Secretary Joseph Williamson, June 28, 1676, *VMHB*, I (1894), 183.

61. "The History of Bacon's and Ingram's Rebellion" [1676] in Charles M. An-

drews, ed., *Narratives of the Insurrections, 1675–1690* (New York, 1915), 94.

62. Captain Thomas Grantham's "Account of my Transactions," Coventry Papers, LXXVII, fo. 301; Andrews, ed., *Narratives*, 92–96; Washburn, *Governor and Rebel*, 87–89; Thomas Grantham, *An Historical Account of Some Memorial Actions* . . . [London, 1716], ed., R. A. Brock (Richmond, 1882). The servants who supported Bacon were punished as runaways (Hening, *Statutes*, II, 395).

63. If Virginia's black population stood at approximately 2500 at the time of Bacon's Rebellion, then the eighty Negroes identified at West's Plantation represented about 3 percent of the blacks in the colony. Since at least two thirds of the Negro population must have been women and children, the eighty holdouts probably represented about nine percent of the adult black males. One contemporary source mentioned that other Negroes were taken with Ingram, but since the exact number in that group is unknown, they were not included in the estimates. It is possible, however, that considerably more than 10 percent of the colony's adult black males were in arms against Berkeley's government (Washburn, *Governor and Rebel*, 80, 209; Andrews, ed., *Narratives*, 94).

64. Andrews, ed., *Narratives*, 96.

65. Winthrop D. Jordan, "Modern Tensions and the Origins of American Slavery," *Journal of Southern History*, XXVIII (1962), 27. The Burgesses passed another act against Negroes carrying weapons in 1680 (Hening, *Statutes*, II, 481–82, 492–93).

66. See Washburn, *Governor and Rebel*, 209.

67. For example, Bailyn, "Politics and Social Structure," 102; Craven, *Southern Colonies*, 394.

68. William L. Saunders, ed., *The Colonial Records of North Carolina* (Raleigh, 1886), I, 261.

69. *Ibid.*, 248, 260–61.

70. Report to the King, October 31, 1681, *VMHB*, XXV (1917), 371; *CSP Colonial, 1681–1685*, 134–35; also *ibid.*, 89; Council of Virginia to the Lords of Trade and Plantations, May 5, 1683, CO 1/50, no. 105; McIlwaine, ed., *Executive Journals of the Council*, I, 4.

71. CO 1/47, no. 106.

72. Sir Henry Chicheley to Sir Leoline Jenkins, May 8, 1682, CO 1/48, no. 68; *VMHB*, XVIII (1910), 249; Blathwayt Papers, XVI, Nicholas Spencer to William Blathwayt, May 29, 1682 (microfilm, Colonial Williamsburg, Inc.).

73. CO 1/48, nos. 69, 74-I, 81, 95, 97; CO 5/1356, 178; Virginia Council Proceedings, May 10, 1682, *VMHB*, XVIII (1910), 248.

74. CO 1/49, no. 25.

75. CO 1/50, no. 68.

76. Blathwayt Papers, XIV, Governor Effingham to Wm. Blathwayt, May 13, 1685.

77. On the rumors, see McIlwaine, ed., *Executive Journals of Council*, I, 105; Nicholas Spencer to Privy Council, April 29, 1689, *VMHB*, XXII (1914), 269–70; Blathwayt Papers, XVI, April 27, 1689.

78. *CSP Colonial, 1696–1697*, 461.

79. L. C. Gray, "The Market Surplus Problems of Colonial Tobacco," *WMQ*, 2nd ser., VII (1927), 233–34; Warren M. Billings, "The Causes of Bacon's Rebellion: Some Suggestions," *VMHB*, LXXVII (1970), 419–22.

80. Morgan, "The First American Boom"; Wertenbaker, *Planters*, 64.

81. *CSP Colonial, 1681–1685*, 406.

82. CO 1/53, no. 67; Blathwayt Papers, XVI, Spencer to Wm. Blathwayt, April 3, 1684.

83. William Fitzhugh to Captain Partis, July 1, 1680, *VMHB*, I (1894), 30; Wertenbaker, *Planters of Colonial Virginia*, 127.

84. A. E. Smith, *Colonists in Bondage*, 74–79.

85. Bodleian Library, Oxford, MS. All Souls 211 (micofilm, Virginia Survey Report, X75).

86. Wertenbaker, *Planters of Colonial Virginia*, 134–35; William Fitzhugh to Nicholas Hayward, January 30, 1687, in Richard Beale Davis, ed., *William Fitzhugh and His Chesapeake World, 1676–1701* (Chapel Hill, 1963), 202. When officials in the mother country suggested forming a settlement of Irish prisoners of war in Virginia, the colonial council rejected the offer because of the "Dangerous Consequence to the Peace and quiett of this their Majesties Dominion, if many Irishmen should be sent into this Colony . . ." (McIlwaine, ed., *Executive Journals of the Council*, I, 139).

87. Davis, ed., *William Fitzhugh*, 15.

88. Beverley, *History of Virginia*, 275.

89. "Report of the Journey of Francis Louis Michel From Berne, Switzerland to Virginia, October 2, 1701–December 1, 1702," *VMHB*, XXIV (1916), 124, 287.

90. *Ibid.*, 129; [Durand of Dauphiné], *A Huguenot Exile in Virginia: or Voyages of a Frenchman exiled for his Religion with a Description of Virginia and Maryland*, ed. Gilbert Chinard (New York, 1934 (orig. publ. The Hague, 1687)), 143; Craven, *White, Red, and Black*, 64–67.

91. [Durand], *A Huguenot Exile*, ed. Chinard, 109, 179–80; Bassett, ed., *Writings of Colonel Byrd*, xxi–xxii.

92. William Fitzhugh to Nicholas Hayward, April 1, 1689, *VMHB*, II (1895), 275; Fairfax Harrison, *Landmarks of Old Prince William: A Study of Origins in Northern Virginia* (Richmond, 1924), I, 177–96. On the large number of small farms in Virginia, see Wertenbaker, *Planters of Colonial*

Virginia, 52–53; Manning C. Voorhis, "Crown Versus Council in the Virginia Land Policy," *WMQ*, 3rd ser., III (1946) 499. Also, on the land speculation of wealthy planters in Maryland, Aubrey C. Land, "Economic Base and Social Structure: The Northern Chesapeake in the Eighteenth Century," *Journal of Economic History*, XXV (1965), 648–49.

93. [Durand], *A Huguenot Exile*, ed. Chinard, 32, 154–55, 157–58.
94. *CSP Colonial, 1693–1696*, 511; Bassett, ed., *Writings of Colonel Byrd*, xi–xiv.
95. "Report of Francis Louis Michel," 135, 289, 290; Wertenbaker, *Planters of Colonial Virginia*, 138–39.
96. See Land, "Economic Base and Social Structure," 639–54, for an estimate of social mobility in Chesapeake society.
97. "Report of Francis Louis Michel," 25; Rainbolt, "Leadership and Constituents in Virginia," 428; Wertenbaker, *Planters of Colonial Virginia*, 130–33.
98. Davies, *Royal African Company*, 131–35, 143–51; Davis, ed., *William Fitzhugh*, 21, 122, 127–28. The development of the Virginia labor force paralleled that of the West Indian colonies, although the Virginians did not become dependent on Negro slaves until twenty or thirty years after the islands had done so (see C. S. S. Higham, *The Development of the Leeward Islands Under the Restoration, 1660–1685* (Cambridge, England, 1921), 144–65; Harlow, *History of Barbados*, 327; Burns, *History of the British West Indies*, 302).
99. Stock, ed., *Proceedings and Debates*, II, 183.
100. Curtin, *Atlantic Slave Trade*, 144; Donnan, ed., *Documents of the Slave Trade*, I, 250; Davies, *Royal African Company*, 143; Craven, *White, Red, and Black*, 100–101.
101. "Report of Francis Louis Michel," 117.
102. *Ibid.*, 116, 117; Bruce, *Economic History*, II, 108–9.
103. *CSP Colonial, 1699*, 261. This evidence supports the Handlins' argument that race prejudice grew as the Negro population in Virginia expanded and as the lower-class whites improved their economic status relative to the blacks. Neither of these developments, however, seems to have greatly affected race relations much before the 1680s ("Southern Labor System," 210, 214–15).
104. Separate living quarters also divided white and black workers. A French visitor in 1687 noted that the planters built separate quarters for "Christian slaves" and "negro slaves" ([Durand], *A Huguenot Exile*, ed. Chinard, 119–20). William Fitzhugh constructed three units of "quarters" for his Negro slaves (R. B. Davis, ed., *William Fitzhugh*, 15).
105. Hening, *Statutes*, III, 456.
106. Cited in Rainbolt, "Leadership and Constituents in Virginia," 429.

107. McIlwaine, ed., *Executive Journals of the Council*, 86–87; *Effingham Papers*, II, October 24, 1687 (microfilm, Colonial Williamsburg, Inc.); Hening, *Statutes*, III, 86; Bruce, *Economic History*, II, 116.

108. On Negro plots, real and imagined, see "Records of Westmoreland Country," *WMQ*, 1st ser., X (1902), 178; Effingham Papers, II, October 24, 1687; Wertenbaker, *Planters of Colonial Virginia*, 128–29.

109. Governor Andros's proclamation calling for the stricter enforcement of acts preventing Negro insurrections was read before the militia in each county (McIlwaine, ed., *Executive Journals of the Council*, I, 317–18). On police powers, see Jordan, *White Over Black*, 82; Hening, *Statutes*, III, 86–87; Morgan, "Slavery and Freedom," 26–27.

110. Hugh Jones, *The Present State of Virginia*, ed., Richard L. Morton (Chapel Hill, 1956), 93.

VIII. Horses and Gentlemen

1. [Durand of Dauphiné], *A Huguenot Exile in Virginia: or Voyages of a Frenchman exiled for his Religion with a Description of Virginia and Maryland*, ed. Gilbert Chinard (New York, 1934 (orig. publ. The Hague, 1687)), 148.

2. Rev. James Fontaine, *Memoirs of a Huguenot Family* . . . , ed. Ann Maury (Baltimore, 1967 (orig. publ. 1853)), 265–66; John Mercer, cited in Jane Carson, *Colonial Virginians at Play* (Williamsburg, 1965), 49, n. 1; H. R. McIlwaine, ed., *Minutes of the Council and General Court of Colonial Virginia, 1622–1632, 1670–1676* . . . (Richmond, 1924), 252, 281, 285.

3. Throughout this essay I use the terms gentry, gentlemen, and great planters as synonyms. In each Virginia county a few gentry families dominated civil, ecclesiastical, and military affairs. While the members of these families were substantially wealthier than the great majority of white planters, they were not a class in a narrow economic sense. Their cultural styles as well as their financial position set them apart. The great planters and their families probably accounted for less than 2 percent of the colony's white population. Louis B. Wright, *The First Gentlemen of Virginia: Intellectual Qualities of the Early Colonial Ruling Class* (San Marino, Calif., 1940), 57, estimates their number at "fewer than a hundred families." While entrance into the gentry was not closed to newcomers, upward mobility into that group became increasingly difficult after the 1690s. See Philip A. Bruce, *Social Life of Virginia in the Seventeenth Century* (New York, 1907), 39–100; Aubrey C. Land, "Economic Base and Social Structure: The Northern Chesapeake in the Eighteenth Century," *Journal of Eco-*

nomic History, XXV (1965), 639–54; Bernard Bailyn, "Politics and Social Structure in Virginia," in James Morton Smith, ed., Seventeenth-Century America: Essays in Colonial History (Chapel Hill, N. C., 1959), 90–115; and Jack P. Greene, "Foundations of Political Power in the Virginia House of Burgesses, 1720–1776," William and Mary Quarterly, 3rd ser., XVI (1959), 485–506.

4. These disturbances are described in Chapter VII. The fullest account of Bacon's Rebellion remains Wilcomb E. Washburn, The Governor and the Rebel: A History of Bacon's Rebellion in Virginia (Chapel Hill, N.C., 1957).

5. Several historians have remarked on the unusual political stability of eighteenth-century Virginia. See, for example, Jack P. Greene, "Changing Interpretations of Early American Politics," in Ray Allen Billington, ed., The Reinterpretation of Early American History: Essays in Honor of John Edwin Pomfret (San Marino, Calif., 1966), 167–68, and Gordon S. Wood, "Rhetoric and Reality in the American Revolution," WMQ, 3rd ser., XXIII (1966), 27–30.

6. The phrase "creole elite" comes from Carole Shammas, "English-Born and Creole Elites in Turn-of-the-Century Virginia," in Thad W. Tate and David L. Ammerman, eds., The Chesapeake in the Seventeenth Century: Essays on Anglo-American Society and Politics (New York, 1979), 274–96. See also David W. Jordan, "Political Stability and the Emergence of a Native Elite in Maryland, 1660–1715," ibid. The process of forming a native-born elite is also discussed in Bailyn, "Politics and Social Structure," in Smith, ed., Seventeenth-Century America, 90–115; John C. Rainbolt, "The Alteration in the Relationship between Leadership and Constituents in Virginia, 1660 to 1720," WMQ, 3rd ser., XXVII (1970), 411–34; and Martin H. Quitt, "Virginia House of Burgesses 1660–1706: The Social, Educational, and Economic Bases of Political Power" (Ph.D. diss., Washington University, 1970).

7. See Chapter VII and Edmund S. Morgan, American Slavery—American Freedom: The Ordeal of Colonial Virginia (New York, 1975), 295–362; Rainbolt, "Leadership and Constituents," WMQ, 3rd ser., XXVII (1970), 428–29. On the social attitudes of the small planters see David Alan Williams, "Political Alignments in Colonial Virginia, 1698–1750" (Ph.D. diss., Northwestern University, 1959), chap. I.

8. A sudden growth of gambling for high stakes in pre-Civil War England is discussed in Lawrence Stone, The Crisis of the Aristocracy, 1558–1641 (Oxford, 1965). For the later period see Robert W. Malcolmson, Popular Recreations in English Society, 1700–1850 (Cambridge, 1973); G. E. Mingay, English Landed Society in the Eighteenth Century (London,

1963), 151–53, 249–50; and E. D. Cuming, "Sports and Games," in A. S. Turberville, ed., *Johnson's England: An Account of the Life and Manners of his Age*, I (London, 1933), 362–83.

9. It is important to stress here that the Virginia gentry did not simply copy English customs. As I argue in this essay, a specific, patterned form of behavior, such as gambling, does not become popular in a society or among the members of a subgroup of that society unless the activity reflects or expresses values indigenous to that culture. In seventeenth-century Massachusetts Bay, for example, heavy betting did not develop. A small amount of gambling seems to have occurred among the poor, especially among servants, but I can find no incidence of gambling among the colony's social, political, or religious leaders. See Nathaniel B. Shurtleff, ed., *Records of the Governor and Company of the Massachusetts Bay . . .* (Boston, 1853–54), II, 180, III, 201, IV, pt. I, 366; *Records of the Suffolk County Court, 1671–1680* (Colonial Society of Massachusetts, *Publications* (Boston, 1933)), XXIX, 131, 259, 263, XXX, 1162; and Joseph H. Smith, ed., *Colonial Justice in Western Massachusetts, 1639–1702: The Pynchon Court Record* (Cambridge, Mass., 1961), 109.

10. Two of Clifford Geertz's essays here helped shape my ideas about Virginia society: "Thick Description: Toward an Interpretive Theory of Culture" and "Deep Play: Notes on the Balinese Cockfight" in Geertz, *The Interpretation of Cultures* (New York, 1973), 3–30, 412–53. Also see Erving Goffman's "Fun in Games" in Goffman, *Encounters: Two Studies in the Sociology of Interaction* (Indianapolis, 1961), 17–81; Raymond Firth, "A Dart Match in Tikopia: A Study in the Sociology of Primitive Sport," *Oceania*, I (1930), 64–96; and H. A. Powell, "Cricket in Kiriwina," *Listener*, XLVIII (1952), 384–85. See also T. Gwynn Jones, *Welsh Folklore and Folk Custom* (London, 1930). Jones provides a remarkable analysis of the eighteenth-century "gwylmabsant," a popular Welsh form of community recreation which "included contests in leaping, running, hurling, wrestling, cock-fighting and foot-ball playing. . . . Rivalry and competition were prominent elements in the Gwylmabsant, which is the reason perhaps, that to this day there is little chance for anything—religion, education, literature, music, drama, art or sport—to thrive in Wales except on lines of competition" (161–62).

11. Philip A. Bruce, *Economic History of Virginia in the Seventeenth Century . . .* , II (New York, 1935 (orig. publ. 1895)), 151.

12. "A Letter from Mr. John Clayton Rector of Crofton at Wakefield in Yorkshire, to the Royal Society, May 12, 1688," in Peter Force, ed., *Tracts and Other Papers Relating Principally to the Origin, Settlement, and Progress of the Colonies in North America . . .* , III (Washington, D. C., 1844), no. 12, p. 21.

13. Richard Beale Davis, ed., *William Fitzhugh and His Chesapeake World,*

1676–1701: The Fitzhugh Letters and Other Documents (Chapel Hill, N. C., 1963), 15.

14. On the independence of the Virginia gentry see Gerald W. Mullin, *Flight and Rebellion: Slave Resistance in Eighteenth-Century Virginia* (New York, 1972), chap. I.

15. William Byrd II to Charles, Earl of Orrery, July 5, 1726, in "Virginia Council Journals, 1726—1753," *Virginia Magazine of History and Biography*, XXXII (1924), 27.

16. [Durand], *A Huguenot Exile*, ed. Chinard, 110.

17. I discuss this theme in greater detail in Chapter VI.

18. Rev. Andrew Burnaby, *Travels through The Middle Settlements In North America, In the Years 1759 and 1760; With Observations Upon the State of the Colonies*, in John Pinkerton, ed., *A General Collection of the Best and Most Interesting Voyages and Travels in All Parts of the World* . . . , XIII (London, 1812), 715.

19. According to John Rainbolt, the gentry's "striving for land, wealth, and position was intense and, at times, ruthless" ("Leadership and Constituents," *WMQ*, 3rd ser., XXVII (1970), 414). See Carole Shammas, "English-Born and Creole Elites," in Tate and Ammerman, eds., *Seventeenth-Century Chesapeake*; Morgan, *American Slavery—American Freedom*, 288–89; and Rhys Isaac, "Evangelical Revolt: The Nature of the Baptists' Challenge to the Traditional Order in Virginia, 1765 to 1775," *WMQ*, 3rd ser., XXXI (1974), 345–53.

20. Louis B. Wright, ed., *Letters of Robert Carter, 1720–1727: The Commercial Interests of a Virginia Gentleman* (San Marino, Calif., 1940), 93–94).

21. Hugh Jones, *The Present State of Virginia Giving a Particular and short Account of the Indian, English, and Negroe Inhabitants of that Colony* . . . (New York, 1865 (orig. publ. 1724)), 48.

22. Quoted in Thomas Jefferson Wertenbaker, *The Old South: The Founding of American Civilization* (New York, 1942), 19.

23. Peter Collinson to John Bartram, Feb. 17, 1737, *WMQ*, 2nd ser., VI (1926), 304.

24. Davis, ed., *Fitzhugh Letters*, 229, 241–42, 244, 246, 249–50. For another example of the concern about outward appearances see the will of Robert Cole (1674), in *WMQ*, 3rd ser., XXXI (1974), 139.

25. Robert Beverley, *The History and Present State of Virginia*, ed., Louis B. Wright (Chapel Hill, N. C., 1947), 226.

26. William Fitzhugh to Oliver Luke, Aug. 15, 1690, in Davis, ed., *Fitzhugh Letters*, 280.

27. William Byrd I to Perry and Lane, July 8, 1686, in "Letters of William Byrd I," *VMHB*, XXV (1917), 132.

28. Louis B. Wright and Marion Tinling, eds., *The Secret Diary of William Byrd of Westover, 1709–1712* (Richmond, Va., 1941), 223–24.

29. Gaming was so popular among the gentry, so much an expression of their culture, that it became a common metaphor, in their discussion of colonial politics. For example, an unsigned essay entitled "The History of Bacon's and Ingram's Rebellion, 1676" described the relationship between Nathaniel Bacon and Governor William Berkeley as a card game. Charles M. Andrews, ed., *Narratives of the Insurrections, 1675–1690* (New York, 1915), 57. In another account of Bacon's Rebellion, written in 1705, Thomas Mathew noted that several members of the House of Burgesses were "not docill enough to Gallop the future Races, that Court seem'd dispos'd to Lead'em." *Ibid.*, 32. In May 1697 William Fitzhugh explained to Captain Roger Jones: "Your self will see what a hard Game we have to play the contrary party that is our Opposers, having the best Cards and the trumps to boot especially the Honor. Yet would my Lord Fairfax there [in England], take his turn in Shuffling and Dealing the Cards and his Lordship with the rest see that we were not cheated in our game, I question not but we should gain the Sett, tho' the game is so far plaid" (Davis, ed., *Fitzhugh Letters*, 352).

30. Rhys Isaac provides a provocative analysis of the relationship between games and gentry culture on the eve of the Revolution in "Evangelical Revolt," *WMQ*, 3rd ser., XXXI (1974), 348–53. See also Mark Anthony de Wolfe Howe, ed., "Journal of Josiah Quincy, Junior, 1773," Massachusetts Historical Society, *Proceedings*, XLIX (1915–16), 467, and William Stith, *The Sinfulness and pernicious Nature of Gaming. A Sermon Preached before the General Assembly of Virginia: At Williamsburg, March 1st 1752* (Williamsburg, 1752), 5–26.

31. The best discussion of these household games in Carson, *Virginians at Play*, 49–89. See also Charles Cotton, *The Compleat Gamester or Instructions How to Play at Billiards, Trucks, Bowls, and Chess . . .* (1674), in Cyril H. Hartmann, ed., *Games and Gamesters of the Restoration: The Compleat Gamester by Charles Cotton, 1674, and Lives of the Gamesters*, by Theophilus Lucas, 1714 (London, 1930).

32. After 1750, however, the gentry's attitude toward household or tavern games seems to have changed. The betting became so heavy that several eminent planters lost fortunes at the gaming tables. A visitor at Williamsburg in 1765 wrote of these men that "they are all professed gamesters, Especially Colonel Burd [William Byrd III], who is never happy but when he has the box and Dices in hand. [T]his Gentleman from a man of the greatest property of any in america has reduced himself to that Degree by gameing, that few or nobody will Credit him for Ever so small a sum of money. [H]e was obliged to sel 400 fine Negroes a few Days before my arrival." "Journal of a French Traveller in the Colonies, 1765, I," *American*

Historical Review, XXVI (1920–21), 742. Byrd was not alone. Robert Wormeley Carter and Robert Burwell were excessive gamblers, and as the aging Landon Carter (Robert "King" Carter's son) observed the wagering of the gentry on the eve of the Revolution, he sadly mused, "they play away and play it all away." Jack P. Greene, ed., *The Diary of Colonel Landon Carter of Sabine Hall, 1752–1778*, II (Charlottesville, Va., 1965), 830. On this generation's addiction to gambling see Emory G. Evans, "The Rise and Decline of the Virginia Aristocracy in the Eighteenth Century: The Nelsons," in Darrett B. Rutman, ed., *The Old Dominion: Essays for Thomas Perkins Abernethy* (Charlottesville, Va., 1964), 68–70.

33. Wright and Tingling, eds., *Secret Diary*, 75, 442, 449.

34. Only one mention of cockfighting before 1730 has come to my attention, and that one refers to contests among the "common planters." Jones, *Present State of Virginia*, 48. See Carson, *Virginians at Play*, 151–52.

35. Jones, *Present State of Virginia*, 48. This observation was repeated in other accounts of Virginia society throughout the eighteenth century. William Byrd II wrote "my Dear Countrymen have so great a Passion for riding, that they will often walk two miles to catch a Horse, in Order to ride One." William K. Boyd, ed., *William Byrd's Histories of the Dividing Line Betwixt Virginia and North Carolina* (Raleigh, N. C., 1929), 258. See also Carson, *Virginians at Play*, 102–5.

36. "A Letter From Clayton," in Force, ed., *Tracts and Other Papers*, no. 12, p. 35.

37. On the development of racing in Virginia, especially the transition from the quarter-mile straight track to the oval course, see W. G. Stanard, "Racing in Colonial Virginia," *VMHB*, II (1894–95), 293–305, and Fairfax Harrison, "The Equine F. F. V.'s: A Study of the Evidence for the English Horses Imported into Virginia before the Revolution," *ibid.*, XXXV (1927), 329–70. I suspect that quarter-horse racing was a sport indigenous to Virginia.

38. Beside Randolph, there were John Stone, William Hardidge, Thomas Yowell, John Hardiman, Daniel Sullivant, Thomas Chamberlain, Rodham Kenner, Richard Kenner, William Soane, and Alexander Swan.

39. Aug. 1690, Henrico County, Order Book, 1678–93, 340. All references to manuscript county records are to the photostat copies at the Virginia State Library, Richmond.

40. Jan. 16, 1666, Accomack Co., Orders, 1666–70, 9.

41. Sept. 10, 1674, York Co., Deeds, Orders, Wills, 1672–94, 85.

42. *Virginia Gazette*, Nos. 19–26, 1736, Sept. 30–Oct. 7, 1737.

43. Bruce, *Social Life*, 195–209; Carson, *Virginians at Play*, 108–10.

44. Apr. 7, 1693, Westmoreland Co., Order Book, 1690–98, 92; "Racing in Virginia in 1700–05," *VMHB*, X (1902–1903), 320.

45. Aug. 1683, Henrico Co. Records [Deeds and Wills], 1677–92, 254.

46. Oct. 16, 1674, Westmoreland Co., Deeds, Patents, etc., 1665–77, 211; Bruce, *Social Life*, 197–98; Carson, *Virginians at Play*, 109.

47. Beverley Fleet, ed., *Richmond County Records, 1704–24*, *Virginia Colonial Abstracts*, XVII (Richmond, Va., 1943), 95–96.

48. Carson, *Virginians at Play*, 105. See Aug. 29, 1694. Westmoreland Co., Order Book, 1690–98, 146.

49. Aug. 22, 1695, Northumberland Co., Order Book, 1678–98, pt. 2, 707–8.

50. Morgan, *American Slavery—American Freedom*, 142, 198, 204.

51. Bruce, *Economic History*, II, 495–512.

52. Aubrey Land's analysis of the probate records in a tobacco-producing area in nearby Maryland between 1690 and 1699 reveals that 74.6 percent of the estates there were worth less than £100 sterling. According to Land, the differences between the social structures of Maryland and Virginia at this time were not "very great." Land, "Economic Base and Social Structure," *Jour. Econ. Hist.*, XXV (1965), 641–44.

53. William Fitzhugh to Dr. Ralph Smith, Apr. 22, 1686, in Davis, ed., *Fitzhugh Letters*, 176.

54. The full covenant is reproduced in Stanard, "Racing in Colonial Virginia," *VMHB*, II (1894–95), 296–98.

55. *Ibid.*, 296.

56. Virginia law prohibited fraudulent gaming, certain kinds of side bets, and gambling by persons who had "no visible estate, profession, or calling, to maintain themselves." William Waller Hening, ed., *The Statutes at Large: Being a Collection of all the Laws of Virginia . . .* , IV (Richmond, 1820), 214–18; George Webb, *Office and Authority of A Justice of Peace . . .* (Williamsburg, Va., 1736), 165–67. Wagers made between two gainfully employed colonists were legal agreements and enforceable as contracts. The courts of Virginia, both common law and chancery, apparently followed what they believed to be standard English legal procedure. Whether they were correct is difficult to ascertain. Sir William Holdsworth explains that acts passed by Parliament during the reigns of Charles II and Anne allowed individuals to sue for gaming debts, but he provides no evidence that English courts regularly settled disputed contests such as horse races. Holdsworth, *A History of English Law* (London, 1966), VI, 404, XI, 539–42.

57. Not until the 1750s did Virginians begin to discuss gambling as a social vice. See Stith, *The Sinfulness . . . of Gaming*; R. A. Brock, ed., *The Official Records of Robert Dinwiddie*, I (Richmond, Va., 1883), 30–31; Samuel Davies, *Virginia's Danger and Remedy. Two Discourses Occasioned by The Severe Drought . . .* (Williamsburg, 1756).

58. Oct. 1690, Henrico Co., Order Book, 1678–93, 351. See also Aug. 28, 1674, Northampton Co., Order Book No. 9, 1664–74, 269, and Nov. 4, 1674, *ibid.*, No. 10, 1674–79.

59. Stanard, "Racing in Colonial Virginia," *VMHB*, II (1894–95), 267; Henrico Co. Records [Deeds and Wills], 1677–92, 466.

60. Carson, *Virginians at Play*, 109–10.

61. "Some Extracts from the Records of York Co., Virginia," *WMQ*, 1st ser., IX (1900–1901), 178–79.

62. Jan. 1694, Northumberland Co., Order Book, 1678–98, Pt. 2, 643.

63. Aug. 29, 1694, Westmoreland Co., Order Book, 1690–98, 146–46a. Also see Oct. 1689, Henrico Co., Order Book, 1678–93, 313, and Stanard, "Racing in Virginia," *VMHB*, II (1894–95), 296.

64. A gentleman could have challenged an opponent to a duel. Seventeenth- and early eighteenth-century Virginians recognized a code of honor of which dueling was a part, but they did everything possible to avoid such potentially lethal combats. I have found only four cases before 1730 in which dueling was even discussed. County courts fined two of the challengers before they could do any harm. ("A Virginian Challenge in the Seventeenth Century," *VMHB*, II (1894–95), 96–97; *Lower Norfolk County Antiquarian*, IV (1904), 106.) And two comic-opera challenges that only generated blustery rhetoric are described in William Stevens Perry, ed., *Historical Collections Relating to the American Colonial Church*, I (Hartford, Conn., 1870), 25–28, and Bond, ed., *Byrd's Histories of the Dividing Line*, 173–75. On the court system see Philip A. Bruce, *Institutional History of Virginia in the Seventeenth Century . . .* , I (Gloucester, 1910), 484–632, 647–89.

65. Aug. 29, 1694, Westmoreland Co., Order Book, 1690–98, 146a.

66. Jan. 1694, Northumberland Co., Order Book, 1678–98, Pt. 2, 643.

67. Sometimes the courts had an extremely difficult time deciding exactly what had occurred at a race. A man testified in 1675 that he had served as the official judge for a contest, and that while he knew which horse had finished first, he was "not able to say much less to Sweare that the Horse did Carry his Rider upon his back over the path." Sept. 16, 1675, Surry County, Deeds, Wills and Orders, 1671–84, 133. For another complex case see Mar. 5, 1685, Rappahannock Co. Orders [no. 1], 1683–86, 103, 120, 153.

68. For evidence of the persistence of these values among the gentry in the Revolutionary period see Isaac, "Evangelical Revolt," *WMQ*, 3rd ser., XXXI (1974), 348–53.

69. The planters' aggressive hospitality may have served a similar function. Hospitality in Virginia should be analyzed to discover its relationship to gentry culture. Robert Beverley makes some suggestive comments about this custom in his *History and Present State of Virginia*, 312–13. An interesting comparison to the Virginia practice is provided in Michael W. Young, *Fighting with Food: Leadership, Values and Social Control in a Massim Society* (Cambridge, 1971).

70. A. R. Radcliffe-Brown, *Structure and Function in Primitive Society: Essays and Addresses* (New York, 1964), chaps. 4, 5.

IX. OF TIME AND NATURE

1. This contrast is developed in Wesley Frank Craven, *The Legend of the Founding Fathers* (Ithaca, 1965), 9–32.

2. Sacvan Bercovitch, *The Puritan Origins of the American Self* (New Haven, 1975); Peter Gay, *A Loss of Mastery: Puritan Historians in Colonial America* (New York, 1966); Perry Miller and Thomas H. Johnson, eds., *The Puritans* (2 vols., New York, 1963), I, 81–90.

3. L. H. Butterfield, ed., *Diary and Autobiography of John Adams* (4 vols., Cambridge, Mass., 1961), III, 195. See also Adams's *Dissertation on the Canon and Feudal Law* in Charles Francis Adams, ed., *The Works of John Adams* (10 vols., Boston, 1850–56), III, 451–54, 484–85.

4. The classic analysis of American Puritan ideas is Perry Miller, *The New England Mind: From Colony to Province* (Cambridge, Mass., 1953). Also David D. Hall, "Understanding the Puritans," in Herbert J. Bass, ed., *The State of American History* (Chicago, 1970), 330–49; George Selement, "Perry Miller: A Note on His Sources in *The New England Mind: The Seventeenth Century*," *William and Mary Quarterly*, 3rd ser., XXXI (1974), 453–64.

5. C. Vann Woodward, "The Southern Ethic in a Puritan World," *WMQ*, 3rd ser., XXV (1968), 343–70; Edmund S. Morgan, "The Puritan Ethic and the American Revolution," *ibid.*, XXIV (1967), 3–43; Babette M. Levy, "Early Puritanism in the Southern and Island Colonies," in American Antiquarian Society, *Proceedings*, LXX (1960), Pt. 1, 60–348; and Perry Miller, *Errand into the Wilderness* (Cambridge, Mass., 1956), chap. IV. The most comprehensive attempt to discover a distinctive "early southern mind" is Richard Beale Davis, *Intellectual Life in the Colonial South, 1585–1763* (3 vols., Knoxville, 1978), esp. I, xxi–xxxi.

6. Louis B. Wright, *The First Gentlemen of Virginia: Intellectual Qualities of the Early Colonial Ruling Class* (Charlottesville, 1964), esp. part one.

7. The literature on the cultural significance of time in various societies is large. My work has profited particularly from Meyer Fortes, "Time and Social Structure: An Ashanti Case Study," in *Social Structure: Studies Presented to A. R. Radcliffe-Brown* (New York, 1963), 54–84; M. J. Finley, "Myth, Memory and History," in *The Use and Abuse of History* (New York, 1975); J. G. A. Pocock, "The Origins of the Study of the Past: A Comparative Approach," *Comparative Studies in Society and History*, IV (1961–62), 209–46; E. J. Hobsbawm, "The Social Function of the Past:

Some Questions," *Past and Present*, No. 55 (1972), 3–17; Paul Bohannan, "Concepts of Time Among the Tiv of Nigeria," *Southwestern Journal of Anthropology*, IX (1953), 251–62; and E. P. Thompson, "Time, Work-Discipline, and Industrial Capitalism," *Past and Present*, No. 38 (1967), 56–97; Ernest Gellner, *Thought and Change* (Chicago, 1964).

8. Clifford Geertz, "On the Nature of Anthropological Understanding," *American Scientist*, LXIII (1975), 47–53; E. E. Evans-Pritchard, *The Nuer: A Description of the Modes of Livelihood and Political Institutions of a Nilotic People* (Oxford, 1940), 94–108; Audrey I. Richards, *Land, Labour and Diet in Northern Rhodesia: An Economic Study of the Bemba Tribe* (Oxford, 1939), 388–98.

9. Florence R. Kluckhohn and Fred L. Strodbeck, *Variations in Value Orientations* (Westport, 1961), 14; Wilbert E. Moore, *Man, Time, and Society* (New York, 1963).

10. See R. B. Davis, *Intellectual Life*, I, 66–102. The contrast between colonial Virginia and many other societies that have been closely studied is striking. See, for example, Laurence Wylie, "The Life and Death of a Myth," in Melford E. Spiro, ed., *Context and Meaning in Cultural Anthropology* (New York, 1965), 164–85; Robert Redfield, "How Human Society Operates," in Harry L. Shapiro, ed., *Man, Culture and Society* (New York, 1971), 419–22; Pocock, "Study of the Past," 211–13; John T. Marcus, "Time and the Sense of History: West and East," *Comparative Studies in Society and History*, III (1960), 123–39; Bernard S. Cohn, "The Pasts of an Indian Village," *ibid.*, 241–49.

11. The words "present state" appeared with great frequency in the titles of essays concerned with colonial Virginia: Robert Beverley, *History and Present State of Virginia* [1705], ed. Louis B. Wright (Chapel Hill, 1947); Henry Hartwell, James Blair, and Edward Chilton, *The Present State of Virginia and the College* [1727], ed. Hunter D. Farish (Williamsburg, 1940); Hugh Jones, *The Present State of Virginia* [1724] (New York, 1865); Ralph Hamor, *A True Discourse of the Present [S]tate of Virginia* [1615], ed. Richard B. Harwell (Richmond, 1957); John Hammond, *Leah and Rachel, or, the Two Fruitfull Sisters Virginia and Mary-land: Their Present Condition, Impartially stated and related* [1656]; ed. Peter Force, *Tracts and Other Papers* (4 vols., Washington, D. C., 1836–46), III, no. 14; "A Perfect Description of Virginia: being a full and true Relation of the present State of the Plantation . . . " [1649], *ibid.*, II, no. 8.

12. Cited in Danial J. Boorstin, *The Lost World of Thomas Jefferson* (New York, 1948), 233. See Richard Dunn, "Seventeenth-Century English Historians of America," in J. M. Smith, ed., *Seventeenth-Century America: Essays in Colonial History* (Chapel Hill, 1959), 195–220; C. Vann Woodward, "The Historical Dimension" and "The Search for Southern Iden-

tity," in *The Burden of Southern History* (New York, 1961, pb. ed.), 3–26, 27–40.

13. T. M. S. Evens, "The Predication of the Individual in Anthropological Interactionism," *American Anthropologist*, LXXIX (1977), 583; also Evon Z. Vogt, *Modern Homesteaders: The Life of a Twentieth-Century Frontier Community* (Cambridge, Mass., 1955), 2–93; Godfrey Lienhardt, *Social Anthropology* (Oxford, 1969), 46–47.

14. The values of Virginia's early settlers are examined in Edmund S. Morgan, "The First American Boom: Virginia 1618 to 1630," *WMQ*, 3rd ser., XXVIII (1971), 169–98; and Chapter VI of this volume. While I would modify some of David Bertelson's conclusions about the culture of colonial Virginia, I found his general discussion of economic values provocative and imaginative (*The Lazy South* (New York, 1967)).

15. See Chapter VIII. According to Rhys Isaac, the breakdown of planter hegemony did not begin until the eve of the American Revolution. He analyzes the cultural divisions in Virginia in "Evangelical Revolt: The Nature of the Baptists' Challenge to the Traditional Order in Virginia, 1765 to 1775," *WMQ*, 3rd ser., XXXI (1974), 345–53. While I find Isaac's interpretation fascinating, I think he overestimates the impact of the Baptist challenge on what he terms the traditional order. I plan to explore the crisis of gentry culture in Virginia in a separate book. The best account of the colony's political structure remains Charles S. Sydnor, *Gentlemen Freeholders: Political Practices in Washington's Virginia* (Chapel Hill, 1952).

16. Richard Hakluyt, "The Discourse on the Western Planting" [1584] in E. G. R. Taylor, ed., *The Original Writings and Correspondence of the Two Richard Hakluyts* (2 vols., London, 1935), II, 317.

17. The play was written by George Chapman, Ben Johnson, and John Marston. The quotation appeared in Alexander Brown, *The Genesis of the United States* (2 vols., Boston, 1900), I, 30–1.

18. [Robert Johnson], *Nova Britannia: Offering Most Excellent Fruites by Planting in Virginia* (London, 1609), in Force, ed., *Tracts*, I, 21. In addition to this pamphlet see [Robert Johnson], *The New Life of Virginia* (London, 1612) in *ibid.*, 9–24; *A True Declaration of the Estate of the Colonie in Virginia* (London, 1610) in *ibid.*, III, 14–23. The promotional literature and the expectation of fabulous wealth easily gained is discussed fully in Edmund S. Morgan, *American Slavery—American Freedom: The Ordeal of Colonial Virginia* (New York, 1975), 1–130.

19. *A True Declaration*, 21.

20. *New Life*, 10, 24.

21. Alden T. Vaughan, *American Genesis: Captain John Smith and the Founding of Virginia* (Boston, 1975); Philip L. Barbour, *The Three Worlds of Captain John Smith* (Boston, 1964).

22. Thomas Jefferson, *Notes on the State of Virginia* (New York, 1964, pb. ed.), 167.

23. John Smith, *Travels and Works*, eds. Edward Arber and A. G. Bradley (2 vols., Edinburgh, 1910), II, 385.

24. *Ibid.*, 571.

25. *Ibid.*, I, 344, 359.

26. *Ibid.*, II, 615.

27. T. H. Breen, "George Donne's 'Virginia Reviewed': A 1638 Plan to Reform Colonial Society," *WMQ*, 3rd ser., XXX (1973), 458.

28. *Ibid.*, 454–55, 459.

29. *Ibid.*, 461, 462.

30. "A Perfect Description," Force, ed., *Tracts*, II, no. 8, p. 10.

31. E. W. Gent, *Virginia: More especially the South part Thereof* [1650], Force, ed., *Tracts*, III, no. 11, p. 15, 49–50.

32. William Bullock, *Virginia Impartially Examined* . . . (London, 1649), intro., 1–34.

33. Hammond, *Leah and Rachel*, Force, ed., *Tracts*, III, no. 14, p. 2–3, 9.

34. *Ibid.*, 17.

35. G[atford], *Publick Good*, 5–34. Also "Anthony Langston on Towns, and Corporations: And on the Manufacture of Iron," *WMQ*, 2nd ser., I (1921), 100–106.

36. Wesley Frank Craven, *The Southern Colonies in the Seventeenth Century, 1607–1639* (Baton Rouge, 1949), 129–32; John C. Rainbolt, "The Absence of Towns in Seventeenth-Century Virginia," *Journal of Southern History*, XXXV (1969), 343–60.

37. Surprisingly, there is no complete, published account of this man's extraordinary career. Aspects of his policies as governor of Virginia are treated in Wilcomb E. Washburn, *The Governor and the Rebel: A History of Bacon's Rebellion* (Chapel Hill, 1957); Sister Joan de Lourdes Leonard, "Operation Checkmate: The Birth and Death of a Virginia Blueprint for Progress, 1660–1676," *WMQ*, 3rd ser., XXIV (1967), 44–74; and John C. Rainbolt, *From Prescription to Persuasion: Manipulation of Eighteenth Century Virginia Economy*, 43–91; Morgan, *American Slavery—American Freedom*, 186–92.

38. William Berkeley, *A Discourse and View of Virginia* (London, 1663), 1–12. The Governor's enemies agreed that Virginia possessed extraordinary potential, but they blamed him for the failure to realize that promise. In a statement circulated by Bacon's supporters, Berkeley was berated, "For having upon specious pretences of publique works raised greate unjust taxes upon the Comonality for the advancement of private favorites & other sinister ends, but noe visible effects in any measure adequate, for not haveing dureing this *long time* of this Gov'nment in any measure advanced this

hopefull Colony either by fortifications Townes or Trade" ("Copy of Mr. Bacons [sic] Declaration in the Name of the People July 30th, 1676," *4 Collections*, MHS, IX, 184 [emphasis added]). The future belonged to a new, responsive government that would quickly transform dreams of general prosperity into reality.

39. Bernard Bailyn, "Politics and Social Structure in Virginia," in James Morton Smith, ed., *Seventeenth-Century America: Essays in Colonial History* (Chapel Hill, 1959), 90–115; David Jordon, "Politics Stability and the Emergence of a Native Elite in Maryland, 1660–1715," and Carole Shammas, "English-Born and Creole Elites," in Thad W. Tate and David Ammerman, eds., *The Chesapeake in the Seventeenth Century: Essays on Anglo-American Society and Politics* (New York, 1979), 274–96; Morgan, *American Slavery—American Freedom*, chaps. 15–17; Allan Kulikoff, "The Rise of the Chesapeake Gentry," (paper presented at the 1978 meeting of the Organization of American Historians), 1–19. I thank Professor Kulikoff for bringing this article to my attention.

40. Richard Beale Davis, ed., *William Fitzhugh and His Chesapeake World 1676–1701* (Chapel Hill, 1963), 224, 326–27.

41. William W. Hening, ed., *The Statutes at Large; Being a Collection of All the Lawes of Virginia . . .* (Richmond, 1819–23), II, 517. Kenneth A. Lockridge provides an estimate of literacy in seventeenth-century Virginia in *Literacy in Colonial New England: An Enquiry into the Social Context of Literacy in the Early Modern West* (New York, 1974), 72–101.

42. Hening, ed., *Statutes*, II, 518.

43. William Stith, *The History of the First Discovery and Settlement of Virginia* (Williamsburg, 1747; New York, 1865), viii.

44. Jack Goody and Ian Watt, "The Consequences of Literacy," *Comparative Studies in Society and History* V (1963), 304–45. Some literate gentry in the late seventeenth century began recording what they believed to be significant scientific observations, eager no doubt to impress English correspondents with their knowledge of New World flora and fauna. These observations required precise measurements, but as William Byrd learned in the spring of 1685 such exactitude was difficult. When Byrd attempted to inform his English friends about a major flood in the colony, he found himself forced to rely upon oral tradition, a vague gauge for someone trying to meet the standards of the Royal Society. In one letter he noted only that the flood was "the biggest . . . knowne since the English seated here." There was no way, of course, for Byrd to verify this claim. In another letter he stated that the water was "20 foot above the common." Again, he wanted to place the event in broad historical perspective, but since he was an immigrant, his understanding of the "common" constituted no more than an informed guess perhaps enriched by conversations with Virginians

older than himself. Considering the colonists' very high mortality rates throughout the century, contacts between old settlers who had actually witnessed distant, but unrecorded, events in the past must have been rare. It is useful to compare this situation with that of contemporary Massachusetts Bay. In the late 1680s men who had participated in the so-called Great Migration with John Winthrop were still ruling the colony. Byrd's confusion about the flood became more evident in a third letter in which he noted only that water rose "above 3 foot higher then ever any knowne before" (Marion Tinling, ed., *The Correspondence of the Three William Byrds of Westover, Virginia 1684–1776* (2 vols., Charlottesville, 1977), I, 40–42). Oral tradition in Chesapeake society helped apparently to settle disputes over land boundaries, especially if the disputants were too poor to hire a surveyor. The contesting parties simply consulted an "Antient Liver," an older resident who supposedly could remember whether the line ran by an oak tree or the head of the springs (Carville V. Earle, *The Evolution of a Tidewater Settlement System: All Hallow's Parish, Maryland, 1650–1783* (Chicago, 1975), 191).

45. [Durand of Dauphiné], *A Huguenot Exile in Virginia: or Voyages of a Frenchman exiled for his Religion with a Description of Virginia and Maryland*, ed. Gilbert Chinard (New York, 1934 (orig. publ. The Hague, 1687)), 105; also see "John Clayton, of James City, Afterwards of Crofton, Yorkshire [1684]," *WMQ*, 2nd ser., I (1921), 114–15.

46. Francis Louis Michel, "Report of the Journey . . . October 2, 1701– December 1, 1702," *Virginia Magazine of History and Biography*, XXIV (1916), 27–29.

47. Hartwell, Blair, and Chilton, *The Present State*, ed. Farish, 3–4. Edward Randolph, an officious royal appointee, wrote an account of the colony in 1696 and asked the same rhetorical question that appeared in so many Virginia writings. He inquired why Virginia "(the first English Settlement upon the continent of America, begun above Eighty Years agoe) is not better Inhabited, considering what vast Numbers of Servants & others, have yearly bin transported thither." After eight decades the colony had failed to achieve its full economic potential. Randolph argued that Virginia might yet prosper if royal officials broke the great planters' monopoly of new land (*Edward Randolph: Including his Letters and Official Papers . . .* , ed. Alfred T. S. Goodrich (7 vols., Boston, 1909), VII, 487). The students of William and Mary College agreed that Virginians had not achieved much of significance over the course of the seventeenth century, and one commencement speaker in 1699 admonished the colony's rulers, "If ever we would equal these our Rivals [Massachusetts, New York, and Pennsylvania], we must contrive to joyn our heads and purses together, and by Companies and Societies to learn to improve our shipping and navigation,

our trade and commerce, our minds and manners, and what no one man can so singly, by a friendly cohabitation and society to do jointly one with another." Like other colonial Americans from Smith to Jefferson, this young man was not depressed by the past. The future was bright despite his predecessors' incompetence, and he was quite willing to advocate a new social policy, the urbanization of Virginia. ("Speeches of Students of the College of William and Mary Delivered May 1, 1699," *WMQ*, 2nd ser., X (1930), 332–33.)

48. Hartwell, Blair, and Chilton, *The Present State*, ed. Farish, 4–7.

49. Francis Makemie, "A Plain & Friendly Perswasive to the Inhabitants of Virginia and Maryland for Promoting Towns & Cohabitations [1705]," *Virginia Magazine of History and Biography*, IV (1897), 255–66.

50. Louis B. Wright provides a good account of Beverley's career in *First Gentlemen of Virginia*, ch. X. Also Dunn, "Seventeenth-Century English Historians," 219–20.

51. Beverley, *History and Present State*, ed. Wright, 55 and Book I.

52. *Ibid.*, 97–113.

53. *Ibid.*, 9 and Book III.

54. *Ibid.*, 10 and Book II.

55. *Ibid.*, 117–56.

56. *Ibid.*, 319.

57. *Ibid.*, 318–19.

58. Ann Maury, *Memoirs of a Huguenot Family* (New York, 1872), 267.

59. Jones, *Present State*, ii, 21–24.

60. *Ibid.*, 10–12.

61. *Ibid.*, 81–151.

62. *Ibid.*, 138–51.

63. Edmund S. Morgan, "Slavery and Freedom: The American Paradox," *Journal of American History*, LIX (1972), 20–23.

64. Wright, *First Gentlemen*, ch. XI.

65. [William Byrd], *An Essay Upon the Government of the English Plantations On the Continent of America* [1701], ed. Louis B. Wright (San Marino, 1945), 29–30. In this pamphlet Byrd noted ". . . a Regular Settlement hath never yet been made, and therefore 'tis time to be done now" (24).

66. William Byrd, *Histories of the Dividing Line*, ed. Percy G. Adams (New York, 1967), 2–3.

67. *Ibid.*, 3.

68. *Ibid.*, 5.

69. [Byrd], *Essay*, ed. Wright, 30.

70. Tinling, ed., *Correspondence of the Three Byrds*, II, 444.

71. [Byrd], *Essay*, ed. Wright, 30.

72. Byrd, *Histories*, 304.

73. William Byrd, *William Byrd's Natural History of Virginia, or the Newly Discovered Eden*, eds. Richard Croom Beatty and William J. Mulloy (Richmond, 1940); William Byrd, *A Journey to the Land of Eden*, ed. Mark Van Doren (New York, 1928).

74. Byrd, *Histories*, 270.

75. Stith, *History*, iii; Craven, *Legend of the Founding Fathers*, 7–8.

76. Stith, *History*, iii–iv.

77. Jefferson, *Notes*, 167.

78. Stith, *History*, 198.

79. *Ibid.*, 161.

80. *Ibid.*, 168.

81. See, for example, Richard Bland, *An Inquiry Into the Rights of the British Colonies* (Williamsburg, 1766), esp., 12–17; Craven, *Legend of the Founding Fathers*, 55.

82. Pauline Maier, "Richard Henry Lee: A Virginian as Revolutionary" in *The Old Revolutionaries* (forthcoming). Maier notes that "Lee's participation in the Revolution, even the language with which he explained his political convictions, was founded, in short, upon a profound and far-reaching alienation from his native Virginia" (19). Lee blamed his predecessors for saddling Virginia with slavery. Because of its reputation as a slave colony, white immigrants had avoided Virginia, and even though it possessed "superior fertility of soil," the other English mainland colonies "are now far beyond us in improvement" (cited on page 21). Lee's rejection of the local past placed him within a long tradition, and his views on Virginia institutions, institutions toward which he felt remarkably little personal loyalty, were similar to those of Jefferson and other Virginia Revolutionaries. I appreciate Professor Maier's kindness in sharing her work with me.

83. These comments refer to a local, specifically Virginia past. Jefferson rejected a body of customs that had evolved in the colony. Jefferson, of course, read deeply in history, but the titles that occupied his attention dealt with a distant, rather abstract past that stretched back to Anglo-Saxon England. This general history of political man, one stripped of local tradition, provided Jefferson with precedents and examples which when taken out of context seemed to support his schemes for social and political reform. History in this sense was a timeless bundle of examples that one could employ to justify almost any course of action. H. Trevor Colbourn provides a fine analysis of Jefferson's use of the past in *The Lamp of Experience: Whig History and the Intellectual Origins of the American Revolution* (Chapel Hill, 1964), esp. chap. VIII. Edmund Pendleton pointed out to Jefferson the radical, even dangerous potential in such an abstracted view of human history. Saxon laws might have served well enough for a simple, eighth-century agrarian society, but they hardly seemed to Pendleton the

best system for eighteenth-century Virginians (*ibid.*, 168–9). On the political uses of history, see J. G. A. Pocock, "Time, Institutions and Action: An Essay on Traditions and their Understanding," in *Politics, Language and Time: Essays on Political Thought and History* (New York, 1971), 233–72.

84. Jefferson, *Notes*, 167, 168–80.

85. Thomas Jefferson, *Autobiography*, intro. Dumas Malone (New York, n. d., pb. ed.), 21; Merrill D. Peterson, *Adams and Jefferson: A Revolutionary Dialogue* (Athens, Ga., 1976), 6; Edmund S. Morgan, *The Meaning of Independence* (Charlottesville, 1976), 72.

86. Jefferson, *Autobiography*, 52; Jefferson, *Notes*, 158–61.

87. Marquis De Chastellux, *Travels in North America in the Years 1780, 1781 and 1782*, ed. Howard C. Rice (2 vols., Chapel Hill, 1963), II, 603.

88. Jefferson, *Autobiography*, 22, 24. Jefferson's contempt for Virginia traditions extended even to certain families who he believed had received undeserved favor from the Crown. He informed John Adams in 1813 that some colonial Virginia families had accumulated substantial fortunes, but their members had truckled to royal appointees, thus earning broad "unpopularity." Jefferson reported with obvious satisfaction that "A Randolph, Carter, or a Burwell must have great personal superiority over a common competitor to be elected by the people, even at this day." In another letter he insisted that "Here youth, beauty, mind and manners are more valued than a pedigree." Jefferson's willingness to dismantle colonial political institutions may in no small part have been bound up with his personal jealousy of pre-Revolutionary, entrenched gentry leaders. (*The Adams-Jefferson Letters: The Complete Correspondence Between Thomas Jefferson and Abigail and John Adams*, ed. Lester J. Cappon (2 vols., Chapel Hill, 1959), II, 389, 390, 402, 424.)

89. Thomas Jefferson, *Papers*, ed. Julian P. Boyd (Princeton, 1950–), XV, 384–97; Boorstin, *Lost World*, 167, 248.

90. Jefferson, *Notes*, 1–72, 157, 159–61.

91. Atkinson to Lyonel and Samuel Lynde, August 25, 1722, *Virginia Magazine of History and Biography*, XV (1908), 352. On the problems with tobacco, Aubrey C. Land, "The Tobacco Staple and the Planters' Problems: Technology, Labor, and Crops," *Agricultural History*, XLIII (1969), 71–80.

92. Philip Vickers Fithian, *Journal and Letters of Philip Vickers Fithian, 1773–1774: A Plantation Tutor of the Old Dominion*, ed. Hunter Dickinson Farish (Williamsburg, 1943), 92.

93. Jefferson, *Autobiography*, 51, 53.

94. *Ibid.*, 55–57. See David John Mays, *Edmund Pendleton, 1721–1803: A Biography* (2 vols., Cambridge, Mass., 1952), II, 126–43.

95. Wesley Frank Craven, *Legend of the Founding Fathers*, 130.